St Petersburg

"All you've got to do is decide to go
and the hardest part is over.

So go!"

TONY WHEELER, COFOUNDER – LONELY PLANET

D0193418

Regis St Louis, Simon Richmond

Contents

Plan Your Trip 4

Explore St Petersburg 50

Understand St Petersburg 197

Survival Guide 241

St Petersburg Maps 270

(left) **St Isaac's Cathedral p82** Known for its lavish mosaic interior.

....

(above) **Grotto Pavilion p180** Located in Catherine Park, Pushkin.

....

(right) **Winter Palace p56** Iconic symbol of the Hermitage.

....

Petrograd & Vyborg Sides
p154

Vasilyevsky Island
p143

Historic Heart
p54

Smolny & Vosstaniya
p121

Sennaya & Kolomna
p104

Welcome to St Petersburg

The sheer grandeur and history of Russia's imperial capital never fail to amaze, but this is also a city with a revolutionary spirit.

City of the Tsars

The creation of westward-looking Peter the Great, St Petersburg was intended from its inception as a display of imperial Russia's growing status in the world. Fine-tuned by Peter's successors, who employed a host of European architects to add fabulous palaces and cathedrals to the city's layout, St Petersburg grew to be the Romanovs' showcase capital and Russia's first great, modern city. The capital may have moved back to Moscow following the revolution, but despite all that history has thrown at it, St Petersburg still feels every bit the imperial city with its historic heart largely frozen in time.

Venice of the North

Whether you're cruising along the elegant canals, crossing one of the 342 bridges in the city, or just watching them being raised in summer over the mighty Neva River at night to allow ships to pass through, you're never far from water in St Petersburg. This has earned the city unsurprising comparisons to Venice, but the similarities don't stop there: walking around the historic centre will reveal canals lined by Italianate mansions and broken up by striking plazas adorned with baroque and neoclassical palaces. North of the city centre there are also pristine beaches fringing the Gulf of Finland.

Artistic Powerhouse

St Petersburg is an almost unrivalled treasure trove of art and culture. You can spend days in the Hermitage, seeing everything from Egyptian mummies to Picassos, while the Russian Museum, spread over four palaces, is perhaps the best collection of Russian art in the world. Add to this world-class ballet, opera and classical concerts at the illustrious performance halls, and a slew of big-name music festivals over the summer months, and you won't be stuck for cultural nourishment. Contemporary art is also available at the fantastic Erarta Museum, the Street Art Museum and in the buzzing gallery scene.

All Seasons City

Summer White Nights are legendary: the northern sun barely dips below the horizon. Revelry begins in May, with parks and gardens greening with flowering trees, and peaks in mid-June when performing arts festivals pack out concert halls and the entire city seems to party all night long. It's the busiest time to visit and the crowds can often be overwhelming. But Piter, as the city is affectionately known, is just as beautiful in early spring, golden autumn and even winter: the skies may be leaden and the ground covered in snow, but the culture still dazzles and delights.

Why I Love St Petersburg

By Simon Richmond, Writer

Little of importance has changed in St Petersburg since I first visited in 1994. It remains a city of majestic architecture, high artistic culture and historical significance. I will never tire of exploring the amazing art collections of the Hermitage and the Russian Museum nor be bored by the grand facades and the reflections of palaces in the canals. Over time it's just got better and better with a brilliant restaurant, bar and cafe scene and exciting creative design clusters. The long nights of partying are simply icing on this, the most elegant of urban cakes.

For more about our writers, see p288

Top: Church of the Saviour on the Spilled Blood (p81)

St Petersburg's
Top 10

White Nights (p24)

1 In mid-June the sun slumps lazily towards the horizon, but never fully sets, meaning that the magical nights are a wonderful whitish-grey. At this time Petersburgers indulge themselves in plenty of all-night revelry; several arts festivals take place including the spectacular Scarlet Sails. Though it's the busiest time to visit the city and most hotels are booked up weeks in advance, there's nothing quite like it, so don't miss out – even if you come in May or July you'll be impressed by how late the sun stays out!

Month by Month

The Hermitage (p56)

2 Perhaps the world's greatest museum, this iconic establishment's vast collection is quite simply mind-boggling, with Egyptian mummies, more Rembrandts than the Louvre, and a collection of early-20th-century art that is unrivalled by almost any other in the world. As if this wasn't enough, your entry ticket allows you to walk around the fascinating apartments and dazzling staterooms of the Romanovs. On top of this, there are still other Hermitage sites: the Winter Palace of Peter I, General Staff Building, Menshikov Palace, Imperial Porcelain factory and the excellent Hermitage Storage Facility. BOTTOM RIGHT: WINTER PALACE INTERIOR

Historic Heart

DROZDIN VLADIMIR / GETTY IMAGES ©

GONZALO AZUMENDI / GETTY IMAGES ©

OLGYSHA / SHUTTERSTOCK ©

St Isaac's View (p82)

3 No other viewpoint of the historic centre beats the one from the rotunda surrounding the stunning gold dome of St Isaac's Cathedral, which rises majestically over the uniformly sized Italianate palaces and mansions around the Admiralty. Well worth the climb up the 262 steps, a panorama of the city opens up to you – with fantastic views over the river, the Winter Palace and the *Bronze Horseman*. The cathedral's interior is also well worth seeing, with a wonderfully over-the-top iconostasis framed by columns of marble, malachite and lazurite.

⊙ *Historic Heart*

Russian Museum (p74)

4 Even though the Hermitage is unrivalled as St Petersburg's most impressive museum, that shouldn't stop you from visiting this superb treasure trove of Russian art, spread out over four stunning palaces in the centre of the city. The main building, the Mikhailovsky Palace, presents a fascinating collection of Russian art from medieval icons to 20th-century avant-garde masterpieces, while the Marble Palace houses a wing of the Ludwig Museum with a focus on contemporary works, and the Stroganov Palace has some of the most spectacular interiors in the city. LEFT: STROGANOV PALACE

⊙ *Historic Heart*

Church of the Saviour on the Spilled Blood (p81)

5 As much a symbol of the city as the Winter Palace, the spellbinding Church of the Saviour on the Spilled Blood never fails to impress. The church was built to commemorate the death of Tsar Alexander II, who, in an event that gave the church its unusual name, was attacked here by a terrorist group and later died of his injuries in 1881. Despite its grisly heritage, the glittering, multicoloured onion domes, and intricate interior and exterior mosaics are quite simply stunning and have to be seen to be believed.

⊙ *Historic Heart*

Tsarskoe Selo (p179)

6 Arguably the most beautiful of the tsarist palace areas that surround St Petersburg, Tsarskoe Selo can be an idyllic place for a day trip. Arrive in good time to see the lavish interiors of the Catherine Palace, including the famous Amber Room, enjoy the gorgeous formal gardens and have a picnic in the landscaped park where Catherine the Great so loved to walk. When it gets impossibly busy at the height of summer, retreat to the nearby scenic estate and palace of Pavlovsk, a beautiful place to escape the crowds.

BELOW: CATHERINE PALACE

⊙ *Day Trips from St Petersburg*

Mariinsky Ballet (p117)

7 What could be more Russian than seeing a ballet or opera at the city's famous Mariinsky Theatre? Formerly known as the Kirov, where Soviet stars such as Nureyev and Baryshnikov danced, the Mariinsky has one of the world's premier ballet troupes as well as a superb orchestra led by artistic director Valery Gergiev. Tickets for productions here are always sought-after, so book online before you travel to ensure you don't miss out. Even if such performances are not your thing, the historic building is a sight in its own right.

☆ *Sennaya & Kolomna*

GIMBAO / SHUTTERSTOCK ©

7

8

Peter & Paul Fortress *(p156)*

8 The city's first major building is on little Zayachy Island. It's immediately recognisable from its extraordinary golden spire, visible all over the city centre at an incredible (for the 18th century) 122m high. A visit to this large complex is a must for history buffs: here you'll find the tombs of the Romanovs and an excellent history museum; make time, too, for a walk along the ramparts. You can even relax on a surprisingly decent beach with stellar views across to the Strelka and Hermitage!

⊙ *Petrograd & Vyborg Sides*

Cruising the Canals *(p32)*

9 St Petersburg is a city that is best appreciated from the water. Despite Peter's efforts, public boat transport by river and canal never quite caught on in the 'Venice of the North'. Even so, don't miss a canal-boat tour or, better yet, paddling yourself in a kayak to see some of the city's architectural gems from a different perspective. While cruising the canals is only possible outside the winter months, if you're here when they're frozen over don't miss wandering along their banks for a visual treat.

🏃 *Tours & Activities*

LYUDMILA2509 / SHUTTERSTOCK ©

ALEKSEI KAZACHOK / SHUTTERSTOCK ©

Taking a Banya *(p33)*

10 For a real cultural immersion, head to one of St Petersburg's *bani* (steam baths), such as the classy Degtyarniye Baths, for the detox of a lifetime. In between basking in the infernal wet heat of the *parilka* (steam room), having your toxins removed through a sound birch-twig whipping and then plunging into ice-cold water, this is a great place to relax and chat with locals for whom the weekly *banya* (steam bath) is considered to be almost a sacred rite.

🏃 *Tours & Activities*

What's New

Creative Clusters

As the decade-old Loft Project ETAGI (p131) expands out into a village of converted shipping containers, other 'creative clusters' are popping up like daisies and include the vibey Golitsyn Loft (p128) on the Fontanka, Artmuza (p153) on Vasilyevsky Island and Hi-Hat (p170) on the Petrograd Side.

New Holland

With the opening of its creative hub the Bottle House in summer 2017, this superb new city park and cultural centre in shaping up to be one of the city's top destinations. (p108)

Secret Bars

The trend for in-the-know speakeasy-style cocktail bars gathers pace with reservation-necessary late night spots such as Kvartira Kosti Kroitsa (p133) and Kabinet (p96).

Craft Beer

Piter has embraced the craft beer revolution sweeping Russia: check out the range of local brews at bars Redrum (p136), Farsh & Bochka (p137) and Beer Boutique 1516 (p152) among other places.

Commode

The logical next step in the anti-cafe phenomena, you pay for time spent at this so-called self-cost bar where drink prices are low. (p136)

Lumiere Hall

Slump into a bean bag to enjoy massive 3D art projections in this 360-degree space, with audio commentary on the works displayed. (p129)

Amazing Scale Models

Grand Maket (p129) is a staggering look at Russia in miniature while the same company has created a mini St Petersburg of the 18th century at Petrovskaya Akvatoria (p91).

Western High-Speed Diameter

Two of Russia's largest suspension bridges, part of a new orbital toll road, facilitate a spectacular crossing of the Neva River's mouth so you can see parts of the city as they never have been seen before. (p199)

Lakhta Center

A free public observation deck will allow you to look down on the city from 357m in Russia's tallest building when it likely opens at the end of 2018 (http://lakhta. center).

New Stage

The Alexandrinky's New Stage offers up contemporary dance, theatre, workshops and roof top cinema in the summer in a gorgeous light-filled building. (p99)

Piter Kayak

Get some early morning or evening excercise and take in the wonderful views on these guided paddles along the city's rivers and canals. (p120)

MISP

Multi-floored gallery staging intriguing exhibitions, showcasing the talents of local artists over the last century. (p111)

For more recommendations and reviews, see **lonelyplanet. com/russia/st-petersburg**

Need to Know

For more information, see Survival Guide (p241)

Currency
Rouble (R)

Language
Russian

Visas
Nearly all visitors need a visa, which will require an invitation. Tourist visas are generally single entry and valid for up to 30 days.

Money
ATMs are widespread, and credit cards accepted in most restaurants, cafes and shops.

Mobile Phones
Local SIM cards (giving internet data as well as calls) can be bought for as little as R200 and used in unlocked phones.

Time
Moscow Time (GMT/USC plus three hours)

Tourist Information
Tourist Information Bureau (Map p272, G5; ☑812-303 0555, 812-242 3909; http://eng.ispb.info; Sadovaya ul 14/52; ◷10am-7pm Mon-Sat; Ⓜ Gostiny Dvor) Maps, tours, information and advice for travellers.

Daily Costs

Budget:
Less than R1500
➡ Dorm bed: R800
➡ Cafe or street-stall meal: R200–R500
➡ Travel on buses and metro: R40-45

Midrange:
R1500–R15,000
➡ Double room in a midrange hotel: R3000-15,000
➡ Two-course meal: R1000
➡ Museum entry fee: R100–R400
➡ City-centre taxi ride: R150

Top End:
Over R15,000
➡ Double room in a top-end hotel: R15000+
➡ Two-course meal with wine: R2000+
➡ Ballet tickets: R3500
➡ First-class train ticket, Moscow–St Petersburg: R7300

Advance Planning

Three months before Get working on your visa. Book hotel rooms for the White Nights.

One month before Book hotel rooms during the rest of the year, Mariinsky and other theatre tickets during the summer months.

One week before Buy your Hermitage ticket online and print it out. Add useful apps such as Google Translate and Yandex Taxi to your smartphone.

Useful Websites

➡ **Lonely Planet** (www.lonely planet.com/russia/st-peters burg) Destination information, hotel bookings, traveller forum and more.

➡ **In Your Pocket St Petersburg** (www.inyour pocket.com/russia/st-petersburg) Excellent local guide.

➡ **Visit Petersburg** (www. visit-petersburg.ru) City's official tourist information site.

➡ **A-a-ah!** Listings for cool places and activities in St Petersburg.

WHEN TO GO

May to September is best, with White Nights the peak. Winter is cold and dark, but beautiful. Go in early May, September and October to avoid the crowds.

St Petersburg

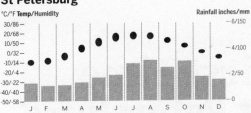

°C/°F Temp/Humidity — Rainfall inches/mm

Arriving in St Petersburg

Pulkovo Airport From St Petersburg's airport, an official taxi to the centre should cost between R800 and R1000; if you book via an app it's likely to be R700. Alternatively, take bus 39 (35 minutes) or 39A (20 minutes) to Moskovskaya metro station for R35, then take the metro from Moskovskaya (Line 2) all over the city for R45.

Moscow Station (Moskovsky vokzal) Easy connection to the nearby pl Vosstaniya (Line 1) and Mayakovskaya (Line 3) metro stations.

Finland Station (Finlyandsky vokzal) Direct connection to the pl Lenina (Line 1) metro station.

Boat Terminals Taxis are easily caught at all terminals in St Petersburg, but all are in walking distance of metro stations or have bus routes passing nearby.

For much more on **arrival** see p242

Etiquette

➔ **Meeting People**
Handshakes are the standard form of greeting. Do not shake hands over thresholds, though, as according to Russian folklore this will lead to an argument down the line! Remove your shoes and coat when arriving in someone's home.

➔ **Presents** If you're visiting friends in their home it's courteous to bring a small present. Flowers are always popular, but do be sure to bring an odd number, as even numbers of flowers are given only at funerals.

➔ **Drinking** You'll be expected to drink a vodka shot in one go if you're a man, but women will not be judged too harshly if they sip. Once a bottle is finished, put it on the floor, not back on the table, as that is considered to bring bad luck.

For much more on **getting around** see p244

Sleeping

St Petersburg has seen an explosion of accommodation options in recent years. However, if you're travelling in summer (particularly during the White Nights), book in advance. Hostels are now plentiful in the city – standards can vary hugely between them, but the very best are superb. Minihotels are a local speciality – usually housed in old apartments with fewer than six guestrooms – and can be both charming and great value. Hotels in St Petersburg tend to be relatively expensive (eye-wateringly so in the four- and five-star categories); the best deals are often available on hotel websites.

Useful Websites

➔ **Airbnb** (airbnb.com) A big player with a big presence in St Petersburg.

➔ **HOFA** (www.hofa.ru) Homestays and apartments.

➔ **Intro by Irina** (www.introbyirina.com) Can arrange both short- and long-term rental apartments.

For much more on **sleeping** see p186

LGBT TRAVELLERS

Despite a Russian law outlawing the 'promotion' of homosexuality to minors, St Petersburg remains a generally safe place for gay travellers. Hotels are normally problem-free about two men or two women sharing rooms, and while discretion is the safest policy on the streets, there is a thriving gay scene that's worth exploring.

First Time St Petersburg

For more information, see Survival Guide (p241)

Checklist

➡ Arrange your visa and check the entry and exit dates on it

➡ Inform your bank if you plan to pay for things or take money out on cards in Russia

➡ Ensure your travel insurance includes coverage in Russia

➡ Book tickets online for the Mariinsky Theatre if you want to see a specific ballet or opera

What to Pack

➡ European plug adaptor if you're travelling from outside mainland Europe

➡ Anti-mosquito spray or tablets (May to September)

➡ Comfortable shoes

➡ Clothing for all weather: temperatures vary massively

➡ Sunglasses for both summer and (surprisingly bright) winter

Top Tips for Your Trip

➡ St Petersburg is a huge city, so don't try to bite off more than you can chew: stagger your sightseeing and allow plenty of time to take it easy and watch the city go by.

➡ Get a metro smart card if you're going to be using the metro a lot. You'll save money and queuing up for tickets.

➡ Take advantage of deals such as the Hermitage's two-day ticket, which allows you access to all its sites over 48 hours, or the Russian Museum's four-palace ticket that does likewise over three days.

➡ Search out discount deals at restaurants Monday to Friday between noon and 4pm for excellent value lunches.

➡ Learning the Cyrillic alphabet repays the effort tenfold, and you'll be able to understand more than you would otherwise. Some basic phrases in Russian go a long way.

What to Wear

Clothing is very important to Russians, many of whom are surprised at how sloppily foreigners dress. Shoes are considered of particular importance, so it's a good idea to keep yours clean. That said, Russians remain quite casual and you'll rarely be expected to be in smart clothing outside the theatre and good restaurants.

Be Forewarned

➡ Foreigners tend to find Russians quite brusque and even unfriendly. Remember, this is a cultural thing, and try not to be offended by it. Russians take a while to warm up, but when they do they're exceptionally friendly.

➡ There is an ongoing epidemic of racist attacks in St Petersburg. If you look very obviously non-Russian, it's a good idea to avoid the suburbs and take taxis at night.

➡ Due to legislation criminalising the 'promotion of homosexuality' to minors, levels of homophobia are higher now than they have been for some time. Gay travellers are advised to remain discreet.

Money

ATMs are everywhere in St Petersburg, and generally accept all major credit and debit cards. You may save on fees by bringing cash in US dollars or euros with you and changing it at any bank or exchange office (обмен валют), where you'll often get a better rate than that offered by credit cards. You can pay by debit and credit cards in most smarter restaurants and shops, but it's never a good idea to rely on being able to do so: always carry some cash.

For more information, see p248.

Taxes & Refunds

There is an 18% VAT rate in Russia, and while it's always included in goods and services, it is sometimes conveniently left off hotel rack rates, so do check before booking, as this could be a very nasty end to your stay.

Tipping

➡ **Restaurants** Leaving 10% on the table is the norm, when service has been good. Not necessary at very cheap places.

➡ **Bars** Not expected unless table service is provided. Then 10%.

➡ **Taxis** Not expected, but round up or add R50 for a long trip.

➡ **Hotels** R50 per bag.

Market stalls near the Church of the Saviour on the Spilled Blood (p81)

Street Names

We use the transliteration of Russian street names to help you when deciphering Cyrillic signs. The following abbreviations are used:

➡ bul – bulvar (бульвар; boulevard)

➡ nab – naberezhnaya (набережная; embankment)

➡ per – pereulok (переулок; lane or side street)

➡ pl – ploshchad (площадь; square)

➡ pr – prospekt (проспект; avenue)

➡ sh – shosse (шоссе; highway)

➡ ul – ulitsa (улица; street)

Staying Connected

Wi-fi is available for free all over the city. All hotels have free wi-fi available to guests, while most restaurants, bars and cafes have this as well.Nearly all mobile phones can roam in Russia, though it is usually expensive. If you want mobile internet, buy a SIM card (SIM karta; about R200) from a phone shop for your unlocked handset.

Language

English is widely, if poorly, spoken. Younger people tend to speak the best English. You don't need to know any Russian to travel here, but learning the alphabet and some basic phrases will be a huge help.

Getting Around

For more information, see Transport (p242)

Metro

The fastest way to cover long distances, the metro has around 70 stations, costs a flat fare of R28 and works from approximately 5.45am to 12.45am each day.

Bus

Better for shorter distances in areas without good metro coverage. Can be slow going, but views are good.

Trolleybus

Trolleybuses are the slowest of the lot, although they're cheap and plentiful.

Marshrutka

The private sector's contribution, these fixed-route minibuses are fast and you can get on or off anywhere along their routes.

Tram

Largely obsolete and little used, trams are still handy in areas such as Kolomna and Vasilyevsky Island where there is little else available.

Key Phrases

How do I get to...?
Как мне добраться до...? (Kak mnye dobrátsa do...)

One ticket, please.
Один билет, пожалуйста. (Adín bilyét pazhálsta.)

Can you tell me when to get off for...?
Подскажите, пожалуйста, когда мне надо выходить на...? (Podskázhitye, pazhálsta, kagdá mnye nada vykhodít na...)

Stop here, please.
Остановитесь здесь, пожалуйста. (Astanavítyes zdyess pazhálsta.)

Key Routes

Metro line 1 Worth getting out at every stop between pl Vosstaniya and Avtovo to admire the very handsomely decorated stations.

Tram 6 Great for travelling between areas north of the river without going through the centre: connects Vasilyevsky Island with the Petrograd Side and the Vyborg Side.

Trolleybus 7 Goes from Smolny along Nevsky pr, over the river, along the Strelka and to the Petrograd Side.

How to Hail a Taxi

➡ Stand on practically any street and stick out your arm: you can be assured that sooner rather than later a car will stop for you.

➡ State your destination and a proposed price.

➡ A short ride in the city centre should be around R200, rising to R300 or R400 for longer ones.

➡ Official taxis are reliable and cheap; order them by phone.

TOP TIPS

➡ For ease of use, buy a smart card (R60) from a machine or the ticket kiosk in any metro station and load it with prepaid journeys.

➡ Be aware that at interchange stations on the metro each station tends to have a different name.

➡ Even if you're staying near a metro station, check local bus, tram and *marshrutka* (minibus) routes, as these can often be more useful.

➡ When entering a metro station, be sure you're using the entrance (вход) rather than the exit (выход).

Cycling

Despite the local traffic being still in the learning stages about basic respect for cyclists, this is a great way to get around this huge and flat city.

➡ Some youth hostels and bike shops, such as Rentbike (p245) and Skladnye Velosipedy (p245), hire bikes for as little as R500 per day.

➡ If you're keen to do a lot of cycling, bring a helmet, bike lights and a good lock from home, as these are hard to come by.

➡ Velogorod (p245) is a handy bike-sharing system with 56 stations across the city. You'll need to use the website or download the app to hire one of their bicycles.

Etiquette

➡ When on the metro escalators, stand on the right and walk on the left.

➡ Do be sure to hold the metro entrance door open if there's someone behind you.

➡ Inside the metro carriages, give up your seat to older or less able travellers when the metro is full.

➡ When getting on to a *marshrutka* (minibus), take a seat and then pass your fare to someone sitting between you and the driver, and they'll pass it along.

➡ If there's an empty seat on a bus and everyone else is standing, it's probably the conductor's seat, so don't take it.

Tickets & Passes

➡ Transport in St Petersburg is very cheap. Single metro tickets cost just R45, while you will save even more by buying rides in bulk on a smart card.

➡ *Marshrutka* (minibus) costs vary: some charge flat fares, while others will charge you according to how far you want to go on their route. You always pay the driver directly.

➡ Trams, buses and trolleybuses all have conductors on board. They will come around the vehicle and sell you tickets, and can usually be recognised by a red sash they wear.

➡ There are no transport passes that are of use for short-term visitors.

For much more on **getting around** see p244

TRAVEL AT NIGHT

Public transport in St Petersburg shuts down some time after midnight, meaning that taxis and walking are your only options for getting around. There's also the issue of some bridges over the Neva River rising nightly between April and November. This means that if you want to cross the river late at night you need to plan accordingly. Now that there is the Western High Speed Diameter highway it's always possible to get from one side of the Neva to the other, although it will involve a possibly long taxi ride across this toll road.

Top Itineraries

Day One

Historic Heart (p54)

☀ Begin your first day by taking a stroll down Nevsky pr, the city's central avenue that connects the Hermitage to the Alexander Nevsky Monastery at the far end. Start at Ploshchad Vosstaniya, cross the lovely Fontanka, drop into the **Church of the Saviour on the Spilled Blood** and the **Kazan Cathedral** and end up at the dazzling ensemble of **Palace Square**, the **Winter Palace** and the **General Staff Building**. Wander along the embankment to the **Summer Garden** and then wander back along the Moyka River.

 Lunch Dine with adorable cuddly toys at cosy Zoom Café (p91).

Sennaya & Kolomna (p104)

☼ Continue along the Moyka to **St Isaac's Cathedral**, visit the astonishingly elaborate interiors and then climb to the top of the dome for superb views of the city. Follow the Moyka down to the **Yusupov Palace** and the **Mariinsky Theatre**, ending up at the beautiful sky-blue **Nikolsky Cathedral**.

✗ **Dinner** Enjoy the antique atmosphere and vegetarian dishes of Idiot (p116).

Historic Heart (p54)

☽ If the dive bars of **Dumskaya ul** don't appeal, **Apotheke Bar** is a convivial spot for cocktails nearby. Alternatively the Belle View rooftop bar at the **Kempinski Hotel Moyka 22** does indeed offer superb views.

Day Two

Historic Heart (p54)

☀ After a hearty breakfast, head to the **Hermitage** and get ready for a day of artistic exhilaration. Choose which parts of the collection you want to see, though leave some room for on-the-spot decision making – the exhibition is so enormous that you'll inevitably discover something new. As well as the art, don't miss the staterooms, and allow yourself plenty of rest stops to avoid exhaustion.

 Lunch Savour some excellent Russian cuisine at Yat (p93).

Historic Heart (p54)

☼ You may still want to spend a few hours in the museum and make the most of your day ticket. But if you leave and still have some energy, wander along before picking up a **sightseeing cruise** around the canals – the best way to sightsee without having to do any more walking!

 Dinner Enjoy a pre- or post-theatre meal at The Répa (p116).

Sennaya & Kolomna (p104)

☽ If you've booked ahead, dress up to spend the evening watching a ballet from the classical repertoire of the **Mariinsky Theatre**. Even if you haven't booked, it's usually quite possible to do so last minute in one of the other theatres in town. For a late-night drink with live jazz drop by **Hat**.

ANTON KUDELIN / SHUTTERSTOCK ©

Summer Garden (p84)

Day Three

Petrograd & Vyborg Sides (p154)

 This is your chance to explore the beautiful Petrograd Side. Start with a visit to the **Peter & Paul Fortress** to see where the city began, wander past the **mosque** and perhaps drop in to see either **Peter's Cabin** or the very interesting **Museum of Political History**. Wander down **Kamennoostrovsky pr** to take in the Russian Style Moderne architecture.

> **Lunch** Enjoy great views over the Neva at Koryushka (p169).

Vasilyevsky Island (p143)

After lunch, walk across to Vasilyevsky Island, and wander the historic ensemble around the **Strelka**. Visit the **Kunstkamera**, Peter the Great's personal cabinet of curiosities, and drop in to the very interesting **Menshikov Palace** to see the oldest standing palace in the city. If you enjoy contemporary art, continue on to the excellent **Erarta Museum of Contemporary Art**.

> **Dinner** Dine in understated Russian elegance at Restoran (p152).

Smolny & Vosstaniya (p121)

Head south to happening Vosstaniya to gallery-, bar- and gig-hop around **Ligovsky pr**. See some new artwork at **Loft Project ETAGI** and, if it's summer, enjoy a drink in the sand and some table football at **Dyuni**.

Day Four

Around St Petersburg (p173)

 Head out of the city early to spend the day in tsarist opulence. Go first to **Tsarskoe Selo** in order to visit the **Catherine Palace** and have a walk in the gardens. If you're still wanting more, head for **Pavlovsk**, a quick bus ride away, where the park is even wilder and more beautiful.

> 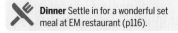 **Lunch** Eat at White Rabbit (p180) in the town of Pushkin.

Historic Heart (p54)

Return to the city in the afternoon and slot in the **Russian Museum**, the perfect complement to the Hermitage. This spectacular (and far more manageable) museum showcases seven centuries of Russian art from church icons to the avant-garde.

> **Dinner** Settle in for a wonderful set meal at EM restaurant (p116).

Smolny & Vosstaniya (p121)

Bar hop from ul Rubinshteyna north along the Fontanka, sneaking into the secret bar **Commode**, followed by **Union** and **Terminal Bar**. Catch a live band at **Fish Fabrique**, **Cosmonaut** or alternative favourite **Griboyedov** for a taste of what's cooking on the local music scene.

If You Like...

Art

Hermitage There's nothing quite like the Hermitage, perhaps the world's greatest art collection. (p56)

General Staff Building The Hermitage's amazing collection of Impressionist and post-Impressionist works continues across Palace Square. (p72)

Russian Museum This survey of all Russian art is also essential, even if you know nothing about the subject before going. (p74)

Erarta Museum of Contemporary Art A stunning museum of modern and contemporary Russian art on Vasilyevsky Island. (p145)

Marina Gisich Gallery One the city's leading private art galleries championing the cream of contemporary Russian artists. (p110)

Pushkinskaya 10 The one-time centre of the city's alternative scene has aged a little, but it's still worth a trip for art lovers. (p127)

Hermitage Storage Facility In case you came out of the Hermitage wanting more, this state-of-the-art space will definitely sate you. (p165)

Street Art Museum The disused part of a factory on the city's edge is now a canvas for colourful and creative street art. (p167)

Architecture

Winter Palace It's hard to beat this spectacular piece of baroque excess. (p56)

Peterhof The spectacular fountains and views of the palace from Water Ave are breathtaking. (p174)

MARCO RUBINO / SHUTTERSTOCK ©

Mikhailovsky Garden (p85)

Smolny Cathedral This soaring Rastrelli masterpiece never fails to inspire awe. (p126)

Admiralty The golden spire of this prime St Petersburg landmark looks handsome from many angles. (p86)

Singer Building Russian Style Moderne at the heart of neo-classical Nevsky pr. (p102)

House of Soviets An unbeatable example of Soviet architectural taste in southern St Petersburg. (p130)

Russian Literature

Bronze Horseman Brought to life in Pushkin's eponymous epic poem, the sculpture that inspired him is a must. (p85)

Site of Pushkin's Duel The scene of great tragedy for anyone who knows the work of Russia's national poet. (p166)

Dostoevsky Museum A wander around Dostoevsky's apartment is a fascinating insight into the writer's life. (p129)

Raskolnikov House *Crime and Punishment* comes to life in the streets of Sennaya. (p112)

Nabokov Museum Visit the house immortalised by the *Lolita* author in his autobiography *Speak, Memory*. (p111)

Anna Akhmatova Museum This museum honours the most quintessential Leningrad poet and survivor of the Great Purge. (p125)

Religious Buildings

Kazan Cathedral See the dramatic interior of this Orthodox stunner. (p83)

Sampsonievsky Cathedral One of the most impressive iconostases in St Petersburg. (p165)

Nikolsky Cathedral Perhaps the prettiest church in the city, this place is stunning both outside and in. (p111)

Church of the Saviour on the Spilled Blood Dazzling domes, incredible mosaics. (p81)

Alexander Nevsky Monastery One of Russia's most important religious centres. (p123)

Buddhist Temple Incense also burns at the world's most northerly *datsan*. (p166)

Naval Cathedral Neo-Byzantine wonder on Kronshtadt island. (p185)

Soviet History

Finland Station (Finlyandsky vokzal) Where Lenin famously arrived to lead the October coup. (p166)

Cruiser Aurora The ship that fired a blank round to signal the start of the October Revolution. (p161)

Winter Palace Where the provisional government was arrested. (p56)

Kirov Museum Home of Sergei Kirov, Stalin's ill-fated man in Leningrad. (p159)

Monument to the Heroic Defenders of Leningrad The moving memorial to the 900-day Nazi blockade. (p130)

Parks & Gardens

Summer Garden The oldest park in St Petersburg has been restored to its original state and looks superb. (p84)

Pavlovsk Park The best tsarist palace grounds to wander around. (p181)

Mikhailovsky Garden The most beautiful park in the centre of St Petersburg. (p85)

For more top St Petersburg spots, see the following:
➡ Eating (p39)
➡ Drinking & Nightlife (p43)
➡ Entertainment (p46)
➡ Shopping (p48)
➡ Tours & Activities (p31)

Botanical Gardens A fascinating botanical garden that's a real pleasure to walk around. (p160)

New Holland The city's newest park sports trees, flower and herb gardens, brilliant kids and toddlers playgrounds and free pétanque (a form of boules). (p108)

Yelagin Island Car-free island park on the Petrograd Side that's a joy to explore on foot or by bicycle. (p172)

Viewpoints

Peter & Paul Fortress Walk along the ramparts of this historic fort for brilliant panoramas of the city. (p156)

Strelka Look down the Neva from between the majestic Rostral Columns at the eastern tip of Vasilyevsky Island. (p147)

St Isaac's Cathedral The colonnade is open until 4.30am during the White Nights season for late-night views of the city. (p82)

Singer Building On specially booked tours it's possible to see the city from inside the glass dome of this iconic Russian Style Moderne building. (p102)

Solaris Lab Magnificent views over the russet rooftops to the glittering dome of St Isaac's from this rooftop tea house. (p117)

Month by Month

February

Intensely cold, with snow and ice everywhere still, February is a great time to see St Petersburg in full winter garb, as long as you don't mind the short days!

✸ Maslenitsa

Akin to Mardi Gras, this celebration kicks off Orthodox Lent and involves eating lots of bliny. Exact dates depend on the dates of Orthodox Easter, but it is usually in February or early March.

March

Expect snow on the ground, though in warmer years March can also see the beginning of the thaw.

✸ International Women's Day

Russia's favourite holiday – 8 March – was founded to honour the women's movement. These days, men buy champagne, flowers and chocolates for their better halves – and for all the women in their lives.

April

Finally the thaw comes, but you might prefer snow to the grey slush that can engulf the city in April. Orthodox Easter and the Mariinsky Ballet Festival brighten the scene.

✸ Easter

Easter Sunday kicks off with celebratory midnight services in which Orthodox churches are jam-packed. Afterwards, people eat special dome-shaped cakes known as *kulichy* and exchange beautifully painted wooden Easter eggs. As with Easter in the West, dates vary year to year, and Orthodox Easter is normally not on the same weekend as Easter elsewhere.

☆ Mariinsky Ballet Festival

The city's principal dance theatre hosts a week-long international festival, where the cream of Russian ballet dancers showcase their talents.

☆ Jazzovaya Vesna

Every April the JFC Jazz Club holds this spring festival featuring local and international artists playing not just jazz but also bossa nova, blues, ragtime and funk.

May

Spring is finally here, and with it a slew of holidays in the first two weeks of the month. Late May is a great time to come to St Petersburg before the summer crowds arrive.

✸ Victory Day

Celebrating the end of WWII, 9 May is a day of huge local importance, when residents remember the 900-day Nazi blockade. Crowds assemble at Piskaryovskoe Cemetery to commemorate the victims, and a parade along Nevsky pr culminates in fireworks over the Neva in the evening.

✸ City Day

Laying flowers at the Monument to Peter I on Senate Sq is a tradition on 27 May, the city's official birthday. Mass celebrations are held throughout the city centre including brass bands, folk dancing and mass drunkenness.

June

This is St Petersburg's high season, and there's certainly no shortage of things to do, as the nights are white, spirits are high and the city has an almost surreal atmosphere.

☆ Festival of Festivals

St Petersburg's annual international film festival takes place during the White Nights in late June. Hosted at the Rodina cinema and others, the festival is a non-competitive showcase of the best Russian and world cinema.

☆ Stars of the White Nights Festival

From late May until mid-July, this annual festival showcases world premieres of opera and ballet. Performances are held around the city, especially at the Mariinsky Theatre. The festival culminates in a fabulous ball at Tsarskoe Selo, which draws the event to a close.

⚑ Scarlet Sails

The highlight of the White Nights season, this one-night festival includes performing arts staged in Palace Square, and crowds of around a million lining the banks of the Neva for a spectacular fireworks display and to see a magnificent red-sailed Swedish frigate float by.

July

High summer is hot and bright – a great time to see the city in all its vividly painted, Italianate glory. There are few festivals during this time, but with weather like this, who needs them?

⚑ Navy Day

On 25 July St Petersburg celebrates its thousands of naval officers and rich maritime history with a flotilla of boats on the Neva outside the Admiralty and a general party along the banks of the river – great if you like a man in uniform.

☆ Usadba Jazz

The musical juggernaut that is Russia's largest open-air festival of jazz and all kinds of other improvised contemporary music makes its way to Yelagin Island.

September

A great month to visit – September is still usually warm and tourist numbers are dropping off. October is cool, if not yet cold, with even fewer visitors.

☆ Early Music Festival

The Early Music Festival aims to revive forgotten masterpieces from the Middle Ages, the Renaissance and the baroque era. The festival features a baroque opera, as well as performances by the Catherine the Great Orchestra. Musicians perform at various venues from mid-September until early October.

November

Winter is already here in November and you can expect to see the first snow on the ground, which gives the city a magical look.

⚑ Day of Reconciliation & Accord

The former October Revolution day – 7 November – is still an official holiday, although it is hardly acknowledged. It still is, however, a big day for flag-waving and protesting by old-school Communist Party members, especially in front of Gostiny Dvor.

December

Christmas isn't such a big deal in Russia (and it's in January anyway), but New Year's Eve is huge. St Petersburg is freezing, snowy and magical.

☆ Arts Square Winter Festival

Maestro Yury Temirkanov presides over this musical highlight, which takes place every year at the Shostakovich Philharmonia. For 10 days in December artists stage both classical and contemporary works, including symphonic music and opera.

⚑ New Year

Petersburgers see in the New Year (Novy God) by trading gifts, drinking champagne and listening to the Kremlin chimes on the radio or TV. A great time to see Russians at their merry best!

With Kids

With its focus on art, history and architecture, St Petersburg may not be an obvious place to bring children, but there are actually plenty of activities that children will love, especially during the summer months when the whole city is something of an outdoor playground.

Central Naval Museum (p110)

Museums & Other Attractions

Top museums for children include the Museum of Zoology (p149), with thousands of stuffed animals (including several mammoths) on display; the Railway Museum (p110), where you can see a range of scale locomotives and model railway bridges; the Central Naval Museum (p110) with its superb collection of model boats; the ghoulish Kunstkamera (p146), which is not suitable for smaller kids; and the Artillery Museum (p161), which is great for any children who love tanks. Three fascinating old Soviet naval craft on Vasilyevsky Island can be great fun to explore: take a tour of the Krasin (p148), an Arctic icebreaker, or either the People's Will (p151) or the C-189 (p147), two Soviet subs now open to the public. Also sure to entrance kids and adults alike are the incredibly detailed scale models of early 18th century St Petersburg at Petrovskaya Akvatoria (p91) and the even more epic model village of Russia's greatest sights at Grand Maket (p129).

The Great Outdoors

One of the best parks to take kids in the city to is on New Holland (p108) where there's a great kids playground, a wooden model of a frigate to climb around, a giant chess set and free pétanque (a form of boules). Amusement parks, boats and bikes for hire, and lots of open space make the Kirovsky Islands (p164), on the Petrograd Side, another great outdoors option just a short journey from the centre of the city. Kids will love the fountains at Peterhof, as well as the hydrofoil ride to get out there. Alexandrovsky Park (p160), on the Petrograd Side, is a great place for youngsters too – with the zoo, planetarium and plenty of other diversions among the trees. Another fun outdoor activity is taking a boat trip on the beautiful canals of the historic heart. For a fun day at the seashore (and eating snacks at beachside vendors) go to Beach Laskovy (p184) in Repino. Take a cruise (with Reeperbahn (p185) among other outfits) to visit various nearby islands in the gulf.

AKEDESIGN / SHUTTERSTOCK ©

Museum of Zoology (p149)

Child-friendly Eating

There is no shortage of family-friendly restaurants with playrooms, children's menus and high chairs for toddlers. Some of our favourites include Yat (p93), Teplo (p115), Botanika (p132), Moskva (p134), Khochu Kharcho (p114), Sadko (p115), Zoom Café (p91), Koryushka (p169), Stroganoff Steak House (p116) and Pryanosti & Radost (p151).

For child-friendly snacks on the hoof, try ubiquitous bliny outlet Teremok (Теремок), found all over the city, for cheap and delicious sweet or savoury pancakes.

Puppet & Circus Shows

Russia has a proud tradition of both puppetry and circus shows that will appeal to adults and children, and to non-Russian and Russian-speakers alike.

The excellent Bolshoy Puppet Theatre (p139) has been producing wonderfully innovative shows since its inception in the dark days of Stalinism, becoming a much-loved local institution. It currently boasts 22 shows for children – including an excellent version of *The Little Prince*.

The Demmeni Marionette Theatre (p100) is also an excellent venue, with a large range of shows, including *Gulliver's Travels* and *Puppets and Clowns* (a lively hour-long circus-style show performed by puppets).

For traditional-style circus shows the historic St Petersburg State Circus (p99) can't be beat; for something more modern, not involving performing animals, check to see if Upsala Circus (p170) has any shows on.

Money-Saving Tips

There's no getting around it: St Petersburg is no longer a cheap destination. Hotels and dining can be expensive, as are admission prices to many top-tier sights. However, there are plenty of free or cheap attractions and activities, as well as discounts and ways to make your budget go further.

No Charge

Visit the Hermitage (p56) for free on the first Thursday of each month. Yelagin Island (p172) is free on weekdays. the following are always free: Nabokov Museum (p111), Alexander Nevsky Monastery (p123), Grand Choral Synagogue (p111), Piskaryovskoe Cemetery (p166), Kazan Cathedral (p83), Sampsonievsky Cathedral (p165), Rizzordi Art Foundation, Geological Museum (p149), Loft Project ETAGI (p131), Red Banner Textile Factory (p161), Nikolsky Cathedral (p111), Mendeleev Museum (p149), Buddhist Temple (p166) and Sigmund Freud Museum of Dreams (p164).

As well as these excellent museums and sights, there's a wealth of gorgeous parks that make great picnic spots. In central St Petersburg try the charming Mikhailovsky Gardens (p85) and Summer Garden (p84); the open spaces of the Mars Field (p87); the overgrown beauty of the gardens at the Alexander Nevsky Monastery (p123); the spacious, pleasant Tauride Palace & Gardens (p128) in Smolny; and the brand new park on New Holland (p108) – all free and perfect on a sunny day.

Also gratis are the daily guided walking tours with St Petersburg Free Tour (p31) and Placemates (p31).

Cheap Frills

The following have charges of R150 or less: the Anna Akhmatova Museum (p125), the Kirov Museum (p159), the Museum of Political History (p159) and the Petersburg Avant-Garde Museum (p160).

Another great-value thing to do is to take yourself on a tour of the city's most impressive metro stations, which will only set you back R45 – or R35 if you have invested in a stored-value metro card!

Great views can be had for the price of a drink or a meal at Gastronomika (p135), Solaris Lab (p117) and rooftop restaurant of Hotel Vedensky (p196) among others.

Discounts

If you're a student, get an ISIC card before you travel, as most places won't accept any other form of student card as evidence of your status. If you want to see a lot of the Hermitage (p56), it's well worth booking the two-day ticket online, which is great value and allows you to visit the museum's other, lesser-known buildings at no extra charge. The same goes for the ticket to the Russian Museum (p74), which allows access to all its four venues over three days. Senior citizens and children also sometimes get free entry, but will need to bring some proof of age with them, such as a passport.

Money Saving

Try to get the Russian price at museums wherever possible – if you have a local friend, go along with them and keep quiet at the ticket office.If you plan to use the metro a lot, buy a magnetic card (R60) and buy trips in bulk to save money.

Eat set business lunches *(biznes lanch)* in restaurants, which are great value and very filling. Many other places offer a discount of around 20% on all bills for meals between noon and 4pm Monday to Friday.

Book in good time for the theatre, opera and ballet to get the best choice of seats and to not be limited to the most expensive.

Visas

You'll almost certainly need a visa to enter Russia – allow at least a month to arrange it. Once in the country you'll also need to make sure your visa is registered; this is usually taken care of by the hotel or hostel you are staying in.

Types of Visa

The primary types of visas are tourist visas (valid for a 30-day stay) and business visas (for 30- to 180-day stays). The specific requirements of Russian embassies in each country differ slightly, so check with the website of the embassy you're planning to apply through. Be aware that unless you live abroad, you won't usually be able to obtain a Russian visa anywhere but in your own country.

Generally for all visas you'll need to submit your passport, a photo, an invitation from either a hotel or a travel agency in Russia, a completed application form (downloadable from the embassy website) and in most cases a certificate of health insurance coverage.

Visa-free Travel

Passport holders of a handful of countries, including Israel, South Africa, South Korea, Thailand and many South American nations, enjoy the positive luxury of 30- to 90-day visa-free travel. Those arriving by cruise ship and ferry in St Petersburg can also take advantage of a 72-hour visa-free regime, though it comes on condition that a tour is purchased through an officially recognised travel agency (which need not be the one offered by the cruise company). This is a restrictive way to travel, but perfect if you just want to spend a few days in St Petersburg.

Invitation

The most annoying part of the visa process is the need to provide an invitation (also called visa support) from a hotel or travel agency. If your hotel doesn't offer this service – most do and you'll sometimes have to pay for it – then you'll need to get in touch with a travel agency. You'll normally need to fill in a form online and give your planned travel dates, but you can leave generous room with these to allow yourself some flexibility. Invitations are normally processed within a week.

ANNA PAKUTINA / SHUTTERSTOCK ©

Pedestrians on Malaya Sadovaya, near Nevsky pr

The following agencies can issue the invitations needed to apply for a Russian visa:

Express to Russia (www.expresstorussia.com)

OstWest.com (www.ostwest.com)

Travel Russia (www.travelrussia.su)

Way to Russia (www.waytorussia.net)

Application

Apply as soon as you have all the documents you need (but not more than two months ahead). Processing time ranges from 24 hours to two weeks, depending on how much you are willing to pay.

It's possible to apply at your local Russian consulate by dropping off all the necessary documents with the appropriate payment or by mailing it all (along with a self-addressed, postage-paid envelope for the return). When you receive the visa, check it carefully – especially the expiry, entry and exit dates and any restrictions on entry or exit points.

A third option is to use a visa agency. It's more expensive than doing it all yourself but it's a great way to delegate the hassles to someone else. Some agencies charge very reasonable fees to submit, track and collect your visa. The following are some recommended ones:

Action-visas.com (www.action-visas.com)

Comet Consular Services (www.cometconsular. com)

IVDS (www.ivds.de)

Real Russia (http://realrussia.co.uk)

VisaHQ.com (http://russia.visahq.com)

VisaCentral (http://visacentral.com)

Registration

On arrival you will be issued with a filled-out immigration card. This will be stamped along with your visa; one half of the card will be given to you, while the immigration officer will retain the other half. When you are checking in at a hotel, you'll have to surrender your passport and immigration card so the hotel can register you with the authorities. Usually they are given back the next morning, if not the same day. Some places (usually hostels) will charge for this service (around R250).

If you're not staying at a hotel, you will need to have your visa registered if you are staying for more than a week. The easiest way to do this is to take it to a travel agency where staff will usually offer registration for between R500 and R1000. If you are staying in Russia for fewer than seven working days, there is no need to register your visa.

Registration is very rarely checked these days, but can theoretically be demanded at any time, including at immigration on your way out of the country. While it's a pain, registering your visa remains wise.

Tours & Activities

St Petersburg offers a fine selection of guided walks, boat tours, bike excursions and more. These provide an introduction to the city, while giving visitors deeper insight into its history and culture. For DIY adventures, St Petersburg has plenty to offer, including kayaking, cycling, and relaxing in a banya (hot bath).

Tour boat on the Moyka River

Walking Tours

There is no shortage of walking tours in St Petersburg, the chief advantage of which is getting a local's perspective on the city. Even though distances are long, walking is a great way to discover courtyards, gardens, quirky sights and side streets that you might otherwise miss. Some operators will provide transport for walking tours as well, meaning that greater areas can be covered. Some highly recommended operators include:

Peterwalk Walking Tours (☑812-943 1229; http://peterswalk.com; from R1320) Going for over 20 years, Peter Kozyrev's innovative and passionately led tours are highly recommended as a way to see the city with knowledgeable locals. The daily Original Peterswalk is one of the favourites and leaves daily from the Julia Child Bistro (p114) at 10.30am from April to end of September. The choice of tours available is enormous and includes a Rasputin Walk and a WWII and the Siege of Leningrad tour.

Sputnik Tours (☑499-110 5266; www.sputnik8.com; price varies) This online tour agency is one with a difference: it acts as a marketplace for locals wanting to give their own unique tours of their city. Browse, select a tour, register and pay a deposit and then you get given the contact number of the guide. A superb way to meet locals you'd never meet otherwise.

Placemates (☑925 845 3747; http://placemates.ru; prices vary) This online portal connects visitors with locals running a variety of tours and interesting experiences around the city, including access to rooftops such as that of the Singer Building, a visit to a glassmaking factory or to a weaver's. They sometimes run free walking tours starting from Admiralteyskaya metro station.

St Petersburg Free Tour (http://petersburgfreetour.com) The central offering of this tour company is its 10.45am daily free city tour, which departs from the Alexander Column on Palace Square. But the company has plenty of other (not free but still reasonably priced) tours on offer, including metro tours, communist Leningrad and the Hermitage.

VB Excursions (☑812-380 4596; www.vb-excursions.com) Offers excellent walking tours with clued-up students on themes including Dostoevsky and Revolutionary St Petersburg. Their 'Back in the USSR' tour (R3850 per person) includes a visit to a typical Soviet apartment for tea and bliny.

Boat Tours

Boat is the ideal way to see such a watery city, though of course these only operate from April to October or so, as the river is frozen over for much of the winter. Most boats leave from the Moyka, Griboyedov Canal and Fontanka near to where Nevsky pr crosses them. There are dozens of operators, and many of them give very loud commentary (in Russian only) that might not exactly enhance your experience.

Anglo Tourismo (☎921-989 4722; www.anglotourismo.com; 27 nab reki Fontanki; 1hr tour adult/student R1900/900; Ⓜ Gostiny Dvor)) Anglo Tourismo is the main operator to run tours with commentary in English. Between May and September the schedule runs every 1½ hours between 11am and 6.30pm. From 1 June to 31 August there are additional night cruises.

City Tour Offers a 'hop on, hop off' boat tour around the main rivers and canals.

Bus Tours

Given the range of far more pleasant ways to see the city, not to mention the issue of St Petersburg's gridlocked traffic, bus tours might not appeal, but the introduction of 'hop-on, hop-off' buses means that they're an option. Alternatively, buy yourself a far cheaper local R40 bus ticket and improvise your own route around the city!

City Tour (☎812-648 1228; https://citytour spb.ru; one day pass adult/child R700/300) The familiar red 'hop on, hop off' double-decker buses you'll see in most big cities in Europe (and beyond) are now well established in St Petersburg. They offer a useful service for anyone unable to walk easily, with buses running along Nevsky pr, passing the Hermitage, going over the Strelka, the Petrograd Side and then back to the historic centre. An adult day ticket costs R700, valid for as many trips as you like, and you can buy tickets when you board the bus.

Bike Tours

Seeing the city by bike is definitely a grand idea, and doing this on a tour can really be great. Several hostels offer bike tours, but the best established in town are those offered by Peterswalk Walking Tours (p31), who offer a tour on Saturday and Sunday at 11am between June and September, departing from Taiga near the Hermitage, and a night bike tour every Tuesday and Thursday from June to August departing the same location at 10.30pm.

Other Tours

Transport enthusiasts will love the 'retro' tours given by the City Electrical Transport Museum, while less mobile travellers will appreciate the existence of Liberty Tour.

Retro Tram Tour (Map p286, D3; ☎812-321 5405; Sredny pr 77; per person R200; ☺ Sat & Sun; Ⓜ Vasileostrovskaya) The City Electrical Transport Museum runs weekend tours in a 1930s tram car. The tours take around two hours, and run across the Petrograd Side then via Sennaya and Kolomna before returning here.

Kopejka World (p142) This new outfit offers guided tours aboard a classic Soviet car – the VAZ-2101, aka the 'Kopejka'. Roof cutouts allow you to get an airy perspective, while guides explain some of the lesser known aspects of St Petersburg.

Liberty (Map p284, D5; ☎812-232 8163; www.libertytour.ru; ul Polozova 12, Office 1; Ⓜ Petrogradskaya) Specialising in wheelchair-accessible tours in and around St Petersburg, this unique-in-Russia company has specially fitted vans. They can also advise on and book hotels with rooms for travellers with disabilities.

Outdoor Activities

As the seasons change so do the types of outdoor activities that are on offer. Winter sees Yelagin Island morph into a top location for ice-skating and cross-country skiing. The same location and Krestovsky Island are both good spots to hire bicycles or go in-line skating. For downhill skiing (nothing too challenging as the terrain is fairly flat) there are small ski resorts in a radius of 10km to 20km around the city, including Ohta Park (www.ohtapark.ru), **Krasnoe Ozero** (☎812-960 0960; www.krasnoeozero.ru; Korobitsyno) and **Tuutari Park** (☎812-380 5062; www.tyytari.spb.ru; Retselya 14; ☺5-10pm Mon-Fri, 10am-9pm Sat & Sun Dec-Mar).

Warmer weather brings the opportunity for kayaking around the city's canals and

6620; www.newarena.spb.ru; pr Pyatiletok 1;
Ⓜ Prospket Bol'shevikov).

Banya

If you're looking for a uniquely Russian experience, then head to the nearest *banya* (steam bath) of which St Petersburg has several, both standard and luxury. Enter the *parilka* (steam room) stark naked and sit back and watch the mercury rise. To eliminate toxins and improve circulation, bathers beat each other (never too hard!) with a bundle of birch branches, known as *veniki*. It's actually an extremely pleasant sensation. When you can't take the heat, retreat. A public *banya* allows access to a plunge pool, usually filled with ice-cold water. The contrast in temperature is invigorating, energising and purifying.

Zenit St Petersburg match, Krestovsky Stadium (p170)

rivers. Contact Wild Russia (p103) to go further afield to Lake Ladoga for yachting and kayaking, as well as off-road biking, parachuting, quad biking and rock climbing outside the city. You can also charter yachts and motorboats via the agency **Solnechny Parus** (Map p276, B8; ☑ 812-327 3525; www.solpar.ru; 2nd fl, Ligovsky pr 94A; Ⓜ Ligovsky Prospekt).

Or you could hit the beach – there's a city-centre one facing the Neva beside the walls of the Peter & Paul Fortress (this is where people famously sunbathe standing up against the stone walls), or head out of town to lovely Beach Laskovy (p184) at Repino.

Spectator Sports

The city's most popular spectator sport is soccer; local team FC Zenit St Petersburg have regularly been champions of the Russian Premier League and winners of both the UEFA Cup and UEFA Super Cup in the past. The team plays at the new 21,500 capacity Krestovsky Stadium (p170), used as one of the venues for the 2018 World Cup as well as other international games. Ice hockey is another crowd pleaser; SKA (www.ska.ru), the premier club, celebrated their 70th anniversary in 2016 and play at the **Ice Palace** (Ледовый Дворец; ☑ 812-718

Best Activities

Piter Kayak (p120) Admire the city's architecture while paddling along its canals and rivers.

Baltic Airlines (p171) Hop in a helicopter on Zayachy Island next to the Peter & Paul Fortress for 10- to 15-minute flights over the city.

Yelagin Island (p172) Take a trip to this Petrograd Side oasis of calm for ice skating in winter and in-line skating in summer.

Wild Russia (p103) Can organise all kinds of local adventure activities including boating, off-road biking and rock climbing.

Piterland (p172) Superb water park where it's balmy whatever the weather outside.

Best Banyas

Krugliye Bani (p172) One of the best spots for a traditional banya; includes a heated open air pool.

Degtyarniye Baths (p142) Central, modern and one of the most foreigner-friendly bani.

Mytninskiye Bani (p142) The oldest communal banya in the city, heated by a wood furnace.

Palace Bridge Wellness Club (p153) Offers several styles of sauna in which to steam away all your stresses.

Visiting on a Cruise

Visiting St Petersburg by ferry or as part of a cruise is an increasingly popular choice, as arriving this way automatically entitles you to enter Russia visa-free for up to 72 hours. This allows you to see St Petersburg without the visa headache and to combine it with other cities in the Baltic.

Visa-free Travel

In order to benefit from the 72-hour visa-free travel rule, you simply have to arrive in St Petersburg by boat at one of the multiple ferry terminals, and have booked a tour with a licensed operator. You can either sleep on your boat, or pay for a hotel, but note that you are also obliged to leave St Petersburg by sea.

If you're on a cruise to St Petersburg, your operator will normally have arrangements in place with a local travel agency, whose tour you will be sold hard. Many cruise-ship passengers have reported being told that visitors need a Russian visa if they do not take the tour sold by the cruise ship. This is in fact not true at all, and any company offering shore excursions is sufficient to avoid the necessity of getting a visa.

Booking Tours

If you're arriving by ferry then **St Peter Line** (☑812-702 0777; https://stpeterline.com) offers a 'tour package', which is really just a bus-transfer service into the city centre for €25 per person. These hourly buses run between the Sea Port and St Isaac's Cathedral, though you can get off at two other stops on Vasilyevsky Island too. There's no guided-tour element, so once you get off the bus, you're free to roam around the city as you please.

It's often both cheaper and a far better experience if you opt out of the cruise-sold excursions, as they rarely offer the best way to spend your brief time in the city. To make the most of things, and to avoid being in an enormous group, consider booking a private tour from one of these shore excursion specialists:

DenRus (www.denrus.ru) This long-established shore excursion operator offers a number of different tours angled specifically towards cruise passengers. Tours can often be adapted to visitor needs and guides are well trained, experienced and speak good English.

Red October (☑812-363 0368; www.redoctober.ru) Operating for 15 years, this experienced tour agency specialises in one- to three-day shore excursions for cruise-ship passengers, including tailor-made programs for private groups.

Wind Surf cruise ship on the Neva River

PHOTO: RUSSIA / GETTY IMAGES ©

Ports of Arrival

There are a number of places where cruise ships arrive in St Petersburg, while all ferries from elsewhere in the Baltic arrive at the Sea Port on Vasilyevsky Island. Anyone on a river cruise from Moscow will arrive at the River Passenger Terminal (p243) in the south of the city, which is a short walk away from the Proletarskaya metro station (Line 3). Upon leaving the metro turn right onto pr Obukhovskoy Oborony and it's five minutes up the road.

Marine Facade Terminal

The **Marine Facade Terminal** (Пассажирский Порт Санкт-Петербург Морской фасад; ☑812-303 6740; www.port spb.ru; 1 Bereg Nevskoy gubi; Ⓜ Primorskaya) at the far end of Vasilyevsky Island is a relatively new facility. It's not in the city centre, but all shore excursion operators have buses or cars for their passengers, and the journey to the Hermitage can be done in 30 minutes. The nearest metro station is Primorskaya, from where it's just two stops to Gostiny Dvor (Line 3) in the historic heart, but it's a good 30-minute walk away and you'd be advised to arrange a taxi. Head down the main road from the Marine Facade, then once you've crossed Nalichnaya ul, take Novosmolenskaya nab and you'll reach the station.

For taxis, an official dispatch stand is in the arrivals area, with fixed rates to various places around town. You'll be given a slip of paper with the price you need to pay the driver: prices average R200 to R400 depending on where in the centre you want to go.

Sea Port

If you're arriving by ferry from Stockholm, Tallinn or Helsinki then you'll arrive at the Sea Port (p244) in the southern corner of Vasilyevsky Island. It's not served by the metro, so your easiest way into the city centre is to take a taxi. Drivers wait outside the terminal or you can order a taxi by phone app; prices average R200 to R400 depending on where in the centre you want to go.

An alternative option is to take bus 7 (R40) from the main road outside. The bus should have pl Vosstaniya (Пл Восстания) written on it, and it goes all the way down Sredny pr, crosses the Neva at the Hermitage and then goes down Nevsky pr to pl Vosstaniya.

St Peter Line (p34) offers a €25 'tour package' bus service that shuttles anyone taking it to St Isaac's Cathedral and back again every hour.

Other Ports

There are three other docks where cruise ships sometimes arrive in St Petersburg. Smaller cruise ships usually dock on either the **English Embankment Passenger Terminal** (Map p280, B2) or the **Lieutenant Schmidt Passenger Terminal** (Map p286, E4). Neither terminal has much in the way of facilities, but both are centrally located and you're within easy walking distance from the sights of the historic heart.

One far less attractive possibility is docking at the **St Petersburg Sea Port** (Морской порт Санкт-Петербурга; www. seaport.spb.ru; Mezhevoy kanal 5), which is the main commercial and industrial port in the city. It's on Gutuyevsky Island and a long way from anything. It's technically possible to walk out of the port to the Narvskaya metro station, but reckon on a 30-minute walk through a fairly miserable industrial area. If you decide to walk, head up Obvodny Canal and then turn right onto Staropetrogovsky pr and you'll see Narvskaya metro station on pl Stachek.

Travelling to Moscow

Many visitors to St Petersburg combine their trip here with one to Moscow. Russia's two largest cities are superbly well connected to each other, with flights leaving at least every hour, Sapsan express trains during the day, slower overnight trains you can sleep on, and even slower boats.

Air

The following airlines fly direct from Pulkovo Airport in St Petersburg to three different Moscow airports. Book in advance and you can get tickets as cheap as R2750 one-way, although normally prices are between R4000 and R7000.

Aeroflot (www.aeroflot.ru) Flies around 20 times a day to Sheremetyevo Airport.

Rossiya Airlines (www.rossiya-airlines.com) Flies to Vnukovo Airport and operates 11 flights per day between the two cities.

S7 Airlines (www.s7.ru) Operates 11 flights per day between St Petersburg and Domodedovo Airport.

UTair (www.utair.ru) Operates four daily flights between St Petersburg and Vnukovo Airport.

Ural Airlines (www.uralairlines.com) Offers two daily flights to Domodedovo Airport.

Boat

Boats from Moscow and elsewhere within Russia arrive at the River Passenger Terminal (p243), which is a short walk away from the Proletarskaya metro station. Leaving the metro, turn right onto pr Obukhovskoy Oborony and it's five minutes up the road.

Train

All trains to Moscow from St Petersburg depart from the Moscow Station (p242). Take your pick from the overnight sleeper trains or the super-fast Sapsan day trains. All train tickets can be bought online at www.rzd.ru, or from the machines at any station in St Petersburg.

Overnight

There are about 10 overnight trains travelling between St Petersburg and Moscow. Most depart between 10pm and 1am, arriving in the capital the following morning between 6am and 8am. On the more comfortable *firmenny* trains, such as the Red Arrow (Красная стрела) or Grand Express (ГРАНД ЭКСПРЕСС) a de-luxe sleeping carriage is between R12,800 and R16,400, 1st-class compartment (two-person cabin) around R16,300, while a 2nd-class *kupe* (four-person cabin) is R2800. Less fancy trains offer 3rd-class *platzkartny* (dorm-style sleeping carriages) for R1570 and even sitting-only carriages for R890.

If in a sleeping carriage you may have to pay a small amount extra for bed linen, although with some tickets this – and breakfast – is included.

Sapsan

These high-speed trains travel at 200km/h to reach Moscow in around four hours. There are six to eight daily departures. Comfortable 2nd-class seats start at R1300, while super-spacious 1st-class seats run from R5000.

Museums & Galleries

St Petersburg is a city of museums and galleries, famed around the world for its world-class collection at the Hermitage, but also for the stellar Russian Museum and the widely renowned Erarta Museum of Contemporary Art. Elsewhere, St Petersburg's smaller institutions focus on everything from the Arctic to zoology, via bread, toys, trams, trains, religion and vodka.

The Big Three

If you're going to visit three museums, make it a triad of galleries: the Hermitage, the Russian Museum and the Erarta Museum of Contemporary Art. The Hermitage needs no introduction – suffice to say that one of the greatest art collections on the planet should be top of your must-see list. The lesser-known Russian Museum displays Russian art from the medieval times until the early 20th century and is the perfect counterpoint to the Hermitage's Western Art collection. Finally, Erarta has established itself as one of world's best collections of modern and contemporary Russian art and should not be missed.

Newer Additions

While many of St Petersburg's museums are bastions of tradition, things are being kept fresh and exciting by several newer arrivals. Top of the list are the galleries at the General Staff Building, a major branch of the Hermitage that's home to a superb collection of Impressionist and Post-Impressionist works by the likes of Monet, Matisse and Picasso. The dazzling Fabergé Museum showcases the apex of Peter Carl Fabergé's jewellery making and features some 1500 of his unique creations including nine Imperial Easter eggs. A rather different tone is set by the exciting Street Art Museum, based on the territory of a laminated plastics factory in the suburb of Okhta. Here the walls act as canvases for celebrated and up-and-coming street artists from across Russia and around the world to create a different themed show each year. An old collection of boats, models and paintings has been rejuvenated by a new location for the Central Naval Museum in Kolomna. Nearby you'll find MISP, the Museum of St Petersburg Art (20th–21st centuries), with regularly changing exhibitions of modern and contemporary works by local artists.

The Best of the Rest

Other smaller and often lesser-known museums that are well worth building into your itinerary include the fascinatingly macabre Kunstkamera, Peter the Great's private cabinet of curiosities (think babies in bottles); the Russian Museum of Ethnography displaying traditional crafts and cultures from across the region; the Museum of Political History in a palace that was home to the famous ballet dancer Mathilda Kshesinskaya; and the excellent complex of museums at the Peter & Paul Fortress, the kernel of 18th-century St Petersburg and home to a good museum covering the city's history.

Art Galleries & House Museums

Some of Russia's most famous artists, including Ilya Repin and Karl Bryullov, trained at the Academy of Arts and the Applied Arts School. Both schools have galleries open to the public that are well worth checking out. You can access the best of modern and contemporary arts at places such as the Kuryokhin Centre, Pushkinskaya 10, the Novy Museum, K-Gallery and Marina Gisich Gallery.

St Petersburg is also a city of literary titans. The flat where Pushkin breathed his last is preserved as a museum. So too are the former homes of the writers Derzhavin, Dostoevsky, Nabokov and Akhmatova.

NEED TO KNOW

Opening Days & Hours

Nearly all museums close at least one day a week. This tends to vary, although Monday and Tuesday are the most common days. Be aware that in addition to this, many museums close one day a month additionally for cleaning; it's worth checking a museum's website for these details.

Language Issues

Things are getting better but few museums have full signage in English. Audioguides, increasingly available in English, are a great way to understand a collection. Guided tours in English vary enormously in quality and usually need to be booked in advance.

Ticket Prices

As a foreigner you will often be charged a 'foreigner price', anything from 50% to 100% more than the Russian price. That said, children, students and pensioners all normally receive discounts on entrance fees, even as foreigners, so it's always worth asking.

Lonely Planet's Top Choices

Hermitage (p56) Everybody's first-choice museum will not fail to amaze even the most jaded traveller.

Russian Museum (p74) Visiting the city's stellar collection of Russian art over the centuries is a sublime experience.

Erarta Museum of Contemporary Art (p145) Trek out to this excellent survey of Soviet underground and contemporary Russian art.

Kunstkamera (p146) See Peter the Great's collection of curiosities, freaks and babies in jars. Not for the faint hearted!

Fabergé Museum (p87) A must for anyone interested in late Imperial Russian jewellery and decorative arts.

Best Museums for Arts & Interiors

Hermitage (p56) Alongside the amazing art collection are the palace's fabulously decorated rooms.

Museum of Decorative & Applied Arts (p126) This little-known gem of a museum contains thousands of beautiful *objets d'art*.

Stroganov Palace (p84) A branch of the Russian Museum with gorgeously restored state rooms.

Yusupov Palace (p107) The location of Rasputin's murder offers some of the city's best 19th century interiors.

Menshikov Palace (p148) Beautiful Petrine interiors at this branch of Hermitage on Vasilyevsky Island.

Best Museums for Kids

Museum of Zoology (p149) Check out the stuffed mammoths here, as well as the thousands of other specimens on display.

Central Naval Museum (p110) Any kids interested in model-making will be in awe of this huge collection of model boats.

Erarta Museum of Contemporary Art (p145) Kids will love the U Space installations that are part of the museum.

Peter & Paul Fortress (p156) Where the city began its life; this fortress contains several fascinating museums.

Best House Museums

Anna Akhmatova Museum at the Fountain House (p125) The unusual house-museum of St Petersburg's most famous modern poet is both tragic and uplifting.

Pushkin Flat-Museum (p86) 'Russia's most famous address' is the house in which its national bard died in 1837.

Dostoevsky Museum (p129) This gloomy museum is a sufficiently suitable place to explore Dostoevsky's troubled and brilliant life.

Derzhavin House-Museum (p131) A wonderful chance to visit an 18th-century mansion brought back to its original splendour.

Kirov Museum (p159) Take a look at how the Bolshevik elite lived in the 1930s, when Kirov was one of Russia's most powerful men.

Cakes and sweets on display, Kupetz Eliseevs (p102)

Eating

There has never been a better time to eat out in St Petersburg. The range and quality of food available seem to increase year on year, making stereotypes about Russian food now seem like bizarre anachronisms. Petersburgers have well and truly caught the foodie bug, and while little of good quality is cheap in this town, the choice is now bigger than ever.

Getting Serious About Food

St Petersburg has become a place where good food is prized and defined not by its high price tag but rather by the talents of the chef. Fresh, local ingredients, inventive combinations, the use of herbs and spices (other than the ubiquitous dill) and a wider range of flavours are a fixture on the city's dining tables, and while there's still plenty of mediocre food out there, visitors today are truly spoiled for choice. We've never had an easier

time recommending restaurants. However, good places are rarely the most obvious and it's recommend to reserve for the very best.

Modern Russian

Russian food, it's fair to say, has an image problem – and if you're not careful you can easily end up with dill-smothered soups, under-seasoned and over-cooked meats, and salads that are more mayonnaise than vegetable. But fret not: there is great Russian cooking to be had in St Petersburg now –

NEED TO KNOW

Opening Hours

Nearly all restaurants are open seven days a week, generally from around 11am or noon until at least 11pm. Many restaurants open 'until the last customer' – a fairly nonspecific term that means as long as someone is still ordering, they'll keep serving.

Reservations

The vast majority of restaurants don't require reservations, though they can be handy on Friday or Saturday evening or for weekend breakfasts in popular places. Reservations are always recommended if you want to sit in a particular place, for example outside on the terrace.

Service

Service has improved; at fancy places it often veers on the over-attentive. The main problem you'll have is that most waiting staff's English is limited.

Tipping

In little cafes and cheap eats, tipping is not expected, though you can easily round up the amount you pay if you're happy with the service. Anywhere more upmarket will usually expect a 10% tip and some add service to the bill.

English Menus

These are a lifeline for non-Russian speakers and are available in nearly all good restaurants, though they're often not available in cheaper cafes (and when they are, they are very badly translated). Bring along a sense of humour and adventure!

both traditional and contemporary, and increasingly a combination of the two. Russian chefs have been rediscovering their own culinary history and have been slowly moving away from the dozen or so standard offerings that are ubiquitous on the country's menus. They're preparing rarer or even forgotten dishes, such as venison and duck cooked in subtle and interesting ways and combined with herbs and fresh, organic vegetables. Economic sanctions on food products from the EU have given a boost to local providers, with places such

as Cococo and EM Restaurant making a virtue of farm-to-table dining principles.

Local Chains

St Petersburg has a number of home-grown restaurant and cafe chains that are well worth knowing about as they provide cheap and reliable eating options all over town. Chief among these is the now international pie chain Stolle (Штолле; www. stolle.ru), a near-ubiquitous cafe where delicious, moist savoury and sweet pies are available to eat in and take away. Similar and equally numerous is the chain of bakery cafes Bulochnye F. Volcheka (Булочные Ф. Вольчека; www.fvolchek.ru). A couple of other chains to look out for are coffee-and-cake specialists Bushe (Буше; www.bushe. ru) and Baltic Bread (Балтийский Хлеб; www.baltic-bread.ru), which does good sandwiches and pastries.

International Cuisine

Long gone are the days when international cuisine in St Petersburg was limited to the odd Georgian or Italian place. As Russians have travelled more and experienced more foreign cuisines, their tastes have widened and there's a healthy mixture of non-Russian cuisine available in St Petersburg today, running from Thai and Indian to American and even Lithuanian. Gourmet burgers are hugely popular and there's plenty of excellent French, German, Italian and pan-Asian food on the city's menus – especially sushi (which is rarely that great). More common, however, is the international menu, where Russian dishes, pizza, sushi and noodles all compete side-by-side for your attention. In many cases this means that all four are pretty average, but increasingly there are places that know what they're doing with multiple cuisines.

Vegetarian Options

There is now a very respectable variety of vegetarian cuisine on offer, both at mainstream restaurants and at an increasing number of meat-free places. Look out for vegetarian chains Troitsky Most and Ukrop, as well as individual restaurants such as Botanika (p132) and Samadeva (p93). Some non-vegetarian restaurants that offer plenty of choice for non-meat eaters include Marketplace (p92), Zoom Café (p91) and Mamaliga (p94). Fish is widely offered on menus, making an excellent alternative for pescatarians. During the 40 days before Orthodox Easter (*veliky post* in Russian), many restaurants also offer a Lent menu that is animal-free.

Like a Local

Locals still disappear to their local *stolovaya* (столовая; canteen) at lunchtime for a supremely cheap and social meal, albeit one that's rarely particularly exciting. These places, hangovers from the Soviet days, are usually signposted in Cyrillic and tend to be located in basements and courtyards, but if you stumble across one (look for the sign столовая), you're normally more than welcome to go in. Experiences don't come much more local than this, and you'll usually find yourself saving plenty of cash if you eat in such places. A sign of their enduring popularity is the recent reinvention of the *stolovaya* in such guises as Marketplace (p92), Obed Bufet (p132) and the chain **Stolovaya No 1 Kopeika** (Столовая No. 1 Копейка; Map p272; http://st1. one; Nevsky pr 25; mains R25-50; set lunch R99; ⊙24hr; MNevsky Prospekt). These modern, attractive spaces that have taken the essential idea of a *stolovaya* and translated it into something appealing for the contemporary St Petersburg diner.

Eating by Neighbourhood

➡ **Historic Heart** (p91) A scattering of gems among many mediocre places.

➡ **Sennaya & Kolomna** (p113) Location of some of the city's best restaurants.

➡ **Smolny & Vosstaniya** (p132) Cool and innovative dining options abound.

➡ **Vasilyevsky Island** (p151) Reasonable selection with a good showing of Caucasus restaurants.

➡ **Petrograd & Vyborg Sides** (p166) Best choices are in Petrograd Side.

Russian mushroom soup

Lonely Planet's Top Choices

EM Restaurant (p116) Contemporary Russian dining at its very best.

Cococo (p94) Culinary creativity run rampant with plenty of local ingredients.

Gräs x Madbaren (p93) Scandi-cool meets Russian locavore at this hip central restaurant.

Yat (p93) Traditional charm in a country-cottage environment moments from the Hermitage.

Duo Gastrobar (p132) Super-stylish fusion food in an equally smart environment.

Koryushka (p169) Stunning Neva views and a great menu featuring St Petersburg's beloved fish speciality.

Best by Budget

€

Marketplace (p92) A smart and great-value cafeteria-style place with oodles of choice and several outlets in the city.

Obed Bufet (p132) Modern take on the Soviet canteen, boasting huge choice and swanky surroundings.

Dekabrist (p116) Well located for a post-Hermitage meal, this modern cafe is excellent value.

Bekitzer (p135) Israel-themed eatery and bar serving the best falafel wraps this side of the Baltic sea.

€€

Chekhov (p167) Excellent Russian food served in a traditional Russian dacha-style environment.

Romeo's Bar & Kitchen (p116) A superb Italian restaurant with a solid reputation.

Hamlet + Jacks (p93) Splits its inventive menu between dishes made with local or international ingredients.

Lev y Ptichka (p167) Friendly Georgian restaurant with delicious and reasonably priced food.

Kuznya House (p115) New Holland's main restaurant offers a creative, globe-trotting menu.

€€€

Mansarda (p117) The dazzling views here don't distract you from the food at this impressive establishment.

The Répa (p116) Elegant dining spot perfect for pre- or post-Mariinsky meals.

Restoran (p152) Ever-reliable Russian restaurant of under-stated style and with songbirds chirping near the lobby.

Best for Breakfast

Zoom Café (p91) This cosy, cuddly-toy filled space in the heart of town serves up a mean Russian breakfast.

Grey's (p135) A pared back but elegant spot for weekend brunch, or a simple weekday breakfast.

Mechtateli (p93) Serves breakfast until 2pm at weekends from a great location overlooking the Fontanka River.

Teplo (p115) Its name translates as 'warm' and you'll quickly understand why: this place feels like a home away from home.

Best 24-hour Eats

Khochu Kharcho (p114) This sprawling Georgian restaurant offers you a filling meal at any time of day.

Jean-Jacques (p169) French favourite that's perfect for very-late-night or early-morning grazing.

Stolovaya No 1 Kopeika (p41) Enjoy round-the-clock access to the Russian dishes at this modern canteen.

Best for Atmosphere

Sadko (p115) With waiters who sing opera between courses, this is a favourite spot for dining near the Mariinsky.

Co-op Garage (p113) Cool spot for creatively topped thin-crust pizzas and craft beers.

Botanika (p132) This place's vegetarianism has translated into a Zen-like calm you won't find elsewhere.

Paninaro (p167) Italian gem inside a striking apartment building on the Petrograd Side.

Best Russian

Banshiki (p133) Serving up a huge variety of nostalgic dishes with a contemporary touch.

Gogol (p93) Conjures up post-revolutionary urban style with fine Russian home cooking.

Staraya Derevnya (p167) Family-run hideaway with intimate atmosphere and delicious meals.

Severyanin (p114) Experience old-fashioned elegance at this top choice for Russian cuisine.

Drinking & Nightlife

It was Vladimir of Kiev, father of the Russian state, who is said to have rejected abstinent Islam in the 10th century. Drinking alcohol remains an integral part of Russian culture and society, with beer far more popular than vodka in the city's many bars. Cafes are also wonderful places to hang out, and pack your dancing slippers as the clubbing scene is vibrant.

Vodka & Beer

The word 'vodka' is the diminutive of *voda,* the Russian word for water, so it means something like 'a wee drop'. Russians sometimes drink vodka in moderation, but more often it's tipped down in swift shots, often followed by a pickle (snacking apparently stops you from getting drunk). Some traditional Russian restaurants in St Petersburg serve their own flavoured vodkas (try the horseradish, cranberry or sea buckthorn, if available) and *polugar,* a historic form of vodka made from bread.

You may be surprised to learn that *pivo* (beer) is actually Russia's most popular alcoholic drink. The market leader is local big brewer Baltika, and another popular local brand is Vasileostrovskaya, named after Vasilyevsky Island, where it is brewed. However, as with the rest of Russia, St Petersburg is in the grip of a craze for craft brewing – small-batch ales from microbreweries both local and international. Craft-beer bars are scattered across the city and worth searching out.

Where to Drink

Back in the day, the equivalent of the local pub was a *ryumochnaya,* which comes from the word *ryumka* (shot). These were pretty grim places, serving up *sto gramm* (100 grams) of a spirit, and little else. There are still a handful of these places around.

In recent years, St Petersburg's drinking possibilities have expanded exponentially. Now, drinkers can take their pick from wine bars, cocktail bars, pubs, sports bars, microbreweries and more. In the summer months, there is an additional assortment of *letniye sady* (summer gardens) scattered around town. It's also perfectly acceptable to go into almost any restaurant and just order drinks.

Nightlife in St Petersburg

St Petersburg boasts a sophisticated array of live-music joints, jazz venues, dance clubs, karaoke places, stylish bars, British- and Irish-style pubs and even its fair share of hipster hangouts. Dumskaya ul, a side street off Nevsky pr, at the junction with ul Lomonosova is St Petersburg's drinking quarter packed with interchangeable dive bars. After midnight at the weekends, it's a sight to see. For more bohemian venues, head to Vosstaniya and along the Fontanka, where you'll find lots of cool bars and clubs. Also get your hotel or Russian friends to make bookings and provide directions to one of the city's uber-cool speakeasy-style bars, typically hidden in secret locations.

Cafes & Anticafes

A few Russian coffee-shop chains have followed their Western counterparts and opened up outlets on every corner. Rest assured, you will never be far from a Coffee House (Кофе Хауз), Ideal Cup (Идеальная Чашка) or Shokoladnitsa (Шоколадница), and can even find well-known international brands such as Starbucks and Costa Coffee. But the independent cafes earn far higher marks for atmosphere and artistry, and are well worth seeking out. Preparation methods include siphon and pour-over, and devotion to creating the perfect brew is nothing short of fanatical.

There's also the local phenomenon known as anti-cafes or time cafes where your bill is based on the time you spend in the venue, and covers free-flowing hot and soft drinks and snacks. The concept has also broadened out into a time-based bar!

Legality

Alcohol is legal on the street, but banned in the metro. The legal drinking age is 18, though it's rarely enforced. It is illegal for shops to sell any alcohol between 10pm and 11am – so buy in advance or drink in a bar or restaurant between these times.

Smoking

Russia introduced a nationwide smoking ban in mid-2014 and it's strictly enforced. You're unable to smoke in restaurants, cafes, bars or hotels, and can only now do so outside.

Drinking & Nightlife by Neighbourhood

➡ **Historic Heart** (p96) An endless choice of smart cafes, cool bars and busy clubs centred on Dumskaya ul.

➡ **Sennaya & Kolomna** (p117) Quiet for the most part; there are still a few excellent bars here.

➡ **Smolny & Vosstaniya** (p136) The city's coolest district is the preferred haunt of hipsters, serious musicians and clubbers.

➡ **Vasilyevsky Island** (p152) Not noted for nightlife, but there are a couple of great places at its eastern tip.

➡ **Petrograd & Vyborg Sides** (p170) Generally quiet after dark, but the Petrograd Side has a couple of interesting places.

Lonely Planet's Top Choices

Union Bar & Grill (p136) Huge and thriving beard-heavy bar on Liteyny pr.

Apotheke Bar (p96) Cosy and sophisticated cocoon for cocktail connoisseurs.

Kabinet (p96) Hidden behind a burger joint is this fun, gambling-themed cocktail bar.

Redrum (p136) Hitting all the right notes with its range of craft beers.

Mod Club (p96) DJs, live music and rooftop movies: this club offers it all.

Big Wine Freaks (p170) Offering an excellent variety of wines, tasty snacks and live music.

Best Cocktail Bars

Dead Poets Bar (p137) Grown-up cocktail bar with plush upholstery and a fanatical approach to mixology.

Bolshoy Bar (p170) Dapper boxcar-sized spot serving first-rate cocktails on the Petrograd Side.

Borodabar (p96) Be sure to be sporting at least stubble when you visit the hip 'beard bar'.

Commode (p136) Clink glasses in this stylish bar where the bill depends on the time you spend here.

Terminal Bar (p137) Mixology is taken seriously at this NYC-style bar.

Best Cafes & Teahouses

Coffee 22 (p96) Could this be the zenith of hipster cafes? We think so.

Solaris Lab (p117) Tea with amazing rooftop views across to St Isaac's.

Bonch Cafe (p97) Great drinks and breakfast spot in the Historic Heart.

Radosti Kofe (p152) Pleasant pit stop for coffee on Vasilyevsky Island.

Kvartira Kosti Kroitsa (p133) There's also a tea salon at this beautiful restaurant and bar secreted away off Nevsky pr.

Double B (p170) Hip coffee station on the Petrograd Side.

Best Clubs

Griboyedov (p139) This long-running bunker club remains a perennial favourite for clubbers in the city.

Kamchatka (p171) This shrine to Kino frontman Viktor Tsoy is a great place to hear new local groups.

Tanzploshchadka (p98) Groove alongside beautiful young things at this on-trend club.

Central Station (p98) Long-running LGBT club with gyrating topless barmen and dancers.

Best Brewpubs

Farsh & Bochka (p137) Wide-ranging line-up of craft brews, with over 30 on draft.

Beer Geek (p138) Tiny basement bar favoured by local craft beer fanatics.

Top Hops (p96) Riverside bar with a regularly changing menu of 20 beers on tap.

Beer Boutique 1516 (p152) Heaven for craft-beer lovers on Vasilyevsky Island.

Yasli (p170) Excellent craft brews on tap and satisfying pub grub on the Petrograd Side.

Best Bohemian Hangouts

The Hat (p136) Live jazz, cocktails and a boho vibe make for a great evening out.

Ziferburg (p137) Anti-cafe with romantic, pre-revolutionary style in Golitsyn Loft.

Stirka 40 (p117) Whether or not you bring your washing to be done, this low-key place is a winner.

Buter Brodsky (p151) Serving ace cocktails, homemade tinctures and their own beer.

Dyuni (p138) Come and join the fun in this hipster sandpit.

⭐ Entertainment

The classical performing arts are one of the biggest draws to St Petersburg. Highly acclaimed professional artists stage productions in elegant theatres around the city, many of which have been recently revamped and look marvellous. Seeing a Russian opera, ballet or classical-music performance in a magnificent baroque theatre is a highlight of any trip.

Ballet & Opera

The beautiful and historic Mariinsky, now with a separate second modern stage and marvellous concert hall, is understandably every visitor's first choice for entertainment. However, if you can't get a ticket, there's no shortage of ballet and opera in other illustrious St Petersburg theatres: try the Mikhailovsky (p98), the Alexandrinsky (p98), the Hermitage Theatre (p99) and the St Petersburg Opera (p119). The key is to ask locally for recommendations, as most educated Petersburgers can give you an idea of which productions are worth buying tickets for. Critics complain that the Russian renditions of well-known Western works often seem naive and overstylised, so steer clear of Mozart. Far more likely to be good are productions of Tchaikovsky, Prokofiev, Rimsky-Korsakov or Shostakovich, all regulars on the playbills at most theatres.

Classical Music

Orchestral music is taken very seriously in St Petersburg, and unsurprisingly so, as most of the Russian genre originated here.

The Rimsky-Korsakov Conservatory (p118) is the beating heart of the classical-music scene, and host concerts given by its students in both its Bolshoy Zal (Big Hall) and Maly Zal (Little Hall). Quality is superb and can be matched only by that at the Shostakovich Philharmonia (p99), under the baton of maestro Yury Temirkanov, where concerts are given in two concert halls with the same names as those at the Conservatory.

Cinema

St Petersburg has long played a central role in Russia's movie-making industry and there are several historic cinemas in town as well as more modern art-house venues and multiplexes. It's possible to see films in their original-language versions and during the summer months attend outdoor screenings on the city's rooftops organised by Roof Cinema (p96), which hosts shows at Mod Club (p96) and the New Stage (p99) in the Historic Centre and Hotel Vedensky (p196) and Hi-Hat (p170) on the Petrograd Side.

Lonely Planet's Top Choices

Mariinsky Theatre (p117) The classic St Petersburg theatre oozes history and has a dazzling interior.

Mikhailovsky Theatre (p98) Another historic theatre in which to see top-quality ballet and opera productions.

Hermitage Theatre (p99) Watching a classical concert inside the Hermitage is a memorable, if pricey, experience.

Yusupov Palace Theatre (p118) This charming minitheatre was once the private stage of the Yusupovs.

Alexandrinsky Theatre (p98) See ballet and drama on the stage where Chekhov's *The Seagull* premiered.

Best Cinemas

Dom Kino (p100) One of the best places to catch international art-house movies in their original language.

Rodina (p99) Two screens and a quality programme of cinema from around the world.

Kino&Teatr Angleter (p99) This modern cinema is comfortable and offers original-language movies.

New Stage (p99) Movies are screened on the roof of this contemporary drama and dance theatre in the summer.

Lendok (p119) Come here to catch international seasons of documentary films.

Live-music Venues

A2 (p171) St Petersburg's top live-music venue is this superb, professionally run Petrograd Side place.

Cosmonaut (p139) Another large and modern venue for seeing live acts.

Kamchatka (p171) A homage to Kino's Viktor Tsoy, this club is where to see new local acts do their thing.

Fish Fabrique (p139) The ultimate St Petersburg music venue, this veritable institution is favoured by a bohemian crowd.

Best for Kids

St Petersburg State Circus (p99) Always a blast for children, this well-established circus puts on a great show.

Feel Yourself Russian Folkshow (p119) An excellent way to see traditional folk dances performed with great flair.

Bolshoy Puppet Theatre (p139) St Petersburg's main puppet theatre has a program of shows aimed at children.

Demmeni Marionette Theatre (p100) Excellent puppet theatre, with performances aimed at kids.

Upsala Circus (p170) Great performing arts project working with vulnerable kids and teens.

Best for Classical Music

Glinka Capella House (p100) The building alone is reason to visit this superb concert venue.

Rimsky-Korsakov Conservatory (p118) Breathe in the history at this illustrious music school.

Mariinsky Concert Hall (p118) A relatively recent addition to the city's concert halls, with fabulous acoustics.

Shostakovich Philharmonia (p99) Home to two world-famous symphony orchestras, this is a classic venue for the classics.

Best for Theatre

Maly Drama Theatre (p140) A small space that sometimes performs plays with English subtitles.

NEED TO KNOW

Tickets

By far the easiest way to buy tickets is online through a performance venue's own website; do this well in advance to make sure you get seats for shows you want to see when you're in St Petersburg. Outside of the busy White Nights season last-minute tickets are generally easy to find. The standard way to buy tickets on the ground is from a theatre kiosk (театральная касса); these kiosks can be found all over the city, or you can also buy them in person from the individual theatre box offices.

Performance Times

Performances generally begin at 7pm or 7.30pm. Arrive in good time to absorb the atmosphere. (Be late and face the wrath of the fearsome babushkas!) As locals live for socialising in the intervals, bars are packed at these times – and there's always at least one interval, sometimes two, per performance.

Etiquette

Dress up for the ballet, opera or theatre. Russians are dolled up to the nines on these occasions and you'll stick out like a sore thumb if you aren't.

St Petersburg Theatre of Musical Comedy (p99) One of the best venues for music and ballet during the White Nights.

Bolshoy Drama Theatre (p100) This venerable theatre is in a beautiful building on the Fontanka River.

Shopping

St Petersburg's shopping scene may lag behind Moscow's glitzy capitalist paradise, but it's a massive improvement on the past, with something for everyone hidden in an ever-increasing array of new shops and malls. If matryoshka (nesting dolls) aren't your thing, you can enliven your souvenir shopping with pieces of Soviet chic, antiques, street fashion and contemporary arts and crafts.

Souvenirs

The city heaves with shops and stalls selling that archetypal souvenir of Russia, the *matryoshka* (nesting dolls). Other traditional souvenirs include amber jewellery, painted wooden eggs, vodka, Russian chocolates and porcelain, the last of which is available from one of Imperial Porcelain's many St Petersburg outlets.

Shopping Centres & Creative Clusters

Two modern palaces of consumerism flank pl Vosstaniya in the heart of the city. The size of Galeria (p140) is something to behold, and with its international designer names as well as local brands it's definitely the easiest one-stop shop for retail therapy in St Petersburg. Nearby Nevsky Centre (p140) is smaller, but equally impressive, and houses a large branch of the Finnish department store Stockmann. At the heart of Nevsky pr Bolshoy Gostiny Dvor (p102), the 18th century forerunner of a mall, is still going strong and worth a browse.

Following in the successful retail footsteps of Loft Project ETAGI and Taiga there has been a rash of creative clusters opening up across the city including Golitsyn Loft (p128), Berthold Center (p110) and Artmuza (p153). Young entrepreneurs are setting up mainly fashion, accessories and home decor boutiques at these places – all well worth a look.

Local Fashion

There's a small but enterprising fashion industry in St Petersburg with a few local designers blazing the trail and selling classy and creative collections to locals interested in expanding their wardrobes beyond the usual international brands. St Petersburg Fashion Week (http://spbfashionweek.com) in October features local designers including Lilya Kissilenko, Natalya Soldatova and Tatyana Sulimina, all of whom have boutiques in the city.

Secondhand & Vintage

Sekond-khand (Сэконд-хэнд) is all the rage in St Petersburg, with fabrics and designs from the Soviet era now being very fashionable among the younger generations. Soviet chic is so in that it goes way beyond clothing – accessories, music, art and (let's face it) a lot of plain junk is on sale all over the city, simply because it's from that era. If you're into Soviet bric-a-brac, then head to Udelnaya Fair (p171) on a Sunday for a truly mind-blowing array of Soviet trash and the odd real treasure.

Shopping by Neighbourhood

→ **Historic Heart** (p101) The city's commercial heart positively throbs with shopping possibilities.

→ **Sennaya & Kolomna** (p119) This quiet neighbourhood offers some truly offbeat, quirky and arty shopping experiences.

→ **Smolny & Vosstaniya** (p140) Dominated by two enormous shopping centres, as well as several creative clusters.

→ **Vasilyevsky Island** (p153) Buy contemporary art at Erarta or Artmuza.

→ **Petrograd & Vyborg Sides** (p171) You'll find St Petersburg's best flea market here.

Lonely Planet's Top Choices

Taiga (p101) This cool collection of shops and businesses just moments from the Hermitage is well worth exploring.

Udelnaya Fair (p171) Find the gems among the junk at this amazing, sprawling place.

Kupetz Eliseevs (p102) Glam deli and confectioners that's great for edible gifts.

Rediska (p119) Eye-catching arts and crafts made in-house or produced by St Petersburg artisans.

Au Pont Rouge (p101) Superglam department store specialising in fashion in a gorgeous Russian Style Moderne building.

Best Souvenirs

Northway (p119) The best place in town for *matryoshki* (nesting dolls) and many other Russian souvenirs.

Tula Samovars (p140) A great selection of these typically Russian traditional hot-water dispensers.

Military Shop (p103) Get Russian Army uniforms and other military paraphernalia here.

Imenno Lavka (p102) Showcase for quirky gifts, accessories, books and interior-design products by local talents.

Snegiri (p142) Traditional felt slippers and booties given a contemporary fashion spin.

Imperial Porcelain (p140) As once patronised by the Russian royal family.

Best Fashion Shops

Day & Night (p171) Emporium of big-name brands and inter-national fashion labels on the Petrograd Side.

Nevsky 152 (p142) A very fancy 'concept store' housing a number of international fashion brands under one roof.

8 Store (p102) Inside Taiga, this is a stylish boutique selling clothes and accessories from local designers.

Tatyana Parfionova (p140) The Nevsky pr boutique of St Petersburg's original and most famous couturier.

21 Shop (p101) Street fashion that's fun and affordable.

Matryoshka (p119) Clothing and accessories inspired by the Russian nesting doll silhouette.

Best Books, CDs, DVDs

Dom Knigi (p103) The city's largest bookshop is a sight in itself, with a huge range to choose from.

Staraya Kniga (p103) Pick your way through two centuries of old books.

Anglia (p140) The best English-language bookshop in St Petersburg.

Phonoteka (p140) Cool range of vinyls, CDs, film and documentary on DVD from around the world.

Best Art Shopping

Erarta (p153) Commercial galleries here are a great place to buy contemporary Russian art.

Borey Art Centre (p141) Take the pulse of the local artistic underground here.

Sol-Art (p141) Attached to the next-door art school, this is a great place to buy paintings by local artists.

NEED TO KNOW

Opening Hours

Shop hours vary, but most open seven days a week and typically from 10am to 9pm, sometimes to as late as 10pm.

Credit Cards

It's pretty common for all shops to take major credit cards and you're seldom far from an ATM if that's not the case.

Caviar

It's the glamorous face of Russian shopping, but the environmentally conscious steer clear of black caviar: overfishing in the Caspian Sea has reached crisis levels and the international trade of wild-sturgeon caviar has been banned since 2006. There is, however, one stall in Bolshoy Gostiny Dvor specialising in farmed caviar.

Artmuza (p153) Plenty of small galleries in this huge creative cluster on Vasilyevsky Island.

Perinnye Ryady (p101) An arcade of art-and-craft shops where you'll find unique souvenirs.

Explore
St Petersburg

ST PETERSBURG'S
TOP SIGHTS

Neighbourhoods at a Glance

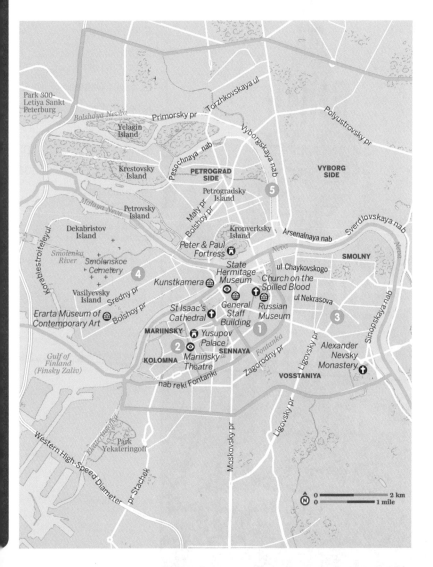

Park 300-
Letiya Sankt
Peterburg

Bolshaya Nevka

Primorsky pr

Torzhkovskaya ul

Polyustrovsky pr

Yelagin
Island

Pesochnaya nab

Vyborgskaya nab

Krestovsky
Island

**PETROGRAD
SIDE**

Petrogradsky
Island

5

**VYBORG
SIDE**

Malaya Neva

Petrovsky
Island

Maly pr

Bolshoy pr

Sverdlovskaya nab

Dekabristov
Island

Kronverksky
Island

Arsenalnaya nab

Koablestroitelejyul

Smolenka
River

Smolenskoe
Cemetery

Peter & Paul
Fortress

Neva

SMOLNY

Vasilyevsky
Island

Srednly pr

4

Kunstkamera

State
Hermitage
Museum

ul Chaykovskogo

Church on the
Spilled Blood

ul Nekrasova

Bolshoy pr

Erarta Museum of
Contemporary Art

St Isaac's
Cathedral

General
Staff
Building

Russian
Museum

3

MARIINSKY

Yusupov
Palace

1

2

Mariinsky
Theatre

SENNAYA

Fontanka

Ligovsky pr

Alexander
Nevsky
Monastery

Sinopskaya nab

KOLOMNA

Zagorodny pr

VOSSTANIYA

Gulf of
Finland
(Finsky Zaliv)

nab reki Fontanki

Ligovsky pr

Zhekatanagofka

Park
Yekateringoff

Western High-Speed Diameter

pr Stachek

Moskovsky pr

0   2 km
0   1 mile

❶ Historic Heart p54

Radiating out from the golden spire of the Admiralty towards the Fontanka River, the Historic Heart has plenty of obvious attractions, such as the Hermitage, Russian Museum and the Church on the Spilled Blood, not to mention the city's most famous avenue: Nevsky Prospekt. There are also quirky gems like the Museum of Soviet Arcade Machines and a quartet of lovely parks. This is where you will be spending most of your time in St Petersburg, especially as the area is also blessed with excellent hotels, dining and drinking options.

❷ Sennaya & Kolomna p104

These two areas adjoin the Historic Heart and are almost as historic themselves. Sennaya is centred on Sennaya Pl (the Haymarket), a traditionally poor area that was immortalised in Dostoevsky's *Crime and Punishment* and has somehow retained its seedy, down-at-heel air despite a big attempt to redevelop it. Kolomna is the largest of seven islands and a quiet, rather out-of-the-way place, although one steeped in history and great beauty. It contains the world-famous Mariinsky Theatre and more canals and rivers than any other part of the city.

❸ Smolny & Vosstaniya p121

This agglomeration of four districts (Smolny, Liteyny, Vosstaniya and Vladimirskaya) is also part of the city centre. The Smolny peninsula is a well-heeled residential district dominated by the Smolny Cathedral, while next-door Liteyny is centred on Liteyny pr, a commercial street between the Smolny and the Fontanka River. South of Nevsky pr are Vosstaniya and Vladimirskaya. Vosstaniya is the focus of St Petersburg's underground art and drinking scene, while Vladimirskaya, named after the stunning Vladimirsky Cathedral, is a mercantile district full of shopping, markets and a clutch of quirky museums.

❹ Vasilyevsky Island p143

The eastern edge of Vasilyevsky Island (or VO as it's usually shortened to) was originally designed to be the administrative heart of the city under Peter the Great. The plan was never carried out but there's still a concentration of historical sights there, including the Strelka) and Kunstkamera. The western side of the island is more industrial, but is also home to the fantastic Erarta Museum of Contemporary Art. Transport fans will be thrilled by the opportunity to tour a couple of submarines and an icebreaker, and by museums devoted to trams and the metro.

❺ Petrograd & Vyborg Sides p154

The Petrograd Side is a fascinating place that includes everything from the Peter and Paul Fortress to an impressive clutch of Style Moderne buildings lining its main drag. It also hosts a beautiful mosque, many interesting museums and huge swaths of parkland on the Kirov Islands, the city's largest green lung. The Vyborg Side is famous for its role in Soviet history and can be a little bleak. That said, a walk around the fascinating postindustrial landscape here will appeal to travellers who have palace fatigue, and a few interesting sights make the trip worthwhile.

Historic Heart

Neighbourhood Top Five

1 State Hermitage Museum (p56) Surveying millennia of global art and culture and being dazzled by the gilded apartments of the Romanovs.

2 Church on the Spilled Blood (p81) Gawping at the jewel-box-bright exterior, then being awestruck by the epic mosaics inside.

3 Russian Museum (p74) Getting to know the world's best collection of Russian art at this fantastic museum with four branches.

4 St Isaac's Cathedral (p82) Climbing the 262 steps to the golden dome for breathtaking views and being amazed by the lavish interior.

5 Anglo Tourismo (p32) Viewing the city from its rivers and canals on a leisurely sightseeing cruise with this or many other boating companies.

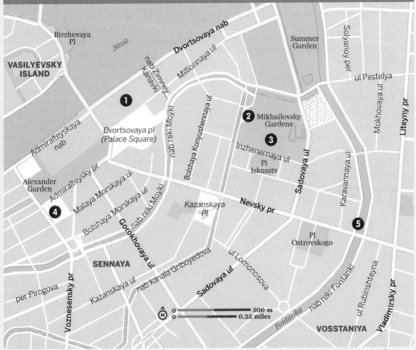

For more detail of this area see Map p272 ➡

Explore the Historic Heart

The Historic Heart is a fast-paced, crowded area that's the commercial and tourist focus of the city. For an unforgettable first impression, head straight to vast Palace Sq: on one side is the Winter Palace (p56), home to the main collection of the Hermitage; on the other, the sweeping grandeur of the General Staff Building (p72).

From here, cherry-pick your way through the rest of the neighbourhood over a couple of days or so. You could spend one day, for example, touring the excellent Russian Museum (p74) and its branches such as the Marble Palace (p84) and Stroganov Palace (p84). If you're speedy (and have the stamina for visual overload) then also squeeze into the same day the dazzling Church of the Saviour on the Spilled Blood (p81) and the splendid view from the cupola of St St Isaac's Cathedral (p82). When you need a breather, take a break from the hubbub in the lush Summer Garden (p84) or Mikhailovsky Garden (p85).

Nevsky pr, the city's main avenue, dominates every itinerary, and you'll find yourself on its broad pavements throughout your visit, popping in and out of shops such as Kupetz Eliseevs (p102). Spend some time off the main drag, though, to find fascinating contrasts, such as the Asian-feeling outdoor market stalls of Apraksin Dvor (p103). In the evening, find high-class entertainment in the theatres around Ploshchad Iskusstv (p91) and Ploshchad Ostrovskogo (p90) or head to the clubs and cocktails bars that are hidden away in unexpected places.

Local Life

→**Parks** The vast Mars Field (p87), Summer Garden (p84), Mikhailovsky Gardens (p85) or Alexander Garden (p86) are delightful green spaces for taking a breather from sightseeing to enjoy a picnic and do some sunbathing on sunny days.

→**Free Art** Locals flock to the Hermitage (p56) on the first Thursday of each month when entrance is free, although the crowds can be huge!

→**Hangouts** See if the Museum of Soviet Arcade Machines (p90) is holding one of its ping-pong DJ nights or if there's a movie screening at the rooftop of Mod Club (p96).

Getting There & Away

→**Metro** This neighbourhood is served by three metro stations: the interconnecting Nevsky Prospekt (Line 2) and Gostiny Dvor (Line 3), and Admiralteyskaya (Line 5) around the corner from the Hermitage.

→**Trolleybus** The number 7 bus, which runs the length of Nevsky pr, goes past Palace Sq and then crosses Dvortsovy most to Vasilyevsky Island.

→**Bus** Hop on buses 7, 10, 24, 27, 181 or 191 to save some footwork along Nevsky.

Lonely Planet's Top Tip

A great boon for time-challenged visitors, or those wanting to avoid daytime crowds – especially tour and school groups – has been the extension of opening hours until 9pm at least once a week at major city museums and galleries, including the Hermitage (Wednesday and Friday) and the Russian Museum (Thursday).

Best Places to Eat

→ Yat (p93)
→ Cococo (p94)
→ Gogol (p93)
→ Gräs x Madbaren (p93)
→ Zoom Café (p91)

For reviews, see p91 →

Best Places to Drink

→ Apotheke Bar (p96)
→ Coffee 22 (p96)
→ Kabinet (p96)
→ Top Hops (p96)
→ Mod Club (p96)

For reviews, see p96 →

Best Places to Shop

→ Au Pont Rouge (p101)
→ Taiga (p101)
→ Kupetz Eliseevs (p102)
→ Perinnye Ryady (p101)
→ DLT (p101)

For reviews, see p101 →

BRIAN KINNEY / SHUTTERSTOCK ©

 TOP SIGHT
THE HERMITAGE

The geographic and tourism centrepiece of St Petersburg is one of the world's greatest art collections and usually most visitors' first stop in the city, even if it is simply to admire the baroque Winter Palace and the extraordinary ensemble of buildings that surround it. No other institution so embodies the opulence and extravagance of the Romanovs.

The Collection

The Hermitage first opened to the public in 1852. Today, for the price of admission, anybody can parade down the grand staircases and across parquet floors, gawping at crystal chandeliers, gilded furniture and an amazing art collection that once was for the Tsar's court's eyes only.

The main complex consists of five connected buildings – the Winter Palace, the Small Hermitage, the Great (Old) Hermitage (also known as the Large Hermitage), the New Hermitage and the Hermitage Theatre (p99) – and is devoted to items from prehistoric times up until the mid-19th century. Impressionist, post-Impressionist and modern works are found in the new galleries of the General Staff Building (p72) across Palace Sq.

The Western European Collection, in particular, does not miss much: Spanish, Flemish, Dutch, French, English and German art are all covered from the 15th to the 18th centuries, while the Italian collection goes back all the way to the 13th century, including the Florentine and Venetian Renaissance, with priceless works by Leonardo da Vinci, Raphael, Michelangelo and Titian. A highlight is the enormous collection of Dutch and Flemish painting, in particular the spectacular assortment of Rembrandt, most notably his masterpiece *Return of the Prodigal Son*.

DON'T MISS

➡ Rembrandt (Room 254)
➡ Great Church (Room 271)
➡ Treasure Gallery
➡ Peacock Clock (Room 204)

PRACTICALITIES

➡ Государственный Эрмитаж
➡ Map p272, C2
➡ www.hermitage museum.org
➡ Dvortsovaya pl 2
➡ joint ticket R700
➡ ⏱10.30am-6pm Tue, Thu, Sat & Sun, to 9pm Wed & Fri
➡ Ⓜ Admiralteyskaya

As much as you will see in the museum, there's about 20 times more in its vaults, part of which you can visit at the Hermitage Storage Facility (p165). Other branches of the museum include the Winter Palace of Peter I (p86), further east along the Neva, Menshikov Palace (p148) on Vasilyevsky Island, and the Imperial Porcelain factory (p140) in the south of the city.

Visiting the Hermitage

The Hermitage is a dynamic institution. Displays change, renovations continue, specific pieces go on tour, and temporary exhibitions occupy particular rooms, displacing whatever normally resides there, so be prepared for slight changes.

The main public entrance is via the courtyard of the Winter Palace off Palace Sq. Groups enter via doors facing onto the Palace Embankment (Dvortsovaya nab).

Ground Floor Exhibits

To get here you'll need to go up to the 1st floor and then down via the stairs between Rooms 153 and 156 or between Rooms 289 and 288.

Rooms 11–24, 27 & 33: Prehistoric Artefacts

The prehistoric collection at the Hermitage contains thousands of artefacts dating from as far back as the Palaeolithic era (500,000 to 12,000 BC). Most of the items were excavated from different regions of the USSR during the Soviet era. The following are the highlights:

Room 12 Carved petroglyphs (dating to 2000 BC) were taken from the northeastern shores of Lake Onega after archaeological expeditions in 1935.

Rooms 13–14 Excavations of a burial mound in the northern Caucasus include the corpse of a nomadic chief, lavishly dressed and covered in jewels.

Rooms 26–32, 38–69: Siberian Antiquities, Central Asia & Caucasus

These excellent galleries present exhibits from Central Asia, Siberia and the Caucasus, dating as far back as the 10th century BC.

Room 26 Contains mummified human corpses that are more than 2000 years old, as well as a fantastically reconstructed wooden cart.

Rooms 47–51 Feature impressive 7th- and 8th-century relics from Panjakent in present-day Tajikistan.

Rooms 67-69 Feature art and artefacts of the Golden Horde, which swept through Russia in the 13th and 14th centuries.

HISTORIC HEART THE HERMITAGE

HERMITAGE TIPS

➡ Avoid possibly long entrance queues by buying your ticket online. The printed-out voucher or PDF on a wi-fi–enabled device is valid for 180 days.

➡ Alternatively pay at the computerised ticket machines in the main entrance courtyard and be sure to wait for your tickets to be printed at the end of the transaction (they come after the payment receipt).

➡ If you leave jackets and bags in the cloakroom, be aware that you can't go back for anything without leaving the museum.

➡ Handbags, small shoulder bags and plastic bags are allowed in the Hermitage, but backpacks aren't.

There is good provision of toilets throughout the Hermitage – don't make the rookie mistake of thinking that those at the foot of the Jordan Staircase as you enter are the only ones available, as the lines (especially for women) can be very long indeed.

The Hermitage

A HALF-DAY TOUR

Successfully navigating the State Hermitage Museum, with its four vast interconnecting buildings and around 360 rooms, is an art form in itself. Our half-day tour of the highlights can be done in four hours, or easily extended to a full day.

Once past ticket control start by ascending the grand **1 Jordan Staircase** to Neva Enfilade and Great Enfilade for the impressive staterooms, including the former throne room St George's Hall and the 1812 War Gallery (Room 197), and the Romanovs' private apartments. Admire the newly restored **2 Great Church** then make your way back to the Neva side of the building via the Western Gallery (Room 262) to find the splendid **3 Pavilion Hall** with its view onto the Hanging Garden and the gilded Peacock Clock, always a crowd pleaser.

Make your way along the series of smaller galleries in the Large Hermitage hung with Italian Renaissance art, including masterpieces by **4 Da Vinci** and **5 Caravaggio**. The Loggia of Raphael (Room 227) is also impressive. Linger a while in the galleries containing Spanish art before taking in the Dutch collection, the highlight of which is the hoard of **6 Rembrandt** canvases in Room 254.

Descend the Council Staircase (Room 206), noting the giant malachite vase, to the ground floor where the fantastic Egyptian collection awaits in Room 100 as well as the galleries of Greek and Roman Antiquities. If you have extra time, it's well worth booking tours to see the special exhibition in the **7 Gold Rooms** of the Treasurey Gallery.

Jordan Staircase
Originally designed by Rastrelli, in the 18th century this incredible white marble construction was known as the Ambassadorial Staircase because it was the way into the palace for official receptions.

The Gold Rooms
One of two sections of the Treasure Gallery, here you can see dazzling pieces of gold jewellery and ornamentation created by Scythian, Greek and ancient Oriental craftsmen.

Great Church
This stunningly ornate church was the Romanovs' private place of worship and the venue for the marriage of the last tsar, Nicholas II, to Alexandra Feodorovna in 1895.

TOP TIPS

➡ Reserve tickets online to skip the long lines.

➡ Bring a sandwich and a bottle of water with you: the cafe isn't great.

➡ Wear comfortable shoes.

➡ Bear in mind the only cloakroom is before ticket control, so you can't go back and pick up a sweater.

Rembrandt
A moving portrait of contrition and forgiveness, *Return of the Prodigal Son* (Room 254) depicts the biblical scene of a wayward son returning to his father.

Da Vinci
Along with the *Benois Madonna*, also here, *Madonna and Child (Madonna Litta;* Room 214) is one of just a handful of paintings known to be the work of Leonardo da Vinci.

St George's Hall

Hermitage Theatre

Pavilion Hall
Apart from the Peacock Clock, the Pavilion Hall also contains beautifully detailed mosaic tables made by Italian and Russian craftsmen in the mid-19th century.

Caravaggio
The Lute Player (Room 237) is the Hermitage's only Caravaggio, and a work that the master of light and shade described as the best piece he'd ever painted.

1. Kazan Cathedral (p83)
Neoclassical cathedral partly modelled on Rome's St Peter's Cathedral.

2. Stroganov Palace (p84)
The Grand Dining Room is a palace highlight.

3. Nevsky Prospekt (p102)
St Petersburg's iconic avenue.

THE HERMITAGE — GROUND FLOOR

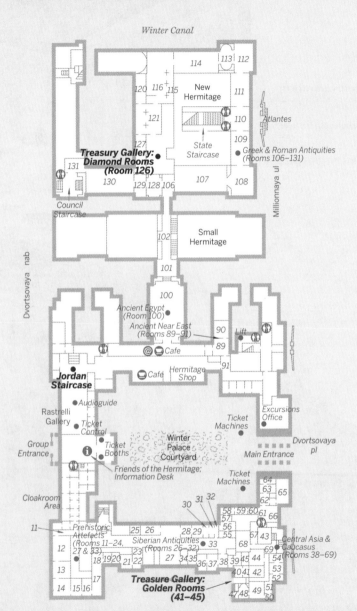

Winter Canal

114 113 112

120 116 115 New Hermitage 111

121

Atlantes

110

State Staircase 109

Treasury Gallery: Diamond Rooms (Room 126) Greek & Roman Antiquities (Rooms 106–131)

127

131 130 129 128 106 107 108

Dvortsovaya nab

Council Staircase

102 Small Hermitage

101

100

Ancient Egypt (Room 100)

Ancient Near East (Rooms 89–91) 90 Lift

89

@ Cafe

91

Jordan Staircase Cafe Hermitage Shop

Audioguide

Rastrelli Gallery Ticket Control Excursions Office

Group Entrance Ticket Booths Winter Palace Courtyard Ticket Machines

Dvortsovaya pl

i *Main Entrance*

Friends of the Hermitage; Information Desk

Ticket Machines

64

63 65

Cloakroom Area 31 32 62

30 58 59 60 61 66

11 57 56 67 43 Central Asia & Caucasus (Rooms 38–69)

Prehistoric Artefacts (Rooms 11–24, 27 & 33) 25 26 28 29 55 68 69 54

12 27 & 33 23 Siberian Antiquities (Rooms 26–32) 33 53

18 19 20 21 22 27 34 35 36 37 38 39 45 44 52

13 17 40 41 42 51

14 15 16 **Treasure Gallery: Golden Rooms (41–45)** 47 48 49 50

Rooms 89–91: Ancient Near East

These rooms house a very impressive collection of cuneiform texts from Babylon and Assyrian limestone reliefs.

Room 100: Ancient Egypt

This large hall houses an incredible collection of ancient Egyptian artefacts uncovered by Russian archaeologists. The display spans the Egyptian era from the Old Kingdom (3000–2400 BC) to the New Empire (1580–1050 BC). There are many painted sarcophagi and tombstones carved with hieroglyphics, as well as a fascinating mummy from the 10th century BC.

Rooms 106–131: Greek & Roman Antiquities

The Hermitage has more than 100,000 items from Ancient Greece and Rome, including thousands of painted vases, antique gemstones, Roman sculpture and Greek gold.

Room 107 The Jupiter Hall is a sumptuous space with portraits of sculptors on the ceiling.

Room 108 Designed by German neoclassicist architect and painter von Klenze to imitate a Roman courtyard.

Room 109 Peter I acquired the sculpture *Aphrodite (Tauride Venus)* from Pope Clement XI. This piece – a Roman copy of a Greek original – was the first antique sculpture ever brought to Russia.

Room 111 Another impressive design by von Klenze, this one was intended to be a library (which explains the philosophers' profiles).

Room 130 Hall of Twenty Columns, containing a fabulous collection of Greco-Roman clay urns.

First-Floor Highlights

On the 2nd floor you'll find the Hermitage's unbeatable Western European collection and its grandest state rooms.

Rooms 151–189: Russian Culture & Imperial Apartments

Most of the western wing of the Winter Palace contains the huge collection from ancient Rus (10th to 15th centuries) through to the 18th century, including artefacts, icons, portraits and furniture. Also here are the private apartments of the last tsar, Nicholas II, and the imperial family. Many of these rooms were completed in 1894, and they now show off elaborate 19th-century interiors.

Rooms 151 & 153 This long corridor, broken up by a vast clock, contains portraits of all the Russian tsars from Peter the Great to Nicholas II.

Rooms 155–156 Moorish Dining Room and Rotunda.

HISTORIC HEART THE HERMITAGE

TAKING A BREAK

Eating options in the Hermitage are not great, limited to busy cafes on the ground-floor between the foot of the Jordan staircase and Room 100. Yat (p93) serves excellent Russian food in a charming atmosphere but a booking is advisable.

If you want to escape the crowds, head to Rooms 1 to 65 on the ground floor which contain prehistoric relics as well as treasures from Siberia, Central Asia and the Caucasus. Due to the layout of the museum, you have to go up to the 1st floor and then down the stairs on the left side of the main entrance to get here. You'll find you have many of the galleries here almost entirely to yourself.

JORDAN STAIRCASE

The main staircase of the Winter Palace – a creation of Bartolomeo Rastrelli – was originally known as the Ambassadorial Staircase. However, in the 19th century it became known as the Jordan Staircase as every year on 6 January the imperial family would descend these stairs to the Neva River for the celebration of Christ's baptism in the River Jordan.

THE HERMITAGE — FIRST FLOOR

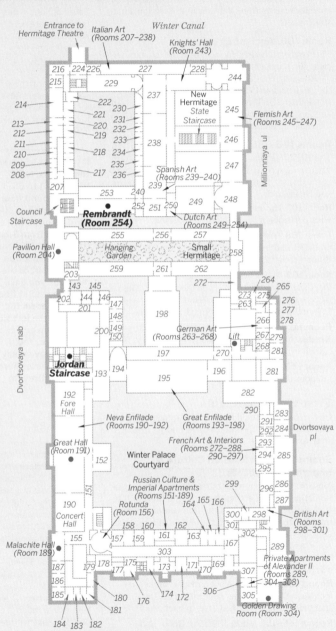

Entrance to
Hermitage Theatre

Italian Art
(Rooms 207–238)

Winter Canal

Knights' Hall
(Room 243)

216 224 226   227   228   244

215   229   237

214   222 230 231 232 233 238   245

213 220 219 218 217   234 235 236   246 247

New Hermitage
State Staircase

Flemish Art
(Rooms 245–247)

Millionnaya ul

Spanish Art
(Rooms 239–240)

239 240   249   248

253 240   251 250   249

252 241

Council
Staircase

**Rembrandt
(Room 254)**

Dutch Art
(Rooms 249–254)

Pavilion Hall
(Room 204)

255 256 257

Hanging
Garden

Small
Hermitage   258

259 261 262

203

143 145   272   264 265

202 144 146   273 275 276

201 147   263   277 278

148

200 149 150   198   266   279

German Art
(Rooms 263–268)

Lift   267 268 281

197   270

Jordan
Staircase   193 194   195   196   281

192
Fore
Hall

282

Neva Enfilade
(Rooms 190–192)

Great Enfilade
(Rooms 193–198)

290 283

291 292 284

Dvortsovaya nab

Great Hall
(Room 191)   152

French Art & Interiors
(Rooms 272–288,
290–297)

293 294 285

295

Winter Palace
Courtyard

Dvortsovaya pl

151

Russian Culture &
Imperial Apartments
(Rooms 151–189)

299

296 286 287

190
Concert
Hall

Rotunda
(Room 156)

164 165 166

300 298

British Art
(Rooms
298–301)

155   158 160 161 162 163 167   301 302

Malachite Hall
(Room 189)

157 159   303   289

187 179 178 175   171 170 169   307

Private Apartments
of Alexander II
(Rooms 289,
304–308)

186 177 173   172   306 305

185 180 176 174

184 183 182 181

Golden Drawing
Room (Room 304)

Rooms 157–162 The Petrovsky Gallery displays personal effects and equipment used by Peter the Great, as well as some beautiful early-18th-century furniture. Look for the ivory chandelier that was partly built by Peter himself.

Room 161 In 1880 there was an attempt on the life of Alexander II in this room. A young revolutionary, Khalturin, planted a bomb in the room below. It killed 11 soldiers when it went off, although the tsar had wandered into another room at the time.

Room 178 Nicholas II spent much of his time in this wonderful Gothic library, topped with a sublime walnut ceiling.

Room 181 The relatively small and intimate Pompeii dining room.

Room 187 The griffin-motif furniture in this palace drawing room dates from 1805.

Room 188 This small dining room is where the Provisional Government was arrested by the Bolsheviks in 1917.

Room 189 Two tonnes of gorgeous green columns, boxes, bowls and urns have earned this room the name 'Malachite Hall', and it is one of the most striking rooms in the entire palace. The handiwork of architect Alexander Bryullov, it was completed in 1839. Three figurines on the wall represent Day, Night and Poetry. This was where the last meeting of the 1917 Provisional Government occurred, on the fateful nights of 25 and 26 October 1917; they were arrested soon after, in the Small Dining Room next door.

Rooms 190–192: Neva Enfilade
These three grand ceremonial halls are often used for temporary exhibitions.

Room 190 This Concert Hall was used for small soirées. The enormous ornate silver tomb was commissioned by Empress Elizabeth for the remains of Alexander Nevsky.

Room 191 As many as 5000 guests could be entertained in the Great Hall (also called Nicholas Hall). The palace's largest room was the scene of imperial winter balls.

Room 192 This anteroom was used for pre-ball champagne buffets.

Rooms 193–198: Great Enfilade
You'll find more state rooms here.

Room 193 Field Marshals' Hall is known for its military-themed chandelier and its portraits of seven of Russia's military leaders.

Room 194 The Hall of Peter the Great contains his none-too-comfy throne.

RUSSIAN ARK

Wander with a ghost through 33 rooms of the Hermitage and 300 years of Russian history in *Russian Ark* (2002). Director Alexander Sokurov shot the movie in one continuous 96-minute take in the Winter Palace.

Rooms 289 and 304–308 comprise the private apartments of Tsar Alexander II. Most spectacular is Room 304, the Golden Drawing Room, which features a fabulous gilt ceiling and a marble fireplace with an intricate mosaic over the mantle.

PEACOCK CLOCK

The centrepiece of the Pavilion Hall (Room 204) is the incredible Peacock Clock, created by James Cox and gifted to Catherine the Great in 1781 by Grigory Potemkin. A revolving dial in one of the toadstools tells the time: as it strikes the hour the automaton peacock spreads its wings and the toadstools, owl and cock come to life. A video beside the clock shows the action in close-up detail should you not be around for the once-weekly performance at 7pm on Wednesday.

Room 195 This gilt Armorial Hall contains chandeliers engraved with the coat-of-arms of all the Russian provinces.

Room 197 The 1812 War Gallery is hung with 332 portraits of Russian and allied Napoleonic war leaders.

Room 198 St George's Hall served as the state rooms where the imperial throne used to sit. With white Carrara marble imported from Italy and floors crafted from the wood of 16 different tree species, it is a splendid affair.

Room 204: Pavilion Hall & Hanging Garden

The ceremonial Pavilion Hall is an airy white-and-gold room sparkling with 28 chandeliers and the famous **Peacock Clock**. The south windows look on to Catherine the Great's **hanging garden** (built over the stables), while the north overlooks the Neva. The amazing floor mosaic in front of the windows is a copy of that in the Roman bath of Otricoli (Ocriculum) near Rome.

Rooms 207–238: Italian Art

Covering 30-plus rooms, the Hermitage's collection of Italian art traverses the 13th to the 18th centuries. The highlights are certainly the works by the Renaissance artists: Leonardo da Vinci, Raphael, Giorgione and Titian. Look also for Botticelli, Caravaggio and Tiepolo.

Room 207 The earliest example in this collection is *The Crucifixion,* painted by Ugolino di Tedice in the second half of the 13th century.

Room 214 Of a dozen or so original paintings by da Vinci that exist in the world, two are here. The very different *Benois Madonna* (1478) and *Madonna Litta* (1490) are named after their last owners. For years, the latter was considered lost. However, in 1909, the Russian architect Leon Benois surprised the art world when he revealed that it was part of his father-in-law's collection.

Room 217 Giorgione is one of the most mysterious painters of the Renaissance, as only a few paintings exist that are known for certain to be his work. A portrait of idealised beauty, *Judith* is said to represent the inseparability of life and death.

Room 221 The work of Titian, the best representative of the Venetian school during the 16th century, is featured here: *Danaya* and *St Sebastian* are widely accepted as two of his masterpieces.

Room 224 Accessed off this room is the Hermitage Theatre; there are lovely views from the connecting corridor over the Neva.

Rooms 226–227: Loggia of Raphael When Catherine the Great visited the Vatican she was so impressed that she commissioned Quarenghi to create this copy of a Vatican gallery; a team of Raphael's students recreated the master's murals on canvas. Note the occasional Russification on these versions: the two-headed eagle of the Romanov dynasty replaces the papal coat-of-arms.

Room 229 Here you'll enjoy two pieces by Raphael, *The Holy Family* and *Madonna and Child,* as well as many pieces by his disciples.

Room 230 Contains the Hermitage's only piece by Michelangelo, a marble statue of a crouching boy.

Rooms 237–238 These Italian Skylight Halls are bathed in natural light, which highlights the ornately moulded ceilings.

Rooms 239–240: Spanish Art

Ranging from the 16th to the 18th centuries, this collection includes the most noteworthy artists of this 'Golden Age' of Spanish painting: Murillo, Ribera and, of course, Velázquez. The collection also includes two remarkable paintings from the 16th century: the marvellous *St Peter and St Paul,* by El Greco, and *St Sebastian Cured by St Irene,* by Ribera.

Room 243: Knights' Hall

Nicholas I started collecting artistic weapons and armaments from around the world. Here is the Western European collection, featuring four impressive 16th-century German knights sitting atop their armoured horses.

Rooms 245–247: Flemish Art

These three rooms dedicated to 17th-century Flanders are almost entirely consumed by three artists: Peter Paul Rubens, Anthony Van Dyck and Frans Snyders.

Rooms 249–254: Dutch Art

Dating from the 17th and 18th centuries, the Dutch collection contains more than 1000 pieces. The 26 paintings by Rembrandt in Room 254 nearly outshine anything else in these rooms. The collection traces his career, starting with *Flora* and *The Descent from the Cross*, which are noticeably lighter but more detailed. His later work tends to be darker and more penetrating, such as the celebrated *The Return of the Prodigal Son*. Painted between 1663 and 1665, it arguably represents the height of Rembrandt's mastery of psychology in his paintings. The solemn baroque masterpiece is a moving portrait of unquestioning parental love and mercy.

Rooms 263–268: German Art

This small collection of German art ranges from the 15th to the 18th centuries. Among the earliest works here are five paintings by Lucas Cranach the Elder.

Room 271: Great Church

Looking splendid following a major renovation completed in 2014, this Rastrelli-designed chapel is one of the Winter Palace's most dazzling spaces, with a white and gilt dome and the ceiling painting *The Ascension of Christ* by Pyotr Basin.

Rooms 272–288 & 290–297: French Art & Interiors

These rooms trace the development of French art from the 15th to the 18th centuries, including tapestries, ceramics, metalwork and paintings. Look for rooms devoted to Nicholas Poussin, founder of French classicism, and Claude Lorrain, master of the classical landscape. Room 282, Alexander Hall, is a testament to the victory over Napoleon in 1812.

Rooms 298–301: British Art

These rooms showcase 15th- to 18th-century British art. Highlights include:

Room 298 *Portrait of a Lady in Blue,* by Thomas Gainsborough, perhaps the most famous piece in the English collection.

Room 300 *The Infant Hercules Strangling the Serpents* by Sir Joshua Reynolds, which was commissioned by Catherine the Great to symbolise the growing strength of Russia.

Second-Floor Highlights

Access to Rooms 314–332, some of which are used for temporary exhibitions, is via stairs off Rooms 269 or 280 on the 1st floor. The Far East, Central Asia and Islamic Near East collections are reached via the stairs off Rooms 302 or 156 also on the 1st floor.

Rooms 351–391: Oriental & Middle Eastern Culture & Art

Art from the Far East, including China, Japan, Tibet, Indonesia, Mongolia and India, can be found in rooms 351 to 376. Rooms 381 to 391 have some wonderful works from Byzantium and Iran including fantastic early 19th-century portraits of Fat'h Ali Shah by Mihr' Ali. Room 391 provides a panoramic view across the Neva from the northwest corner of the Winter Palace.

History of the Hermitage

When, in 1764, Catherine the Great purchased the art collection of Johann Gotzkowski, which contained a large number of works by Rubens, Rembrandt and Van Dyck, little did anyone suspect that this would form the basis of one of the world's most celebrated art museums, the repository of millions of artistic masterpieces from around the world.

A New Winter Palace

Some 30 years earlier, it was Empress Anna who engaged a young Bartolomeo Rastrelli to incorporate the existing royal buildings on the Neva into a proper palace. Her successor, the ever-extravagant Empress Elizabeth, wanted something grander so in 1754 she signed a decree ordering the creation of a winter palace, closely supervising its design and construction. Her inopportune death in 1761 occurred only a few months before the Winter Palace was finally completed, but her legacy has been confirmed by what is arguably St Petersburg's most strikingly beautiful palace.

Visitors and residents were wowed by the capital's newest addition: 'visible from a distance, rising above the rooftops, the upper storey of the new Winter Palace, adorned with a host of statues', as it was described by one 18th-century visitor to the capital. But the palace, of course, was a private residence. After the death of Empress Elizabeth, Peter III lived here for only three months before he was overthrown in a palace coup and replaced by Catherine the Great. This grand baroque building thenceforth became the official residence of the imperial family.

The Imperial Art Collection

Collecting art was an obsession for Catherine, who purchased some of the most extensive private collections in Europe, including those of Heinrich von Brühl, Lord Robert Walpole and Baron Pierre Crozat. By 1774 Catherine's collection included over 2000 paintings, and by the time of her death in 1796 that number had doubled.

Catherine and her successors didn't much care for Rastrelli's baroque interiors and had most of the rooms completely remodelled in classical style. To display her art, Catherine first had built the Small Hermitage and later the so-called Old Hermitage, and allowed prominent people to privately visit the collection on application. In the 1780s Giacomo Quarenghi added the Hermitage Theatre, which served as the private theatre for the imperial family; it is still used today although now for public performances.

The early 19th century saw the expansion of the collection, particularly in the field of classical antiquity, due both to the continued acquisition of

....

1. Flemish paintings in the Snyders Room (Room 245) **2.** Small Throne Hall (Peter the Great Memorial Hall), Winter Palace

other collections and rich finds being discovered in southern Russia. More acquisitions followed Russia's victory over Napoleon in 1812 and included the private collection of Napoleon's consort, Joséphine de Beauharnais.

In December 1837 a devastating fire broke out in the heating shaft of the Field Marshals' Hall; it burned for over 30 hours and destroyed a large portion of the interior. Most of the imperial belongings were saved, thrown out of windows or dragged outside to sit in the snow. Nicholas I vowed to restore the palace as quickly as possible, employing architect Vasily Stasov and thousands of workers to toil around the clock. Their efforts were not in vain, as the project was completed in a little over a year. Most of the classical interiors in the ceremonial rooms that we see today, including the Grand Hall, the Throne Room and the Armorial Hall, were designed by Stasov.

Russia's First Public Art Museum

While Peter the Great opened the Kunstkamera (p146), his private collection of curiosities, to the public in the early 18th century, it was Nicholas I who eventually opened the first public art museum in Russia. During a visit to Germany in 1838 he was impressed by the museums he saw in Munich – specifically, by the idea of buildings that were architectural masterpieces in themselves, designed specifically to house and preserve artistic masterpieces. He employed German architect Leo von Klenze and local boy Vasily Stasov to carry out such a project in the proximity of the Winter Palace. The result was the 'neo-Grecian' New Hermitage, adorned by statues and bas-reliefs depicting great artists, writers and other cultural figures. After 11 years of work, the museum was opened to the public in 1852.

1. Kunstkamera (p146) 2. East Wing, General Staff Building (p72)

At this time, the first director of the Hermitage was appointed and the collection as a museum, rather than the tsar's private gallery, began to take shape. Various further acquisitions in the late 19th and early 20th centuries meant that the Hermitage had truly arrived as a world-class museum. Particularly important caches of paintings included the two Leonardo da Vinci Madonnas (acquired in 1865 and 1914), Piotr Semionov-Tien-Shansky's enormous collection of Dutch and Flemish art, purchased in 1910, and the Stroganov collection of Italian old masters.

Expanding the Collection

It was the postrevolutionary period that saw a threefold increase in the Hermitage's collection. In 1917 the Winter Palace and the Hermitage were declared state museums, and throughout the 1920s and 1930s the Soviet state seized and nationalised countless valuable private collections, including those of the Stroganovs, Sheremetyevs, Shuvalovs, Yusupovs and Baron Stieglitz. In 1948 it incorporated the renowned collections of post-Impressionist and Impressionist paintings of Moscow industrialists Sergei Shchukin and Ivan Morozov, including works by Matisse and Picasso.

During WWII, Soviet troops in Germany and Eastern Europe appropriated enormous numbers of paintings that had belonged to private collectors. In 1995, after years of keeping the paintings in storage, the Hermitage finally put these works, including those by Monet, Degas, Renoir, Cézanne, Picasso and Matisse, on public display. In recent years, the museum has been building a collection of contemporary art that currently numbers around 1500 pieces, some of which are displayed in the General Staff Building (p72) – a tiny fraction of the three million items listed in the Hermitage's inventory.

◉ TOP SIGHT
GENERAL STAFF BUILDING

The east wing of this magnificent building, wrapping around the south of Palace Sq and designed by Carlo Rossi in the 1820s, marries immaculately restored interiors with contemporary architecture to create a series of galleries displaying the Hermitage's amazing collection of Impressionist and post-Impressionist works. Contemporary works are displayed here, too, often in temporary exhibitions by major artists.

New Grand Enfilade

Entry to the galleries is via a new marble staircase, which doubles as an amphitheatre for musical performances. On the 1st floor a 'New Grand Enfilade' of lofty exhibition rooms has been created by throwing a glass ceiling over the building's interior courtyards. Among the giant works on display here are Ilya and Emilia Kabakov's *Red Wagon* installation and the restored 19th-century German and Austrian canvases from the Steiglitz Mansion on the English Embankment.

Off this central corridor are smaller galleries for temporary exhibitions as well as a beautifully restored trio of rooms that once housed the Imperial Russian Ministry of Finance.

Impressionists & Post-Impressionists

The 3rd-floor galleries house the Hermitage's collection of Impressionist and post-Impressionist paintings, arguably the best in the world. Much of this artwork was displayed for the first time in the 1990s, when the museum revealed some fabulous pieces, kept secret since seizure by the Red Army from Germany at the end of WWII.

DON'T MISS

- ➡ Monet (3rd floor)
- ➡ Picasso (4th floor)
- ➡ Matisse (4th floor)
- ➡ Restored Russian ministry rooms.

PRACTICALITIES

- ➡ Здание Главного штаба
- ➡ Map p272, D3
- ➡ www.hermitage museum.org
- ➡ Dvortsovaya pl 6-8
- ➡ R300, incl main Hermitage museum & other buildings R700
- ➡ ⊙10.30am-6pm Tue, Thu, Sat & Sun, to 9pm Wed & Fri
- ➡ Ⓜ Admiralteyskaya

Barbizon School

Next to **Room 452** (where you'll find three sculptures by Rodin) is a series of unnumbered rooms displaying works from the Barbizon School, named for the village in France where this group of artists settled. They were reacting against romanticism, the prevailing school of art for the earlier part of the 19th century, and making a move towards realism. Gustave Courbet, Jean-Baptiste-Camille Corot, Théôdore Rousseau and Jean-François Millet are all represented.

Russian Avant-Garde

Russian avant-garde art is not a strong point of the Hermitage (if this is what you're looking for, try the Russian Museum). That said, the General Staff Building does display a couple of Kandinsky's early works in **Room 444** along with Kazimir Malevich's *Black Square* (1915), the most striking painting of the Petrograd avant-garde. Malevich created several variants of the simple black square against a white background throughout his career, of which this is the fourth and last. It was taken by many as a nihilistic declaration of the 'end of painting', causing both awe and outrage.

20th Century

Rooms 430 to 440 are where the big guns of the Hermitage's 20th-century works are shown. On display are over 40 paintings by Matisse and almost as many by Picasso. Henri Matisse was initially classified as a Fauvist, but he continued to paint in his own particular style, even as Fauvism declined in the early 20th century. Around this time, Matisse met Pablo Picasso and the two became lifelong friends. Picasso is best known as the founder and master of cubism, but again his work spanned many styles.

A turning point for Matisse – and perhaps his most famous work – is *The Dance* (1910). The intense colours and the dancing nudes convey intense feelings of freedom. This panel – along with the accompanying *The Music* – was painted specifically for Russian businessman Sergei Shchukin. While these panels are certainly commanding, don't miss *The Red Room* and *Portrait of the Artist's Wife*.

Picasso's blue period is characterised by sombre paintings in shades of blue. When he was only 22, he painted *The Absinthe Drinker*, a haunting portrait of loneliness and isolation. The sensuous *Dance of the Veils* (1907) and *Woman with a Fan* (1908) are excellent representations of his cubist work, as are the ceramics on display here.

BLACK SQUARE

Kazimir Malevich's *Black Square* went missing during the Soviet period, mysteriously reappearing in southern Russia in 1993. Oligarch Vladimir Potanin bought the painting for $US1 million and donated it to the Hermitage in 2002.

Inspired by romanticism, a group of painters in the 1860s began experimenting with painting modern life and landscapes, endeavouring to capture the overall effect of a scene instead of being overly concerned with details. The new trend – radical in its time – was known as Impressionism.

TAKE A BREAK

Unlike at the Winter Palace, the General Staff Building's **Cafe Hermitage** (Кафе Эрмитаж; ☏812-703 7528; General Staff Builidng, 8 Dvortsovaya pl; mains R250-450; ⏰11am-11pm Tue, Thu, Sat & Sun, until 8pm Wed & Fri; Ⓜ Admiralteyskaya) is a pleasant self-serve place for light refreshments or an affordable meal.

TOP SIGHT
RUSSIAN MUSEUM

Focusing solely on Russian art, from ancient church icons to 20th-century paintings, the Russian Museum's collection is magnificent and can easily be viewed in half a day or less. The collection is less overwhelming than that of the Hermitage, but the masterpieces nonetheless keep on coming as you tour the Mikhailovsky Palace and the attached Benois Wing.

The Museum's Collection

Mikhailovsky Palace was designed by Carlo Rossi and built between 1819 and 1825. It was a gift for Grand Duke Mikhail (brother of Tsars Alexander I and Nicholas I) as compensation for missing out on the throne. Nicholas II opened it as a public gallery on 7 March 1898.

The museum originated from the collection begun by Tsar Alexander III, whose bust greets you on the magnificent main staircase. The collection now numbers around 400,000 pieces (the Russian Museum also manages several other palaces, plus the Mikhailovsky and Summer Gardens). On display are a superb range of ancient icons, paintings, graphic art, sculpture, and folk, decorative and applied art. The collection of avant-garde works is particularly notable, including pieces by Nathan Altman, Natalya Goncharova, Kazimir Malevich and Alexander Rodchenko.

The museum's Benois Wing houses pieces from the 20th century as well as temporary exhibitions. It was constructed between 1914 and 1919 and is connected to the original palace. It is accessible through an entrance on nab kanala Griboyedova.

DON'T MISS

→ *The Wave* – Ivan Aivazovsky

→ *Barge Haulers on the Volga* – Ilya Repin

→ *Last Day of Pompeii* – Karl Bryullov

→ *Portrait of the Poetess Anna Akhmatova* – Nathan Altman

PRACTICALITIES

→ Русский музей

→ Map p272, F3

→ ☎812-595 4248

→ www.rusmuseum.ru

→ Inzhenernaya ul 4

→ adult/student R450/200

→ ⊙10am-8pm Mon, 10am-6pm Wed & Fri-Sun, 1-9pm Thu

→ Ⓜ Nevsky Prospekt

Visiting the Russian Museum

Enter the Mikhailovsky Palace's lower floor to the right of the main facade. Pick up a museum map before ascending the magnificent main staircase to the 1st floor, as this is where the chronological ordering of the exhibits from the 10th to the 20th century begins.

Galleries close for restoration and rehangings from time to time, and works are sometimes loaned out, so be prepared for slight changes to the following.

Rooms 1–4: Religious Icons

The first four rooms of the museum encapsulate a succinct but brilliant history of Russian icon painting, including work from the three major schools of Russian icon painting: Novgorod, Muscovy and Pskov. Room 2 has *St Nicholas the Miracle Worker with Life,* while Room 3 features Russian master Andrei Rublev's massive paintings of the apostles Peter and Paul as well as his *Presentation.* Room 4 is notable in its departure from earlier styles. Compare *Old Testament Trinity with Scenes from Genesis* (c. 1408) with the completely atypical *Our Father* (1669).

Rooms 5–7: Petrine & Post-Petrine Art

Peter the Great was a great patron of the arts and almost single-handedly brought the Western eye to Russian painting, as witnessed by the massive jump in style from ecclesiastical to secular subjects between Rooms 4 and 5. The rooms include three busts of Peter and two portraits.

Room 6 includes some charmingly odd canvases in very strange shapes as well as mosaic portraits of both Peter and Catherine the Great, as well as of Elizabeth I, Peter's daughter. The centre of the room is taken up by a huge portrait of the ill-fated Peter III, but look out for the impressive bust of Prince Menshikov. Room 7 has an amazingly ornate ceiling. The room houses a sculpture of *Empress Anna with an Arab Boy* and a few impressive tapestries, including one that depicts Peter the Great at the Battle of Poltava, his greatest military victory.

Rooms 8–11: Rise of the Academy

These rooms display the early works of the St Petersburg Academy of Arts. These artists borrowed the European classical aesthetic for their work. Look for portraits in Rooms 8 and 10 (including two portraits and a full-sized sculpture of Catherine the Great in Room 10) and biblical themes in Room 9.

Room 11 is the Rossi-designed White Hall, which was Grand Duke Mikhail's drawing room. Here, the interior is the art – in this case representing the Empire epoch. It's wonderfully ornate and shiny – a perfect place to host musical greats like Strauss and Berlioz, who performed here.

OTHER BRANCHES OF THE RUSSIAN MUSEUM

The Russian Museum also manages three other impressive palaces in the city centre, where you can view temporary exhibits, permanent collections and grand state rooms: the Marble Palace (p84), the Stroganov Palace (p84) and Mikhailovsky Castle (p85). Of the palaces, the Marble Palace has the best art collection, while the Stroganov Palace has the best interiors.

Combined tickets, available at each palace, covers entrance either to your choice of two the same day (adult/ student R600/270) or to all four within a three-day period (R850/400).

RUSSIAN MUSEUM — GROUND FLOOR

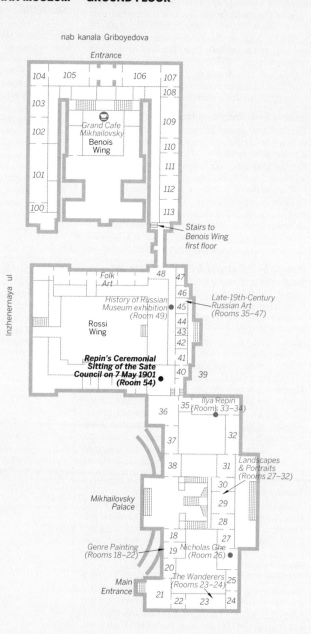

nab kanala Griboyedova

Entrance

104 | 105 | 106 | 107
108
103
Grand Cafe Mikhailovsky
102 | Benois Wing | 109
110
101 | 111
112
100 | 113

Stairs to Benois Wing first floor

Inzhenernaya ul

Folk Art | 48 | 47
46
History of Russian Museum exhibition (Room 49) | 45 | Late-19th-Century Russian Art (Rooms 35–47)
44
Rossi Wing | 43
42
Repin's Ceremonial Sitting of the Sate Council on 7 May 1901 (Room 54) | 41
40 | 39

36 | 35 | Ilya Repin (Rooms 33–34)
32
37
38 | 31 | Landscapes & Portraits (Rooms 27–32)
30
Mikhailovsky Palace | 29
28
18 | 27
Genre Painting (Rooms 18–22) | 19 | Nicholas Ghe (Room 26)
20
Main Entrance | The Wanderers (Rooms 23–24) | 25
21 | 22 | 23 | 24

The Last Day of Pompeii, Karl Bryullov

Rooms 12–17: Dominance of the Academy

By the early 19th century the Academy of Arts was more and more influenced by Italian themes, given the unfashionability of France. In Room 12 look for Vladimir Borovikovsky's magnificent *Catherine II Promenading in Tsarskoe Selo* and his *Portrait of Murtaza Kuli,* his picture of the brother of the Persian Shah. Room 13 is full of paintings of peasant subjects with uplifting titles such as *Peeling Beetroot.*

Room 14 is truly spectacular, including enormous canvases such as Karl Bryullov's incredible *The Last Day of Pompeii* and *The Crucifixion*, and Ivan Aivazovsky's terrifying *The Wave.*

Room 15 is also impressive, with the far wall made up of studies for Alexander Ivanov's masterpiece *The Appearance of Christ Before the People* (1837–57), which hangs in Moscow's Tretyakov Gallery. Ivanov spent 20 years on this work, but it was met with a negative critical reception. However, later generations appreciated the work, and even these studies, many of which mark a notable departure in terms of detail and representation.

Rooms 18–22: Genre Painting

At the turn of the 19th century, it became fashionable for 'genre painting' to look to themes from (an incredibly idealised) rural Russia, which you can see in Rooms 18 and 20. Room 19 has some beautiful portraits by Ivan Kramskoi, including ones of his daughter Sofia and fellow painter Ivan Shishkin.

PETER I INTERROGATING TSAREVICH ALEXEY IN PETERHOF

Ghe's masterpiece captures the tumultuous relationship between Peter the Great and his son Alexey, whom he had imprisoned and tortured to death as he tried to extract information about 'plotters' against him. It foreshadows Alexey's brutal end in the Peter and Paul Fortress. Initially the painting was met with such critical coldness Ghe declared that art should not be for sale, became a follower of Tolstoy, bought a farm and began painting portraits for a pittance so that anyone who wanted one could afford them.

The best place to eat within the museum is **Grand Cafe Mikhailovsky** (Map p272; Benois Wing, Russian Museum, nab kanala Griboyedova; mains R300; ☺10am-5pm Mon, Wed, Fri-Sun 10am-5pm, Thu 1-8pm; Ⓜ Nevsky Prospekt), in the Benois Wing, where you can enjoy a coffee and cake or a more substantial meal of three courses plus tea for just R380 between noon and 3pm.

RUSSIAN MUSEUM — FIRST FLOOR

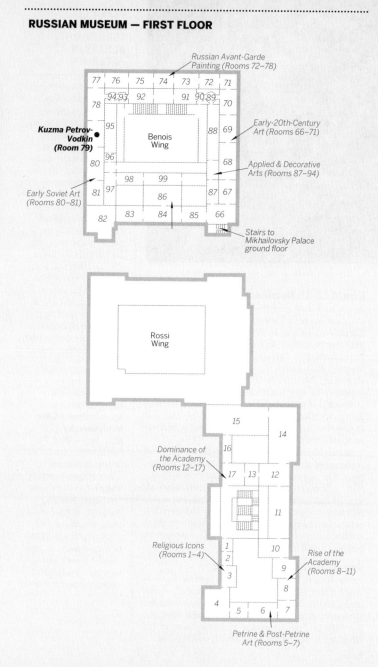

Russian Avant-Garde Painting (Rooms 72–78)

Kuzma Petrov-Vodkin (Room 79)

Benois Wing

Early-20th-Century Art (Rooms 66–71)

Applied & Decorative Arts (Rooms 87–94)

Early Soviet Art (Rooms 80–81)

Stairs to Mikhailovsky Palace ground floor

Rossi Wing

Dominance of the Academy (Rooms 12–17)

Religious Icons (Rooms 1–4)

Rise of the Academy (Rooms 8–11)

Petrine & Post-Petrine Art (Rooms 5–7)

Room 21 contains some enormous canvases: *Phrina at the Poseidon Celebration in Elesium* by Genrikh Semiradsky, *Christian Martyrs at the Colosseum* by Konstantin Flavitsky and *Nero's Death* by Vasily Smirnov. Room 22 is dominated by a huge rendition of *Pugachev's Judgement* by Vasily Perov.

Rooms 23–24: The Wanderers

In these galleries you'll find works by the Wanderers (Peredvizhniki), a group of Academy artists who saw their future outside the confines of that institution. They wandered among the people, painting scenes of realism that had never been seen before in Russian art. Prime examples include Nikolai Perov's animated *Hunters at Rest* and the *Monastery Refectory,* a scathing critique of the Church establishment's greed. Also keep an eye out for Pavel Christiakov's serene *Jovannina Sitting on Window Sill.*

Rooms 25 & 26: Konstantin Makovsky & Nicholas Ghe

Room 25 is devoted to Konstantin Makovsky (1839–1915), who painted the incredibly cinematic *Festivity During the Carnival on Admiralty Sq in St Petersburg* at the age of just 30. Also a standout is his portrait of his wife Julija.

Ghe's masterpiece, *Peter I Interrogating Tsarevich Alexey in Peterhof,* is usually found in Room 26 along with other dark Ghe works such as *The Last Supper.*

Rooms 27–32: Landscapes & Portraits

Contemporaries of the Wanderers, landscape artists such as Ivan Shishkin were still popular. These rooms also document the rise of populist art, which had a strong social conscience and sought to educate the public. Examples of this are Konstantin Savitsky's *To War* (Room 31) and Grigory Myasoyedov's lyrical *Harvest Time.*

In Room 28 pause to take in the talent of Ukrainian artist Marie Bashkirtseff (1858–84) who died young but not before painting striking portraits, such as *Umbrella* and the *Three Smiles* series.

Rooms 33–34: Ilya Repin

Take your time viewing several masterpieces by Ilya Repin (1844–1930), one of Russia's most famous painters. The iconic *Barge Haulers on the Volga* is an incredible picture, as is *Cossacks Writing a Letter to the Turkish Sultan.* There is also his marvellous portrait of a barefoot Leo Tolstoy.

Rooms 35–47: Late-19th-Century Russian Art

These rooms display the large number of contradictory styles that were fashionable in St Petersburg before the explosion of the avant-garde. These include

ILYA REPIN

One of Russia's greatest artists, Ilya Repin was born in Chuhuiv, now part of Ukraine. Originally a member of the Wanderers, he outgrew the movement and went on to produce key works of Russian realist and populist art. His masterpiece, *Barge Haulers on the Volga*, an unrivalled portrait of human misery and enslavement in rural Russia, shows why the early Soviet authorities held him in high regard as a model for the Socialist Realist painters to come.

Vasily Surikov, a master of the historical painting that was in vogue in the late 19th century. His portrayals of *Yermak's Conquest of Siberia* and *Suvorov Crossing the Alps* (Room 36) are particularly dramatic, but the lifelike rendition of Cossack rebel *Stepan Razin* (Room 37) is undoubtedly his most evocative.

Rooms 48–49: Antokolsky's Sculptures & Folk Art

Mark Antokolsky's statues *Ivan the Terrible* and *Death of Socrates* are on display either side of a souvenir stand. From here you enter the Benois Wing to your right or continue straight ahead for the comprehensive account of Russian folk art, a really lovely display featuring everything from kitchen equipment to giant carved house gables. Room 49 is a long corridor devoted to the museum's history showcasing old photos and posters from past exhibitions.

Rooms 66–71: Early-20th-Century Art

On the 1st floor of the Benois Wing, the collection moves into the 20th century with works by the father of modern Russian art, Mikhail Vrubel (1856–1910) in Room 66. Some of his groundbreaking works include *Epic Hero (Bogatyr)* and *Flying Demon*.

Rooms 67 to 71 include works by important early-20th-century painters including Kuzma Petrov-Vodkin, Nikolai Sapunin, Mikhail Nesterov and Boris Kustodiev, whose *Merchant's Wife at Tea* is perhaps the most well-known picture here.

Rooms 72–78: Russian Avant-Garde Painting

Between 1905 and 1917, the Russian art world experienced an explosion of creative inspiration that defied the stylistic categorisation that had existed before. Room 72 is home to Nathan Altman's gorgeous, semi-cubist *Portrait of the Poetess Anna Akhmatova*, painted in 1914, and it remains one of his most famous works even though Akhmatova apparently didn't care for it herself. In the same room is Altman's striking *Self Portrait* (1911). Room 74 contains primitivist paintings by artist couple Natalya Goncharova and Mikhail Larionov.

Futurism and suprematism, including works by Malevich such as *Black Square* and Vladimir Tatlin's *Counter Relief*, can be found in Rooms 75 to 76. Room 77 is devoted to constructivism and features works by Alexander Rodchenko and Vladimir Lebedev. Room 78 displays the bright, ethereal work of Pavel Filonov.

Rooms 80–81: Early Soviet Art

Most paintings from the Stalin era may have been censored beyond meaning, but there are some interesting portraits of daily life here, such as Alexander Samokhvalov's *Militarised Komsomol* (1932–33) and various pictures from WWII showing heroic resistance and national unity.

Rooms 82–86: Late Soviet Art

With Stalin gone and the 'thaw' under way in the 1950s, Soviet art recovered somewhat from the severity of socialist realism. Idealised images of rural life and peasants still feature very strongly, however. Look for Alexei Sundukov's *Queue* which captures the failed economy of the times and Dmitry Zhilinsky's *The Artist's Family*, showing several generations of a family.

Rooms 87–94: Applied & Decorative Art

Works in these galleries range from a beautifully glazed ceramic fireplace by Mikhail Vrubel and other art nouveau–inspired pieces, to Soviet-era porcelain and textiles printed with ingenious patterns made out of tiny tractors or planes.

Rooms 101–109: Temporary Exhibitions

The Russian Museum's temporary exhibitions are hung on the ground-floor galleries either side of entrance to the Benois Wing. To reach these from the 1st floor of the Benois Wing (following your tour of the museum's main collection), use the stairs down off rooms 91 and 92.

TOP SIGHT
CHURCH ON THE SPILLED BLOOD

This five-domed dazzler is St Petersburg's most elaborate church, with a classic Russian Orthodox exterior and an interior decorated with some 7000 sq m of mosaics. Officially called the Church of the Resurrection of Christ, its full colloquial name (Church of the Saviour on the Spilled Blood) references the assassination attempt on Tsar Alexander II here in 1881.

Restored Beauty

The church, which was was consecrated in 1907, incorporates elements of 18th-century Russian architecture from Moscow and Yaroslavl, and is so lavish it took 24 years to build and went over budget by 1 million rubles – an enormous sum for the times. Decades of abuse and neglect during most of the Soviet era ended in the 1970s when restoration began. When the doors reopened 27 years later on what is now a museum, visitors were astounded by the spectacular mosaics covering the walls and ceilings. Designs for the mosaics came from top artists of the day including Victor Vasnetsov, Mikhail Nesterov and Andrey Ryabushkin.

The Exterior

The polychromatic exterior – decorated with mosaics of detailed scenes from the New Testament and the coats of arms of the provinces, regions and towns of the Russian Empire of Alexander's time – is equally showstopping. Twenty granite plaques around the facade record the main events of Alexander's reign.

DON'T MISS

➡ Canopy marking the spot of the assassination
➡ The mosaic murals
➡ The 20 granite plaques on the outside
➡ Taking a photo from the footbridge

PRACTICALITIES

➡ Храм Спаса на Крови
➡ Map p272, F3
➡ ☏812-315 1636
➡ http://eng.cathedral.ru/spasa_na_krovi
➡ Konyushennaya pl
➡ adult/student R250/150
➡ ⊘10.30am-6pm Thu-Tue
➡ Ⓜ Nevsky Prospekt

TOP SIGHT
ST ISAAC'S CATHEDRAL

Named after St Isaac of Dalmatia, on whose feast day Peter the Great was born, this is one of the largest domed buildings in the world. Most people bypass the museum to climb the 262 steps to the kolonnada (colonnade) around the drum of the dome; the outlook across the city is superb.

Controversial Design

French architect Auguste de Montferrand began designing the cathedral in 1818. Due partly to technical issues, it took so long to build (until 1858) that Nicholas I was able to insist on an even more grandiose structure than Montferrand had originally planned. More than 100kg of gold leaf was used to cover the 21.8m-high dome alone, while the huge granite pillars on the building's facade each weigh over 120 tonnes. There's a statue of Montferrand holding a model of the cathedral on the west facade, although Nicholas I denied the architect his dying wish, to be buried here, considering it too high an honour for a mere artisan.

Interior Decoration

The cathedral's interior is lavishly decorated with 600 sq m of mosaics, 16,000kg of malachite, 14 types of marble and an 816-sq-m ceiling painting by Karl Bryullov. Look out for some interesting photographs of the cathedral throughout its history, too.

DON'T MISS

➡ Views from the dome

➡ Lavish interiors

➡ Display of historic photos

➡ Statue of Montferrand

PRACTICALITIES

➡ Исаакиевский собор

➡ Map p272, B5

➡ ☎ 812-315 9732

➡ www.cathedral.ru

➡ Isaakievskaya pl

➡ cathedral adult/student R250/150, colonnade R150

➡ ⊙ cathedral 10.30am-10.30pm Thu-Tue May-Sep, to 6pm Oct-Apr; colonnade 10.30am-10.30pm May-Oct, to 6pm Nov-Apr

➡ Ⓜ Admiralteyskaya

⊙ SIGHTS

STATE HERMITAGE MUSEUM MUSEUM
See p56.

GENERAL STAFF BUILDING MUSEUM
See p72.

RUSSIAN MUSEUM MUSEUM
See p74.

**CHURCH OF THE SAVIOUR
ON THE SPILLED BLOOD** CHURCH
See p81.

ST ISAAC'S CATHEDRAL MUSEUM
See p82.

PALACE SQUARE SQUARE
Map p272 (Дворцовая площадь; Dvortsovaya pl; ⓂAdmiralteyskaya) This vast expanse is simply one of the most striking squares in the world, still redolent of imperial grandeur almost a century after the end of the Romanov dynasty. For the most amazing first impression, walk from Nevsky pr, up Bolshaya Morskaya ul and under the **triumphal arch** (Map p272).

In the centre of the square, the 47.5m **Alexander Column** (Александровская колонна; Map p272; Palace Sq; ⓂAdmiralteyskaya) was designed in 1834 by Montferrand. Named after Alexander I, it commemorates the 1812 victory over Napoleon.

The square's northern end is capped by the Winter Palace (Zimny Dvorets), a rococo profusion of columns, windows and recesses, topped by rows of larger-than-life statues. A residence of tsars from 1762 to 1917, it's now the largest part of the State Hermitage Museum.

Curving an incredible 580m around the south side of the square is the Carlo Rossi–designed General Staff Building (p72) completed in 1829. The east wing now houses a branch of the Hermitage while the west wing is the headquarters of the Western Military District. The two great blocks are joined by a triumphal arch over Bolshaya Morskaya ul, topped by the Chariot of Glory by sculptors Stepan Pimenov and Vasily Demuth-Malinovsky, another monument to the Napoleonic Wars.

NEVSKY PROSPEKT STREET
Map p272 Nevsky Prospekt is Russia's most famous street, running 4km from the Admiralty to Alexander Nevsky Monastery, from which it takes its name. The inner 2.5km to Moskovsky vokzal is the city's shopping centre and focus of its entertainment and street life. Walking Nevsky is an essential St Petersburg experience. If you're here on a holiday evening (such as 27 May – City Day), the sight of thousands of people pouring like a stream down its middle is one you'll not forget.

Nevsky Prospekt was laid out in the early years of St Petersburg, as the start of the main road to Novgorod, and soon became dotted with fine buildings, squares and bridges. At the beginning of the 1900s, it was one of Europe's grandest boulevards, with cobblestone footpaths and a track down the middle for horse-drawn trams. On either side of the tracks were wooden paving blocks to muffle the sound of horse-drawn carriages – an innovation that was a world-first and for which the avenue was dubbed the quietest main street in Europe.

Today, things are quite a bit noisier. The traffic and crowds can become oppressive and, after a while, you'll find yourself going out of your way to avoid the street.

KAZAN CATHEDRAL CHURCH
Map p272 (Казанский собор; ☎812-314 4663; http://kazansky-spb.ru; Kazanskaya pl 2; ⊗8.30am-7.30pm; ⓂNevsky Prospekt) **FREE** This neoclassical cathedral, partly modelled on St Peter's in Rome, was commissioned by Tsar

HISTORIC HEART SIGHTS

WITNESS TO HISTORY

Palace Square has been the location for some of the most dramatic moments in St Petersburg's history. On Bloody Sunday (9 January 1905), tsarist troops fired on workers who were peaceably gathered in the square, sparking the 1905 revolution. And it was across Dvortsovaya pl that the storming of the Winter Palace took place during the 1917 October Revolution, an event re-enacted by Lenin and thousands of Red Guards in 1920 and later filmed in 1927 for Sergei Eisenstein's *October,* commissioned by the government to celebrate the 10th anniversary of the Bolshevik Revolution.

Paul shortly before he was murdered in a coup. Its 111m-long colonnaded arms reach out towards Nevsky pr, encircling a garden studded with statues. Inside, the cathedral is dark and traditionally Orthodox, with a daunting 80m-high dome. There is usually a queue of believers waiting to kiss the icon of Our Lady of Kazan, a copy of one of Russia's most important icons.

Look for the victorious Napoleonic War field marshal Mikhail Kutuzov (whose remains are buried inside the cathedral) and his friend and aide Mikhail Barclay de Tolly.

The cathedral's design reflects Paul's eccentric desire to unite Catholicism and Orthodoxy in a kind of 'super-Christianity' as well as his fascination with the Knights of Malta, of which he was a member.

STROGANOV PALACE   MUSEUM

Map p272 (Строгановский дворец; www.rusmuseum.ru; Nevsky pr 17; adult/student R300/150; ⊙10am-6pm Wed & Fri-Mon, 1-9pm Thu; ⓜNevsky Prospekt) One of the city's loveliest baroque exteriors, the salmon-pink Stroganov Palace was designed by court favourite Bartolomeo Rastrelli in 1753 for one of the city's leading aristocratic families. The building has been superbly restored by the Russian Museum, and you can visit the impressive state rooms upstairs, where the Grand Dining Room, the Mineralogical Study and the Rastrelli Hall, with its vast frieze ceiling, are the obvious highlights.

Famously, the Stroganov's chef created here a beef dish served in a sour cream and mushroom sauce that became known to the world as 'beef stroganoff'.

MARBLE PALACE   PALACE

Map p272 (Мраморный дворец; ☑812-595 4248; www.rusmuseum.ru; Millionnaya ul 5; adult/student R300/150; ⊙10am-6pm Mon, Wed & Fri-Sun, 1-9pm Thu; ⓜNevsky Prospekt) This branch of the Russian Museum (p74) features temporary exhibitions of contemporary art and a permanent display of paintings from the Ludwig Museum in Cologne that includes works by Picasso, Warhol, Basquiat and Liechtenstein. The palace, designed by Antonio Rinaldi, gets its name from the 36 kinds of marble used in its construction. Highlights include the Gala Staircase, made of subtly changing grey Urals marble; and the impressive Marble Hall, with walls of lapis lazuli and marble in a range of colours from yellow to pink.

Built between 1768 and 1785, the palace was a gift from Catherine the Great to Grigory Orlov for suppressing a Moscow rebellion. Outside it stands the equestrian statue of Alexander III.

SUMMER GARDEN   PARK

Map p272 (Летний сад; ☑812-314 0374; https://igardens.ru; nab reki Moyki; tours from R1200; ⊙10am-10pm May-Sep, 10am-8pm Oct-Mar, closed Apr; ⓜGostiny Dvor) **FREE** The city's oldest park, these leafy, shady gardens can be entered either at the northern Neva or southern Moyka end. Early-18th-century architects designed the garden in a Dutch baroque style, following a geometric plan, with fountains, pavilions and sculptures studding the grounds. The ornate cast-iron fence along the Neva side was a later addition, built between 1771 and 1784.

The gardens functioned as a private retreat for Peter the Great (his modest **Summer Palace** (Map p272; ☑812 314 0374; Muzey Letny Dvorets Petra1), closed for renovations, is here) before becoming a strolling place for St Petersburg's 19th-century leisured classes.

MONUMENT TO ALEXANDER III

'I don't care about politics. I simply depicted one animal on another,' said sculptor Paolo Trubetskoy defending his equestrian statue of Alexander III when it was unveiled in 1909. Originally erected on pl Vosstaniya, the unflattering giant bronze of the stout, unpopular tsar had caused a scandal among St Petersburg society who were divided on its artistic merits. Alexander's son Nicholas II considered shipping it off to Irkutsk, but when rumours started that he wanted to send his dad into Siberian exile, he changed his mind.

In 1937 the statue was removed from pl Vosstaniya and sent to languish in an interior courtyard of the Russian Museum. In post-communist Russia, when the Marble Palace ceased to house the Lenin Museum, the statue was moved to the forecourt there, replacing Lenin's armoured car (which now can be seen at the Artillery Museum (p161).

Only in the 20th century were commoners admitted.

Tours can be booked in advance or at the Teahouse (p97) which is the best of several cafes to be found in the gardens and which occasionally hosts music concerts on summer evenings.

The 92 marble statues, busts and sculptural groups that decorate parts of the garden are replicas: the 18th-century originals are housed in the Mikhailovsky Castle.

MIKHAILOVSKY CASTLE   MUSEUM

Map p272 (Михайловский замок; ☑812-595 4248; www.rusmuseum.ru; Sadovaya ul 2; adult/student R300/150; ◷10am-6pm Mon, Wed & Fri-Sun, 1-9pm Thu; ⓂGostiny Dvor) A branch of the Russian Museum (p74), the castle is worth visiting for its temporary exhibits as well as a few finely restored state rooms, including the lavish burgundy and gilt throne room of Tsar Paul I's wife Maria Fyodorovna.

Rastrelli's original fairytale wooden palace for Empress Elizabeth was knocked down in the 1790s to make way for this bulky edifice, a bizarre take on a medieval castle, quite unlike any other building in the city.

The son of Catherine the Great, Tsar Paul I, was born in the wooden palace and he wanted his own residence on the same spot. He specified a defensive moat as he (quite rightly) feared assassination. But this erratic, cruel tsar only got 40 days in his new abode before he was suffocated in his bedroom in 1801.

In 1823 the palace became a military engineering school (hence its Soviet-era name, Engineer's Castle, or Inzhenerny Zamok), whose most famous pupil was Fyodor Dostoevsky.

MIKHAILOVSKY GARDEN   PARK

Map p272 (Михайловский сад; https://igardens.ru; ◷10am-10pm May-Sep, 10am-8pm Oct-Mar, closed Apr; ⓂNevsky Prospekt) **FREE** Administered by the Russian Museum, these 8.7-hectare gardens are lovely and offer an impressive perspective of Mikhailovsky Castle. They are famous for their Style Moderne wrought-iron fence and gates, a profusion of metallic blooms and flourishes that wrap around one side of the Church on the Spilled Blood.

BRONZE HORSEMAN   MONUMENT

Map p272 (Senatskaya pl; ⓂSadovaya) The most famous statue of Peter the Great was immortalised as the Bronze Horseman in the epic poem by Alexander Pushkin. With his horse (representing Russia) rearing above the snake of treason, Peter's enormous statue was sculpted over 12 years for Catherine the Great by Frenchman Etienne Falconet. Its inscription reads 'To Peter I from Catherine II – 1782'.

Many have read significance into Catherine's linking of her own name with that of the city's founder: she had no legitimate claim to the throne and this statue is sometimes seen as her attempt to formalise the link (philosophical, if not hereditary) between the two monarchs. The significance of the inscription in both Latin and Cyrillic alphabets would not have been lost on the city's population, which was still in the process of Westernisation during Catherine's reign.

Despite completing his lifework here, Falconet departed Russia a bitter, angry man. Years of arguing with the head of the Academy of Fine Arts over the finer details of the sculpture had taken its toll, and he didn't even bother staying for the unveiling.

It's tradition for local newlyweds to be photographed here after their weddings, so expect to see plenty of jolly wedding parties.

RUSSIAN MUSEUM OF ETHNOGRAPHY   MUSEUM

Map p272 (Российский Этнографический музей; ☑812-570 5421; www.ethnomuseum.ru; Inzhenernaya ul 4/1; adult/student R300/100, treasure room R250; ◷10am-9pm Tue, 10am-6pm Wed-Sun; ⓂGostiny Dvor) This excellent museum displays the traditional crafts, customs and beliefs of more than 150 cultures that make up Russia's fragile ethnic mosaic. It's a marvellous collection with particularly strong sections on the Jews of Russia, Transcaucasia and Central Asia, including rugs and two full-size yurts (nomads' portable tent-houses). Galleries are accessed either side of the magnificent 1000-sq-m Marble Hall, flanked by rows of pink Karelian-marble columns, in which events and concerts are held.

You need to buy an extra ticket to view the treasure room, which has some great weapons and rare devotional objects.

WINTER PALACE OF PETER I   MUSEUM

Map p272 (Зимний дворец Петра Первого; www.hermitagemuseum.org; Dvortsovaya nab 32; admission R150; ⊙10.30am-5pm Tue-Sat, 10am-4pm Sun; ⓜAdmiralteyskaya) Excavations beneath the Hermitage Theatre in the late 1970s revealed remains of the principal residence of Peter the Great, including a large fragment of the former state courtyard, as well as several suites of palace apartments. Some rooms have been restored to their appearance during Peter's era, complete with Dutch tiles and parquet floors, and are used to exhibit some of Peter's personal items from the Hermitage collection.

The cobbled courtyard has one of Peter's official carriages and a sledge. In the last room before you leave, don't miss the wax effigy of Peter made by Bartolomeo Rastrelli after the tsar died in the palace in 1725.

ADMIRALTY   ARCHITECTURE

Map p272 (Адмиралтейство; Admiralteysky proezd 1; ⓜAdmiralteyskaya) The gilded spire of the Admiralty is a prime St Petersburg landmark, visible from Gorokhovaya ul, Voznesensky pr and Nevsky pr, as all of these roads radiate outwards from this central point. From 1711 to 1917, this spot was the headquarters of the Russian navy; now it houses the country's largest military naval college and is closed to the public.

The building itself was reconstructed between 1806 and 1823 to the designs of Andreyan Zakharov. With its rows of white columns and its plentiful reliefs and statuary, it is a foremost example of the Russian Empire style. Get a close look at the globe-toting nymphs flanking the main gate. Despite the spire's solid-gold appearance, it's actually made from wood and was almost rotted through before restoration efforts began in 1996.

ALEXANDER GARDEN   PARK

Map p272 (Александровский сад; Admiralteysky pr; ⓜAdmiralteyskaya) FREE Laid out from 1872 to 1874, these pleasant gardens, named after Alexander II, wrap around the Admiralty and are mentioned in Pushkin's famous verse novel *Eugene Onegin* as a fashionable place for a stroll. They remain so, dotted with statues of Glinka, Lermontov, Gogol and other cultural figures, as well as a fountain that dates to 1879. Opposite St Isaac's there's a very good **children's playground** within the garden.

PUSHKIN FLAT-MUSEUM   MUSEUM

Map p272 (Музей-квартира А.С. Пушкина; ☏812-571 3531; www.museumpushkin.ru; nab reki Moyki 12; adult/student R250/150; ⊙10.30am-5pm Wed-Sun; ⓜAdmiralteyskaya) Alexander Pushkin, Russia's national poet, had his last home here on one of the prettiest curves of the Moyka River. He only lived here four months, and died here after his duel in 1837. The little house is now the Pushkin Flat-Museum, which has been reconstructed to look exactly as it did in the poet's last days. You can only visit on a tour (run hourly on the hour), given in Russian only.

On display are his death mask, a lock of his hair and the waistcoat he wore when he died.

STATE RUSSIAN MUSEUM AND EXHIBITION CENTRE ROSPHOTO   GALLERY

Map p272 (РОСФОТО; ☏812-314 1214; www.rosphoto.org; Bolshaya Morskaya ul 35; admission R150-300; ⊙11am-7pm Mon, Wed, Fri-Sun, noon-9pm Tue & Thu; ⓜAdmiralteyskaya) This gallery showcases rotating exhibitions of photography, videography and other mixed media drawn from across Russia and around the world. It's definitely one of the best spaces for seeing contemporary photographic work in St Petersburg. Note the beautiful stained-glass windows on the stairwell of the handsome building the gallery is located in, which housed an insurance company before the revolution.

The gallery's well-stocked art bookshop and pleasant cafe are also worth a look.

ST PETERSBURG STATE MUSEUM OF THEATRE & MUSIC   MUSEUM

Map p272 (Санкт-Петербургский музей театрального и музыкального искусства; ☏812-571 2195; http://theatremuseum.ru; Ostrovskogo pl 6; tickets to halls R80-150; ⊙Thu-Mon 11am-7pm, Wed 1-9pm; ⓜGostiny Dvor) This museum is a treasure-trove of items relating to the Russian theatre including model sets, posters and costumes. You'll have to buy separate tickets to its three sections, the best of which is the Legends of St Petersburg exhibition (R150). Also worth a look is the gallery devoted to the painter, scenery and costume designer Leon Bakst (R100).

A section aimed at children (R80) has great models of the Mariinsky stage and antique contraptions used to create effects like the sound of wind, rain and trains.

TOP SIGHT
FABERGÉ MUSEUM

The magnificently restored Shuvalovsky Palace is home to the world's largest collection of pieces manufactured by the jeweller Peter Carl Fabergé (including nine Imperial Easter eggs) and fellow master craftspeople of pre-revolutionary Russia.

Fabergé founded his jewellery business in St Petersburg in 1842. At its height he employed 700 people across many factories and in four shops in Russia and one in London. The tradition of tsars giving their wives jewelled Easter eggs began in 1885 when Alexander III commissioned the 37-year-old Fabergé to create a present for his Danish wife Maria Feodorovna. From 1897, the new tsar Nicholas II asked the jeweller to continue making the eggs for his mother, now the Dowager Empress, and his own wife Alexandra Feodorovna.

As dazzling as these brilliant baubles are, they are just a prelude to a series of other lavishly decorated halls in which thousands of other pieces are displayed, including silver tea services, enamelled and jewelled cigarette cases and belt buckles, jade bowls and Russian Impressionist paintings. Look out for pieces by Fyodor Rückert, whose cloisonné enamel work is highly distinctive and beautiful.

DON'T MISS

➡ Imperial Easter eggs
➡ Fyodor Rückert cloisonné enamel pieces
➡ Grand Staircase
➡ Knights' Hall
➡ Red Room

PRACTICALITIES

➡ Музей Фаберже
➡ Map p272, H5
➡ http://fabergemuseum.ru
➡ nab reki Fontanki 21
➡ R450, incl tour R600
➡ ⊙10am-8.45pm Sat-Thurs
➡ Ⓜ Gostiny Dvor

KARL BULLA
PHOTOGRAPHY STUDIO   GALLERY

Map p272 (Фонд исторической фотографии им. Карла Буллы; ☎812-970 5103; www.bulla fond.ru; 4th fl, Nevsky pr 54; admission R50; ⊙10am-8pm; ☎; Ⓜ Gostiny Dvor) Karl Bulla (1853–1929) was one of the city's most famous photographers and is immortalised in a life-sized **statue** (Map p272; Malaya Sadovaya ul; Ⓜ Gostiny Dvor) on Malaya Sadovaya ul. Around the corner, his studio is still in operation at the top of this building where there's also a gallery of evocative black-and-white images of the city, shot by Bulla and his sons in the late 19th and early 20th century, alongside photographic portraits of the likes of the imperial family, Tolstoy and Chaliapin.

MUSEUM OF THE HISTORY OF
POLITICAL POLICE   MUSEUM

Map p272 (Музей политической полиции; ☎812-312 2742; www.polithistory.ru; Admiralteysky pr 6; adult/child R100/free; ⊙10am-6pm Mon-Fri; Ⓜ Admiralteyskaya) In the very same building that housed the tsarist and the Bolshevik secret police offices, this small museum recounts the history of this controversial institution and includes one room that recreates the office of Felix Dzerzhinsky, founder of the Cheka (Bolshevik secret police). Each of the remaining three rooms is devoted to the secret police during a different period of history: the tsarist police, the Cheka and the KGB.

Exhibitions are heavy on photographs and documents, but some of them are fascinating. Some explanatory materials are available in English.

MARS FIELD   PARK

Map p272 (Марсово поле; nab Lebyazhey kanavki; Ⓜ Nevsky Prospekt) Named after the Roman god of war and once the scene of 19th-century military parades, the grassy Mars Field is a popular spot for strollers, even though in the early 20th century it was used as a burial ground for victims and heroes of the revolution. At its centre, an **eternal flame** (Map p272) has been burning since 1957 in memory of the victims of all wars and revolutions in St Petersburg.

LUTHERAN CHURCH   CHURCH

Map p272 (☎812-312 0798; www.petrikirche.ru; Nevsky pr 22; ⊙9am-9pm; Ⓜ Nevsky Prospekt)

POPOVA VALERIYA / SHUTTERSTOCK ©

1. Anichkov most **2.** Troitsky most **3.** Griffin statue, Bankovsky most

St Petersburg's Bridges

A city threaded with canals and rivers needs bridges. St Petersburg has made a virtue of this necessity, crafting bridges that are both practical and beautiful to look at. Here are a few of our favourites:

Anichkov most (Аничков мост)

Named after its engineer and featuring rearing horses at all four corners, the striking ornamentation of this bridge symbolises humanity's struggle with and taming of nature.

Bankovsky most (Банковский мост)

This charming footbridge is suspended by cables emerging from the mouths of golden-winged griffins. The name comes from the Assignment Bank (now a further-education institute), which stands on one side of the bridge.

Lviny most (Львиный мост)

Another suspension footbridge over Griboyedov Canal, this one is supported by pairs of regal lions, hence its name.

Panteleymonovsky most (Пантелеймоновский мост)

At the confluence of the Moyka and the Fontanka, this beauty features lamp posts bedecked with the double-headed eagle and railings adorned with the coat of arms.

1-y Inzhenerny most (Первый Инженерный мост)

While there is no shortage of adornment on the cast-iron bridge leading to Mikhailovsky Castle, the highlight is the Chizhik-Pyzhik, the statue of the little bird that hovers over the Moyka.

Troitsky most (Троицкий мост)

Opened in 1903, this Franco-Russian codesign is a Style Moderne classic. Like most other spans across the Neva it is a drawbridge, raised every evening during the shipping season at designated times to allow the passage of river traffic.

LOCAL KNOWLEDGE

MUSEUM OF SOVIET ARCADE MACHINES

Museum of Soviet Arcade Machines (Map p272; ☏812-740 0240; http://15kop. ru; Konyushennaya pl 2; adult/student R450/350; ⊙11am-8pm, until 9pm May-Sep; ⬤; ⓂNevsky Prospekt) Giving new meaning to 'back in the USSR', this 'museum' is sure to be one of the most entertaining ones you will visit in St Petersburg. Admission includes a stack of 15 kopek coins used to operate the 50-odd game machines in its collection, which date to the Brezhnev era.

Have great fun joining local kids and their nostalgic parents as they play games such as *Morskoi Boi* (Battleships), table ice hockey and *Repka*, based on a Russian fable about pulling a giant radish out of the ground!

There's a pleasant cafe here too and at least once a month they host late-night DJ parties when ping-pong tables are rolled out to add to the fun.

`FREE` Tucked in a recess between Bolshaya and Malaya Konyushennaya uls is this lovely church, in the Romantic-Gothic style, built for St Petersburg's thriving German community in the 1830s. It's distinguished by a four-column portico and topped with a discreet cupola. Concerts are also held here, including free ones when the church organ is played.

There's an exhibition in the upstairs gallery about the city's German population and the church, which during Soviet times housed a swimming pool (the high diving board was placed in the apse).

BRODSKY HOUSE-MUSEUM   MUSEUM

Map p272 (Музей-квартира И.И. Бродского; www.nimrah.ru/musbrod; pl Iskusstv 3; adult/student R300/100; ⊙noon-7pm Wed-Sun; ⓂNevsky Prospekt) This is the former home of Isaak Brodsky, Repin's favourite student and one of the favoured artists of the revolution (not to be confused with Joseph Brodsky, one of the least-favourite poets of the same regime). Besides being a painter himself, Brodsky was also an avid collector, and his house-museum contains his collection of thousands of works, including lesser-known paintings by top 19th-century artists such as Repin, Levitan and Kramskoy.

ARMENIAN CHURCH OF ST CATHERINE   CHURCH

Map p272 (Церковь св. Екатерины; ☏812-570 4108; http://armenian-church.org; Nevsky pr 40-42; ⊙8am-6.30pm Mon-Fri, 9.30am-1.30pm Sat; ⓂNevsky Prospekt) Continuing with a tradition of non-Orthodox churches being built on Nevsky pr, the Armenian merchant Ovanes Lazarian paid for the city's first Armenian church to be erected here in 1771. Designed by German architect Georg Veldten and completed in 1780, the church's intimate interior was destroyed during Soviet times, but has since been restored.

PLOSHCHAD OSTROVSKOGO   SQUARE

Map p272 (Площадь Островского; ⓂGostiny Dvor) Created by Carlo Rossi in the 1820s and 1830s, this square is named for Alexander Ostrovsky (1823–86), a celebrated 19th-century playwright. An enormous **statue of Catherine the Great** (Map p272; pl Ostrovskogo; 1873) stands amid the chess, backgammon and mah-jong players who crowd the benches here. At the Empress' heels are renowned statesmen of the 19th century, including her lovers Orlov, Potemkin and Suvorov.

The most prominent building on the square is Rossi's neoclassical Alexandrinsky Theatre (p98).

The square's west side is taken up by the **National Library of Russia** (Map p272; ☏812-310 7137; www.nlr.ru; pl Ostrovskogo 1/3; ⊙9am-9pm Mon-Fri, 11am-7pm Sat & Sun; ⬤; ⓂGostiny Dvor).

PLOSHCHAD LOMONOSOVA   SQUARE

Map p272 (Площадь Ломоносова; ⓂGostiny Dvor) Named after the great scientist Mikhail Lomonosov, this small square forms the southwestern end of the Carlo Rossi–designed ensemble and is the best spot from which to admire the ideal symmetrical proportions of ul Zodchego Rossi: the buildings on this street are 22m wide, 22m apart and 220m long.

The **Vaganova School of Choreography** at No 2 is the Mariinsky Ballet's training school, where Pavlova, Nijinsky, Nureyev and others learned their art.

From the square you can also admire **Most Lomonosova**, a stone drawbridge (no longer functioning) dating from 1787 with four Doric pavilions that housed the drawbridge mechanism.

PLOSHCHAD ISKUSSTV · SQUARE

Map p272 (Площадь Искусств; MNevsky Prospekt) In the 1820s and 1830s, Carlo Rossi designed Ploshchad Iskusstv (Arts Square), named after the cluster of museums and concert halls that surrounds it, and the lovely Mikhailovskaya ul, which joins the square to Nevsky pr. There is invariably a pigeon perched atop the **statue of Pushkin** (Map p272; pl Iskusstv), erected in 1957, which stands in the middle of the tree-lined square.

VORONTSOV PALACE · HISTORIC BUILDING

Map p272 (Воронцовский дворец; Sadovaya ul 26; MGostiny Dvor) Opposite Gostiny Dvor, this palace (1749–57) is another noble town house by Rastrelli. From 1810 it was the most elite military school in the empire and is still used as a military school for young cadets. The palace is occasionally opened for concerts and such, details of which are posted out the front.

ANICHKOV PALACE · PALACE

Map p272 (Аничков дворец; ☎812-314 9555; www.anichkov.ru; Nevsky pr 39a; MGostiny Dvor) Built between 1741 and 1751, with input from a slew of architects, including Rastrelli and Rossi, the Anichkov Palace is now officially known as the St Petersburg City Palace of Youth Creativity. It's the location for over 1000 hobby classes and after-school clubs for the city's children. There's a small museum inside, but it is only open sporadically for tours.

The palace was twice a generous gift for services rendered: Empress Elizabeth gave it to her favourite Count Razumovsky and later Catherine the Great presented it to Potemkin. This was also Tsar Nicholas II's favourite place to stay in St Petersburg – he far preferred the cosy interiors to the vastness of the Winter Palace.

PETROVSKAYA AKVATORIA · SHOWROOM

Map p272 (Петровская Акватория; ☎812-933 4152; www.peteraqua.ru; Malaya Morskaya ul 4/1; adult/child R400/200; ⊙10am-10pm; MAdmiralteyskaya) For an idealised view of what parts of St Petersburg looked like back in the early 18th century, this interactive model village is a small revelation. The scaled models of the Peter and Paul Fortress, Vasilyevsky Island, Peterhof, Oranienbaum etc are incredibly detailed with moving horse and carriages and sailing ships.

The ensemble is laid out to reflect the four seasons and lit for both night and day. You'll find it on the 6th floor above the metro entrance.

CHURCH OF THE SAVIOUR
NOT MADE BY HUMAN HAND · SQUARE

Map p272 (Храм Спаса Нерукотворного Образа на Конюшенной Площади; 1 Konyushennaya pl; ⊙9am-7pm; MNevsky Prospekt) On the north side of Stables Sq, this church – named after a legendary Byzantine icon – is where Pushkin's funeral service was held in 1837. The square was where the imperial court once kept its horses and transportation.

EATING

★ZOOM CAFÉ · EUROPEAN $

Map p272 (☎812-612 1329; www.cafezoom.ru; Gorokhovaya ul 22; mains R350-550; ⊙9am-midnight Mon-Fri, from 11am Sat, from 1pm Sun; 🛜🖶♿; MNevsky Prospekt) A perennially popular cafe (expect to wait for a table at peak times) with a cosy feel and an interesting menu, ranging from Japanese-style chicken in teriyaki sauce to potato pancakes with salmon and cream cheese. Well-stocked bookshelves, a range of board games and adorable cuddly toys (each with its own name) encourage lingering.

CLEAN PLATES SOCIETY · INTERNATIONAL $

Map p272 (Общество чистых тарелок; ☎812-934 9764; www.cleanplatescafe.com; Gorokhovaya ul 13; mains R400-600; ⊙11am-1am; 🛜🖶; MAdmiralteyskaya) Burgers, curry, borsch and burritos all get a look in on this stylish and relaxed restaurant's menu. The horseshoe bar and the inventive cocktail and drinks list are its prime attractions.

UKROP · VEGAN $

Map p272 (☎812-946 3035; www.cafe-ukrop.ru; Malaya Konyushennaya ul 14; mains R280-360; ⊙9am-11pm; 🛜🖶; MNevsky Prospekt) Proving veggie, vegan and raw food can be inventive and tasty as well as wholesome, Ukrop (meaning dill) also makes an effort with its bright and whimsical craft design, which includes swing seats and lots of natural materials.

JACK & CHAN INTERNATIONAL $

Map p272 (☑812-982 0535; http://jack-and-chan.com; Inzhenernaya ul 7; mains R350-420; ⓧ11am-midnight Sun-Thu, until 2am Fri & Sat; 🛱; Ⓜ Gostiny Dvor) The restaurant name, a punning reference to Jackie Chan in Russian, neatly sums up the burger-meets-Asian menu at this fine and stylish casual diner. Try the sweet-and-sour fish and the prawn-and-avocado salad with glass noodles.

CHAIKI ITALIAN $

Map p272 (Чайки; ☑812-949 7737; www.chaykibar.ru; nab reki Moyki 19; mains R350; ⓧnoon-midnight Sun-Thu, until 3am Fri & Sat; 🛱; Ⓜ Admiralteyskaya) Whitewashed brick walls set the tone for this relaxed basement cafe-bar which does excellent pizza and decent salads. Wash the food down with locally made craft beers and fruit ciders.

PATISSERIE GARÇON FRENCH $

Map p272 (www.garcon.ru; Malaya Morskaya ul 20; mains R400-600; ⓧ9am-10pm; Ⓜ Admiralteyskaya) Branch of this excellent French bistro-cafe, which provides a relaxed Parisienne atmosphere to enjoy decent coffee, fresh bakes and lights meals.

MARKETPLACE RUSSIAN, INTERNATIONAL $

Map p272 (http://market-place.me; Nevsky pr 24; mains R200-300; ⓧ8am-5.30am; 🛱🖉; Ⓜ Nevsky Prospekt) The most central branch of this minichain that brings a high-class polish to the self-serve canteen concept, with many dishes cooked freshly on the spot to order. The hip design of the multilevel space is very appealing, making this a great spot to linger, especially if you indulge in one of the desserts or cocktails served on the 1st floor.

BIBLIOTEKA INTERNATIONAL $

Map p272 (☑812-244 1594; www.ilovenevsky.ru; Nevsky pr 20; mains R250-600; ⓧ8am-11pm Sun-Thu, to midnight Fri & Sat; 🛱; Ⓜ Nevsky Prospekt) You could spend the better part of a day here. Ground floor is a waiter-service cafe where it's difficult to avoid being tempted by the cake and dessert display by the door; next up is a more formal restaurant; and on the top floor there's a multiroom lounge bar (closed Monday and Tuesday) with live music and DJs until 1am on Friday and Saturday.

PELMENIYA RUSSIAN $

Map p272 (Пельмения; nab reki Fontanki 25; mains R300; ⓧ11am-11pm; 🛱; Ⓜ Gostiny Dvor) All kinds of dumplings are on the menu here – Georgian *khinkali*, Uzbek *manti*, Ukrainian *vareniki* and of course the eponymous *pelemni* – prepared fresh in a pleasant, contemporary design space near the main boat-tour dock.

CAFÉ SINGER CAFE $

Map p272 (Кафе Зингеръ; ☑812-571 8223; www.singercafe.ru; Nevsky pr 28; mains 400-500; ⓧ9am-11pm; 🛱; Ⓜ Nevsky Prospekt) On the 2nd floor of the iconic Singer Building (p102) is this great cafe, with fantastic views of the Kazan Cathedral and the bustle of Nevsky pr through its huge windows. As well as a sumptuous cake counter there's actually a more formal dining area around the corner, where you can order from a largely Russian menu.

TROITSKY MOST VEGETARIAN $

Map p272 (Троицкий мост; ☑812-925 5978; www.t-most.ru; nab reki Moyki 30; mains R200-300; ⓧ9am-11pm; 🛱🖉; Ⓜ Admiralteyskaya) This is the most central branch of the excellent veggie-cafe chain. It serves up the same excellent fare, including great vegetarian lasagne, in a cosy interior.

SOUP VINO MEDITERRANEAN $

Map p272 (☑812-312 7690; www.supvino.ru; Kazanskaya ul 24; mains R310-410; ⓧnoon-11pm; 🖉; Ⓜ Nevsky Prospekt) This tiny place is a foodie dream. Fresh daily specials such as artichoke salad and gazpacho complement a large range of freshly made soups. There are also several pasta dishes and delicious panini that can be taken away or enjoyed in the cute, wood-heavy premises.

PATISSERIE GARÇON FRENCH $

Map p272 (www.garcon.ru; nab kanala Griboyedova 25; mains R400-600; ⓧ9am-9pm; Ⓜ Nevsky Prospekt) Convenient branch of the city's best-value French bistro-cafe, providing a relaxed Parisienne atmosphere to enjoy decent coffee, fresh bakes and lights meals.

There's another one, a hop from St Isaac's Cathedral, too, as well as a branch in the Au Pont Rouge (p101) department store.

POTATOES WITH MUSHROOMS INTERNATIONAL $

Map p272 (Картофель с грибами; ☑812-994 0983; Gorokhovaya ul 12; mains R240-360; ⓧ11am-11pm Sun-Thu, 11am-2am Fri & Sat; 🛱🖉; Ⓜ Admiralteyskaya) Come here for a good-value, light bite, such as its various *kapsalon* dishes (a Dutch-style meal in a tin bowl).

The potato pancakes are excellent and there's a nice line in cocktails and wine too.

SAMADEVA
VEGETARIAN **$**

Map p272 (www.samadevacafe.ru; Kazanskaya ul 10; mains R200-300; ⏰9am-11pm; 🔌📶; Ⓜ️Nevsky Prospekt) The food isn't the tastiest vegetarian fare you'll find in the city, but this self-proclaimed 'philosophical cafe' is a pleasant enough spot for a meal and provides a blissful break from the sightseeing grind.

RUSSKAYA ZABAVA
RUSSIAN **$**

Map p272 (Русская забава; 📞812-570 0405; Gorokhovaya ul 3; mains R270-340; ⏰11am-11pm, from noon Sat & Sun; 🔌; Ⓜ️Admiralteyskaya) This kitschy cafe, whose name translates as Russian Fun, specialises in traditional dumplings *(pelmeni)* which come stuffed with beef, pork, salmon or mushrooms. Choose a soup or a salad as a starter, and you've got a filling and good-value meal.

⭐GRÄS X MADBAREN
FUSION **$$**

Map p272 (📞812-928 1818; http://grasmadbaren.com; ul Inzhenernaya 7; mains R420-550, tasting menu R2500; ⏰1-11pm Sun-Thu, until 1am Fri & Sat; 🔌; Ⓜ️Gostiny Dvor) Anton Abrezov is the talented exec chef behind this Scandi-cool meets Russian locavore restaurant where you can sample dishes such as a delicious corned beef salad with black garlic and pickled vegetables or an upmarket twist on ramen noodles with succulent roast pork.

The connected cocktail bar Madbaren is equally inventive, offering libations such as Siberian Penicillin (horseradish vodka, pollen syrup and rhubarb).

⭐YAT
RUSSIAN **$$**

Map p272 (Ять; 📞812-957 0023; www.eatinyat.com; nab reki Moyki 16; mains R370-750; ⏰11am-11pm; 🔌♿; Ⓜ️Admiralteyskaya) Perfectly placed for eating near the Hermitage, this country-cottage-style restaurant has a very appealing menu of traditional dishes, presented with aplomb. The *shchi* (cabbage-based soup) is excellent, and there is also a tempting range of flavoured vodkas. There's a fab kids area with pet rabbits for them to feed.

⭐GOGOL
RUSSIAN **$$**

Map p272 (Гоголь; 📞812-312 6097; http://restaurant-gogol.ru; Malaya Morskaya ul 8; mains R350-690; ⏰9am-3am; 🔌; Ⓜ️Admiralteyskaya) Like its sibling restaurant Chekov, Gogol whisks diners back to the genteel days of prerevolutionary Russian home dining. The menu comes in a novel, with chapters for each of the traditional courses. Salads, soups, dumplings and classics such as chicken Kiev are all very well done and served in charming, small dining rooms.

MECHTATELI
EUROPEAN **$$**

Map p272 (Мечтатели; 📞8-921-761 3155; www.thedreamerscafe.ru; nab reki Fontanki 11; mains R340-890; ⏰8am-11pm Sun-Thu, until 2am Fri & Sat; 🔌; Ⓜ️Gostiny Dvor) If you've been dreaming of a place with a delicious menu based on local produce – including deer, salmon and duck – and that's also a great spot for a leisurely breakfast, a good coffee or glass of wine, then 'the dreamers' restaurant has it all wrapped up very nicely in a minimalist-styled package.

HAMLET + JACKS
INTERNATIONAL **$$**

Map p272 (📞812-907 0735; http://hamletandjacks.com/; Volynsky per 2; mains R480-1170; ⏰1pm-midnight Sun-Thu, until 2am Fri & Sat; 🔌; Ⓜ️Nevsky Prospekt) Named after its owners, this new restaurant splits its menu between inventive dishes made with local products, such as fish from Murmansk and deer from Siberia, and those made with international ingredients. We enjoyed a perfectly cooked duck breast with beetroot and parsnip purees.

GOSTI
RUSSIAN **$$**

Map p272 (Гости; 📞812-312 5820; Malaya Morskaya ul 13; mains R600-800; ⏰9am-midnight; 🔌; Ⓜ️Admiralteyskaya) Whether you drop by for bakery treats and its homemade teas, or for a full meal of delicious and well-presented Russian classics, you can't go wrong at Gosti. Friendly service, a comfy, cosy and colourful interior on two levels, and live piano music on some nights all add to its considerable charm.

ARKA BAR & GRILL
INTERNATIONAL **$$**

Map p272 (📞812-339 8939; www.arka.spb.ru; Bolshaya Konyushennaya ul 27; mains R340-1620; ⏰9am-6am; 🔌; Ⓜ️Nevsky Prospekt) Sip your drink at the 13m-long bar that runs down to a double-storey restaurant at the rear. This sophisticated place keeps long hours and covers many bases, from a pastry and coffee for breakfast to a main meal (the Russian food is good) to house-made chocolates.

MAMALIGA
CAUCASIAN $$

Map p272 (Мамалыга; ☑812-571 8287; www.mamaliga-mamaliga.ru; Kazanskaya ul 2; mains R400-850; ◷10am-midnight; 🛜🖉; Ⓜ Nevsky Prospekt) This stylish, bright and spacious cafe has wooden floors, deeply distressed walls and understated old-world furnishings. Its mouth-watering pictorial menu covers a wide range of dishes from the Caucasus.

CAFÉ KING PONG
ASIAN $$

Map p272 (Кинг Понг; ☑812-315 8256; www.kingpong.ru; Bolshaya Morskaya ul 16; mains R400-700; ◷noon-midnight; 🛜🖉; Ⓜ Admiralteyskaya) This fun pan-Asian diner, occupying sleek and luminous premises with a retro-glamorous feel just off Nevsky, offers a large menu of very-good-quality dishes taking in dim sum, noodles, soups and rice dishes. There are also plenty of veggie options.

YEREVAN
ARMENIAN $$

Map p272 (☑812-703 3820; http://erivan.ru; nab reki Fontanki 51; mains R500-1000; ◷noon-midnight; 🛜; Ⓜ Gostiny Dvor) Top-class Armenian restaurant, with an elegant ethnic design and delicious traditional food made with ingredients it promises are from 'ecologically pure' regions of Armenia. Live traditional music is performed after 8pm.

TERRASSA
EUROPEAN $$

Map p272 (☑812-640 1616; http://ginza.ru/spb/restaurant/terrassa; Kazanskaya ul 3a; mains R600-1000; ◷11am-1am, from noon Sat & Sun; 🛜🖉; Ⓜ Nevsky Prospekt) Sleek and buzzing, Terrassa is centred on its namesake terrace, which boasts unbelievable views (open only in warmer months). Inside you can watch the chefs, busy in the open kitchen, preparing fresh fusion cuisine that exhibits influences from Italy, Asia and beyond.

You'll usually need reservations to sit on the terrace, but you can just drop by and hope to get lucky.

KILIKIA
ARMENIAN $$

Map p272 (Киликия; ☑812-327 2208; www.kilikia.spb.ru; nab kanala Griboyedova 40; mains R650; ◷10.30am-6am; Ⓜ Sennaya Ploshchad) An excellent option for the late-night munchies, Kilikia is famous for its shashlyk, which is the real thing – deliciously seasoned, fresh meat served with a range of traditional Armenian dishes. The place has a welcoming, cosy atmosphere and there's live music between 8pm and 11pm on Friday and Saturday nights.

TANDOORI NIGHTS
INDIAN $$

Map p272 (☑812-312 8772; http://tandoorinightsspb.com; Voznesensky pr 4; meals R500-900; ◷noon-11pm; 🛜🖉; Ⓜ Admiralteyskaya) One of Piter's most authentic Indian restaurants offering a mix of traditional and modern recipes in a range of spice levels. It's a great choice for vegetarians.

★ COCOCO
RUSSIAN $$$

Map p272 (☑812-418 2060; www.kokoko.spb.ru; Voznesensky pr 6; mains R650-1300; ◷7-11am, 2pm-1am; 🛜; Ⓜ Admiralteyskaya) Cococo has charmed locals with its inventive approach to contemporary Russian cuisine. Your food is likely to arrive disguised as, say, a small bird's egg, a can of peas or a broken flowerpot – all rather gimmicky, theatrical and fun. The best way to sample what it does is with its tasting menu (R2900). Bookings are advised.

Every Thursday at 7pm the chef pushes out the boundaries with a special 10-course tasting menu (R5000). If that all sounds too much, consider popping in here for a pleasant breakfast: the space doubles as the in-house restaurant of the W Hotel (p191).

SINTOHO
ASIAN $$$

Map p272 (☑812-339 8043; www.sintoho.ru; Four Seasons Hotel Lion Palace, 1 Voznesensky pr; mains R1500-3400; ◷4pm-midnight; ❄🛜; Ⓜ Admiralteyskaya) Classic dishes, with creative twists, from Singapore, Hong Kong and Tokyo (hence the SinToHo name) are served in the Four Seasons' luxurious and contemporary-styled restaurant. There's a sushi counter and tepanyaki grill where you can watch the chefs at work close up.

If this doesn't appeal, the hotel also has a lovely winter garden for meals and afternoon tea and the gentleman's-club-like **Xander bar**, with a double-sided central fireplace – the perfect place to hole up on a wintery night.

BAKU
AZERBAIJANI $$$

Map p272 (Баку; ☑812-941 3756; http://restoran-baku.ru; Sadovaya ul 12/23; mains R600-1600; ◷noon-midnight; 🖉📶; Ⓜ Gostiny Dvor) Baku's ornate decor – tiled walls, arched doorways and throw pillows – whisks you to old Azerbaijan. Try Azeri shashlyk (kebabs), traditional *plov* (rice and lamb spiced with cumin

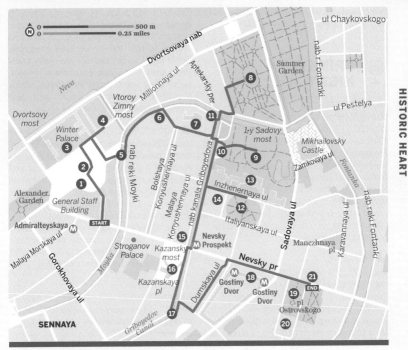

Neighbourhood Walk
Historic Heart

START DVORTSOVAYA PL
END KUPETZ ELISEEVS
LENGTH 2KM; THREE HOURS

Approach ❶ **Palace Square** (p83) on Dvortsovaya pl, from Bolshaya Morskaya ul. Turning the corner from Nevsky pr, behold the ❷ **Alexander Column** (p83), perfectly framed under the triumphal arch with the ❸ **Winter Palace** (p56) as its backdrop. Turn right at the square's northeast corner to find the ❹ **Atlantes** holding aloft the portico of the New Hermitage.

At the Moyka River, cross to the eastern bank using either span of the ❺ **Pevchesky Most**. Head north to the final residence of Russia's most celebrated poet and now the ❻ **Pushkin Flat-Museum** (p86). Around the corner, Konyushennaya pl is dominated by the 18th-century court stables, currently under restoration. In the middle of the complex, visit the ❼ **Church of the Saviour Not Made by Human Hand** (p91) where Pushkin's funeral was held.

Rest in the ❽ **Mars Field** (p87), the former imperial guard parade grounds back over the Moyka River, or in the canal-side ❾ **Mikhailovsky Gardens** (p85). You'll now be ready for the spectacular ❿ **Church on the Spilled Blood** (p81). View the church from ⓫ **Teatralny most** near the intersection of the Moyka and Griboyedov Canal.

Detour off nab kanala Griboyedova to find a statue of Pushkin in the middle of pretty ⓬ **pl Iskusstv** (p91). The square is ringed by celebrated cultural institutions, including the ⓭ **Russian Museum** (p74) and ⓮ **Mikhailovsky Theatre** (p98).

At the junction of Nevsky pr and nab kanala Griboyedova admire the Style Moderne ⓯ **Singer Building** (p102). It's a contrast to the formidable ⓰ **Kazan Cathedral** (p83) opposite. Behind the church, ⓱ **Bankovsky most** (p89) is the city's most picturesque and photographed bridge.

Head up Dumskaya ul to Nevsky pr and navigate along the exterior gallery surrounding the ⓲ **Bolshoy Gostiny Dvor** (p102). A short walk along Nevsky pr is Ploshchad Ostrovskogo, with a ⓳ **statue of Catherine the Great** (p90) and a view of the ⓴ **Alexandrinsky Theatre** (p98). Opposite, finish up at the food hall ㉑ **Kupetz Eliseevs** (p102).

and raisins), as well as delicious *kutab* (thin pancakes stuffed with different fillings).

⬤ DRINKING &
⬤ NIGHTLIFE

★ COFFEE 22   CAFE

Map p272 (https://vk.com/coffeeat22; ul Kazanskaya 22; ☺8.30am-11pm Mon-Thu, until 1am Fri, 10am-1am Sat, 10am-11pm Sun; 🛜; MNevsky Prospekt) In an area heavily saturated with hipster cafes, Coffee 22 – with its tattooed baristas and service staff, arty decor (piercing portrait of poet Joseph Brodsky, a rustic wall of dried mosses) and fashion-forward customers – is perhaps the hippest of them all. Listen to its DJs via its mixcloud.com/coffee22 soundtrack.

★ TOP HOPS   CRAFT BEER

Map p272 (📞8-966-757 0116; www.tophops.ru; nab reki Fontanki 55; ☺4pm-1am Mon-Thu, 2pm-2am Fri-Sun; 🛜; MGostiny Dvor) One of the nicer craft-beer bars in town, this riverside space with friendly staff serves up a regularly changing menu of 20 beers on tap and scores more in bottles. The tasty Mexican snacks and food (go for nachos and chilli) go down exceptionally well while you sample your way through their range.

★ APOTHEKE BAR   COCKTAIL BAR

Map p272 (📞812-337 1535; http://hatgroup.ru/apotheke-bar; ul Lomonosova 1; ☺8pm-6am Tue-Sun; MGostiny Dvor) The antithesis of the nearby dive bars, Apotheke is a calm, cosy cocoon for cocktail connoisseurs. Its slogan is 'think what you drink' so there's no official menu but a friendly young bartender, most likely in a white jacket and sporting a hipster moustache, to make suggestions or simply surprise you.

★ KABINET   COCKTAIL BAR

Map p272 (📞8-911-921 1944; www.instagram.com/kabinet_bar; Malaya Sadovaya ul 8; ☺8am-6pm; MGostiny Dvor) Bookings are essential for this speakeasy cocktail bar styled as a secret poker joint and hidden beneath the Grill Brothers burger restaurant. It's a fun, sophisticated place with the waiters dealing sets of cards to determine your choice of cocktail.

★ BORODABAR   COCKTAIL BAR

Map p272 (📞911 923 8940; www.facebook.com/Borodabar; Kazanskaya ul 11; ☺5pm-2am Sun-Thu, to 6am Fri & Sat; 🛜; MNevsky Prospekt) Boroda means beard in Russian, and sure enough you'll see plenty of facial hair and tattoos in this hipster cocktail hang out. Never mind, as the mixologists really know their stuff – we can particularly recommend their smoked Old Fashioned, which is infused with tobacco smoke, and their colourful (and potent) range of shots.

★ MOD CLUB   BAR, CLUB

Map p272 (www.modclub.info; nab kanala Griboyedova 7; cover R150-350; ☺6pm-6am; MNevsky Prospekt) A popular spot for students and other indie types who appreciate the fun and friendly atmosphere and a cool mix of music both live and spun. Laid-back and great fun, this is a solid choice for a night out.

The club's roof is also one of the venues for the summer programme of screenings organised by **Roof Cinema** (📞812-645 1040; http://roofcinema.com; tickets R300-800).

MESTO VSTRECHI
KAZANSKAYA 7   ANTI-CAFE

Map p272 (Место встречи Казанская 7; 📞812-941 7553; https://vk.com/mv_k7; Kazanskaya ul 7; minimum charge R150; ☺noon-midnight; MNevsky Prospekt) Occupying several of the lofty upper-floor rooms of this grand building, you pay R3 per minute for the time spent at this spacious cafe covering as much as you like of soft drinks and snacks.

Each of the spaces has been given a different theme – music, art, library etc – and various events are held here through the week.

LYUBLYU: LED WINE LOVE'S   WINE BAR

Map p272 (ЛЮБЛЮ: LED Wine Love's; 📞812-913 3783; http://yourstream.ru; nab reki Fontanki 45; ☺3pm-midnight; 🛜; MGostiny Dvor) Only good-quality Russian wines are served by the glass or bottle at this compact wine bar with a view across the Moyka River. Try the light, sparkling Abrau-Durso Blanc de Blanc (R340) or go for the tasting set of four wines (R500).

Snacks are available and, should you need a plant, a shop selling terrariums.

CRAFT BREW CAFE   CRAFT BEER

Map p272 (📞812-938 9193; www.reca.su; Malaya Morskaya ul 15; ☺11am-1pm Sun-Thu, until 6am Fri & Sat; @🛜; MAdmiralteyskaya) One of the largest (in terms of floor space) of the craft-beer bars popping up like daisies across the city, this handy place offers an industrial chic feel, DJs at the weekends and a reasonable range of local and international beers on tap and in bottles.

BONCH CAFE — CAFE
Map p272 (☎812-740 7083; www.bonchcoffee.ru; Bolshaya Morskaya ul 16; ◷8.30am-midnight Mon-Fri, from 10am Sat & Sun; 🛜; Ⓜ Admiralteyskaya) Coffee is brewed just the way you like it at this pleasantly designed cafe occupying a large corner space in a handy location. It's a great place for breakfast as well as late-night sweet treats as there's 30% off all desserts after 10pm.

GRAN — CAFE
(Gorkhovaya ul 46; ◷8.30am-9pm Mon-Fri, from 11am Sat & Sun; 🛜; Ⓜ Sennaya Ploschad) Gran is a great little neighbourhood cafe that prepares excellent cups by your brew method of choice – Aeropress, Chemex or Hario pour-overs. Of course, if you prefer just a latte or a flat white, the baristas here have you covered. It's a small, raw space with flowers and touches of artwork softening the brick and concrete.

Coffees aside, Gran has waffles, granola and other breakfast fare (served til 4pm), plus panini, bagel sandwiches and desserts.

TEA HOUSE — TEAHOUSE
Map p272 (Чайный Домик; ☎812-314 0374; Summer Garden, nab reki Moyki; ◷10am-9pm Wed-Mon; Ⓜ Nevsky Prospekt) The nicest of several cafes located within the Summer Garden, where you can also watch free musical performances on some nights during the summer months.

This is also where you can arrange tours of the garden.

CLUB L.U.X — CLUB
Map p272 (☎8-981-972 9342; http://lux-klub.ru; nab kanala Griboyedova 7; ◷11.30pm-6am Fri & Sat) One of the city's largest dance clubs offers a hangar-like space hung with crystal chandeliers, wrapped in swathes of satin and gauze and padded with faux leather. Take your pick between popular house music on the main dance floor, and deep-house on the second 'luxury' floor.

VNVNC — CLUB
Map p272 (☎8-981-845 0741; https://vk.com/vnvnc; Konyushennaya pl 2b; admission R100-200; ◷11pm-6am Fri & Sat; 🛜; Ⓜ Nevsky Prospekt) 'Abandon hope all ye who enter here,' warns the sign on the door – and it's putting no one

off cramming into this popular club that occupies a former chapel in the courtyard area south of the square. In warmer months patrons linger outside where there's a greasy burger bar to help soak up the alcoholic excesses.

KOFE NA KUKHNE — CAFE
Map p272 (Кофе на Кухне; https://vk.com/morecoffee; nab reki Fontanki 13; ◷8.30am-10pm Mon-Fri, 10am-11pm Sat & Sun; 🛜; Ⓜ Gostiny Dvor) Go on, spoil yourself with one of the vegan muffins and other baked goodies at 'Coffee in the Kitchen', which has a variety of ways to prepare your cup of joe. It's a comfy space with a multicoloured communal table in the back.

PIF PAF — BAR
Map p272 (☎812-312 6227; http://pifpafhair.wixsite.com/pifpaf; nab kanala Griboyedova 31; ◷10am-3am Sun-Thu, until 6am Fri & Sat; 🛜; Ⓜ Nevsky Prospekt) It's a happening bar, it serves a mean burger and there's a hairdresser at the back – should you fancy a new 'do' part-way through the night. Oh, and there's a fussball table, if conversation lags and you fancy a bit of hand-twisting action.

CAFE-BAR PRODUCKTY — CAFE
Map p272 (Продукты; ☎812-312 5754; www.facebook.com/fontanka17; nab reki Fontanky 17; ◷2pm-2am Sun-Thu, to 6am Fri & Sat; Ⓜ Gostiny Dvor) Retro movie posters, mix-and-match furniture and a working juke box provide the shabby-chic wrapper for this relaxed cafe-bar serving hot drinks, beer and cocktails.

DOUBLE B — CAFE
Map p272 (ДаблБи; ☎812-928 0818; http://vk.com/doublebspb; Millionnaya ul 18; ◷9am-10pm Mon-Fri, 11am-10pm Sat & Sun; 🛜; Ⓜ Admiralteyskaya) The young baristas are friendly and take their coffee brewing seriously at this serene hipster hang-out, with specially roasted beans from Ethiopia, Costa Rica and Kenya and methods including Aeropress and drip. They also offer a few artisan teas.

GOLUBAYA USTRITSA — GAY
Map p272 (☎8-921-332 5161; www.boyster.ru; ul Lomonosova 1; ◷7pm-6am; Ⓜ Gostiny Dvor) Loud, lewd and lots of fun, this is the coolest gay place in town. Take your pick from the main bar, where the uninhibited crowd is often quite literally hanging from the

rafters, the *Priscilla Queen of the Desert* karaoke bar, or the other upstairs bars and dancefloors.

Meaning Blue Oyster, the bar is named after the leather bar that featured in the 1980s *Police Academy* movies, but is as unlike it as vinyl is to velvet.

BERMUDY BAR DISCO BAR

Map p272 (https://vk.com/bar_bermudy; Bankovsky per 6; ⊗6pm-6am; ⓜSennaya Ploshchad) Resurrecting the time-honoured St Petersburg practice of dancing on the tables, this friendly bar does indeed become more of a disco than a bar after midnight. With low prices, good cocktails, table football and a trashy, fun atmosphere, Bermudy is an anything-goes destination if you want a late night.

W TERRACE BAR

Map p272 (☑812-610 6155; www.wstpetersburg. com; W Hotel, Voznesensky pr 6; ⊗noon-1am Sun-Thu, noon-2am Fri & Sat May-Sep; ☎; ⓜAdmiralteyskaya) The W's rooftop cocktail bar and terrace offers fantastic city views to be enjoyed over top-notch libations. Bookings are advised for the outdoor space with seating in cosy cabanas and views straight onto St Isaac's Cathedral.

TANZPLOSHCHADKA CLUB

Map p272 (Танцплощадка; www.tancplo.com; Konyushennaya pl 2a; ⊗8pm-6am Fri & Sat; ⓜNevsky Prospket) Beloved by beautiful young things, this is the dance club of the moment with a shabby-chic indoor space beneath a lofty vaulted brick ceiling and plenty of outdoor space should it get too hot inside. Find it at the back, through the archway and courtyard complex south of Konyushennaya pl.

CENTRAL STATION GAY

Map p272 (☑812-312 3600; http://central station.ru; ul Lomonosova 1/28; cover after midnight R100-300; ⊗6pm-6am; ⓜNevsky Prospekt) Huge, with several bars and dance floors, as well as a men-only dark room, this is a stalwart of the St Petersburg gay scene. There are events on throughout the week. Music is mainly at the pop and house end of the spectrum and there's usually plenty of topless eye-candy gyrating at weekends.

WARSZAWA BAR

Map p272 (www.facebook.com/warszawabufet; Kazanskaya ul 11; ⊗10am-2am Sun-Thu, to 4am Fri & Sat; ⓜNevsky Prospekt) Russian urbanites have always harboured a special admiration for the quaint provincialism of Eastern Europe, hence this smallish bar with old-fashioned wallpaper, vintage furniture and portraits of 20th-century Polish film stars. Polish beer is on tap and cocktails are based on liquors you may have never heard of. Good for deep, vodka-infused philosophical conversations.

DACHA BAR

Map p272 (Дача; https://vk.com/bardacha; Dumskaya ul 9; ⊗6pm-6am; ⓜGostiny Dvor) This is the joint that kicked off the whole Dumskaya dive-bar scene in 2004. We'd say it's showing its age, but truth is that it was never about keeping up appearances here – just drinking and dancing the night through in a packed-to-the-gills space.

FIDEL CLUB

Map p272 (https://vk.com/barfidel; Dumskaya ul 9; ⊗6pm-6am; ⓜGostiny Dvor) This long-running dive bar is a sort of musical and alcoholic tribute to the ruler who 'outlived six presidents of America and six leaders of the Soviet Union and Russia'.

☆ ENTERTAINMENT

★MIKHAILOVSKY THEATRE PERFORMING ARTS

Map p272 (Михайловский театр; ☑812-595 4305; www.mikhailovsky.ru; pl Iskusstv 1; tickets R500-5000; ⓜNevsky Prospekt) This illustrious stage delivers the Russian ballet or operatic experience, complete with multitiered theatre, frescoed ceiling and elaborate productions. Pl Iskusstv (Arts Sq) is a lovely setting for this respected venue, which is home to the State Academic Opera & Ballet Company.

It's generally easier and cheaper to get tickets to the performances staged here than those at the Mariinsky (p117).

★ALEXANDRINSKY THEATRE THEATRE

Map p272 (☑812-710 4103; www.alexandrinsky. ru; pl Ostrovskogo 2; tickets R900-6000; ⓜGostiny Dvor) This magnificent venue is just one part of an immaculate architectural ensemble designed by Carlo Rossi. The theatre's interior oozes 19th-century elegance and style, and it's worth taking a peek even if you don't see a production here.

This is where Anton Chekhov premiered *The Seagull* in 1896; the play was so badly received on opening that the playwright fled to wander anonymously among the crowds on Nevsky pr. Chekhov is now a beloved part of the theatre's huge repertoire, ranging from Russian folktales to Shakespearean tragedies.

Head through the archway in the southwest corner of the square to find the Alexanderinsky's New Stage.

NEW STAGE
PERFORMING ARTS

Map p272 (Новая сцена; ☑812-401 5341; http://alexandrinsky.ru; nab reki Fontanki 49a; MGostiny Dvor) The New Stage at Alexandrinsky (p98), which opened in 2013, is a strikingly modern building for the historic city center but one that keeps a low profile due to the architect's ingenious use of glass and a secluded courtyard space. Come here to see contemporary dance, music, film, lectures and other events.

The theatre's roof is also one of the venues for the summer programme of screenings organised by Roof Cinema (p96).

SHOSTAKOVICH PHILHARMONIA
CLASSICAL MUSIC

Map p272 (Санкт-Петербургская филармония им. Д.Д.Шостаковича; www.philharmonia.spb. ru; tickets R800-2500; MNevsky Prospekt) Under the artistic direction of world-famous conductor Yury Temirkanov, the Philharmonia represents the finest in orchestral music. The **Bolshoy Zal** (Большой зал; Map p272; ☑812-240-01-80; Mikhailovskaya ul 2; MNevsky Prospekt) is the venue for a full program of symphonic performances, while the nearby **Maly Zal** (Малый Зал; Map p272; ☑812-571 8333; Nevsky pr 30; MGostiny Dvor) hosts smaller ensembles. Both venues are used for numerous music festivals.

RODINA
CINEMA

Map p272 (Родина; ☑812-571 6131; http://rodinakino.ru; Karavannaya ul 12; ⊘tickets R150-300; MGostiny Dvor) Art-house movie theatre that shares a grand building (a former concert hall) with Dom Kino (p100).

There are two screens and they often show films in their original language with subtitles.

KINO&TEATR ANGLETER
CINEMA

Map p272 (Кино&Театр Англетер; ☑812-494 5063; www.angleterrecinema.ru; Angleterre Hotel, Malaya Morskaya ul 24; tickets R330;

MAdmiralteyskaya) This cinema inside the Angleterre Hotel is one of the best places in the city to see movies in their original language, with subtitles rather than dubbing. The program, which includes several different features every day, focuses on current art-house releases.

DOM 7
JAZZ

Map p272 (☑812-314 8250; http://vk.com/dom_7; nab kanala Griboyedova 7; ⊘noon-midnight Tue-Thu & Sun, noon-5am Fri & Sat; MNevsky Prospekt) This low-key Russian restaurant and bar has very popular live jazz sets at 9.30pm and 11.30pm on Friday and Saturday, when it's practically standing room only.

ST PETERSBURG THEATRE OF MUSICAL COMEDY
THEATRE

Map p272 (Санкт-Петербургский государственный театр музыкальной комедии; ☑812-570 5316; http://web.muzcomedy.ru; Italyanskaya ul 13; tickets from R3800; MNevsky Prospekt) Dating back to 1929, this theatre, as its name implies, specialises in musical and comedic plays and performances. Over the White Nights tourist season you'll likely find Swan Lake on here. At other times check it out for its high-quality musical productions.

HERMITAGE THEATRE
BALLET

Map p272 (☑812-408 1084; https://hermitagetheater.com; Dvortsovaya nab 32; online tickets from R8300; MAdmiralteyskaya) Designed by Giacomo Quarenghi, this intimate neoclassical auditorium was once the private theatre of the imperial family, and stands on the site of the original Winter Palace of Peter I. Book early if you'd like to see a ballet (usually classics such as *Swan Lake* and *Giselle*) at a discount, but still be prepared to pay well over the odds compared to other theatres in the city.

Access to the theatre is via an entrance to the Large (Old) Hermitage on Dvortsovaya nab; look for the door on the southwest side of the stone bridge over the small water channel.

BOLSHOI ST PETERSBURG STATE CIRCUS
CIRCUS

Map p272 (☑812-570 5198; www.circus.spb.ru; nab reki Fontanki 3; tickets R500-6000; MGostiny Dvor) Russia's oldest permanent circus complex (built in 1877) is looking splendid since a recent major renovation. Circus

RAISING OF THE BRIDGES

It's quite a sight to witness the raising of the bridges over the Neva river during the navigation period. **Dvortsovy most** (Palace Bridge; Дворцовый мост; Map p272; Ⓜ Admiralteyskaya), beside the Winter Palace, is one of the most popular spots to watch this event from as there is classical music broadcast and a carnival atmosphere with street vendors and plenty of sightseeing boats bobbing in the Neva. One company offering these late-night cruises with or without live jazz and blues music is **Astra Marine** (Map p272; ☑ 812-426 1717; www.boattrip.ru; tours R400-800).

troupes and artists from other cities and countries perform shows here, too.

DOM KINO
CINEMA

Map p272 (☑ 812-314 5614; www.domkino.spb.ru; Karavannaya ul 12; ⊘ tickets from R100; Ⓜ Gostiny Dvor) One of the handful of cinemas in the city where you can see foreign films and some higher-brow Hollywood productions with subtitles, as well as arty Russian movies. It is also where the British Council holds its British Film Festival. Despite a refit, the whole place remains remarkably Soviet in a charming way.

The cinemas are small so book ahead or get here early if there's a film you particularly want to see. In the same building is Rodina (p99), another classy cinema with two screens.

AVRORA
CINEMA

Map p272 (☑ 812-315-52-54; www.avrora.spb.ru; Nevsky pr 60; tickets R300-700; Ⓜ Gostiny Dvor) Opening in 1913 as the Piccadilly Picture House, this was the city's most fashionable cinema in the early years of Russian film, and it has retained its position pretty consistently ever since. Today most premieres (to which you can nearly always buy tickets) take place here. Foreign films are dubbed into Russian, though sometimes you'll find the odd subtitled one.

Renamed the more Soviet-sounding Avrora in 1932, it was here that a young Dmitry Shostakovich played piano accompaniment to silent movies.

GLINKA CAPELLA HOUSE
CLASSICAL MUSIC

Map p272 (☑ 812-314 1058; www.glinka-capella.ru; nab reki Moyki 20; Ⓜ Admiralteyskaya) This historic hall was constructed for Russia's oldest professional choir, the Emperor Court Choir Capella, founded in 1473. Originally based in Moscow, it was transferred to St Petersburg upon the order of Peter the Great in 1703. These days,

performances focus on choral and organ music.

BOLSHOY DRAMA THEATRE
THEATRE

Map p272 (BDT; ☑ 812-244 1071; https://bdt.spb.ru; nab reki Fontanki 65; ⊘ tickets R500-3000; Ⓜ Sennaya Ploshchad) The BDT, which will celebrate its centenary in 2019, has a reputable repertoire and is a good place to see Russian drama. Recently renovated, it is one of the city's grandest theatres, and its location on the Fontanka River is delightful.

DEMMENI
MARIONETTE THEATRE
PUPPET THEATRE

Map p272 (☑ 812-310 5879; www.demmeni.ru; Nevsky pr 52; ⊘ tickets from R500; Ⓜ Gostiny Dvor) Since 1917, this venue under the arches on central Nevsky is the city's oldest professional puppet theatre. Mainly for children, the shows are well produced and professionally performed.

PRIYUT KOMEDIANTA
THEATRE

Map p272 (Приют комедианта; ☑ 812-310 3277; www.pkteatr.ru; Sadovaya ul 27/9; ⊘ tickets R600-1800; Ⓜ Sennaya Ploshchad) This delightful theatre's name means 'the actor's shelter' and it does a pretty good job of fulfilling its role, providing refuge for some of the city's best up-and-coming actors, directors and producers. It was founded by actor Yury Tomashevsky in the late 1980s, when the city turned over a defunct cinema that the group still uses.

Productions are in Russian.

KOMISSARZHEVSKAYA THEATRE
THEATRE

Map p272 (Театр им В.Ф.Комиссаржевской; ☑ 812-315 5355; www.teatrvfk.ru; Italiyanskaya ul 19; Ⓜ Gostiny Dvor) Named after Vera Komissarzhevskaya, a great actress who gained her reputation as leading lady in Vsevolod Meyerhold performances during the late 19th century, this theatre is known for its modern treatment of classic plays. Productions are in Russian.

SHOPPING

★ AU PONT ROUGE · DEPARTMENT STORE
Map p272 (https://aupontrouge.ru; nab reki Moyki 73-79; ☺10am-10pm; ⓜAdmiralteyskaya) Dating from 1906–7, the one-time Esders and Scheefhaals department store has been beautifully restored and is one of the most glamorous places to shop in the city. This glorious Style Moderne building is now dubbed Au Pont Rouge after the **Krasny most** (Red Bridge) it stands beside. Inside you'll find choice fashions and accessories and top-notch souvenirs.

The restoration included the rebuilding of the glass cupola, destroyed in the 1930s so as not to clutter the view towards the Admiralty down Gorokhovaya ul. On the ground floor there's a branch of the French cafe Patisserie Garçon.

★ TAIGA · FASHION & ACCESSORIES
Map p272 (Тайга; http://taiga.space; Dvortsovaya nab 20; ☺1-9pm; ☎; ⓜAdmiralteyskaya) Like several other of the city's trendy hangouts, Taiga keeps a low profile despite its prime location close by the Hermitage. The warren of small rooms in the ancient building are worth exploring to find cool businesses ranging from a barber to fashion and books. 8 Store (p102) is one of the best, a stylish boutique stacked with clothes and accessories by local designers.

Also great for original design gifts and souvenirs is Imenno Lavka (p102).

TYKVA · FASHION & ACCESSORIES
Map p272 (www.facebook.com/tykvastore; Bolshaya Konyushennaya ul 9; ☺10am-10pm; ⓜNevsky Prospekt) Contemporary Russian designers for both men and women are represented in this stylishly minimalist boutique on the 2nd floor of a grand building that's undergoing something of a revamp as another creative cluster of arty, boho businesses and cafes.

You'll also find branches in the creative clusters of Golytsin Loft and at ul Vosstaniya 24.

MAKER DESIGN LOFT · FASHION & ACCESSORIES
Map p272 (☎8-911-113 4138; www.makerdesignloft.com; Marsovo pole 7; ☺10am-9pm; ⓜNevsky Prospekt) Not in the same sprawling, raggedy league as other St Petersburg creative clusters, Maker is really one big shop selling mainly locally designed clothes and accessories, aimed at 'normal people' by which it means its prices are not out of this stratosphere. There's a cafe and a beauty salon here, too.

21 SHOP · FASHION & ACCESSORIES
Map p272 (https://21-shop.ru; Bolshaya Konyushennaya ul 19/8; ☺11am-8pm; ⓜNevsky Prospekt) Pick up a locally designed T-shirt, sweatshirt, bag or other item of streetwear or accessory at this large unisex boutique with its entrance just off Bolshaya Konyushennaya – an affordable antidote to the high fashion of nearby department store DLT.

It also has a branch in the Galeria (p140).

PIF PAF SUPER SHOP · FASHION & ACCESSORIES
Map p272 (☎812-571 7036; nab kanala Griboyedova 31; ☺noon-10pm; ⓜNevsky Prospekt) Next to the cafe-bar (p97) of the same name, this is one of the best second-hand fashion stores in the city – it has a good eye for quality labels and a stylish look, but consequently you'll pay more than the average for the goods.

UNTSIYA · TEA
Map p272 (Унция; ☎812-325 5800; www.chay.info; Nevsky pr 5; ☺10am-9pm; ⓜAdmiralteyskaya) There are many branches of this purveyor of quality loose-leaf teas and coffees across the city – this is a handy central one. The design is pleasantly antique and their souvenir gift boxes make great presents.

PERINNYE RYADY · ARTS & CRAFTS
Map p272 (Перинные, арт-центр; ☎812-440 2028; http://artcenter.ru; Dumskaya ul 4; ☺10am-8pm; ⓜGostiny Dvor) Scores of arts-and-craft stores can be found in this arcade in the middle of Dumskaya ul. Among them are **Collection**, with a wide range of painted works, several by members of the Union of Artists of Russia, and **Pionersky Magazin**, specialising in Soviet-era memorabilia, where you're guaranteed to find a bust of Lenin and colourful propaganda and art posters.

DLT · DEPARTMENT STORE
Map p272 (ДЛТ; ☎812-648 0848; www.dlt.ru; Bolshaya Konyushennaya ul 21-23; ☺10am-10pm; ⓜNevsky Prospekt) This historic department store is a temple to prestige fashion and

HISTORIC SHOPS OF NEVSKY PROSPEKT

Nikolai Gogol described it as 'Petersburg's universal channel of communication' in his story *Nevsky Prospekt*. Some 300 years on from its creation, little has changed. Nevsky remains the city's most famous street, running 4.7km from the Admiralty to the Alexandr Nevsky Monastery, from which it takes its name. Taking a stroll along it is an essential St Petersburg experience and particularly special at dusk as the low light casts shadows and picks out silhouettes from the elegant mix of architecture.

The inner 2.5km to Moscow Station (Moskovsky vokzal) is the city's prime shopping drag that pulses with street life. Here you'll find baroque palaces, churches in a range of denominations, all manner of entertainments and, above all, shops, some historic in their own right. These are the key ones not to miss:

Singer Building (Map p272; Nevsky pr 28; Ⓜ Nevsky Prospekt) The former headquarters of the Singer sewing machine company, which opened a factory in the Russian capital in 1904, is one of St Petersburg's most gorgeous buildings. Its Style Modern architecture, designed by Pavel Suzor, and topped with a glass tower and scupIture, also housed the American consulate for a few years prior to WWI. It's possible to access the offices part of the building including the interior of the glass dome on a tour (R6000 for up to three people) organised with Placemates (p31).

Bolshoy Gostiny Dvor (Большой Гостиный Двор; Map p272; ☑812-630 5408; http://bgd.ru; Nevsky pr 35; ⊘10am-10pm; Ⓜ Gostiny Dvor) One of the world's first indoor shopping malls, the 'Big Merchant Yard' dates from between 1757 and 1785 and stretches 230m along Nevsky pr (its perimeter is more than 1km long). This Rastrelli creation is not as elaborate as some of his other work, finished as it was by Vallin de la Mothe in a more sober neoclassical style. At its height at the turn of the 20th century, Gostiny Dvor contained over 170 shops.

Passage (Пассаж; Map p272; ☑812-313 7400; http://passage.spb.ru; Nevsky pr 48; ⊘10am-9pm; Ⓜ Gostiny Dvor) Built between 1846 and 1848, this arcade has a glass roof spanning the entire block from Nevsky to Italiyanskaya ul. Dostoevsky wrote a story about a man who was swallowed by a crocodile in Passage, after a live crocodile exhibited here in 1864. Look for the small exhibition on the 1st floor with historical photos and other items related to the arcade. The handsomely restored ground floor has several good souvenir and antique shops.

Kupetz Eliseevs (Map p272; ☑812-456 6666; www.kupetzeliseevs.ru; Nevsky pr 56; ⊘10am-11pm; 🛜; Ⓜ Gostiny Dvor) This Style Moderne stunner is St Petersburg's most elegant grocery store. Built in 1904 as the flagship of the Eliseev Brothers' highly successful chain of food emporiums, little expense or design flourish was spared in its construction. In recent years the building has been restored to its full grandeur with huge plate-glass windows providing glimpses into a dazzling interior of stained glass, chandeliers, polished brass and a giant pineapple palm. The building's exterior is no less lavish, graced with four allegorical sculptures representing industry, trade and commerce, art and science. The building also included a theatre, which is still functioning.

beauty brands, most of them foreign. Even if you're not up for a pricey shopping expedition, the interior, with twin atriums, is amazing and worth a look.

IMENNO LAVKA GIFTS & SOUVENIRS
Map p272 (Именно-лавка; ☑8-921-581 0466; www.imenno-lavka.ru; TAIGA, Dvortsovaya nab 20; ⊘11am-7pm; Ⓜ Admiralteyskaya) In front of this design office is a small boutique showcasing interesting gifts, accessories, books and interior-design products by local talents. Look

out for the bear and wolf heads and wooden beard masks by Alexander Kanygin.

8 STORE FASHION & ACCESSORIES
Map p272 (☑8-981-741 1880; http://8-store.ru; Dvortsovaya nab 20; ⊘1-9pm; Ⓜ Admiralteyskaya) If you're looking for affordable Russian designer fashions, accessories, interior objects and souvenirs, this chic boutique, an anchor tenant of the Taiga (p101) creative space, is worth searching out.

MILITARY SHOP
CLOTHING

Map p272 (Товары для военных; ☑812-309 3924; http://voentorg-spb.ru; Sadovaya ul 26; ☺10am-8pm; MGostiny Dvor) In a city with men in uniform on every street corner, this is where you can get yours (the uniform that is!). Buy stripey sailor tops, embroidered badges, big boots, camouflage jackets and snappy caps at decent prices. Look for the circular green and gold sign with 'Military Shop' written in English; the entrance is in the courtyard.

YAKHONT
JEWELLERY

Map p272 (Яхонт; ☑812-314 6415; www.juvelirtorg.spb.ru; Bolshaya Morskaya ul 24; ☺10am-8pm; MAdmiralteyskaya) From this building, Carl Fabergé dazzled the imperial family and the rest of the world with his extraordinary bespoke designs. Yakhont has no link to the Fabergé family, but it is carrying on the tradition anyway. This long, dark salon provides an impressive showcase of the work.

STARAYA KNIGA
BOOKS

Map p272 (Старая книга; ☑812-315 1151; http://staraya-kniga.ru; Nevsky pr 3; ☺10am-7pm; MAdmiralteyskaya) This long-established antique bookseller is a fascinating place to rummage around. The stock ranges from fancy, mint-edition books to second-hand, well-worn Soviet editions, maps and art (in the section next to the art-supplies shop). It's a great place to look for an unusual, unique souvenir. Find it in the courtyard off the main road.

APRAKSIN DVOR
MARKET

Map p272 (☑812-310 5608; http://apraksinmarket.ru/; Sadovaya ul 30; ☺10am-7pm; MGostiny Dvor) There's been a market here since the 18th century. Although parts of it are being upgraded, it remains mostly a gritty and chaotic Dostoevsky-style warren of stalls offering mainly cheap clothes, shoes and leather goods, as well as food and snacks beloved by the multiethnic traders who work here.

If you're hungry look for **Chufalnya** (Map p272; Korpus 27, Apraksin Dvor, Sadovaya ul 30 (enter from Apraksin per); mains R240-360; ☺10am-10pm; MSennaya Ploshchad), a Chinese grocery and cafe on the upper floor of the Korpus 27 block.

DOM KNIGI
BOOKS

Map p272 (☑812-448 2355; www.spbdk.ru; Nevsky pr 28; ☺9am-1am; ☎; MNevsky Prospekt) A stalwart of the city's bookshops, Dom Knigi is housed in part of the wonderful, whimsical Singer Building (p102). On the ground floor you'll find lots of English-language coffee-table books that make good souvenirs.

🏃 SPORTS & ACTIVITIES

RENTBIKE
CYCLING

(☑812-981 0155; www.rentbike.org; Naberezhnaya fontanki 77; per hr/day from R100/500; ☺10am-10pm; MSennaya Ploshchad) This centrally located company rents out well-maintained bikes at good rates. You'll need to leave a passport or ID card with them, along with a deposit of R2000 per bike. The place is in a courtyard off Naberezhnaya fontanki.

WILD RUSSIA
ADVENTURE SPORTS

Map p272 (☑812-313 8030; www.wildrussia.spb.ru; office 224, nab reki Fontanki 59; MGostiny Dvor) Yachting and kayaking on Lake Ladoga can be arranged through the friendly and capable guys at Wild Russia. They can also arrange many other outdoor activities including off-road biking, parachuting, quad biking and rock climbing outside the city.

Sennaya & Kolomna

SENNAYA | KOLOMNA

Neighbourhood Top Five

1 Mariinsky Theatre (p106) Seeing a Russian ballet or opera classic in one of Russia's most celebrated performing arts halls.

2 Yusupov Palace (p107) Exploring sumptuous art-filled interiors of this mansion on the Moyka and hearing tales of Rasputin's grizzly end.

3 New Holland Island (p108) Relaxing amid the peaceful setting of St Petersburg's newest green space, then returning by night for dining, outdoor concerts and DJs.

4 Nikolsky Cathedral (p111) Visiting one of St Petersburg's prettiest churches, a picturesque sky-blue and gold design framed by canals and gardens.

5 Sennaya Ploshchad (p110) Wandering the atmospheric streets around this buzzing square, the setting of some of Dostoevsky's most famous literary works.

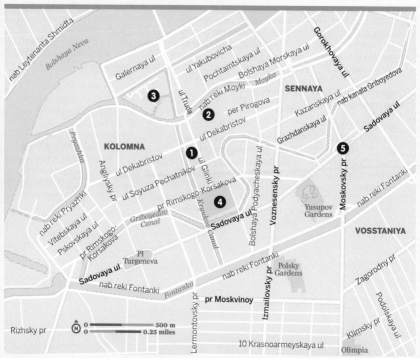

For more detail of this area see Map p280 ➡

Explore Sennaya & Kolomna

Stretching north and south of the meandering Moyka River, these two neighbourhoods may lack the dense concentration of sights found in the Historic Heart, but are still blessed with some spectacular sights. By day, you can explore the lavish interiors of the Yusupov Palace or bask in the greenery and art-filled spaces of New Holland Island, then return by night for magnificent concerts at one of three performing arts venues under the Mariinsky umbrella.

There's also much history hidden in these scenic streets. Russophiles can wander the lanes off Sennaya Ploschad, a region where Dostoevesky – and some of his best known characters – lived and roamed, and explore pivotal domestic achievements at the Central Naval Museum and the Railway Museum. There are plenty of lesser known attractions as well, including one of the city's most photogenic cathedrals and Russia's most impressive synagogue.

You could spend a few days exploring the area, or simply base yourself here. The district offers proximity to the Historic Heart – with more of a local feel – and plenty of great dining options as well.

Local Life

➡ **Canal Life** Sennaya and Kolomna are home to some of the prettiest canals in the city, well away from the crowds. Check out the gorgeous Kryukov Canal, the far ends of the Griboyedov Canal and the Fontanka River.

➡ **Free Concerts** Check out the Maly Zal (small hall) at the Rimsky-Korsakov Conservatory (p118), where you'll often see fantastic free concerts from students and alumni.

➡ **Transport Issues** Get to know the bus and *marshrutka* routes if you're going to be spending any time in Kolomna, where there's no metro and distances on foot can be very long.

➡ **Day at the Park** Take a break from sightseeing and join locals for a leisurely spell in New Holland (p108). Play chess, ping pong, pétanque or join a yoga or fitness class.

Getting There & Away

➡ **Metro** Sennaya is served by the interconnecting Sennaya pl (Line 2), Spasskaya (Line 4) and Sadovaya (Line 5) stations, the city's biggest interchange. Kolomna is not served by the metro at all at the time of writing, though an extension to the Mariinsky is planned. Currently the nearest stations are those on Sennaya pl or Admiralteyskaya station in the Historic Heart.

➡ **Bus** Bus 3 connects the Mariinsky with Nevsky pr via Bolshaya Morskaya ul, while Trolleybus 5 connects pl Truda with Nevsky pr via Konnogvardeysky bul.

Lonely Planet's Top Tip

Book ahead of time to see the ballet or opera performance you're interested in at the **Mariinsky Theatre** (p117), especially during the White Nights, when performances of popular productions sell out months in advance. You can book and pay for tickets on the website, and then collect them at the box office before the performance, which is much better than trying to find what's available once you're in town.

SENNAYA & KOLOMNA

Best Palaces

➡ Yusupov Palace (p107)
➡ House of Music (p113)
➡ Old Yusupov Palace (p110)
➡ Rumyantsev Mansion (p111)

For reviews, see p106 ➡

Best Places to Eat

➡ EM Restaurant (p116)
➡ The Répa (p116)
➡ Severyanin (p114)
➡ Kuznya House (p115)
➡ Teplo (p115)
➡ Co-op Garage (p113)

For reviews, see p113 ➡

Best Places to Drink

➡ Stirka 40 (p117)
➡ Solaris Lab (p117)
➡ Crocodile (p117)

For reviews, see p117 ➡

TOP SIGHT
MARIINSKY THEATRE

The Mariinsky Theatre has played a pivotal role in Russian ballet ever since it was built in 1859, and it remains one of Russia's most loved and respected cultural institutions. Its pretty green-and-white main building on aptly named Teatralnaya pl (Theatre Sq) is a must for any visitor wanting to see one of the world's great ballet and opera stages.

A Glittering History

The building you see today opened its doors in 1860, and was named in honour of Maria Alexandrovna, the wife of Tsar Alexander II. Since its inception, the Mariinsky has seen some of the world's greatest musicians, dancers and singers on its stage. Petipa choreographed his most famous works here, including *Swan Lake* and *The Nutcracker,* and the premieres of Tchaikovsky's *The Queen of Spades* and Prokofiev's *Romeo & Juliet* were also held here. The Soviets initially closed the Mariinsky down, but as the renamed Kirov Ballet it became a major force in promoting the Soviet Union abroad, and is still the main reason that ballet and Russia remain synonymous worldwide.

DON'T MISS

➡ Russian 'champagne' during show intervals
➡ White Nights Festival
➡ Small Mariinsky II performances

PRACTICALITIES

➡ Мариинский театр
➡ Map p280, C4
➡ ☎812-326 4141
➡ www.mariinsky.ru
➡ Teatralnaya pl
➡ ☉ box office 11am-7pm
➡ Ⓜ Sadovaya

Performance

The best way to experience the building as its designers intended is to see an opera or ballet. Outside performance times you can wander into the theatre's foyer and maybe peep into the lovely auditorium. As well as the main Mariinsky Theatre, there is also the newer, world-class Mariinsky II next door, a 2000-seat, six-stage theatre that marks the Mariinsky's arrival in the 21st century.

TOP SIGHT
YUSUPOV PALACE

This spectacular palace on the Moyka River has some of the best 19th-century interiors in the city, in addition to a fascinating and gruesome history. The palace's last owner was the eccentric Prince Felix Yusupov, a high-society darling and at one time the richest man in Russia. Most notoriously, this palace is where Grigory Rasputin was murdered in 1916.

DON'T MISS

➜ White Column Room
➜ Private theatre
➜ Oak Dining Room
➜ Rasputin tour

PRACTICALITIES

➜ Юсуповский дворец
➜ Map p280, D3
➜ ☎921-970 3038
➜ www.yusupov-palace.ru
➜ nab reki Moyki 94
➜ adult/student incl audio guide R700/500, Rasputin tour adult/student R350/250
➜ ⏱11am-6pm
➜ ⓂSadovaya

Amazing Interiors

The palace was built by Vallin de la Mothe in the 1770s, but the current interiors date from a century later, when it became the residence of the illustrious Yusupov family. The palace interiors are sumptuous and rich, with many halls painted in different styles and decked out with gilded chandeliers, silks, frescoes, tapestries and some fantastic furniture. Your visit begins on the 2nd floor, which features an amazing ballroom (the White Column Room), banquet hall, the delightful Green Drawing Room and the ornate rococo private theatre. The tour continues on the ground floor, where you will see the fabulous Turkish Study (used by Felix as a billiards room), the Prince's study and the Moorish Drawing Room, among many other rooms.

The Mad Monk

In 1916 Rasputin was murdered here by Felix Yusupov and some fellow plotters, who considered the Siberian mystic to have become too powerful. To see the room where Rasputin's murder began (he was poisoned and shot to no avail, finally succumbing to drowning) you have to pay for an extra 90-minute tour, which takes place at 5pm daily.

TOP SIGHT
NEW HOLLAND ISLAND

Closed to the public for much of the past three centuries, New Holland Island has been transformed into a stunning new green space and cultural complex. Come to check out art installations on the grounds, have a meal or a drink in one of the historic brick buildings, and take part in some of the many events happening year-round.

Background

In Peter's time, the complex was used for shipbuilding (its name refers to the place where he learned the trade). The impressive red-brick-and-granite arch, designed by Jean-Baptiste Vallin de la Mothe in the late 18th century, is one of the city's best examples of Russian classicism. In the 19th century, a large basin was built in the middle of the island and experiments were conducted by scientist Alexey Krylov in an attempt to build a boat that couldn't be capsized. In 1915 the navy built a radio transmitter here – the most powerful in Russia at the time. It was from there that Lenin gave his famous 1917 broadcast, announcing the revolution had begun. During WWII, the island suffered heavy damage during bomb raids and artillery fire. The buildings that did survive fell into ruin in the post-war years, and remained largely derelict until the 21st century.

Buildings & Grounds

Near the entrance to the island, the newly built **Pavilion** houses temporary exhibitions and is also the place to hear lectures, artist presentations and other events. Around the corner, the handsomely restored **Foundry**, dating from the mid-19th century, is built on the site that some believe was used as Peter the Great's original blacksmith shop. Today it houses the casual Volkonsky Deli (p115) and the more stylish Kuznya House

DON'T MISS

➡ Foundry
➡ Bottle
➡ Pavilion

PRACTICALITIES

➡ Новая Голландия
➡ Map p280, B3
➡ www.newhollandsp.ru
➡ nab Admiralteyskogo kanala
➡ ⊙9am-10pm Mon-Thu, to 11pm Fri-Sun
➡ Ⓜ Sadovaya

(p115), a sit-down restaurant that transitions into a late-night lounge with DJs on weekends. In front of the Foundry, a herb garden adds beauty to the setting, with its lavender, dill, thyme, mint and other plants. A small pond at the centre of New Holland invites contemplation (and ice skating in winter). A path skirts the perimeter, while stairs lead down to pontoons, getting you close to the water.

Work continues on New Holland, with 2017 seeing the opening of the **Bottle**, a brick, three-storey, ring-shaped building dating from the 19th century that has cafes, stores (including an excellent art-minded bookseller) and workshops. An inner courtyard has a small stage with its own line-up of concerts and other events.

Events

There are loads of events happening in New Holland. Outdoor concerts are the big draw in the summer, and past years have brought out top names from SPB's music scene as well as international artists like Ane Brun from Stockholm and hip-hop trio Digable Planets from Brooklyn. It's a peaceful place to perfect your sun salutations during yoga sessions on the grass, hone your drawing skills at a sketching class, or work up a sweat during 'Sports Days' when trainers give free fitness classes. You can also catch periodic film screenings and lectures on art and architecture.

Hands-on Activities

Aside from lounging on the grass on warm sunny days, the island is a fine spot for a bit of ping pong, pétanque or chess. New Holland even hosts occasional tournaments – all are welcome to join. You can hire out games from the visitor centre. In the winter, there's also ice skating on the pond.

Playground

A photogenic playground pays homage to New Holland's shipbuilding days with a model of the *Petr and Pavel* frigate, built to 80% scale. Stretching 26m long and 6m high, this open wooden structure has rope bridges, platforms, a wooden steering wheel, and a telescope, making it a fantastic setting for kids to explore. Next to it is a smaller playground better suited to younger kids, with swings and slides.

TOP TIPS

➡ A handy visitor centre (to the left after crossing the bridge) can tell you what events are on and give you the lay of the land.

➡ The visitor centre is also the place to hire out essentials for pétanque, ping pong and chess.

➡ Return on a weekend night to join the party crowd at Kuznya House.

The nearest metro is Admiralteyskaya, 2km northeast. If you don't want to walk, hop on bus 3, 22 or 27 to pl Truda.

TAKE A BREAK

Grab a sandwich, pastry or coffee at the lively Volkonsky Deli (p115). Kuznya House (p115) serves excellent globally inspired cuisine, and bartenders mix up fine cocktails.

SENNAYA & KOLOMNA NEW HOLLAND ISLAND

◉ SIGHTS

◉ Sennaya

SENNAYA PLOSHCHAD
SQUARE

Map p280 (Сенная площадь; Ⓜ Sennaya Ploshchad) Immortalised by Dostoevsky, who lived all over the neighbourhood and set *Crime and Punishment* here, St Petersburg's Haymarket was once the city's filthy underbelly. Indeed, until a much-needed facelift just over a decade ago, the square was overloaded with makeshift kiosks and market stalls, which made it a magnet for the homeless, beggars, pickpockets and drunks. These days, you'll have to look hard to find vestiges of its once insalubrious days.

The peripatetic Dostoevsky, who occupied some 20 residences in his 28-year stay in the city, once spent a couple of days in debtors' prison in what is now called the Senior Officers' Barracks, just across the square from the Sennaya pl metro station.

Alyona Ivanovna, the elderly moneylender murdered in *Crime and Punishment*, lived a few blocks west of here, at nab kanala Griboyedova 104. Her flat would have been No 74, in the courtyard on the 3rd floor.

RAILWAY MUSEUM
MUSEUM

Map p280 (Музей железнодорожного транспорта; www.cmzt.narod.ru; Sadovaya ul 50; adult/student Mon-Fri R300/150, Sat & Sun R400/200; ⊙ 10.30am-5.30pm; Ⓜ Sadovaya) This museum near Sennaya pl is a must for train-set fans and modellers. It houses a collection of scale locomotives and model railway bridges, often made by the engineers who built the real ones. The oldest such collection in the world, the museum dates to 1809, 28 years before Russia had its first working train!

Come on weekends for the free Russian-language tours of the museum (held at 11am and 2pm), when guides raise little drawbridges, ring station bells and operate mechanised trains along various tracks in the galleries.

Look out for the fantastic map of Russia hanging above the main museum staircase showing all the train lines in the country, which almost makes up for the total lack of signage in English.

YUSUPOV GARDENS
PARK

Map p280 (Юсуповский сад; Sadovaya ul; ⊙ sunrise-sunset; Ⓜ Sadovaya) West of Sennaya pl along Sadovaya ul you'll find the charming Yusupov Gardens, a pleasant park with a big lake in the middle. The flower-filled grounds are a popular place to stroll, sit and sunbathe. The building set back behind the gardens is the **Old Yusupov Palace** (Map p280; not to be confused with the Yusupov Palace on the Moyka River), which is closed to the public and is used mainly for official receptions.

BERTHOLD CENTRE
ARTS CENTRE

Map p280 (Бертгольд Центр; www.vk.com/bertholdcentre; Grazhdanskaya ul 13; Ⓜ Sadovaya) One of St Petersburg's newest 'art clusters', the Berthold Centre has a handful of shops, cafes and galleries spread around a former foundry. There's a courtyard in the centre of the complex that gathers a young, bohemian crowd – especially during special events and concerts (bands sometimes play on a rooftop just overlooking the courtyard).

MARINA GISICH GALLERY
GALLERY

Map p280 (☎ 812-314 4380; www.gisich.com; nab reki Fontanki 121; ⊙ 11am-7pm Mon-Fri, noon-5pm Sat; Ⓜ Sadovaya) **FREE** A small gallery that puts on worthwhile contemporary shows.

◉ Kolomna

MARIINSKY THEATRE
THEATRE

See p106.

NEW HOLLAND
ISLAND

See p108.

YUSUPOV PALACE
PALACE

See p107.

CENTRAL NAVAL MUSEUM
MUSEUM

Map p280 (Центральный военно-морской музей; ☎ 812-303 8513; www.navalmuseum.ru; pl Truda; adult/student R600/400; ⊙ 11am-6pm Wed-Sun; Ⓜ Admiralteyskaya) Following a move to this beautifully repurposed building opposite the former shipyard of New Holland, the Central Naval Museum has moved into the 21st century and is now one of St Petersburg's best history museums. The superb, light-bathed building houses an enormous collection of models, paintings and other artefacts from three centuries of Russian naval history, including *botik*, the small boat known as the 'grandfather of the Russian navy' – stumbling across it in the late 17th century was Peter the Great's inspiration to create a Russian maritime force.

The real attraction here is the superb collection of model boats, some of which are simply extraordinary in size and detail. There's sadly little signage in English, so it's worthwhile paying extra for an audio guide (R600 to R800) if you're interested in really understanding what you're seeing. The entrance to the museum is opposite New Holland on nab Kryukova kanala.

NIKOLSKY CATHEDRAL   CATHEDRAL
Map p280 (Никольский собор; Nikolskaya pl 1/3; ⊙9am-7pm; Ⓜ Sadovaya) Surrounded on two sides by canals, this ice-blue cathedral is one of the most picture-perfect in the city, beloved by locals for its baroque spires and golden domes. It was one of the few churches that still operated during the Soviet era, when organised religion was effectively banned.

Nicknamed the Sailor's Church (Nicholas is the patron saint of sailors), it contains many 18th-century icons set against rich green columns, and a fine carved wooden iconostasis, though visitors are limited to only a small area of the church's interior.

A graceful bell tower overlooks the Griboyedov Canal, which is crossed by Staro-Nikolsky most. From this bridge, you can see seven other bridges, more than from any other spot in the city.

MISP   GALLERY
Map p280 (Музей Искусства Санкт-Петербурга XX-XXI Веков; www.mispxx-xxi.ru/eng; nab kanala Griboyedova 103; R150; ⊙2-9pm Wed-Fri, noon-8pm Sat & Sun; Ⓜ Sadovaya) This multi-floored gallery near the Griboyedov Canal stages intriguing exhibitions that showcase the talents of Russian artists of the 20th and 21st centuries. The content changes roughly every two months, and past shows have delved into Russian symbolism, Soviet depictions of femininity, Russian futurism, and portraits and landscapes from the Leningrad school.

NABOKOV MUSEUM   MUSEUM
Map p280 (Музей Набокова; www.nabokov.museums.spbu.ru/En; Bolshaya Morskaya ul 47; ⊙11am-6pm Tue-Fri, to 5pm Sat; Ⓜ Admiralteyskaya) **FREE** This 19th-century townhouse was the suitably grand childhood home of Vladimir Nabokov, infamous author of *Lolita* and arguably the most versatile of 20th century Russian writers. Here Nabokov lived with his wealthy family from his birth in 1899 until the revolution in 1917, when they left the country. Nabokov artefacts on display include family photographs, first editions of his books and parts of his extensive butterfly collection.

The house features heavily in Nabokov's autobiography *Speak, Memory,* in which he refers to it as a 'paradise lost'. Indeed, he never returned, dying abroad in 1977. Aside from the various Nabokov artefacts, there's actually relatively little to see of the former home itself, save for some charming interiors (ask to see the gorgeous stained-glass windows in the stairwell, which are not technically part of the museum, but staff may allow you to take a peek).

RUMYANTSEV MANSION   MUSEUM
Map p280 (Особняк Румянцева; www.spbmuseum.ru; Angliyskaya nab 44; adult/student R200/100; ⊙11am-6pm Thu-Mon, to 5pm Tue; Ⓜ Admiralteyskaya) History buffs should not miss this oft-overlooked but superb local museum. Part of the State Museum of the History of St Petersburg, the mansion contains an exhibition of 20th-century history, including displays devoted to the 1921 New Economic Policy (NEP), the industrialisation and development of the 1930s, and the Siege of Leningrad during WWII. Exhibitions are unusual in that they depict everyday life in the city during these historic periods. Each room has an explanatory panel in English.

The museum is housed in the majestic 1826 mansion of Count Nikolai Petrovich Rumyantsev, a famous diplomat, politician and statesman, as well as an amateur historian whose personal research library became the basis for the Russian State Library in Moscow. The history of the mansion and its owners is fascinating in itself, and the few restored staterooms at the front of the house suggest daily life for the Rumyantsevs was an opulent affair.

GRAND CHORAL SYNAGOGUE   SYNAGOGUE
Map p280 (Большая хоральная синагога; ☑921-978 4464; www.eng.jewishpetersburg.ru; Lermontovsky pr 2; ⊙10am-6pm Sun-Fri, services 10am Sat; Ⓜ Sadovaya) Designed by Vasily Stasov, the striking Grand Choral Synagogue opened in 1893 to provide a

DOSTOEVSKY'S DOMAIN

Dostoevsky lived all over this area; he resided in three flats on tiny Kaznacheyskaya ul alone. From 1861 to 1863, he lived at No 1. In 1864, he spent one month living in the faded red building at No 9, before moving to No 7. Here, he lived from 1864 to 1867 and wrote *Crime and Punishment*; indeed, the route taken by the novel's antihero Raskolnikov to murder the old moneylender passed directly under his window.

Speaking of *Crime and Punishment*, one of the most infamous addresses in the neighbourhood is an innocuous house on the corner of Stolyarny per (called 'S... lane' in the book). Known as the **Raskolnikov House** (Дом Раскольникова; Map p280; Stolyarny per 5; M Sennaya Ploshchad), it's one of two possible locations of the attic apartment of Dostoevsky's troubled protagonist. Those who claim this is the place go further, saying that Rodion retrieved the murder weapon from a street-sweeper's storage bin inside the tunnel leading to the courtyard.

The house, not open to the public, is marked by a sculpture of Dostoevsky. The inscription says something to the effect of 'The tragic fate of the people of this area of St Petersburg formed the foundation of Dostoevsky's passionate sermon of goodness for all mankind'. Other Dostoevsky connoisseurs argue that it would be more appropriate if Raskolnikov's attic apartment was located further down the street at No 9, which is otherwise unmarked.

central place of worship for St Petersburg's growing Jewish community. Its lavishness (particularly notable in the 47m-high cupola and the decorative wedding chapel) indicates the pivotal role that Jews played in imperial St Petersburg. The synagogue was fully revamped in 2003. Visitors are welcome except on the Sabbath and other holy days. Men and married women should cover their heads upon entering.

Also on-site are the Small Synagogue (generally opened for guided tours only), the Jewish restaurant Le'chaim (p116) and a Kosher Shop. In summer, the synagogue also hosts performances with a Jewish cantor and other musicians performing *chaaznut* and *klezmer* music. The synagogue organises English-language tours of the building, as well as Jewish heritage tours of St Petersburg, all of which need to be organised in advance – see the website.

RUSSIAN VODKA MUSEUM   MUSEUM

Map p280 (Музей русской водки; www.vodka museum.su; Konnogvardeysky bul 4; with/without tour R450/200, unguided/guided tasting tour R450/600; ⊙noon-7pm; M Admiralteyskaya) This excellent private museum tells the story of Russia's national tipple in an interesting and fun way, from the first production of 'bread wine' to the phenomenon of the modern international vodka industry, complete with waxwork models and some very cool bottles. You can guide yourself through the exhibit, or be accompanied

by an English-speaking guide who'll liven things up a bit. If you'd like to sample the exhibits, too, take a tasting tour!

There's an excellent restaurant (p117) in the same building, and if you eat there, you can get a discount on museum entry.

MANEGE CENTRAL
EXHIBITION HALL   GALLERY

Map p280 (Центральный выставочный зал Манеж; ☏812-611 1100; www.manege.spb.ru; Isaakievskaya pl 1; R300; ⊙11am-7pm; M Admiralteyskaya) Formerly the Horse Guards' Riding School, this large white neoclassical building was constructed between 1804 and 1807 from a design by Giacomo Quarenghi. It now houses rotating art and commercial exhibitions, often featuring contemporary and local artists. Check the website to see what's on while you're in town. There's a good cafe and a bookshop on the basement level.

MUSEUM OF THE
HISTORY OF RELIGION   MUSEUM

Map p280 (Государственный музей истории религии; www.gmir.ru; Pochtamtskaya ul 14; adult/student/child R400/200/100, audio guide R180; ⊙10am-6pm Thu-Mon, 1-9pm Tue; M Admiralteyskaya) Back in the day, this was called the Museum of Atheism; it had a very strong anti-religious bent and was housed in the Kazan Cathedral. Now the name has changed, as has the location, but the fascinating exhibition remains, describing the history of various world religions, including Islam, Judaism, Hinduism, Buddhism and Christianity, and taking in everything from Russian icons to Pacific cults and Greek gods. Very little is signed in English, but there is a good-value audio guide.

HOUSE OF MUSIC PALACE

Map p280 (Дом музыки; ☑812-400 1400; www.spdm.ru; nab reki Moyki 211; tours R350; ⊙ticket office 11am-6pm Mon-Thu, to 5pm Fri; ⓂSadovaya) This fabulous and fully restored mansion on the Moyka River belonged to Grand Duke Alexey, the son of Alexander II. The wrought-iron-and-stone fence is one of its most stunning features, with the Grand Duke's monogram adorning the gates. Tours of the house usually take place once or twice a week, but the dates vary and tickets often sell out in advance, so check the website. Another way to visit the interior is to attend a concert here.

The palace was built in 1895 by Maximilian Messmacher, and each facade represents a different architectural style. The interior is equally diverse, and since renovation has housed the House of Music (Dom Muzyki), where popular classical concerts (R200 to R1000) are regularly held in the building's English Hall. Guided tours are given in Russian and German only.

ST ISIDORE'S CHURCH CHURCH

Map p280 (Свято-Исидоровская церковь; ul Rimskogo Korsakova 24; ⊙9am-6.30pm; ⓂSadovaya) The last great church to have been built in St Petersburg before the revolution, this neo-Byzantine beauty dates from 1907 and creates one of the most gorgeous silhouettes in the entire city, best viewed from the nearby Pikalov Bridge, or the Griboyedov Canal. There's little to see inside, but it's worth a detour to see its onion domes.

MARIINSKY PALACE PALACE

Map p280 (nab reki Moyki) The last neoclassical palace constructed in St Petersburg, the Mariinsky Palace (not to be confused with the theatre) was built between 1839 and 1844. Today it houses the Legislative Assembly of Saint Petersburg, and is closed to the public.

ALEXANDER BLOK
HOUSE-MUSEUM MUSEUM

Map p280 (Музей-квартира Блока; www.spbmuseum.ru; ul Dekabristov 57; adult/student R150/100; ⊙11am-6pm Thu-Mon, to 5pm Tue;

ⓂSadovaya) This museum occupies the flat where poet Alexander Blok spent the last eight years of his life (1912–20). The 4th-floor apartment has been preserved much as it was when Blok lived here with his wife Lyubov (daughter of chemist and inventor Mendeleev). When the poet fell ill in 1920, his family moved into the 2nd-floor apartment where he died a year later. An exhibition demonstrates the influence of Blok's work, as well as some original copies of his poems; signage in Russian only.

The revolutionary Blok believed that individualism had caused a decline in society's ethics, a situation that would only be rectified by the communist revolution he lived to see, though he died before he could become truly disillusioned with post-revolutionary Russia. The room where Blok died contains his death mask and a drawing of Blok on his deathbed, sketched on the last page of the poet's pad. Chamber concerts and poetry readings occasionally take place here; ask downstairs for the schedule.

POPOV
COMMUNICATIONS MUSEUM MUSEUM

Map p280 (Музей связи Попова; www.rustelecom-museum.ru; Pochtamtsky per 4; adult/student R200/100; ⊙10.30am-6pm Tue-Sat; ⓂAdmiralteyskaya) Housed in the fabulous 18th-century palace of Chancellor Bezborodko, this museum of communications is the perfect addition to Pochtamtskaya ul (Post Office St). It is named for Professor Alexander Popov, inventor of the radio, and it covers all manner of communication, from the Pony Express to the modern era.

Exhibits are interactive and interesting, including an antique telephone switchboard that still works, the first civil communications satellite, Luch-15, which occupies a prominent place in the atrium, and plenty of multimedia explanations of how things work. Stamp collectors will have a field day admiring the national philatelic collection.

✖ EATING

✖ Sennaya

CO-OP GARAGE PIZZA $

Map p280 (www.cooperativegarage.com; Gorokhovaya 47; pizzas R260-390; ⊙noon-midnight Sun-Thu, to 2am Fri & Sat; 🛜🖉) Tucked into an unmarked courtyard off Gorokhovaya, this sprawling restaurant and drinking den is the go-to spot for creatively topped thin-crust pizzas and craft beers. The industrial setting draws a chatty crowd of tatted-up hipsters and style mavens, with a mostly rock soundtrack playing in the background. On warm days you can take a table in the courtyard.

There's also a small take-out window opposite the pizza spot, where you can get tasty wok-fried noodles and draught beer.

JULIA CHILD BISTRO
INTERNATIONAL $

Map p280 (☑812-929 0797; Grazhdanskaya ul 27; mains R310-490; ⊙9am-11pm Mon-Fri, from 10am Sat & Sun; 🐕🍴; MSadovaya) This neighbourhood charmer is a fine anytime spot, with good coffees, teas and snacks, plus creative thoughtfully prepared dishes like *kasha* (porridge) with mushrooms and feta for breakfast, or halibut with lemon cabbage and celery mousse later in the day. Kindly staff and a laid-back setting will make you want to stick around for a while.

Despite the name, there isn't much of a Julia Child connection – aside perhaps from the emphasis on quality ingredients and an interior that vaguely resembles the cookbook virtuoso's studio kitchen.

TESTO
ITALIAN $

Map p280 (Тесто; www.testogastronomica.ru; per Grivtsova 5/29; mains R310-550; ⊙11am-11pm; 🐕🍴; MSennaya Ploshchad) This pleasant little place is good value and yet takes Italian cookery very seriously. Choose from a wide range of homemade pastas and top them with your favourite sauce, whether tomato-based bolognese or a rich, creamy salmon sauce. A few options for soup, salad and pizza round out the menu, but the pasta is the main focus.

KHOCHU KHARCHO
GEORGIAN $$

Map p280 (Хочу харчо; ☑812-640 1616; Sadovaya ul 39/41; mains R620-1280; ⊙24hr; 🐕🍴👶; MSennaya Ploshchad) This sparkling, friendly and capacious offering right on the Haymarket is a major draw for diners at all hours. Like many other Ginza restaurants, Khochu Kharcho has a fully photographic menu of delicious comfort food, focused on Mingrelian (West Georgian) cooking. Come for calorific *khachapuri* (cheese-stuffed bread), *khinkali* (dumplings), and of course the eponymous *kharcho,* a beef, rice, tomato and walnut soup.

OH! MUMBAI
INDIAN $$

Map p280 (☑812-314 0340; per Grivtsova 2; mains R380-880; ⊙noon-11pm; 🐕🍴; MAdmiralteyskaya) Headed by a chef from New Delhi, this attractive eatery, decorated with colourful metal lamps and strung with prayer flags, serves up some of the best Indian cooking in the city. You'll find filling and satisfying curries, tandoors and a delicious selection of vegetarian options – all go nicely with piping hot naan (flatbread).

Service can be slow, so order some papadums or samosas, and sip that mango lassi slowly while you wait.

★SEVERYANIN
RUSSIAN $$

Map p280 (Северянин; ☑921-951 6396; www.severyanin.me; Stolyarny per 18; mains R620-1300; ⊙noon-midnight; 🐕; MSennaya Ploshchad) An old-fashioned elegance prevails at Severyanin, one of the top choices for Russian cuisine near Sennaya ploshchad. Amid vintage wallpaper, mirrored armoires and tasselled lampshades, you might feel like you've stepped back a few decades. Start off with the excellent mushroom soup or borscht, before moving on to rabbit ragout in puff pastry or Baltic flounder with wine sauce.

Excellent but friendly service and fair prices.

KARAVAN
CENTRAL ASIAN $$

Map p280 (Караван; Voznesensky pr 46; mains R420-790; ⊙10am-1am; 🍴; MSadovaya) Despite the somewhat kitschy decor, Karavan is a superb Central Asian restaurant with a lovely location overlooking the Fontanka River. Open grills line the dining room, giving an optimum view (and scent) of the kebabs that are on the menu. Meat aside, there's also satisfying *vareniki* (dumplings), mushroom soup and rich Adjarian *khachapuri* (cheese bread topped with egg).

You'll also find good Georgian wines on hand and Weihenstephaner on tap.

✖ Kolomna

1818 KAFE AND BIKES
INTERNATIONAL $

Map p280 (Кафе и Велосипеды; www.cafe1818.ru; ul Dekabristov 31; mains R240-420; ⊙10am-11pm Mon-Fri, from 11am Sat & Sun; 🐕🍴; MSadovaya) 🚲 Combining a love of bicycles and street food from around the globe, Kafe and Bikes serves up delicious cooking amid upbeat grooves, exposed bulbs and those slate grey walls so prevalent in St Petersburg. *Shawarmas*, wok-fried buckwheat noodles with vegetables, pizzas, *khachapuri* (Georgian cheese bread) and *syrniki* (sweet cheese fritters) are all served up in a hurry by friendly staff.

Don't miss the pedal-powered blender in the corner – a fine way to get in a workout while making your own smoothie. You can also hire a bicycle here (per hour from R150).

VOLKONSKY DELI INTERNATIONAL $
Map p280 (www.newhollandsp.ru/en/foundry; nab Admiralteyskogo kanala; mains R280-450; ⊘11am-10pm; 🛜🍴) The best place for a quick bite on New Holland Island is this buzzing little self-serve deli, which offers soups, salads, sandwiches and heavenly baked goods. On warm days the tables out front are the place to be.

DEDUSHKA KHO SOUP $
Map p280 (Дедушка Хо; Lermontovsky pr 10; mains R170-290; ⊘11am-11pm; ⓜSadovaya) When the weather sours, retreat to this snug, casual spot just west of Nikolsky Cathedral for warming bowls of *pho* (Vietnamese noodle soup) topped with veal, and shrimp-filled *tom yum* (spicy soup with lemongrass).

The soups are filling and served up in a hurry, but if you're famished throw in an order of summer rolls (filled with shrimp, chicken and vegetables).

★TEPLO MODERN EUROPEAN $$
Map p280 (✆812-570 1974; www.v-teple.ru; Bolshaya Morskaya ul 45; mains R360-940; ⊘9am-midnight Mon-Fri, from 11am Sat & Sun; ❄🛜🐾; ⓜAdmiralteyskaya) This much-feted, eclectic and original restaurant has got it all just right. The venue itself is a lot of fun to nose around, with multiple small rooms, nooks and crannies. Service is friendly and fast (when it's not too busy) and the peppy, inventive Italian-leaning menu has something for everyone. Reservations are usually required, so call ahead.

The restaurant is full of unexpected props, from table football to a child's playroom. Dishes come from all over the world and there are plenty of vegetarian choices, as well as breakfasts served until noon (1pm on weekends).

KUZNYA HOUSE INTERNATIONAL $$
Map p280 (www.facebook.com/kuznyahouse; nab Admiralteyskogo kanala; mains R450-890;

⊘noon-11pm Sun-Thu, to 6am Fri & Sat; 🛜🍴) Set in the atmospheric Foundry building, Kuznya House has a creative menu that hopscotches around the globe, with tasty dishes like salmon ceviche with fennel, tandoori chicken, and mussels with frites. It's a stylish but easygoing spot for a meal or a drink, and it transforms into a lounge spot on weekends when DJs spin until the early hours.

Breakfast is served from noon to 2pm (till 4pm on weekends).

SADKO RUSSIAN $$
Map p280 (✆812-903 2373; www.sadko-rst.ru; ul Glinki 2; mains R540-1200; ⊘noon-1am; 🐾; ⓜSennaya Ploshchad) Serving all the Russian favourites, this impressive restaurant's decor combines traditional Zhostovo floral designs and Murano glass chandeliers amid vaulted ceilings and elegantly set tables. It's popular with theatregoers (reserve ahead in the high season), as it's an obvious pre- or post-Mariinsky dining option.

The waiters, all music students at the nearby Conservatory, give 'impromptu' vocal performances (usually Thursday to Sunday nights around 7pm).

There's a great children's room and a full children's menu to boot, so families are very well catered for.

GRAF-IN INTERNATIONAL $$
Map p280 (www.graf-in.com; Konnogvardeysky bul 4; mains R480-990; ⊘11am-midnight Sun-Thu, to 2am Fri & Sat; 🛜; ⓜAdmiralteyskaya) This smart, funky but informal restaurant offers an international selection of food focused mainly on Modern European cooking, with sections of the menu devoted to Josper, pasta and Asian food, among others. The dishes are prepared in the glass-walled kitchen and are all beautifully presented, while the art direction budget attracts a young and chic crowd.

ENTRÉE FRENCH $$
Map p280 (✆812-992 4220; Nikolskaya pl 5; sandwiches R320-480, mains R490-960; ⊘11am-midnight; 🛜; ⓜSadovaya) Charming Entrée comes in two parts: the cafe-cum-deli to the right has a chessboard floor, rustic decor, delicious éclairs and sandwiches and, for some reason, Michael Douglas' signature scrawled on the wall. Behind the curtain is a more formal restaurant with a European menu (duck confit, risotto with wild mushrooms) and a sizeable wine list.

Service could be a little friendlier, but otherwise this place is a great find in a rather desolate stretch of the city centre. Breakfast is served all day.

ROMEO'S BAR & KITCHEN   ITALIAN $$

Map p280 (☑812-572 5448; www.romeosbarand kitchen.ru; pr Rimskogo-Korsakova 43; mains R480-990; ⊗9am-midnight; 🛜; MSadovaya) This stylish Italian-run restaurant on one side of the charming Kryukov Canal offers a full menu of traditional Italian cooking, from its large meat selection to main courses such as grilled salmon with red caviar, cherry tomatoes and fennel. Ask for the pizza menu (R360 to R740), as it's separate to the main one. Breakfast is served daily until noon.

IDIOT   RUSSIAN $$

Map p280 (☑921-946 5173; www.idiot-spb.com/ eng; nab reki Moyki 82; mains R300-1000, brunch R690; ⊗11am-1am; 🛜🍴; MSennaya Ploshchad) Something of an expat favourite, the Idiot is a charming place that has been serving up high-quality Russian fare for years now. The friendly basement location is all about atmosphere, relaxation and fun (encouraged by the complimentary vodka coming with each meal). You can't go wrong here, whether opting for bliny with caviar, grilled trout or *pelmeni* (Russian-style ravioli) with mushrooms and sour cream.

The cosy subterranean space, the antique furnishings and crowded bookshelves make it an extremely pleasant place to come for a bite or for drinks.

STROGANOFF STEAK HOUSE   STEAK $$

Map p280 (☑812-314 5514; www.stroganoff steakhouse.ru; Konnogvardeysky bul 4; mains R490-3200; ⊗8am-midnight Mon-Fri, from 10am Sat & Sun; 🛜🧒; MAdmiralteyskaya) Beef lovers can indulge their habit at this 12,000-sq-metre restaurant, the city's biggest. Thanks to clever design, though, it doesn't feel overwhelmingly large or impersonal, with the huge space divided into six stylish yet informal dining spaces. The steaks menu is impressive and there's a large list of side orders, salads and other main courses to choose from as well.

There's a fun children's playroom here, making it a good choice for young families.

LE'CHAIM   JEWISH $$

Map p280 (Лехаим; ☑812-572 5616; www. spb-lehaim.ru; Lemontovsky pr 2; mains R390-620; ⊗10am-10pm Sun-Thu) St Petersburg's only kosher restaurant, Le'chaim whips up carefully prepared Jewish and European dishes. Start off with *forshmak* (an appetizer made with herring) or potato kugel, followed by baked trout, or chicken and matzo ball soup. It's located directly behind the Grand Choral Synagogue in the same gated complex.

DEKABRIST   MODERN EUROPEAN $$

Map p280 (www.decabrist.net; ul Yakubovicha 2; mains R320-670; ⊗8am-11pm; 🛜; MAdmiralteyskaya) A decent-value, modern and stylish cafe just moments from St Isaac's Cathedral, Dekabrist sounds like it might be too good to be true. The menu is simple but eclectic, and includes burgers, grilled salmon, pork schnitzel, falafel and a range of salads and desserts, while the two-floor space is comfortable and sociable, even if the lighting is borderline interrogatory.

MIGA   KOREAN $$

Map p280 (Мига; Lermontovsky pr 6; mains R460-1340; ⊗noon-midnight; 🛜🍴; MSadovaya) The authentic (read: no frills) Korean restaurant is a great find in this quiet residential neighbourhood. There's a wide-ranging, pictorial menu that includes delicious *bulgogi* (Korean beef barbecue), *bossam* (spicy pork belly) and *bajon* (seafood pancakes), as well as perennial favourite *bibimbap*. Service is fast and friendly, and there's a private banquet room, which draws in the foreign groups.

EM RESTAURANT   EUROPEAN $$$

Map p280 (☑921-960 2177; http://emrestaurant. ru; nab reki Moyki 84; set menu R3500; ⊗7-11pm Tue-Sun; 🛜🍴; MAdmiralteyskaya) Bookings are essential for this superb restaurant where the chefs calmly prepare seven beautifully presented courses in an open kitchen. Be prepared for such exotic elements as reindeer, smoked perch, red cabbage sorbet and fois gras coloured with squid ink. Individual food preferences can be catered to and every Sunday they work their culinary magic on a vegan menu.

THE RÉPA   RUSSIAN $$$

Map p280 (☑812-640 1616; http://ginza.ru/spb/ restaurant/therepa; Teatralnaya pl 18/10; mains R370-1490; ⊗5pm-1am Mon-Fri, 2pm-1am Sat & Sun; 🛜; MSadovaya) Repa may be Russian for turnip but this delightful restaurant, cheek-by-jowl with the Mariinsky, is anything but rustic. Beautifully painted murals of dancers grace the walls as waiters glide by delivering glasses of sparkling wine and plates of bliny, Kamchatka crab or whole baked fish to elegantly attired customers.

If you have a ticket to the Mariinsky you'll also receive 20% off most items on the bill.

RUSSIAN VODKA ROOM NO 1   RUSSIAN **$$$**

Map p280 (✆812-570 6420; www.vodkaroom.ru; Konnogvardeysky bul 4; mains R490-1530; ✳🖭; Ⓜ Admiralteyskaya) This charming, welcoming place is the restaurant of the Russian Vodka Museum (p112), but it's good enough to be a destination in its own right. The interior enjoys a grand old-world dacha feel, as does the menu: rack of lamb in pomegranate sauce, whole fried Gatchina trout and Kamchatka crab with porcini mushrooms take you back to imperial tastes and tsarist opulence.

As you'd expect there's a huge vodka list (shots R100 to R500) and the knowledgeable staff will help you match your meal to one of the many bottles they sell.

MANSARDA   INTERNATIONAL **$$$**

Map p280 (Мансарда; ✆812-946 4303; www.ginza.ru; Pochtamskaya ul 3; mains R590-1690; ⏱noon-1am; ✳🖭; Ⓜ Admiralteyskaya) It's all about glass at the rooftop restaurant of the Gazprom building. This impressive place definitely has the best views in town and you can almost touch the dome of St Isaac's Cathedral from the nicest tables (book in advance). Yet despite the fixation, the food is no afterthought, with a delicious range of international fare and a superb wine list on offer.

To get here, enter the Gazprom building and take the dedicated lift to the top floor.

🍷 DRINKING & NIGHTLIFE

SOLARIS LAB   CAFE

Map p280 (www.facebook.com/solarislab11; per Pirogova 18, 4th fl; ⏱1pm-midnight; Ⓜ Sadovaya) Set inside a glass, semi-spherical dome, Solaris Lab has magnificent views over the russet rooftops of St Petersburg to the glittering dome of St Isaac's. It draws a mixed crowd of families and hipsters, who linger over pots of high-quality tea

and tasty desserts (try the lemon tart). On warm days, there's outdoor seating on the rooftop.

Head up to the top floor to find this remarkable cafe.

SCHUMLI   CAFE

Map p280 (www.schumli.ru; Kazanskaya ul 40; ⏱9.30am-10pm Mon-Fri, from noon Sat & Sun; 🖭; Ⓜ Sennaya Ploshchad) With its large range of coffees, sumptuous selection of cakes and – best of all – freshly made Belgian waffles, this small but friendly cafe is a great place to regain flagging energy when wandering around the city. There's an upstairs dining room for full meals (mains R320 to R640), but coffee with a side of something sweet is the real reason to come.

CROCODILE   BAR

Map p280 (Крокодил; Galernaya ul 18; ⏱12.30pm-midnight; 🖭; Ⓜ Admiralteyskaya) This pleasant place is a fine low-key setting for a drink. Enjoy a dimly lit but artsy interior (including a piano just waiting to be played) and an interesting, eclectic menu (mains R480-920) when hunger strikes.

STIRKA 40   BAR

Map p280 (Стирка; Kazanskaya ul 26; ⏱11am-midnight Sun-Thu, to 4am Fri & Sat; 🖭; Ⓜ Sennaya Ploshchad) This friendly joint, whose name means 'washing', has three washing machines, so you can drop off a load and have a few beers while you wait. A novel idea, though one few people seem to take advantage of. Its small and unassuming layout makes it a great place for a quiet drink with a cool young crowd.

☆ ENTERTAINMENT

★**MARIINSKY THEATRE**   BALLET, OPERA

Map p280 (Мариинский театр; ✆812-326 4141; www.mariinsky.ru; Teatralnaya pl 1; tickets R1200-6500; Ⓜ Sadovaya) St Petersburg's most spectacular venue for ballet and opera, the Mariinsky Theatre is an attraction in its own right. Tickets can be bought online or in person; book in advance during the summer months. The magnificent interior is the epitome of imperial grandeur, and any evening here will be an impressive experience.

Known as the Kirov Ballet during the Soviet era, the Mariinsky has an illustrious history, with troupe members including such ballet greats as Nijinsky, Nureyev, Pavlova and Baryshnikov. In recent years the company has been invigorated by the current artistic and general director, Valery Gergiev, who has worked hard to make the company solvent while overseeing the construction of the impressive and much-needed second theatre, the Mariinsky II, across the Kryukov Canal from the company's green-and-white wedding cake of a building. It is pretty certain that the Mariinsky Theatre will close at some point in 2018 or 2019 for a full (and, again, much needed) renovation, so visit the building's faded grandeur while you can.

MARIINSKY II   BALLET, OPERA

Map p280 (Мариинский II; ☑812-326 4141; www.mariinsky.ru; ul Dekabristov 34; tickets R350-6000; ⊘ticket office 11am-7pm; Ⓜ Sadovaya) Finally opening its doors in 2013 after more than a decade of construction, legal wrangles, scandal and rumour, the Mariinsky II is a showpiece for St Petersburg's most famous ballet and opera company. It is one of the most technically advanced music venues in the world, with superb sightlines and acoustics from all of its 2000 seats.

There's no denying that the modern-yet-not-modern-enough-to-be-interesting exterior is no great addition to St Petersburg's magnificent wealth of buildings. Inside, though, it's a different story. The interior is a beautifully crafted mixture of backlit onyx, multi-level public areas between which staircases, lifts and escalators weave, limestone walls, marble floors and Swarovski chandeliers. The simple yet superbly designed auditorium boasts plenty of legroom, three stages that can be combined to form one, and an orchestra pit that can hold no fewer than 120 musicians. Serious music fans should come here to see a state-of-the-art opera and ballet venue, while anyone curious to see the results of a decade of building work will also not leave disappointed.

As well as the main auditorium, there are also several smaller venues within the venue (Prokofiev Hall, Stravinsky Foyer, Shchedrin Hall, Mussorgsky Hall), all of which host regular concerts that can be a cheaper alternative to seeing a performance in the main hall.

MARIINSKY CONCERT HALL   CLASSICAL MUSIC

Map p280 (Мариинский концертный зал; www.mariinsky.ru; ul Dekabristov 37; tickets R700-1800; ⊘ticket office 11am-8pm; Ⓜ Sadovaya) Opened in 2007, this concert hall is a magnificent multifaceted creation. It manages to preserve the historic brick facade of the set and scenery warehouse that previously stood on this spot, while the modern main entrance, facing ul Dekabristov, is all tinted glass and angular lines, hardly hinting at the beautiful old building behind.

Its array of classical orchestral performances is superb, but be aware that it's a modern venue, and won't provide your typical 'night at the Mariinsky' atmosphere.

RIMSKY-KORSAKOV
CONSERVATORY   CLASSICAL MUSIC

Map p280 (Консерватория имени Н. А. Римского-Корсакова; ☑812-312 2519; www.conservatory.ru; Teatralnaya pl 3; tickets R300-2000; Ⓜ Sadovaya) This illustrious music school was the first public music school in Russia. The Bolshoy Zal (Big Hall) on the 3rd floor is an excellent place to see performances by up-and-coming musicians throughout the academic year, while the Maly Zal (Small Hall) often hosts free concerts from present students and alumni; check when you're in town for what's on.

Founded in 1862, the Conservatory counts Pyotr Tchaikovsky among its alumni and Nikolai Rimsky-Korsakov among its former faculty. Dmitry Shostakovich and Sergei Prokofiev are graduates of this institution, as are countless contemporary artistic figures, such as Mariinsky artistic director Valery Gergiev.

YUSUPOV PALACE THEATRE   THEATRE

Map p280 (Театр Юсуповского дворца; ☑812-314 9883; www.yusupov-palace.ru; nab reki Moyki 94; tickets R700-3200; Ⓜ Sadovaya) Housed inside the outrageously ornate Yusupov Palace, this elaborate yet intimate venue was the home entertainment centre for one of the city's foremost aristocratic families. While you can visit the theatre when you tour the palace, seeing a performance here is a treat, as you can imagine yourself the personal guest of the notorious Prince Felix himself.

The shows are a mixed bag – usually a 'Gala Evening' that features fragments of various Russian classics.

ST PETERSBURG OPERA OPERA
Map p280 (Санкт-Петербургская Опера; ☑812-312 3982; www.spbopera.ru; ul Galernaya 33; tickets R700-2000; ⓂAdmiralteyskaya) Housed in the sumptuous (and dare we say, rather bizarre) former home of Baron von Derviz, the St Petersburg Opera performs regular operas in its intimate and grandly lavish former ballroom. With just 187 seats, you're guaranteed a good view of the Russian, Italian and German classics, even if the quality can't compare to other more established opera houses in the city.

FEEL YOURSELF
RUSSIAN FOLKSHOW DANCE
Map p280 (☑812-312 5500; www.folkshow.ru; ul Truda 4, Nikolayevsky Palace; ticket incl drinks & snacks R4900; ⊘box office 11am-9pm, shows 7pm; ⓂAdmiralteyskaya) Terrible title, but not a bad show of traditional Russian folk dancing and music. The pricey two-hour performance features four different folk groups, complete with accordion, balalaika and Cossack dancers. As a bonus, it's held inside the spectacular Nikolayevsky Palace.

LENDOK CINEMA
Map p280 (Лендок; ☑812-714 0806; www.lendoc.ru; nab Kryukova kanala 12; tickets R150-350; ⊘11am-11pm; ⓂSenaya) Occupying a grand former mansion, this cinema and working film studio specialises mainly in documentary films, including international ones, although they do also screen feature films.

The lobby bar is also a pleasant spot for a drink or something to eat – when they have a week specialising in a nation's cinema here, the menu features dishes from that country.

🛍 SHOPPING

REDISKA ARTS & CRAFTS
Map p280 (Grazhdanskaya ul 13, Berthold Centre; ⊘noon-10pm; ⓂSadovaya) Near the courtyard of the Berthold Centre, this delightful shop has lots of eye-catching objects, much of it made in-house or produced by St Petersburg artisans. You'll find jewellery imprinted with famous paintings, whimsical wooden clocks, ceramics, tiny Konstructor kits (a kind of miniature Lego), artfully painted flasks, backpacks, sunglasses and hand-made soaps, lotions and candles.

Don't miss the handsome fabric pouches and passport covers by Anton Tut Ryadom, a craft-making collective composed of people with disabilities.

MOMENTOGRAFIYA PHOTOGRAPHY
Map p280 (www.momentography.ru; ul Grazhdanskaya 15; ⊘noon-8pm Mon-Sat; ⓂSennaya Ploschad) Lomography fans shouldn't miss this handsome little shop in the Berthold Centre. You'll find a whole range of eye-catching cameras and accessories, from vintage-looking instant cameras to handy bags, photo albums and film.

MATRYOSHKA FASHION & ACCESSORIES
Map p280 (www.matryoshkadesign.com; ul Dekabristov 28; ⊘11am-8pm; ⓂSadovaya) Designer Natalia Larchenko has taken the classic Russian nesting doll silhouette and transformed it into a tiny work of art in her attractive necklaces, bracelets, earrings – including works in amber from the Kaliningrad region. The curvy design also features in both bold and subtle patterns on silk scarves and shawls, as well as soft pullovers.

Quality materials (rose gold, sterling silver) and fine craftsmanship (most products are made in Italy) are essential to the brand.

NORTHWAY GIFTS & SOUVENIRS
Map p280 (Angliyskaya nab 36/2; ⊘9am-8pm; ⓂAdmiralteyskaya) There is quite simply no bigger collection of *matryoshki* (nesting dolls), amber, fur and other Russian souvenir staples than that on offer at this very impressive and stylish shop right on the Neva embankment. Look no further for Russian gifts to take home.

MARIINSKY ART SHOP GIFTS & SOUVENIRS
Map p280 (www.mariinsky.ru; Mariinsky Theatre, Teatralnaya pl 1; ⊘11am-6pm on performance days, also open during interval; ⓂSadovaya) Opera and ballet lovers will delight at the theatre-themed souvenirs for sale in the Mariinsky gift shop. None of it is cheap, but the selection is impressive. Also on sale: a comprehensive collection of CDs, DVDs, books and posters that you won't find elsewhere.

GALLERY OF DOLLS GIFTS & SOUVENIRS
Map p280 (Галерея кукол; Bolshaya Morskaya ul 53/8; entry R50; ⊘noon-7pm Tue-Sat; ⓂSennaya Ploschad) Featuring ballerinas and

babushkas, clowns and knights, this gallery depicts just about every fairy-tale character and political persona in doll form. The highly creative figures are more like art than toys and make unusual souvenirs (although they're admittedly an acquired taste).

KOSHER SHOP   FOOD & DRINKS

Map p280 (www.en.jeps.ru; Lermontovsky pr 2; ⊙10am-9pm Sun-Fri; MSadovaya) Serving St Petersburg's Jewish community, the Kosher Shop is conveniently located next to the Grand Choral Synagogue. Although its emphasis is on hard-to-find kosher food, the shop also sells some souvenirs (Jewish-themed *matryoshki*), Jewish music and art.

SENNOY MARKET   FOOD & DRINKS

Map p280 (Moskovsky pr 4; ⊙8am-7pm; MSennaya Ploshchad) Cheaper and less atmospheric than Kuznechny Market (p142), Sennoy Market is also centrally located. You'll find fruit and vegies, as well as freshly caught fish and fresh meat, which makes it a useful spot for self-caterers.

MIR ESPRESSO   FOOD & DRINKS

Map p280 (Мир Эспрессо; ul Dekabristov 12/10; ⊙9am-8pm Mon-Fri, from 10am Sat & Sun; MSadovaya) Come for the aroma and stay for the amazing coffee from all over the world. There are espresso machines and every type of coffee-maker and caffeine-related accessory.

🏃 SPORTS & ACTIVITIES

★ **PITER KAYAK**   KAYAKING

Map p280 (☎921-435 9457; http://piterkayak.com; nab Kryukova kanala 26; tours R1700-R2500; ⊙tours at 7am Tue-Sun Apr-Sep) Experienced kayaker Denis and his friendly young team lead these excellent early morning tours which last around four hours and cover 11km. The canals and rivers are at their quietest at this time and, unlike on regular boat tours, the slower pace allows you to admire the wonderful surroundings at your leisure.

On Wednesday and Friday at 6pm they also run a 3½-hour kayak tour over on the Petrograd side, paddling around Kamenny and Yelagin islands. Bespoke tours can also be arranged.

Smolny & Vosstaniya

SMOLNY & LITEYNY | VLADIMIRSKAYA & VOSSTANIYA

Neighborhood Top Five

❶ Alexander Nevsky Monastery (p123) Exploring the beating heart of Orthodox St Petersburg in this complex of churches and atmospheric cemeteries – the final resting place of many of Russia's greatest artists.

❷ Museum of the Defence & Blockade of Leningrad (p125) Learning about the incredible suffering and unyielding resourcefulness of citizens during the longest siege in modern history.

❸ Smolny Cathedral (p126) Taking in the spectacular powder-blue and white exterior of Rastrelli's baroque masterpiece.

❹ Museum of Decorative & Applied Arts (p126) Savouring the superb collection of gorgeous objects inside one of the neighbourhood's most elegant interiors.

❺ Dostoevsky Museum (p129) Seeing the room where Fyodor Dostoevsky wrote *The Brothers Karamazov* at this 'memorial flat'.

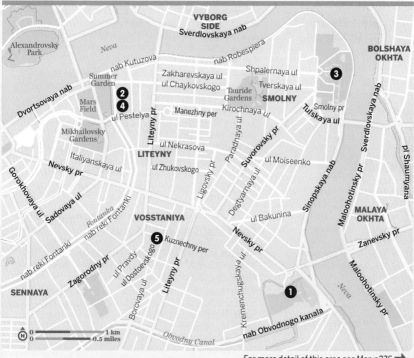

For more detail of this area see Map p276 ➡

Lonely Planet's Top Tip

Walking the busy streets of St Petersburg can sometimes be pure sensory overload. For a more peaceful vantage point, head up to one of the rooftop restaurants and bars overlooking the city. **Gastronomika** (p135) serves up excellent cuisine to memorable views.

✕ Best Places to Eat

➡ Banshiki (p133)

➡ Khachapuri i Vino (p132)

➡ Kvartira Kosti Kroitsa (p133)

➡ Duo Gastrobar (p132)

➡ Tartarbar (p133)

➡ Vsyo na Svyom Mestye (p133)

For reviews, see p132 ➡

🍷 Best Places to Drink

➡ Commode (p136)

➡ Redrum (p136)

➡ Hat (p136)

➡ Union Bar & Grill (p136)

➡ Dead Poets Bar (p137)

For reviews, see p136 ➡

◉ Best Museums

➡ Museum of Decorative & Applied Arts (p126)

➡ Anna Akhmatova Museum at the Fountain House (p125)

➡ Museum of the Defence & Blockade of Leningrad (p125)

➡ Dostoevsky Museum (p129)

For reviews, see p125 ➡

Explore Smolny & Vosstaniya

This area, bisected by the second half of Nevsky pr, breaks down into four districts: Smolny, Liteyny, Vosstaniya and Vladimirskaya. An extremely varied place, it contains the closest thing St Petersburg has to a creative hub, as well as its political and diplomatic heart. You could easily spend a few days taking in the major sights of this vast district and still only scratch the surface.

Among the big draws here are the Alexander Nevsky Monastery, worth a half-day visit in the southeast corner, and the collection of museums and historic sites in Liteyny near the Fontanka River, which could warrant a full day (or more) of exploration. Aside from delving into history and culture, there's much to discover just on neighbourhood wanders – from browsing record stores and indie booksellers on streets a few blocks north and south of Nevsky to cafe-hopping on restaurant-lined ul Rubinshteyna. By night, the district has just as much to offer, with some of the best bars in the city, particularly around the Liteyny area.

Slowly gentrifying Vosstaniya still feels a bit rundown, but is the closest Petersburg has to a creative and alternative culture hub, with art galleries, bars and clubs.

Local Life

➡ **Creative Kicks** Make the most of being in St Petersburg's most creative area: enjoy an exhibition at Loft Project ETAGI (p131), gallery hopping at Pushkinskaya 10 (p127) and memorable installations at Lumiere Hall (p129).

➡ **Shopping Mayhem** Smolny and Vosstaniya boast two of the city's biggest shopping centres – Galeria (p140) and Nevsky Centre (p140).

➡ **Park Life** When the weather is fine, join locals in the Tauride Garden (p128), one of St Petersburg's most laid-back green spaces.

➡ **Nightlife** Save at least one night for a bar crawl in the Liteyny area. Here, you'll find some of St Petersburg's best concentration of nightlife, from live music joints and swanky lounges to craft beer halls and buzzing cocktail bars.

Getting There & Away

➡ **Metro** Accessed by Pl Vosstaniya/Mayakovskaya, Vladimirskaya/Dostoevskaya, Pl Alexandra Nevskogo, Chernyshevskaya and Ligovsky Prospekt.

➡ **Bus** Handy for getting up or down Nevsky pr in minutes, dozens of buses and trolleybuses run this route, including buses 24 and 191, which run the entirety of Nevsky.

TOP SIGHT
ALEXANDER NEVSKY MONASTERY

Named after the patron saint of St Petersburg who led the Russian victory over the Swedes in 1240, the Alexander Nevsky Monastery is the city's oldest and most eminent religious institution. Today it is a working monastery that attracts scores of devout believers, as well as being the burial place of some of Russia's most famous artistic figures.

Historic Victory

Founding the monastery in 1710, Peter the Great sought to link St Petersburg to the historic battle against the Swedes, and thus to underscore Russia's long history with the newly captured region. Even though the site of Nevsky's victory was further upstream by the mouth of the Izhora River, the monastery became the centre of the Nevsky cult – his remains were transferred here from Vladimir in 1724 and remain the most sacred item in the cathedral here. In 1797 the monastery became a *lavra*, the most senior grade of Russian Orthodox monasteries.

Cemeteries

Coming into the monastery complex, you'll first arrive at the opposing cemeteries, which hold the remains of some of Russia's most famous names. You'll find Dostoevsky, Tchaikovsky, Rimsky-Korsakov, Borodin and Mussorgsky within the walls of the **Necropolis of Art Masters** (Некрополь Мастеров Искусств; Map p276; www.gmgs.ru; Nevsky pr 179/2; incl Necropolis of the 18th Century R400; ⊘9.30am-6pm May-Sep, 11am-4pm Oct-Apr; МPloshchad Aleksandra Nevskogo), which is on your right after you enter the monastery's main gate. Across the way in the **Necropolis of the 18th Century** (Некрополь XVIII века; Map p276; Nevsky pr 179/2; incl Necropolis of Art Masters

DON'T MISS
- ➡ Necropolis of Art Masters
- ➡ Trinity Cathedral
- ➡ Annunciation Church

PRACTICALITIES
- ➡ Александро-Невская лавра
- ➡ Map p276, F8
- ➡ www.lavra.spb.ru
- ➡ Nevsky pr 179/2
- ➡ cemetery R400, pantheon R150
- ➡ ⊘grounds 6am-11pm in summer, 8am-9pm in winter, churches 6am-9pm, cemeteries 9.30am-6pm in summer, 11am-4pm in winter, pantheon 11am-5pm Tue, Wed & Fri-Sun
- ➡ МPloshchad Aleksandra Nevskogo

TOP TIPS

➡ You can wander for free around most of the grounds and the main church, but you must buy tickets to enter the two most famous cemeteries as well as the Blagoveshchenskaya Burial Vault.

➡ The route to the Nikolsky Cemetery is not signed. Take one of the passages on either side of Trinity Cathedral's main entrance – marked with туалет (toilet) signs.

➡ At the Blagoveshchenskaya Burial Vault ask the docent for info in English, which is available on a small touchscreen in the corner.

Anyone wanting to visit the Trinity Cathedral should dress respectfully (no shorts, or sleeveless tops, for example) and women should cover their heads before entering.

TAKE A BREAK

The monastery's on-site **canteen** (open 9am to 7pm) has snacks, as well as inexpensive cafeteria-style lunch fare from 1pm to 2pm. For sandwiches, pastas and snacks, **Bien Cafe & Bar** (Map p276; Nevsky pr 166; mains R340-480; ⊗8am-11pm Mon-Fri, from 10am Sat & Sun; ⓂPl Alexandra Nevskogo) is a 10-minute walk up Nevsky pr.

R400; ⊗9.30am-6pm May-Sep, 11am-4pm Oct-Apr; ⓂPloshchad Aleksandra Nevskogo), you'll find far more graves, though fewer famous names – look out for polymath Mikhail Lomonosov and Natalya Lanskaya (Pushkin's wife) as well as the graves of the St Petersburg architects Quarenghi, Stasov and Rossi.

Monastery Complex

The monastery itself is within a further wall beyond the cemeteries. The centrepiece is the classical **Holy Trinity Alexander Nevsky Lavra** (Свято-Троицкая Александро-Невская Лавра; Map p276; Nevsky pr 179/2; ⊗6am-9pm; ⓂPloshchad Aleksandra Nevskogo), which was built between 1776 and 1790. Hundreds crowd in here on 12 September to celebrate the feast of St Alexander Nevsky, whose remains are in the silver reliquary by the elaborate main iconostasis, which you'll find to the right of the main altar, under a red and gold canopy. Behind the cathedral is the **Nikolsky Cemetery** (Map p276; Nevsky pr 179/2; ⊗9.30am-6pm May-Sep, 11am-4pm Oct-Apr; ⓂPloshchad Aleksandra Nevskogo) FREE, a beautiful spot with a little stream running through it, where more recently deceased Petersburgers can be found, including former mayor Anatoly Sobchak and murdered Duma deputy Galina Starovoytova.

Opposite the cathedral is the **Metropolitan's House** (Map p276; Nevsky pr 179/2) (built 1775–78), the official residence of the spiritual leader of St Petersburg's Russian Orthodox community. In the surrounding grounds is a smaller cemetery where leading Communist (ie atheist) Party officials and luminaries are buried. On the far right of the grounds facing the canal is St Petersburg's **Orthodox Academy** (Map p276; Nevsky pr 179/2), one of only a handful in Russia (the main one is at Sergiev Posad, near Moscow).

Annunciation Church

Between the cemeteries and the main church, you'll pass a ticket kiosk with a separate admission to the old **Annunciation Church** (Map p276; Nevsky pr 179/2; R150; ⊗11am-5pm Tue, Wed & Fri-Sun; ⓂPloschad Alexandra Nevskogo), aka the Blagoveshchenskaya Burial Vault. This was actually the sight of St Petersburg's first stone temple, completed in 1725, though it's been modified over the years. Intended as a burial chamber for the royal family, the ground floor today houses the remains of various minor royals, statesmen and tsarist generals. One of the most impressive tombs belongs to Alexander Golitsyn, who served as a governor of St Petersburg from 1780 to 1783. You'll also find the oldest tombstones in the monastery here – Ivan and Darya Ryevsky, who died in the early 1700s.

◉ SIGHTS

◉ Smolny & Liteyny

MUSEUM OF THE DEFENCE & BLOCKADE OF LENINGRAD   MUSEUM

Map p276 (Музей обороны и блокады Ленинграда; www.blokadamus.ru; Solyarnoy per 9; R250, audio guide R300; ⊙10am-6pm Thu-Mon, 12.30pm-8.30pm Wed; Ⓜ Chernyshevskaya) The grim but engrossing displays here contain donations from survivors, propaganda posters from the blockade period and many photos depicting life and death during the siege. You'll see the meagre bread rations as they dwindled by the month, drawings made by children trying to cope with the loss of family members, and snapshots taken during Shostakovich's Symphony No.7 – composed and played during the siege (by famished musicians), to show the world that Leningrad was not down for the count.

There's decent English signage, though it's worth investing in the audio guide which delves deeper into the experience of life during those horrific 900 days. This museum opened just three months after the blockade was lifted in January 1944 and boasted 37,000 exhibits, including real tanks and aeroplanes. But three years later, during Stalin's repression of the city, the museum was shut, its director shot, and most of the exhibits destroyed or redistributed. Not until 1985's *glasnost* was an attempt made once again to gather documents to reopen the museum; this happened in 1989.

ANNA AKHMATOVA MUSEUM AT THE FOUNTAIN HOUSE   MUSEUM

Map p276 (Музей Анны Ахматовой в Фонтанном Доме; www.akhmatova.spb.ru; Liteyny pr 51; adult/child R120/free, audio guide R200; ⊙10.30am-6.30pm Tue & Thu-Sun, noon-8pm Wed; Ⓜ Mayakovskaya) Housed in the south wing of the Sheremetyev Palace, this touching and fascinating museum celebrates the life and work of Anna Akhmatova, St Petersburg's most famous 20th-century poet. Akhmatova lived here from 1926 until 1952, invited by the art scholar Nikolai Punin, who lived in several rooms with his family. The two had a long-running affair, somewhat complicated by the tight living situation – Punin didn't want to separate from his wife.

The apartment is on the 2nd floor and is filled with mementos of the poet and correspondence with other writers, as well as elements from the life of Punin (like the overcoat hanging in the entry) and other boarders who lived here; sadly Punin would die in a gulag in 1953. A visit to this place also provides a glimpse of the interior of an (albeit atypical) apartment from the early to mid-20th century, even if relatively few pieces of original furniture have survived. Particularly moving is the study where, in her own words, Akhmatova 'quite unexpectedly' started her masterpiece *Poem Without a Hero* in 1940, and her living room where the poet had a famous all-night conversation with British diplomat Isaiah Berlin during the height of Stalinism, an event that had become legendary in Russian literary history. There are information panels in English in each room, as well as an audio guide available in English and several other languages.

Admission also includes the Josef Brodsky American Study. Brodsky did not live here, but his connection with Akhmatova was strong. For lack of a better location, his office has been recreated here, complete with furniture and other artifacts from his adopted home in Massachusetts. Funds are currently being collected to open a Josef Brodsky Museum at the poet's former home a few blocks away on Liteyny pr.

When coming to the museum, be sure to enter from Liteyny pr, rather than from the Fontanka River, where the main palace entrance is, as it's not possible to reach the museum from there.

RIMSKY-KORSAKOV FLAT-MUSEUM   MUSEUM

Map p276 (Мемориальный музей-квартира Римского-Корсакова; ☑812-713 3208; www.theatremuseum.ru; Zagorodny pr 28; R100, audio guide R100; ⊙11am-6pm Thu-Sun, 1-9pm Wed; Ⓜ Vladimirskaya) Home of Nikolai Rimsky-Korsakov for the last 15 years of his life (1893–1908), this is where he composed 11 of his 15 operas, including the *Fairy Tale of the Tsar Saltan* and the *Golden Rooster*. The memorial flat (a branch of the State Museum of Theatre & Music) includes four rooms that have been lovingly restored to their original appearance.

A Becker grand piano graces the living room, played over the years by Rachmaninov, Glazunov, Scriabin, Stravinsky – and of course by Rimsky-Korsakov himself. The composer maintained a tradition of hosting musical soirées at his home; this tradition continues today, with periodic concerts (although you are unlikely to see Chaliapin perform today). Enter from the courtyard.

MUSEUM OF THE
ARCTIC & ANTARCTIC MUSEUM

Map p276 (Музей Арктики и Антарктики; www.polarmuseum.sp.ru; ul Marata 24A; adult/child R300/80; ⊙10am-6pm Wed-Sun; MVladimirskaya) This museum is devoted to polar expeditions, wildlife, cultures and history. The enormous collection includes scientific equipment, maps, taxidermy, photographs, clothing and artefacts from polar cultures. Apart from the stuffed polar bears and penguins, the most impressive exhibit is a 1930s wooden seaplane hanging from the ceiling, used during the Soviet exploration of the 'Red North' under Stalin. As you'd expect there's a strong focus on Soviet polar exploration, and very little signage in English.

Its location in the former Old Believers' Church of St Nicholas is not well disguised, and the premises are very impressive, especially the upper floor, a round gallery overlooked by a crumbling cupola.

SMOLNY CATHEDRAL CHURCH

Map p276 (Смольный собор; ☑812-577 1421; pl Rastrelli 3/1; belltower adult/child R150/50; ⊙church 7am-8pm, bell-tower 10am-6pm; MChernyshevskaya) If baroque is your thing, then look no further than the sky-blue Smolny Cathedral, an unrivalled masterpiece of the genre that ranks among Bartolomeo Rastrelli's most amazing creations. The cathedral is the centrepiece of a convent mostly built to Rastrelli's designs between 1748 and 1757. His inspiration was to combine baroque details with the towers and onion domes typical of an old Russian monastery. You'll get a fascinating perspective over the church and city beyond from the 63m-high belltower.

There's special genius in the proportions of the cathedral (it gives the impression of soaring upwards), to which the convent buildings are a perfect foil. In stark contrast, the interior is a rather austere plain white as Rastrelli fell from favour before he was able to begin work on it. Recent years, however, have seen ongoing restoration and the transformation of the cathedral (used as a concert hall and exhibition space) back into a working church.

Access to the 277 steps leading up to the belltower is inside the cathedral on the right-hand side.

SHEREMETYEV PALACE MUSEUM

Map p276 (Шереметьевский дворец; ☑812-272 4441; www.theatremuseum.ru; nab reki Fontanki 34; one/two exhibitions R300/370; ⊙11am-7pm Thu-Mon, 1-9pm Wed; MGostiny Dvor) Splendid wrought-iron gates facing the Fontanka River guard the entrance to the Sheremetyev Palace (built 1750–55), now a branch of the **State Museum of Theatre & Music**, which has a collection of musical instruments from the 19th and 20th centuries. The Sheremetyev family was famous for the concerts and theatre performances they hosted at their palace, which was a centre of musical life in the imperial capital.

Upstairs, you'll find a lovely collection of 18th-century mahogany furniture, Italian renaissance paintings and rare instruments (including a grand piano that belonged to Glinka), spread among handsomely restored rooms. The most impressive, such as the green drawing room, were designed in second empire baroque style. The ground floor is given over to an enormous collection of more instruments (separate admission fee), but is probably only of great interest to collectors.

MUSEUM OF DECORATIVE &
APPLIED ARTS MUSEUM

Map p276 (Музей прикладного искусства; ☑812-273 3258; www.spbghpa.ru; Solyanoy per 15; adult/student R300/150, excursion in Russian R2000; ⊙11am-5pm Tue-Sat; MChernyshevskaya) Also known as the Stieglitz Museum, this fascinating establishment is as beautiful as you would expect a decorative arts museum to be. An array of gorgeous objects is on display, from medieval furniture to 18th-century Russian tiled stoves and contemporary works by the students of the Applied Arts School (also housed here). This museum is less visited than some of its counterparts in the city, but the quiet atmosphere only adds to its appeal.

In 1878 the millionaire Baron Stieglitz founded the School of Technical Design and wanted to surround his students with world-class art to inspire them. He began a collection that was continued by his son and was to include a unique array of European and Oriental glassware, porcelains, tapestries, furniture and paintings. It eventually grew into one of Europe's richest private collections. Between 1885 and 1895, a building designed by architect Maximilian Messmacher was built to house the collection and this building also became a masterpiece. Each hall is decorated in its own unique style, including Italian, Renaissance, Flemish and baroque. The Terem Room, in

ART GALLERIES

This is a great area for exploring St Petersburg's contemporary art scene. Highlights include the following.

Pushkinskaya 10 (Арт-Центр Пушкинская 10; Map p276; www.p-10.ru; Ligovsky pr 53; R500; ⊙4-8pm Wed-Fri, noon-8pm Sat & Sun; MⓂPloshchad Vosstaniya) This now legendary locale is a former apartment block – affectionately called by its street address despite the fact that the public entrance is actually on Ligovsky pr – that contains studio and gallery space, as well as music clubs **Fish Fabrique** (p139) and **Fabrique Nouvelle** (p138), plus an assortment of other shops and galleries. It offers a unique opportunity to hang out with local musicians and artists, who are always eager to talk about their work.

One ticket gives admission to all the galleries.

Kuryokhin Centre (Map p276; ☑812-322 4223; www.kuryokhin.net; 4th flr, Ligovsky pr 73; R100; ⊙11am-9pm Mon-Sat; MⓂPloshchad Vosstaniya) Named after Sergey Kuryokhin (1954–96), a legend of the Russian contemporary arts and music scene, this is the temporary home of the arts centre until its new home on Vasilevsky Island is ready (late 2019). You can view some of the talented avant-garde artist's work and that of his contemporaries including the band Kino and performance artist Vladislav Mamyshev-Monroe. You can also see exhibitions of new works that push the artistic boundaries.

The centre also organises SKIF, an international music and arts festival held in September with shows at the New Stage of the Alexandrinsky Theatre.

Gallery MArt (Галерея МАрт; Map p276; ☑812-710 8835; www.gallerymart.ru; ul Marata 35; ⊙noon-7pm Tue-Fri, to 6pm Sat; MⓂVladimirskaya) This small two-room gallery is a fine spot to check out up-and-coming artists from St Petersburg, Kazakhstan, Belarus and beyond. Call or visit the website to see what's on. It's tucked into a courtyard, though the gallery is signed off ul Marata.

K-Gallery (Map p276; ☑812-273 0056; www.kgallery.ru; nab reki Fontanki 24; R200; ⊙11am-8pm Mon-Fri, noon-6pm Sat & Sun; MⓂGostiny Dvor) Opened in 2005, K-Gallery houses one of the largest private collections of Russian artwork in the city. The two-floor space features a changing array of exhibitions (with three to five shows per year) featuring pieces dating from the late 19th-century to the Soviet avant-garde.

the style of the medieval Terem Palace of Moscow's Kremlin, is an opulent knockout.

After the revolution the school was closed, the museum's collection redistributed to the Hermitage and the Russian Museum, and most of the lavish interiors were brutally painted or plastered over or even destroyed (one room was used as a sports hall). The painstaking renovation continues to this day, despite receiving no state funding.

To find the museum, take the second entrance to the Academy as you walk up Solyanoy per from ul Pestelya. After buying tickets, head up the main staircase, turn right at the top, walk through two halls and then go down the lovely fresco-covered staircase to your left. Once you've visited the museum, feel free to wander around the grand halls and corridors of the Applied Arts School. If you continue the way you came to get to the museum and turn right

you'll get to the school's main hall, with its signature skylights, where exhibitions of students' work are often held.

CATHEDRAL OF THE TRANSFIGURATION OF OUR SAVIOUR
CATHEDRAL

Map p276 (Спасо-Преображенский собор; Preobrazhenskaya pl; ⊙8am-8pm; MⓂChernyshevskaya) The interior of this 1743 cathedral, which has been beautifully restored and repainted both outside and in, is one of the most gilded in the city. The grand gates bear the imperial double-headed eagle in vast golden busts, reflecting the fact that the cathedral was built on the site where the Preobrazhensky Guards (the monarch's personal protection unit) had their headquarters.

Architect Vasily Stasov rebuilt the cathedral from 1827 to 1829 in the neoclassical style. It is dedicated to the victory over the Turks in 1828–29; note the captured Turkish cannons, wrapped in chains, in the gate surrounding the cathedral.

SMOLNY INSTITUTE HISTORIC BUILDING

Map p276 (Смольный институт; pl Proletarskoy Diktatury 3; MChernyshevskaya) Built by Giacomo Quarenghi between 1806 and 1808 as a school for aristocratic girls, the Smolny Institute was thrust into the limelight in 1917 when it became the headquarters for the Bolshevik Central Committee and the Petrograd Soviet. From here, Trotsky and Lenin directed the October Revolution, and in the **Hall of Acts** (Aktovy zal) on 25 October, the All-Russian Congress of Soviets conferred power on a Bolshevik government led by Lenin.

The Smolny Institute served as the seat of Soviet power until March 1918, when the capital was relocated to Moscow. In 1934, the powerful Leningrad Party chief Sergei Kirov was assassinated in its corridors, on orders from Stalin, ridding the Soviet leader of a perceived rival and simultaneously providing the perfect pretext for the notorious Leningrad purges. Today St Petersburg's governor continues to run the city from here. Although it's closed to the public, some of the big tour companies, such as SPB Tours (www.spb-tours.com), include a short visit inside the Smolny Institute on multiday tours around St Petersburg.

TAURIDE PALACE & GARDENS PARK

Map p276 (Таврический дворец и сад; ⊙8am-8pm Aug-Mar, to 10pm May-Jul, closed Apr; MChernyshevskaya) Catherine the Great had this baroque palace built in 1783 for Grigory Potemkin, a famed general and her companion for many years. Today it is home to the Commonwealth of Independent States and is closed to the public. The gardens, on the other hand, are open to all; once the romping grounds of the tsarina, they became a park for the people under the Soviets, and their facilities include a lake, several cafes and an entertainment centre.

The palace was named after Tavria (another name for Crimea, the region that Potemkin conquered) and was a thank-you present to Potemkin from Catherine. Catherine's bitter son, Paul I, turned the palace into a barracks after his ascension to the throne in 1796, which ruined most of the lavish interiors. Between 1906 and 1917 the State Duma, the Provisional Government and the Petrograd Soviet all met here; in the 1930s it housed the All-Union Agricultural

Communist University, a fate that would have no doubt horrified Catherine the Great.

GOLITSYN LOFT CULTURAL CENTRE

Map p276 (nab reky Fontanki 20; MGostiny Dvor) The new epicentre of creativity on the Fontanka River is this mazelike complex of shops, bars, cafes, beauty salons, tattoo parlours, galleries and even a hostel with capsule-style bunks. Enter via the archway into a large courtyard, which is spread with outdoor eating and drinking spots in the summer, then head up any of the stairwells into the five buildings for a bit of urban exploration. On weekends the centre stages one-off events, such as craft markets, concerts and film screenings.

According to legend, literary salons were held here in the early 1800s and Pushkin was a regular guest – some claim he even wrote his political screed 'Volnost' ('Freedom') in the rooms today occupied by the Ziferburg (p137) cafe.

LENINGRAD CENTRE ARTS CENTRE

Map p276 (Ленинград центр; ☑812-242 9999; www.leningradcenter.ru; Potyomkinskaya ul 4; ⊙noon-1am; 🛜; MChernyshevskaya) This new high-tech entertainment complex houses two theatres, a gallery, a top-floor restaurant and two bars on the ground floor. It's set in a former mansion that was converted into a massive cinema during the Soviet era. In 2014, the building reopened in its present form and hosts a wide-ranging repertoire of concerts, dance performances, musical theatre and film screenings. You can't miss the video wall in the foyer – said to be the largest in Europe.

It's worth stopping by if in the area. Most exhibitions in the gallery are free.

BOLSHOY DOM HISTORIC BUILDING

Map p276 (Большой дом; Liteyny pr 4; MChernyshevskaya) Noi Trotsky's monolithic design for the local KGB headquarters (and currently the St Petersburg headquarters of the Federal Security Service, or FSB, its successor organisation) is referred to by everyone as the 'Bolshoy Dom' or 'Big House'. It's a fierce-looking block of granite built in 1932 in the late-constructivist style and was once a byword for fear among the people of the city: most people taken here during the purges were never heard from again. Obviously, the building is not open to the public.

Employees who have worked here include Vladimir Putin during his KGB career. The

Bolshoy Dom made the news in 2010, when the subversive art collective Voina (War) drew a 65m-long penis on the nearby Liteyny Bridge, which, when the bridge was raised, made a very clear statement towards the FSB.

ANNA AKHMATOVA MONUMENT   MONUMENT
Map p276 (Памятник Анне Ахматовой; nab Robespierre; MChernyshevskaya) This moving statue of St Petersburg's most famous 20th-century poet was unveiled in 2006, across the river from the notorious Kresty holding prison, to mark the 40th anniversary of Akhmatova's death. The location is no coincidence – Kresty Prison was where Akhmatova herself queued for days in the snow for news of her son after his multiple arrests during Stalin's terror.

The inscription on the monument comes from her epic poem 'Requiem', in which she describes life during the purges. It reads: 'That's why I pray not for myself/But for all of you who stood there with me/Through fiercest cold and scorching July heat/Under a towering, completely blind red wall.'

MONUMENT TO THE VICTIMS OF
POLITICAL REPRESSION   MONUMENT
Map p276 (Памятник жертвам политических репрессий; nab Robespierre; MChernyshevskaya) This gruesome piece of sculpture by Russian artist Mikhail Shemyakin was unveiled in 1995, shortly after the end of the Soviet Union, and during a time of relative lustration. The scultpure is centred on two sphinxes, both of which look, from one side, like beautiful creatures. However, view them from the other side (facing the infamous Kresty Prison across the water) and it's clear the beauty has been corrupted beyond recognition and half the face is a mere skull.

Lines of writing from many of the Soviet system's victims are engraved on the monument's granite base. It's a sad and deeply moving place.

⦿ Vladimirskaya & Vosstaniya

ALEXANDER NEVSKY
MONASTERY   MONASTERY
See p123.

GRAND MAKET ROSSIYA   MUSEUM
(☎812-495 5465; www.grandmaket.ru; Tsvetochnaya ul 16; adult/child R480/280, audio guide or binoculars R250; ◷10am-8pm; MMoskovskoe

Vorota) Russia in all its grit and glory – from the industrial sprawl of Magnitogorsk to the glittering domes of Moscow – is on full display at this vast recreation of the motherland in miniature. One huge room contains mountains, cities, rivers and lakes, with lots of mechanised action that you can observe while strolling around the perimeter of the varied landscape. Tiny trains shuttle around the countryside, helicopters ascend, and trucks and cars move across bridges, up mountain roads and along industrial sites.

The level of detail is staggering, from the spot-on recreations of Soviet-style apartment blocks, to the clothing worn by waiting passengers at the train depot. It's hard not to be charmed by this ambitious, miniaturised work of art.

DOSTOEVSKY MUSEUM   MUSEUM
Map p276 (Литературно-мемориальный музей Ф.М. Достоевского; www.md.spb.ru; Kuznechny per 5/2; adult/student R250/100, audio guide R250; ◷11am-6pm Tue-Sun, 1-8pm Wed; MVladimirskaya) ✏ Fyodor Dostoevsky lived in flats all over the city (mostly in Sennaya), but his final residence is this 'memorial flat' where he lived from 1878 until he died in 1881. The apartment remains as it was when the Dostoevsky family lived here, including the study where he wrote *The Brothers Karamazov,* and the office of Anna Grigorievna, his wife, who recopied, edited and sold all of his books.

The objects here include an image of Raphael's Sistine Virgin, which Doestoevsky was quite fond of; a clock that belonged to Dostoevsky's younger brother, which shows the hour and time when Dostoevsky died; and various family photos (including Dostoevsky's daughter Liubov Fyodorovna, who also became a writer). Apart from the six-room flat, there are two other rooms devoted to his novels, his travels and his legacy. A rather gloomy sculpted likeness of the man himself (as if there's any other kind) is just outside the nearby Vladimirskaya metro station.

LUMIERE HALL   ARTS CENTRE
(☐8-812-407 1731; www.lumierehall.ru/spb; nab Obvodny kanala 74; R500; ◷11am-11pm; MFruzenskaya) In a once-industrial part of the city, Lumiere Hall hosts large-format multimedia exhibitions – basically massive 3D projections in a 360-degree space, with audio commentary on the works displayed and the artists behind the creations. Take a seat on

THE SOVIET SOUTH

Sprawling southern St Petersburg was once planned to be the centre of Stalin's new Leningrad, and anyone interested in Stalinist architecture should make the easy trip down here to the Moskovskaya metro station for a wander around and to see a clutch of sights all within easy walking distance.

House of Soviets (Дом советов; Moskovsky pr 212; Ⓜ Moskovskaya) Right outside the Moskovskaya metro station you'll see the House of Soviets, a staggeringly bombastic Stalinist beauty. Planned to be the central administrative building of Stalin's Leningrad, it was built with the leader's neoclassical tastes in mind. Begun by Noi Trotsky in 1936, it was not finished until after the war, by which time the architect had been purged. Nonetheless, this magnificent, sinister building is a great example of Stalinist design, with its columns and bas-reliefs and an enormous frieze running across the top. Today it houses the Moskovsky Region's local administration and is closed to the public.

Monument to the Heroic Defenders of Leningrad (Монумент героическим защитникам Ленинграда; www.spbmuseum.ru; pl Pobedy; R200; ⊙10am-6pm Thu-Mon, until 5pm Tue; Ⓜ Moskovskaya) Due south of the House of Soviets, on Moskovsky pr is this awe-inspiring monument. Centred around a 48m-high obelisk, the monument, unveiled in 1975, is a sculptural ensemble of bronze statues symbolising the city's encirclement and eventual victory in WWII. On a lower level, a second bronze ring 40m in diameter surrounds a very moving sculpture standing in the centre. Haunting symphonic music creates a sombre atmosphere to guide you downstairs to the underground exhibition in a huge, mausoleum-like interior.

Here, the glow of 900 bronze lamps creates an eeriness matched by the sound of a metronome (the only sound heard by Leningraders on their radios throughout the war save for emergency announcements), showing that the city's heart was still beating. Twelve thematically assembled showcases feature items from the war and siege. An electrified relief map in the centre of the room shows the shifting front lines of the war.

Park Pobedy (Moskovsky pr; ⊙6am-midnight; Ⓜ Park Pobedy) This large green space gathers a cross-section of Petersburgers, including young families, teens and canoodling couples who stroll the leafy paths and enjoy the views over the ponds and flower gardens. Built to celebrate Russia's victory in WWII, the park is full of statues of Soviet war heroes and has a beneficent depiction of Lenin interacting with small children. To get to the Park, walk 1.7km north up Moskovsky pr, or hop on a bus or tram heading north.

beanbags and enjoy the show. Recent installations have included projections of paintings by Ivan Aivazovsky, Van Gogh and Gustav Klimt. It's a 1km walk from the metro station. Head up to the canal and turn right.

On Friday and Saturday, Lumiere Hall also has late-night screenings of popular Hollywood and foreign films. These kick off around 11.30pm.

VLADIMIRSKY CATHEDRAL   CATHEDRAL
Map p276 (Владимирский собор; Vladimirsky pr 20; ⊙8am-6pm, services 6pm daily; Ⓜ Vladimirskaya) This fantastic, five-domed cathedral, ascribed to Domenico Trezzini, is the namesake of this neighbourhood. Incorporating both baroque and neoclassical elements, the cathedral was built in the 1760s, with Giacomo Quarenghi's neoclassical belltower added later in the century.

One famous member of the congregation was Dostoevsky, who lived around the corner. The cathedral was closed in 1932 and the Soviets turned it into an underwear factory, but in 1990 it was reconsecrated and resumed its originally intended function.

The baroque iconostasis was originally installed in the private chapel of the Anichkov Palace, but was transferred here in 1808. For an impressive perspective on the onion domes, have a drink in Birreria (p139) across the road.

**MUSEUM OF THE IMPERIAL
PORCELAIN FACTORY**   MUSEUM
(www.ipm.ru; pr Obukhovsky Oborony 151; R300; ⊙10am-7pm Mon-Fri; Ⓜ Lomonosovskaya) Run as an outpost of the Hermitage, this superb museum has a stellar display of the various designs the factory has produced over

LOFT PROJECT ETAGI

Loft Project ETAGI (Лофт проект ЭТАЖИ; Map p276; ☎812-458 5005; www.loft projectetagi.ru; Ligovsky pr 74; rooftop R100; ⊙9am-11pm; ⓂLigovsky Prospekt) This fantastic conversion of the former Smolninsky Bread Factory has plenty to keep you interested, including many of the original factory fittings seamlessly merged with the thoroughly contemporary design. A young creative crowd flock to the mazelike space that includes galleries and exhibition spaces, eye-catching shops, a hostel, a bar and a cafe with a great summer terrace all spread out over five floors. In the yard, converted shipping containers house yet more pop-up clothing shops, record sellers, cafes and eateries whipping up creative street food.

Keep an eye out for stores like **Krakatau** (p141) for stylish men's wear, and **Laser B** (p141), which sells T-shirts, dresses and accessories featuring bold graphic works. In the summer months the roof of the building is open 24 hours a day for views overlooking the city; there are also occasional open-air concerts held here. Enter through the doors to one side of the main gate and you'll find ETAGI in the courtyard.

SMOLNY & VOSSTANIYA SIGHTS

the centuries and will appeal to anyone interested in this very Russian handicraft. Among the collection you'll find everything from bespoke dinner services used by the tsars to unique constructivist tea sets created in the 1920s, indicative of the factory's versatility in serving its various political masters.

Don't miss the exquisite collection of porcelain statuettes depicting the various peoples of Russia and beyond, with clothing so beautifully rendered it looks like fabric. There's also a porcelain shop here where prices are slightly lower compared to the factory's city-centre outlets. To get here, turn left out of the metro station and walk under the bridge. Turn left on the embankment and you'll see the factory ahead.

DERZHAVIN HOUSE-MUSEUM MUSEUM

(Музей-усадьба Державина; nab reki Fontanki 118; adult/student R300/200; ⊙10am-6pm Wed & Fri-Mon, noon-8pm Thu; ⓂTekhnologichesky Institut) This grand old Petersburg residence was the home to court poet Gabriel Derzhavin (1743–1816), one of Russia's greatest early writers, who recognised the genius of Alexander Pushkin during Pushkin's own childhood. Having been divided into some 60 communal apartments under the Soviets, the mansion was fully renovated in 2003 and is now a charming museum. The focus of the house is Derzhavin's own study, with its three secret entrances.

After exploring the house, you can take a stroll in the pretty gardens with its little bridges and tiny canals; you can also enter the greenery via Derzhavinksy per.

STATE MUSEUM OF URBAN SCULPTURE MUSEUM

Map p276 (Государственный Музей Городской Скульптуры; www.gmgs.ru; Chernoretsky per 2; R150; ⊙noon-6pm Sat-Wed) Despite the name, this two-storey gallery typically has more than just sculpture on display at its changing exhibitions. You may find paintings, video art and mixed media – most of which are created by avant-garde St Petersburg artists. There are a few sculptures in front of the gallery – and occasional installations tucked in the museum courtyard (staff will be sure to take you there if so). Enter from just outside the monastery walls off pl Alexandra Nevskogo.

TRINITY CATHEDRAL CATHEDRAL

(Троицкий собор; Izmailovsky pr 7A; ⊙9am-7pm Mon-Sat, 8am-8pm Sun, services 10am daily & 5pm Fri-Sun; ⓂTekhnologichesky Institut) The Trinity Cathedral boasts stunning blue cupolas emblazoned with golden stars. A devastating fire in 2006 caused the 83m-high central cupola to collapse, but it has been restored and now looks even better than it did before. Construction of the vast cathedral began in 1828, according to a design by Vasily Stasov. The cathedral was consecrated in 1835 and functioned as the chapel for the Izmailovsky Guards, who were garrisoned next door.

In honour of the Russian victory in the Russo-Turkish War in 1878, the memorial Column of Glory was constructed out of 128 Turkish cannons. (The present monument was erected on the north side of the cathedral in 2003: it is an exact replica of the original, which was destroyed by Stalin.)

The cathedral was famed for its immense collection of icons, as well as several silver crosses dating from the 18th and 19th centuries. After the revolution, most of these treasures were looted, the ornate interiors were destroyed and the cathedral was finally closed in 1938.

Trinity Cathedral was returned to the Orthodox Church in 1990, but the interior is decidedly bare, especially compared with its previous appearance. It was here that Fyodor Dostoevsky married his second wife, Anna Snitkina, in 1867.

✖ EATING

✖ Smolny & Liteyny

★DUO GASTROBAR   FUSION $
Map p276 (☑812-994 5443; www.duobar.ru; ul Kirochnaya 8A; mains R350-500; ☉1pm-midnight; ⓂChernyshevskaya) Boasting a minimalist Scandinavian design scheme, Duo Gastrobar has wowed diners with its outstanding cooking that showcases quality ingredients with global accents in delectable plates such as crab bruschetta, duck breast with smoked cheese and tomato, and rich French onion soup. There's an excellent wine list (over a dozen by the glass) as well.

Run by two chefs who have worked all over the city, Duo is a great place to experiment with new flavours and combinations in a pleasant and friendly atmosphere. Reserve ahead.

KHACHAPURI I VINO   GEORGIAN $
Map p276 (☑812-273 6797; Mayokovskogo 56; mains R310-390; ☉noon-midnight; 🛜🖉; ⓂChernyshevskaya) This welcoming, warmly lit space serves outstanding Georgian fare. The recipes aren't overly complicated and the fine ingredients speak for themselves in flavour-rich dishes like aubergine baked with *suluguni* (a type of cheese), pork dumplings, and tender lamb stew with coriander. Don't miss the excellent *khachapuri* (cheese bread), which comes in a dozen varieties and is whipped up by the bakers in front.

Top it off with a Georgian wine, like the full-bodied mukuzani. Over the bar, a row of French horns transformed into lampshades adds a whimsical touch.

LA CELLETTA   ITALIAN $
Map p276 (☑921-788 0069; www.lacelletta.ru; Fontanka 30; mains R320-540; ☉noon-midnight; 🛜🖟; ⓂChernyshevskaya) La Celletta has gained a strong local following for its beautifully executed risottos, pastas and desserts (including a rich tiramisu) – all served up at excellent prices (reservations advised). The pizza, however, is the star of the show.

The Italian team behind the casual, bright-yellow eatery turns out perfectly pillowy crusts, topped with juicy cherry tomatoes, plump porcini mushrooms and thin-sliced prosciutto (as well as mystifying Russian favourites like potatoes and boiled eggs). Don't overlook the gelato counter near the entrance.

BOTANIKA   VEGETARIAN $
Map p276 (Ботаника; ☑812-272 7091; www.cafebotanika.ru; ul Pestelya 7; mains R360-650; ☉11am-midnight; 🛜🖉; ⓂChernyshevskaya) This vegetarian charmer lives up to its green-minded name, with zesty fresh salads, veggie curries and ingredient-rich soups, plus a menu that takes in Russian, Indian and Italian dishes, all of which are handsomely executed. It's a friendly space, with plants and flower vases sprinkled about, and there's even a playroom and menu for the kids.

UKROP   VEGETARIAN $
Map p276 (Укроп; ul Marata 23; mains R280-360; ☉9am-11pm; 🛜🖉; ⓂMayakovskaya) One of various Ukrop restaurants around town, this place draws in the veg-minded crowds who come for creative salads, pastas, panini and soups, all served at excellent prices.

OBED BUFET   CAFETERIA $
Map p276 (Обед Буфет; 5th fl, Nevsky Centre, Nevsky pr 114; mains R250-380; ☉10am-11pm; 🛜; ⓂMayakovskaya) Just what St Petersburg needs: a well-organised, central and inviting cafeteria run by the city's most successful restaurant group. Here you'll find an extraordinary range of salads, soups, sandwiches, pizzas and meat dishes. There is even a 50% discount until noon and 30% after 9pm, making this a superb deal (come at 9pm for the latter, otherwise there will be no food left).

Don't miss the kitschy 'Snacks' machine out front. Insert coins for ready-made soups, sandwiches and bliny.

MARKET PLACE   INTERNATIONAL **$**

Map p276 (www.market-place.me; Nevsky pr 92; mains R320-640; ⊙8.30am-11pm Sun-Thu, to 6am Fri & Sat; 🛜; Ⓜ Mayakovskaya) This buzzing, two-story space on Nevsky has wide-ranging appeal, with six different food counters, behind which prep staff stand at the ready to whip up your order. Delicious salads, steaming stir-fried noodles, grilled meats and seafood, pastas, sandwiches and baked dishes mean you'll never run out of options. There's also a juice bar.

CAFFE ITALIA   ITALIAN **$**

Map p276 (Bakunina 5; mains R350-800; ⊙9am-2am Mon-Fri, from 10am Sat & Sun; 🛜; Ⓜ Ploschad Vosstaniya) Set with Italian icons (a Vespa and very cute vintage Fiat 500), this sprawling cafe and eatery always draws a crowd, whether in the morning for cappuccinos and pastries and later in the day for pastas, filling pizzas and creamy gelato. Things get lively at night, with an adjoining bar (Evo Music Bar) that draws revellers come the weekend. Cash only.

JIVA   VEGETARIAN **$**

Map p276 (4th fl, ul Belinskogo 9; mains around R280; ⊙noon-10pm; 🛜🍃♿; Ⓜ Gostiny Dvor) A major draw for vegetarians and vegans, Jiva whips up delicious cruelty-free burgers, in eight varieties (including lentil, chickpea, spinach and red bean), served on unique homemade buns (try the Asafoetida with Indian spices). The setting is relaxed, with meditative music and potted plants, and you can cap the meal with tea or a rich cheesecake. To get there, follow the signs off Belinskogo.

★ SCHENGEN   INTERNATIONAL **$$**

Map p276 (Шенген; 📞812-922 1197; ul Kirochnaya 5; mains R480-850; ⊙9am-midnight Mon-Fri, from 11am Sat & Sun; 🛜; Ⓜ Chernyshevskaya) A breath of fresh air just off Liteyny pr, Schengen represents local aspirations to the wider world. The wide-ranging menu is packed with temptations, from tender halibut with tomatoes and zucchini to slow-cooked venison with parsnip cream and plums in red wine. It's served up in a cool and relaxing two-room space where efficient staff glide from table to table.

★ BANSHIKI   RUSSIAN **$$**

Map p276 (Банщики; 📞921-941 1744; www.banshiki.spb.ru; Degtyanaya 1; mains R500-1100; ⊙11am-11pm; 🛜; Ⓜ ploschad Vosstaniya)

Although it opened in 2017, Banshiki has already earned a sterling reputation for its excellent Russian cuisine, serving up a huge variety of nostalgic dishes with a contemporary touch. Everything is made in house, from its refreshing *kvas* to dried meats and eight types of smoked fish. Don't overlook cherry *vareniki* (dumplings) with sour cream, oxtail ragout or the rich borscht.

There's a 20% discount at lunch. Just downstairs from the *banya,* Banshiki (which means 'banya masters') makes a fine setting for a post-steam feast.

TARTARBAR   RUSSIAN **$$**

Map p276 (Тартарбар; 📞911-922 5606; www.tartarbar.ru; Vilensky per 15; mains R450-650; ⊙1pm-midnight) The same team behind the celebrated Duo Gastrobar recently opened this clever dining space to showcase a creative menu of small plates. Rawness features in various forms (lamb tartare, tuna ceviche, beef carpaccio), though you'll also find grilled octopus, oxtail with morels, and flounder in garlic sauce.

The eclectic setting mixes exposed brick and mid-century Scandinavian furnishings with artful whimsy – concrete panels with plants dangling over the side.

VSYO NA SVYOM MESTYE   INTERNATIONAL **$$**

Map p276 (Всё на Своём Месте; 📞812-932 0256; Liteyny pr 7; mains R380-740; ⊙noon-midnight) A hip little gastrobar with warm ambiance, tables made of converted sewing machines, and a record player providing the tunes. Stop in for creative market-fresh fare, which might include cod filet on cauliflower purée, ramen soup, or polenta with roast chicken and oyster mushrooms – all goes nicely with the craft brews and easygoing vibe.

KVARTIRA KOSTI KROITSA   INTERNATIONAL **$$**

Map p276 (Квартира Кости Кройца; www.kreutzflat.com; 5th fl, apt 8, ul Marata 1, 921-651 7788; mains R450-730; ⊙24hr; 🛜🍃; Ⓜ Mayakovskaya) A beautifully designed bourgeois hideaway, Kvartira Kosti comprises a stylish restaurant with views over Nevsky pr, a small handsomely designed bar, and a surprising tea salon tucked in the back, with a stained-glass skylight and elegant furnishings set amid a circular room. The menu features Asian-style noodle dishes, creative salads, risotto, fish and chips, and a full breakfast lineup.

A GIFT TO YOUNG HOUSEWIVES

The most popular cookbook in 19th-century Russia was called *A Gift to Young Housewives*, a collection of favourite recipes and household management tips that turned into a bestseller. The author, Elena Molokhovets, a housewife herself, was dedicated to her 10 children, to the Orthodox Church, and to her inexperienced 'female compatriots' who might need assistance keeping their homes running smoothly.

This book was reprinted 28 times between 1861 and 1914, and Molokhovets added new recipes and helpful hints to each new edition. The last edition included literally thousands of recipes, as well as pointers on how to organise an efficient kitchen, how to set a proper table and how to clean a cast-iron pot.

Molokhovets received an enormously positive response from readers who credited her with no less than preserving their family life. The popular perception of the time was that a wife's primary responsibility was to keep her family together, and keeping her husband well fed seemed to be the key. As one reader wrote, 'A good kitchen is... not an object of luxury. It is a token of the health and well-being of the family, upon which all the remaining conditions of life depend'. Molokhovets included some of these letters in later editions as testimony to her work.

The cookbook was never reprinted during the Soviet period. The details of sumptuous dishes and fine table settings – let alone questions of etiquette and style – would certainly have been considered bourgeois by the Soviet regime. Yet still, copies of this ancient tome survived, passed down from mother to daughter like a family heirloom. Today, the book reads not only as a cookbook, but also as a lesson in history and sociology.

The big draw, though, is the secretive setting. You need to reserve ahead, and then you'll have to call/text to receive a code and instructions that give access to the building. There's also one plush apartment adjoining the restaurant, though you'll have to share the bathroom (shower attached) with the restaurant guests.

SUNDUK
INTERNATIONAL **$$**

Map p276 (Сундук; www.cafesunduk.ru; Furshtatskaya ul 42; mains R450-780; ☉10am-midnight Mon-Fri, from 11am Sat & Sun; 🔊; ⓂChernyshevskaya) This self-termed 'art cafe' is tucked into a tiny basement, its two rooms crowded with mismatched furniture, musical instruments, mannequins and lots of other junk (or 'art'), creating a bohemian atmosphere. The European menu has a hearty selection of meat and fish, with plenty of Russian classics, plus the odd Asian dish to spice things up. There is live music nightly at 8.30pm.

GIN NO TAKI
JAPANESE **$$**

Map p276 (www.ginnotaki.ru; pr Chernyshevskogo 17; mains R340-1250; ☉9am-1am Mon-Fri, from 11am Sat & Sun; 🔊🖊; ⓂChernyshevskaya) In a city awash with wannabe Japanese restaurants, this large, lively operation is one of the most authentic, with a wide range of sushi, sashimi, kebabs, tempura and bento box lunches. A photo menu makes ordering

no hassle at all, and their homemade beer is an excellent accompaniment to any meal.

MOSKVA
INTERNATIONAL **$$**

Map p276 (Москва; 🗹812-640 1616; www.moskvavpitere.ru; 6th fl, Nevsky Centre, Nevsky pr 114; mains R420-1480; ☉10am-midnight; ❄🔊🖊📶; ⓂPloshchad Vosstaniya) On the top floor of the Nevsky Centre shopping mall on Petersburg's main street, Moskva has a handy location and tons of space. The pictorial menu is incredibly large: whatever you're in the mood for, you'll find it here, including a children's playroom. The best seats are on the terrace overlooking the city outside, but you'll need to reserve ahead for these.

FRANCESCO
ITALIAN **$$**

Map p276 (🗹812-275 0552; Suvorovsky pr 47; mains R530-2050; ☉9am-midnight Mon-Fri, from 11am Sat & Sun; 🔊; ⓂChernyshevskaya) Made to feel like a large family home, this charmingly decorated Italian restaurant comes complete with birds in cages, sideboards full of crockery and old photographs on the wall. The service is very good, food is excellent and there's an altogether lovely atmosphere.

BUREAU
BURGERS **$$**

Map p276 (Бюро; www.blog.barbureau.ru; ul Zhukovskogo 29; burgers R310-490; ☉1pm-midnight; 🔊) Among the many new burger joints sprouting up around SPB, stylish Bureau stands out for its quality offerings, with delicious toppings (carmelised onions, blue cheese), craft beer on tap and appealing sides (rosemary potatoes, antipasti plates). There's also a brunch inside the Street Art Museum (p167).

MECHTA MOLOKHOVETS
RUSSIAN $$$

Map p276 (Мечта Молоховецъ; ☑812-929 2247; www.molokhovets.ru; ul Radishcheva 10; mains R950-2200; ⊙noon-11pm; ❄☏; Ⓜ Ploshchad Vosstaniya) Inspired by the cookbook of Elena Molokhovets, the menu at 'Molokhovets' Dream' covers all the classics from borsch to beef stroganoff, as well as less frequently seen dishes such as venison tenderloin with juniper sauce or wild mushrooms with sour cream and pickled onions. Whatever you have here, you can be sure it's the definitive version.

PALKIN
RUSSIAN $$$

Map p276 (Палкинъ; ☑812-703 5371; www.palkin.ru; Nevsky pr 47; mains R1200-3700; ⊙noon-midnight; ☏⑂; Ⓜ Mayakovskaya) This historic restaurant, which has roots dating back to 1785, evokes a touch of royal grandeur with its elegantly set dining room, exquisite cuisine and rather theatrical service. Start off with caviar or foie gras, before moving on to grilled Ladoga white fish or beef Stroganoff a la Palkin.

BLOK
STEAK $$$

Map p276 (Блок; ☑812-415 4040; www.blok.restaurant; Potyomkinskaya ul 4; mains R750-5800; ⊙noon-1am; ☏; Ⓜ Chernyshevskaya) On the top floor of the Leningrad Centre, Blok aims to dazzle with big, bold artworks, a sculptural chandelier running down the glass-covered ceiling, and two terraces with sweeping skyline views. None of this detracts from the star of the show: perfectly grilled steak, which comes in 23 varieties – including *muromets,* a tender perfection which is dry-aged in house.

✖ Vladimirskaya & Vosstaniya

BEKITZER
ISRAELI $

Map p276 (Бекицер; ☑812-926 4342; www.facebook.com/bktzr; ul Rubinshteyna 40; mains R180-450; ⊙noon-6am Mon-Fri, from noon Sat & Sun; ☏⑂; Ⓜ Dostoyevskaya) Always crowded and spilling out into the street, this Israel-themed eatery and drinking den lures hip and joyful people with its creative cocktails, Israeli Shiraz and the best falafel wraps this side of the Baltic sea. Other culinary temptations include sabich salad (with eggplant, egg, hummus and tahini), appetiser spreads with baba ghanoush and pitas, and rather imaginative matzah pizzas.

BGL CAFE & MARKET
BAGELS $

(nab reki Fontanki 96; mains R170-340; ⊙11am-11pm; ☏⑂) Finally, somewhere decent to enjoy bagels! This sunny little cafe is popular with a young, well-read crowd, and has a great location overlooking the Fontanka River. Start the day off with a bagel stuffed with omelette, bacon and cheese; salmon and avocado; or hummus and baked peppers. There's also decent coffee, desserts and kindhearted staff.

GREEN ROOM CAFE
RUSSIAN $

Map p276 (Кофейня Зелёная Комната; Ligivosky pr 74; mains R170-260; ⊙9am-11pm; ☏⑂; Ⓜ Ligovsky Prospekt) You'll find the in-house cafe of the super cool Loft Project ETAGI on the 3rd floor (go through the courtyard). The centrepiece here is a fantastic summer terrace, which is a fine place for snacks and drinks. The converted industrial space has an airy interior, with plants and other organic elements, and an excellent-value menu.

GREY'S
BISTRO $

Map p276 (www.greys-bistro.ru; Konnaya ul 5/3; mains R380-580; ⊙11am-11pm; ☏; Ⓜ Pl Vosstaniya) The name may be literal (the walls are an understated light grey that complements the dark timber floors and stylish lighting), but the food is far from dour. Grey's excels at uncomplicated classics like fish soup, homemade roasts, rack of lamb and grilled trout, along with popular desserts like berry tart – all quite reasonably priced.

GASTRONOMIKA
INTERNATIONAL $$

Map p276 (☑812-640 1616; 6th fl, Stremyannaya ul 21; mains R560-1290; ⊙noon-1am; ☏⑂; Ⓜ Vladimiriskaya) On the top floor of the Olympic Plaza shopping complex, Gastronomika is the go-to spot for a wide-ranging menu of pizzas, barbecue brisket, Asian noodle soups and salmon or halibut with rich sauces. The cooking gets solid reviews, but the real draw is the outstanding view over the rooftops of St Petersburg.

A party vibe prevails on weekends, when DJs spin from 9pm onward, and diners receive a welcome drink.

TASTE TO EAT
RUSSIAN **$$**

(Вкус Есть; ☎812-983 3376; http://tastetoeat. tastetoeat.ru; nab reki Fontanki 82; mains R480-680; ⊙1-11pm; 🛜) This popular, handsomely designed restaurant along the Fontanka River serves up quality ingredients from across Russia in innovative dishes like smoked mackerel paté, orzo with crab from Kamchatka, and curry with lamb stewed in *kvas*. With its sun-filled big windows, comfy leather seating and good wine list, it makes a fine setting for a leisurely meal, day or night.

GEOGRAFIYA
INTERNATIONAL **$$**

Map p276 (География; ☎812-340 0074; www. geo-rest.com; ul Rubinshteyna 5; R450-700; ⊙noon-midnight; 🛜🖊; Ⓜ Mayakovskaya) True to its name, this hip place takes diners on a culinary journey around the globe, with a standout menu of Singapore-style noodles with seafood, Szechuan beef with jasmine rice and Thai coconut soup, plus plenty of Russian classics (like homemade dumplings).

An equally eclectic soundtrack, vintage travel posters, and a huge cocktail menu all set the stage for a fine start to the night. DJs spin on Friday and Saturday nights (from 9pm).

SCHASTYE
ITALIAN **$$**

Map p276 (Счастье; ☎812-572 2675; www. schastye.com; ul Rubinshteyna 15/17; mains R420-800; ⊙9am-midnight Mon-Fri, from 10am Sat & Sun; 🛜🖊; Ⓜ Mayakovskaya) 'Happiness' comes in several forms here: a multiroomed venue full of cosy nooks and crannies to huddle up in, an expansive Italian menu, delicious pastries and tempting sweets, and lavish and thoroughly warm (if somewhat random) decor (think jars full of pasta and photo frames with stock shots of family members).

BAKLAZHAN
GEORGIAN **$$**

Map p276 (Баклажан; ☎812-677 7372; www. ginza.ru; Ligovsky pr 30A; mains R500-900; ⊙8am-11pm; 🛜🖊; Ⓜ Ploshchad Vosstaniya) On the fourth floor of the posh Galeria shopping center, Baklazhan is another success from the Ginza chain. The stylish setting, piping hot *khachapuri* (cheese bread) and excellent Georgian cuisine will make you forget you're dining in a mall. *Baklazhan* (eggplant) plays a starring role in tasty roasted eggplant salads and stuffed eggplant with cheese.

🍺 DRINKING & NIGHTLIFE

🍸 Smolny & Liteyny

★ UNION BAR & GRILL
BAR

Map p276 (www.facebook.com/barunion; Liteyny pr 55; ⊙6pm-4am Sun-Thu, to 6am Fri & Sat; 🛜; Ⓜ Mayakovskaya) The Union is a glamorous and fun place, characterised by one enormous long wooden bar, low lighting and a New York feel. It's all rather adult, with a serious cocktail list and designer beers on tap. The hip 20- and 30-something crowd packs in on weekends to catch live bands, but it's generally quiet during the week.

There's good snack fare (burgers, hummus with pita, shawarma) from the grill in the back room, and a tiny rear patio for the smoking crowd.

★ HAT
BAR

Map p276 (ul Belinskogo 9; ⊙7pm-5am; Ⓜ Gostiny Dvor) The wonderfully retro-feeling Hat is a serious spot for jazz and whiskey lovers, who come for the nightly live music and the cool cat crowd that makes this wonderfully designed bar feel like it's been transported out of 1950s Greenwich Village. A very welcome change of gear for St Petersburg's drinking options, but it can be extremely packed at weekends.

★ COMMODE
BAR

Map p276 (www.commode.club; ul Rubinshteyna 1, 2nd fl; per hr R180; ⊙4pm-2am Sun-Thu, to 6am Fri & Sat) Stopping in for drinks at Commode feels more like hanging out in an upper-class friend's stylish apartment. After getting buzzed up, you can hang out in various high-ceilinged rooms, catch a small concert or poetry slam, browse books in the quasi-library room, play a round of table football, or chat with the easygoing crowd that have fallen for the place.

Drink and snack prices and are kept low (cocktails run R100 to R150), but you'll pay by the hour – not unlike an anticafe – for time spent at this so-called self-cost bar.

★ REDRUM
BAR

Map p276 (☎812-416 1126; www.facebook.com/ redrumbarspb; ul Nekrasova 26; ⊙4pm-1am Sun-Thu, to 3am Fri & Sat; Ⓜ Mayakovskaya) One of St Petersburg's best drinking dens, Redrum hits all the right notes. It has a cosy, white brick interior, a welcoming, easygoing crowd, and a stellar line-up of craft brews (some two dozen on tap). There's also good pub fare on hand to go with that creative line-up of Session Indian Pale Ales, sour ales, Berliner Weisse and porters.

Have a seat at the small circular bar and get ordering tips from the friendly bartenders, who will be happy to point you in the right direction.

DEAD POETS BAR   COCKTAIL BAR

Map p276 (☏812-449 4656; www.deadpoetsbar. com; ul Zhukovskogo 12; ☺2pm-2am Sun-Thu, to 8am Fri & Sat; ☎; MMayakovskaya) This very cool place has a sophisticated drinks menu and an almost unbelievable range of spirits stacked along the long bar and served up by a committed staff of mixologists. It's more of a quiet place, with low lighting, a jazz soundtrack and plenty of space to sit down.

TERMINAL BAR   BAR

Map p276 (ul Belinskogo 11; ☺2pm-4am; ☎; MMayakovskaya) A slice of New York bohemia on one of the city's most happening streets, Terminal is great for a relaxed drink with friends, in a small, intimate setting. Bar staff take their cocktails seriously.

MISHKA   BAR

Map p276 (Мишка; www.facebook.com/bar. mishka; nab reki Fontanki 40; ☺6pm-2am Mon-Thu, 2pm-6am Fri-Sun; ☎; MGostiny Dvor) Hipster ground zero in St Petersburg is this two-room basement place that is massively popular with a cool student crowd. The frenetic front room becomes a dancefloor later in the evening, while the quiet backroom is a chill-out area. DJs spin nightly and there's a big cocktail list.

BAR 812   COCKTAIL BAR

Map p276 (www.bar812.ru; ul Zhukovskogo 11; ☺6pm-1am Mon-Thu, until 4am Fri & Sat; ☎;

MMayakovskaya) The brass bar here is one of the most popular in the city (not to mention one of the more pricey). It has beautifully made cocktails and draws a heaving crowd on weekends. Come during the week for a more laid back and relaxed sipping experience.

FREEDOM   ANTICAFE

Map p276 (Nevsky pr 88; per min R2; ☺noon-midnight Sun-Thu, until 6am Fri & Sat; ☎; MMayakovskaya) In a courtyard off Nevsky pr, this very popular anticafe is spacious and friendly and full of rooms where you can play board games, watch TV, hang out and meet like-minded boho types.

There are occasional music jams, and a piano and guitar if you wish to play.

ZIFERBURG   ANTICAFE

Map p276 (nab reki Fontanki 20; per min R3; ☺11am-midnight; MGostiny Dvor) Tucked inside the Golitsyn Loft, this is one of St Petersburg's loveliest spots to while away an afternoon. Elegant furnishings, huge windows and a piano in the corner set the scene. Like other anti-cafes, you'll pay by the minute, with drinks and cookies part of the deal.

The price tops out at R540, meaning you won't pay more than that even if you spend all day here.

FARSH & BOCHKA   BAR

Map p276 (www.beercard.ru; ul Belinskogo 11; ☺5pm-midnight Mon-Thu, noon-2am Fri & Sat, noon-midnight Sun) On bar-lined ul Belinskogo, Farsh & Bochka stands out for its wide-ranging line-up of craft brews, with over 30 on draft, including SPB and Russian varieties. It's a noisy, buzzing place – a fine spot to catch a game or have a low-key night while sipping a full-bodied Vienna-style lager and munching on barbecued meats, rosemary fries or shrimp tacos.

SMOLNY & VOSSTANIYA DRINKING & NIGHTLIFE

DRINKS WITH A VIEW

Sky Bar (Top fl, Hotel Azimut, Lermontovsky pr 43/1; ☺5pm-1am; ☎; MBaltiyskaya) The top floor of the Soviet-era Azimut Hotel, one of the city's biggest eyesores, is also home to the Sky Bar, quite simply the best place to get a bird's-eye view of the city. Taking up much of the 18th floor, the bar has plenty of space to sit back and enjoy the incredible view of the historic centre through its vast floor-to-ceiling windows. In addition to cocktails and coffee, there's also a full food menu.

Even the nearest metro is some distance away, however, so it's best to wander here along the Fontanka from the centre.

NA ZDOROVYE!

'To your health!' is what Russians say when they throw back a shot of vodka. But this pronouncement hardly suffices as a proper toast in a public forum or an intimate drinking session among friends. A proper toast requires thoughtfulness and sincerity.

A few themes prevail. The first toast of the night often acknowledges the generosity of the host, while the second usually recognises the beauty of the ladies present. In mixed company, you can't go wrong raising your glass to international friendship (*za mezhdunarodnuyu druzhbu*) or world peace (*za miravoy mir*). But in all cases, the toast requires a personal anecdote or a profound insight, as well as a bit of rambling preamble to make it meaningful.

In Russia, drinking vodka is a celebration of life in all its complexity – the triumph, the tragedy and the triviality. A toast is a vocalisation of that celebration, so say it like you mean it. And drink it in the same way – *zalpom* – bottoms up!

PIVNAYA KARTA
BAR

Map p276 (www.beercard.ru; ul Vosstaniya 55; ◷noon-11pm; ⓜChernyshevskaya) A mecca for beer lovers, Pivnaya Karta has over 400 varieties of beer from around the globe, with some 20 different rotating draft selections. That said, it's a small stand-up space that feels more bottle shop than bar, and of interest for only a small slice of SPB society.

🍺 Vladimirskaya & Vosstaniya

★ZIFERBLAT
ANTICAFE

Map p276 (Циферблат; ☎981-180 7022; www.ziferblat.net; 2nd fl, Nevsky pr 81; per min R3, after first hr R2 per min; ◷11am-midnight; 🛜; ⓜPloshchad Vosstaniya) A charming multiroom 'free space' that has started a worldwide trend, Ziferblat is the original anticafe in St Petersburg. Coffee, tea, soft drinks and biscuits are included as you while away time playing chess and other board games, reading, playing instruments (help yourself to the piano and guitar) or just hanging out with the arty young locals who frequent its rooms.

The unsigned entrance is hard to find. Look for the big #81 sign on Nevsky pr, then find the door with buzzers just east of there. Ring Циферблат (labelled in Russian only).

BEER GEEK
CRAFT BEER

Map p276 (Биргик; ☎812-643 2484; https://vk.com/beergeekspb; ul Rubinshteyna 2/45; ◷noon-midnight; ⓜMayakovskaya) Duck into the courtyard to find this very cosy basement bar that's recommended by local beer fanatics for its regularly updated range of 12 local and international craft ales on tap and curated selection of bottles to drink in or take out.

Sit either on the couple of stools at the bar or on some wooden tiered steps alongside three cuddly toy tigers and a moose!

DYUNI
BAR

Map p276 (Дюны; www.facebook.com/dunes.on.ligovsky; Ligovsky pr 50; ◷noon-3am Sun-Thu, to 6am Fri & Sat; 🛜; ⓜPloshchad Vosstaniya) What looks like a small suburban house sits rather incongruously here amid repurposed warehouses in this vast courtyard. There's a cosy indoor bar and a sand-covered outside area with table football and ping pong, which keeps the cool kids happy all night in the summer months. To find it, simply continue 300m in a straight line from the courtyard entrance on Ligovsky pr.

DJs spin from Wednesdays to Sundays, with the odd band from time to time.

FISH FABRIQUE NOUVELLE
LIVE MUSIC

Map p276 (www.fishfabrique.spb.ru; Ligovsky pr 53; ◷3pm-late; ⓜPloshchad Vosstaniya) This legendary bar is set in the building that's the focus of the avant-garde art scene – it attracts an interesting crowd who give this cramped space its edge. Live bands kick up a storm most nights around 10pm.

ETO BAR
BAR

Map p276 (Vladimirsky per 14; ◷6pm-2am Sun-Thu, to 6am Fri & Sat; ⓜVladimirskaya) An easygoing newcomer to the nightlife scene, Eto is a cosy, brick-walled space with a wooden bar (recycled from the theatre stage next door) and live music nightly from 9pm to midnight. Stop in for good wines by the glass (from R270), classic cocktails and an eclectic lineup of jazz, blues and rockabilly.

If you play an instrument, ask about joining in. Look for the archway entrance just visible from the street.

GRIBOYEDOV · CLUB

Map p276 (Грибоедов; www.griboedovclub. ru; Voronezhskaya ul 2a; ⊙noon-6am Mon-Fri, from 2pm Sat & Sun; ☎; ⓂLigovsky Prospekt) Griboyedov is hands-down the longest-standing and most respected music club in the city. Housed in a repurposed bomb shelter, this one was founded by local ska collective Dva Samolyota. It's a low-key bar in the early evening, gradually morphing into a dance club later in the night. Admission varies from free to upwards of R400, depending on who's playing or spinning.

BIRRERIA · BAR

Map p276 (Биррерия; www.facebook.com/ birreriaspb; 2nd fl, Vladimirsky pr 19, Vladimirsky Passage; ⊙noon-2am; ⓂVladimirskaya) On the second floor of the Vladimirsky Passage shopping complex, this upscale place has an excellent line-up of Belgian, German and English beers on tap and far more selections by the bottle. Good bistro fare and great views of the Vladimirsky Cathedral.

 # ★ ENTERTAINMENT

JFC JAZZ CLUB · JAZZ

Map p276 (☏812-272 9850; www.jfc-club.spb.ru; Shpalernaya ul 33; cover R200-500; ⊙7-10pm; ⓂChernyshevskaya) Very small and very New York, this cool club is the best place in the city to hear modern, innovative jazz music, as well as blues, bluegrass and various other styles (see the website for a list of what's on). The space is tiny, so book a table online if you want to sit down.

RED FOX JAZZ CAFÉ · JAZZ

Map p276 (Красный лис; ☏812-275 4214; www. rfjc.ru; ul Mayakovskogo 50; cover R200-300; ⊙10am-11am Mon-Fri, from 1.30pm Sat, from 4.30pm Sun; ⓂChernyshevskaya) The fun and friendly Red Fox Jazz Café is a subterranean space that showcases various jazz styles in the old-fashioned 1920s to '50s sense: big band, bebop, ragtime and swing. Sunday changes it up with a jam session, featuring anybody who wants to participate. The menu is extensive and affordable and you can reserve a table for free. Music starts at 8.30pm.

FISH FABRIQUE · LIVE MUSIC

Map p276 (http://fishfabrique.ru; Ligovsky pr 53; ⊙noon-4am daily, concerts from 8pm Thu-Sun; ☎; ⓂPloshchad Vosstaniya) There are St Peters-burg institutions and then there's Fish Fabrique, the museum of local boho life that has been going for over two decades. Here, in the dark underbelly of Pushkinskaya 10, artists, musicians and counter-culturalists of all ages meet to drink beer and listen to music.

Nowadays, the newer Fabrique Nouvelle in the same courtyard hosts concerts nightly, while the old Fish Fabrique only has them on weekends; whichever one you're in, you're sure to rub shoulders with an interesting crowd.

CABARET · LIVE PERFORMANCE

Map p276 (Кабаре; www.cabarespb.ru; Razyezzhaya ul 43; cover R300-600; ⊙11pm-6am Thu-Sat; ⓂLigovsky Prospekt) This latest incarnation of a gay club that has been going in various forms for over a decade is a great place for a campy, old-school experience, with a very popular drag show featuring lip-synching drag queens who come on stage at 2.30am each club night and impersonate Russian and international stars. Lots of silly fun, but massively popular.

COSMONAUT · LIVE MUSIC

(Космонавт; www.cosmonavt.su; ul Bronnitskaya 24; tickets R300-800; ☎; ⓂTekhnologichesky Institut) This fantastic conversion of a Soviet-era cinema in a rather nondescript part of town is a great venue for medium-sized concerts and a good place to see live acts in St Petersburg. There's air-conditioning, which is a godsend in summer, and a very comfortable VIP lounge upstairs, with seating throughout.

JAZZ PHILHARMONIC HALL · JAZZ

(www.jazz-hall.com; Zagorodny pr 27; cover R1200-1500; ⊙concerts 7pm or 8pm Wed-Sun; ⓂVladimirskaya) Founded by legendary jazz violinist and composer David Goloshchokin, this venue represents the more traditional side of jazz. Two resident bands perform straight jazz and Dixieland in the big hall, which seats up to 200 people. The smaller Ellington Hall is used for occasional acoustic performances. Foreign guests also appear doing mainstream and modern jazz; check the website for details.

BOLSHOY PUPPET THEATRE · PUPPET THEATRE

Map p276 (Большой театр кукол; www.puppets. ru; ul Nekrasova 10; tickets R350-600; ⓂChernyshevskaya) This 'big' puppet theatre is indeed the biggest in the city, and has been active

SMOLNY & VOSSTANIYA ENTERTAINMENT

since 1931. The repertoire includes a wide range of shows for children and for adults.

MALY DRAMA THEATRE
THEATRE

Map p276 (Малый драматический театр; www.mdt-dodin.ru; ul Rubinshteyna 18; Ⓜ Vladimirskaya) Also called the Theatre of Europe, the Maly is St Petersburg's most celebrated theatre. Its director Lev Dodin is famed for his long version of Fyodor Dostoevsky's *The Devils,* as well as Anton Chekhov's *Play Without a Name,* which both toured the world to great acclaim. It's also one of the few theatres that does (some) performances with subtitles.

🛍 SHOPPING

IMPERIAL PORCELAIN
HOMEWARES

(Императорский Фарфор; www.ipm.ru; pr Obukhovsky Oborony 151; ⊘10am-8pm; Ⓜ Lomonosovskaya) Dating back to the mid-18th century, this is the company that made tea sets for the Russian royal family. Formerly known as Lomonosov China, the company continues to produce innovative designs – the speciality being contemporary takes on traditional themes. The stuff is expensive, but the quality is high and the designs can be spectacular.

PHONOTEKA
MUSIC

Map p276 (Фонотека; www.phonoteka.ru; ul Marata 28; ⊘10am-10pm; Ⓜ Mayakovskaya) This store will thrill anyone interested in music and cinema, as it sells a very cool range of vinyls from all eras (it's particularly strong on rare Soviet discs), a great selection of CDs from around the world and a discerning choice of film and documentary on DVD, making it an excellent place to buy Russian films.

ANGLIA
BOOKS

Map p276 (nab reki Fontanki 30; ⊘10am-8pm Mon-Fri, from 11am Sat, noon-7pm Sun; Ⓜ Gostiny Dvor) The city's only dedicated English-language bookshop has a good selection of contemporary literature, classics, dictionaries, history and travel writing – plus a dedicated section on Russia. It also hosts small art and photography displays, organises book readings and generally is a cornerstone of expat life in St Petersburg.

TULA SAMOVARS
GIFTS & SOUVENIRS

(Тульские самовары; www.samovary.ru; ul Gorokhovaya 69; ⊘10am-8pm; Ⓜ Pushkinskaya) Nearly all samovars (metal containers holding boiling water) in Russia are made in the town of Tula, south of Moscow, but this beautiful showroom is the place in St Petersburg to buy a unique souvenir of your visit. The samovars range from small, simple designs to enormous and elaborate ones with precious stones and other embellishments.

GALERIA
SHOPPING CENTRE

Map p276 (Галерея; www.galeria.spb.ru; Ligovsky pr 30A; ⊘10am-11pm; Ⓜ Ploshchad Vosstaniya) This extraordinary place has rather changed everything for shopping in St Petersburg – there are probably as many shops here as elsewhere in the entire city centre. Spread over five floors, with around 300 shops (including H&M, Michael Kors, Marks & Spencer, Kiehl's and Zara), this really is a one-stop shop for pretty much all your shopping needs.

When hunger strikes, head up to the excellent Georgian restaurant Baklazhan (p136), on the fourth floor.

NEVSKY CENTRE
SHOPPING CENTRE

Map p276 (Невский Центр; www.nevskycentre.ru; Nevsky pr 112; ⊘10am-11pm; Ⓜ Ploshchad Vosstaniya) Nevsky Centre is a smart, central multifloor shopping centre. It houses some 70 shops over seven floors, including the city's largest department store, Stockmann, which includes the excellent basement Stockmann supermarket. Elsewhere there's a food court and well-known clothing shops, including H&M, Lacoste and Tommy Hilfiger, plus a Thai-style massage centre on the sixth floor.

IMPERIAL PORCELAIN
HOMEWARES

Map p276 (Императорский Фарфор; www.ipm.ru; Vladimirsky pr 7; ⊘10am-8pm; Ⓜ Vladimirskaya) This is one of many convenient city-centre locations of the famous porcelain factory that once made tea sets for the Romanovs. If you're determined to get a bargain, head out to the factory outlet where prices are a bit cheaper.

TATYANA PARFIONOVA
FASHION & ACCESSORIES

Map p276 (Татьяна Парфёнова; www.parfionova.ru; Nevsky pr 51; ⊘noon-8pm; Ⓜ Mayakovskaya) Tatyana Parfionova was the first St Petersburg designer to have her own fashion house back in 1995, when New Russians turned up their noses at anything that was not straight from Paris or Milan. Now this local celebrity showcases her stuff at her Nevsky pr boutique, where you'll find her striking monochromatic *prêt-à-porter* designs as well as her famous scarves.

Each scarf is an extraordinary work of art – one of a kind, made from silk and elaborately hand-embroidered in a painstaking process that takes three to four months (with prices from R179,000). Less expensive in-store items include shoes, pillowcases and duvet covers.

BOREY ART CENTRE ART

Map p276 (Борей Артцентр; www.borey.ru; Liteyny pr 58; ☺noon-8pm Tue-Sat; MMayakovskaya) There is never a dull moment at this underground (in both senses of the word) art gallery. In the front room, you'll see some fairly mainstream stuff for sale, but the back rooms always house creative contemporary exhibitions by local artists.

SOL-ART ART

Map p276 (www.solartgallery.com; Solyanoy per 15; ☺10am-6pm; MChernyshevskaya) In the sumptuous surroundings of the Museum of Decorative & Applied Arts, this is a great place to buy contemporary local art. You'll find quite extensive selections here, from small prints (starting at R500) to large-format works by acclaimed painters that cost hundreds of times that. In business for over 20 years, Sol-Art has a solid reputation, and also ships worldwide.

OFF VINTAGE

(www.offoffoff.ru; nab Obvodnogo kanala 60; ☺noon-9pm Sun-Tue, to 10pm Wed-Sat; MObvodny Kanal) Inside the Tkachi 'Cultural Space' is this paradise for anyone after some Soviet accessories, vintage jackets and secondhand clothes of varying styles. The friendly owner may take it upon herself to find just the right outfit for you – and she clearly knows what she's doing judging by her own appearance.

BEE-KEEPING FOOD & DRINKS

Map p276 (Пчеловодство; www.pchelovodstvo-spb.ru/kontakti; Liteyny ul 46; ☺9am-9pm; MSennaya Ploshchad) This quirky shop sells honey, beeswax and even beekeeping outfits. You can sample many different flavours of honey *(myod)* from all over Russia, and there are also natural remedies, creams and teas made from beeswax and pollen.

IMPERIAL PORCELAIN CERAMICS

Map p276 (Императорский Фарфор; www.ipm shop.com; Nevsky pr 160; ☺10am-9pm; MPloshchad Vosstaniya) The famed porcelain makers have been in business since the 1740s (but was of course nationalised during the Soviet period). One of several shops in St Petersburg, here you'll find exquisite tea sets, plates and decorative items with Russian themes (Anna Akhmatova, Pushkin, Russian fairytales). Worldwide shipping available.

TKACHI SHOPPING CENTRE

(Ткачи; www.tkachi.com; nab Obvodnogo kanala 60; ☺10am-10pm; MObvodny Kanal) In an otherwise derelict part of town, 'Weavers' is an impressive conversion of a warehouse into a 'creative space', which more often than not in Petersburg means shops and cafes with a vague nod in the direction of art. On the ground floor you'll find gifts, clothes, bikes and electronics, while the 5th floor is a huge exhibition space and restaurant.

RUSSKAYA STARINA ANTIQUES

Map p276 (Русская старина; ul Nekrasova 6; ☺11am-9pm, from noon Sun; MMayakovskaya, Chernyshevskaya) This fascinating place is a repository of local antiques and has a wide range of stock running from furniture and paintings to medals and samovars. It's well worth a look, and the low-pressure sales technique invites browsing.

IMAGINE CLUB MUSIC

Map p276 (www.imagine-club.com; ul Zhukovskogo 20; ☺10am-10pm; MPloshchad Vosstaniya) St Petersburg's largest record shop, and by record we do actually mean vinyl as well as CDs, is a great place to buy some quality Russian music souvenirs. LPs from all over the former Soviet Union can be found here, as well as an impressive choice of imports from Western Europe and the US.

KRAKATAU FASHION & ACCESSORIES

Map p276 (www.krakatau.ru; Ligovsky pr 74; ☺noon-9pm; MLigovsky Prospekt) Handsomely tailored men's wear is sold from this Russian outfitter in Loft Project ETAGI. Ruggedlooking jackets, trousers and sneakers come in muted colour schemes – making them easy additions to the wardrobe.

LASER B FASHION & ACCESSORIES

Map p276 (www.laserb.ru; Ligovsky pr 74; ☺noon-9pm; MLigovsky Prospekt) Inside the Loft Project ETAGI complex, Laser B has Russian-made designs you won't find elsewhere, including boldly patterned T-shirts, dresses and button-downs, plus whimsical backpacks and other accessories.

SMOLNY & VOSSTANIYA SHOPPING

SNEGIRI
FASHION & ACCESSORIES

Map p276 (Снегири; ☎812-987 7669; www.sne girivalenki.ru; ul Vosstaniya 24; ⓜPloshchad Vosstaniya) The traditional craft of Russian felt slippers and booties made from thick-fibred wool from Romanov sheep has been given a contemporary spin here. Their cosy footwear comes in a range of colours and styles and can be bought from a cut wooden cabin in the Fligel creative courtyard complex, behind the post office on the main street.

KUZNECHNY MARKET
MARKET

Map p276 (Кузнечный рынок; Kuznechny per 3; ⊙8am-8pm Mon-Sat, to 7pm Sun; ⓜVladimirskaya) The colours and atmosphere of the city's largest fruit-and-vegetable market are a wonderful experience: the vendors will ply you with free samples of fresh fruits, homemade *smetana* (sour cream) and sweet honey. You'll also find a few souvenir stalls as well as a tempting chocolate counter.

BAT NORTON
CLOTHING

Map p276 (www.batnorton.com; nab reki Fontanki 50; ⊙10am-10pm; ⓜDostoevskaya) This local streetwear brand has the tagline 'made in Russia' and its bright, psychedelic and playful unisex clothing is popular with a cool, younger crowd.

NEVSKY 152
FASHION & ACCESSORIES

Map p276 (www.nevsky152.ru; Nevsky pr 152; ⊙11am-9pm) This is a one-stop 'concept store' for big-name international fashion brands in St Petersburg, as the well-dressed doorman will make abundantly clear. Come here for boutiques from such names as Chanel, Fendi and Armani.

🏃 SPORTS & ACTIVITIES

COACHMEN'S BANYA
BATHHOUSE

Map p276 (Yamskiye Bani; ☎812-312 5836; www.yamskie.ru; ul Dostoevskogo 9; R300-600; ⊙8am-11pm, last entrance 9pm; ⓜVladimirskaya) Multilevel complex with both ordinary and lux *banya* as well as private rooms and saunas for you to rent with up to eight friends. The attendants are friendly and the patrons take their bathing very seriously. Last entry to all baths is 9pm.

DEGTYARNIYE BATHS
BATHHOUSE

Map p276 (Дегтярные Бани; ☎812-985 1983; www.d1a.ru; Degtyarnaya ul 1a; per hr R400-750, private banya R4500-17,500; ⊙8.30am-10pm; ⓜPloshchad Vosstaniya) These modern baths are divided up into men's and women's sections, or you can book private unisex *bani* (hot baths) of varying degrees of luxury (these accommodate up to 14 people). Prices are cheaper before 1pm on weekdays. Minimum charge of two hours.

MYTNINSKIYE BANI
BATHHOUSE

Map p276 (Мытнинские бани; www.mybanya. spb.ru; ul Mytninskaya 17-19; per hr R200-350; ⊙8am-10pm Fri-Tue; ⓜPloshchad Vosstaniya) Unique in the city, Mytninskiye Bani is heated by a wood furnace, just like the log-cabin bathhouses that are still found in the Russian countryside. It's actually the oldest communal *banya* (hot bath) in the city, and in addition to a *parilka* (steam room) and plunge pool, the private 'lux' *banya* (R1000 to R2000 per hour) includes a swanky lounge area with leather furniture and a pool table.

KAZACHIYE BANI
BATHHOUSE

(Казачьи бани; www.kazbani.ru; Bolshoy Kazachy per 11; per 2hr R100-300, private banya per hr R850-1700; ⊙8am-10pm Tue-Sun; ⓜPushkinskaya) Following a trend that is occurring throughout the city, the communal *banya* is something of an afterthought here. The majority of the venue is given over to very swanky, private *bani*, which are an excellent option for groups of up to 10 people. The cheaper communal *banya* is good value though.

Tuesday, Thursday and Saturday are for women; Wednesday, Friday and Sunday are for men.

KOPEJKA WORLD
SCENIC DRIVE

(Копейка Мир; ☎931-585 1021; www.kopejkaworld.com; 2hr tour R6000) This new outfit offers guided tours from aboard its classic Soviet cars – the VAZ-2101, aka the 'Kopejka'. Roof cutouts allow you to get a different perspective on St Petersburg, while guides explain some of the lesser-known aspects of this grand city.

Vasilyevsky Island

Neighbourhood Top Five

❶ Strelka (p147) Taking in one of the best views of the city from the historic spit of land that crowns Vasilyevsky Island and boasts flaming Rostral Columns during national holidays.

❷ Kunstkamera (p146) Exploring Peter the Great's ghoulish collection of anatomical oddities as well as other ethnographic curiosities.

❸ Erarta Museum of Contemporary Art (p145) Checking out St Petersburg's best modern art museum, with a huge collection of Russian works from the late Soviet and post-Soviet era.

❹ Menshikov Palace (p148) Visiting this beautifully preserved palace, St Petersburg's first stone building.

❺ Icebreaker Krasin (p148) Hearing tales of Soviet exploration in the Arctic aboard this retired icebreaker.

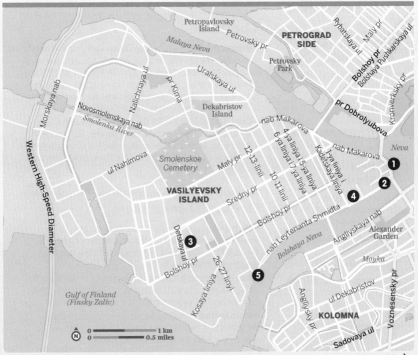

For more detail of this area see Map p286 ➡

Lonely Planet's Top Tip

The **Palace Bridge Wellness Club** (p153) is one of the city's best places for a sauna and swimming. If you're travelling with children under three, drop in on a Wednesday when it's parents and under-threes only from 7am to 6.30pm. Every day, children under three pay nothing and those between three and 14 get in for half-price, but only before 6pm; after that it's adults only.

Best Places to Eat

➡ Restoran (p152)

➡ Buter Brodsky (p151)

➡ Marketplace (p151)

➡ Khachapuri i Vino (p151)

➡ Pryanosti & Radosti (p151)

For reviews, see p151 ➡

Best Places to Drink

➡ Beer Boutique 1516 (p152)

➡ Radosti Kofe (p152)

➡ Birzha Bar (p153)

For reviews, see p152 ➡

Best Museums

➡ Erarta Museum of Contemporary Art (p145)

➡ Kunstkamera (p146)

➡ Museum of Zoology (p149)

➡ Menshikov Palace (p148)

For reviews, see p147 ➡

Explore Vasilyevsky Island

This large, triangular island is among the oldest neighbourhoods in St Petersburg, especially the eastern tip known as the Strelka (p147) ('tongue of land'). Crammed with classical buildings housing institutions, excellent museums such as the Kunstkamera (p146) and Menshikov Palace (p148), and the sprawling campus of St Petersburg State University, this is the best place to start your exploration of the island.

Further back from the Strelka, Vasilyevsky Ostrov (or VO as it's commonly shortened to) is an orderly, residential place, with a grid system of wide roads lined with shops, restaurants and cafes. Make a beeline for the Russian Academy of Arts Museum (p148), the historic St Andrew's Cathedral (p149), the stunningly decorated Temple of the Assumption (p148), and the compact Novy Museum (p147) showcasing late-20th-century art from the Soviet Union.

The northern and western ends of the island are rather post industrial and remote. Even so, there are things worth coming out this way to see, including the fantastic Erarta Museum of Contemporary Art (p145), and the chance to tour around the Icebreaker Krasin (p148) and two submarines. Transport wonks will also be thrilled to find museums devoted to the city's metro and tram systems.

Local Life

➡**Bridge Advice** If you're staying on Vasilyevsky Island, remember that in the summer months the bridges go up at night. Dvortsovy most's timetable is up at 1.10am and down for 20 minutes at 2.50am before going up again until 4.55am. Blagoveshchensky most is crossable from 2.45am until 3.10am and then not again until 5am.

➡**Cool Street** Hang with the locals on 6-ya and 7-ya liniya, the main pedestrian and commercial street of Vasilyevsky Island. Lined with cafes, bars, restaurants and shops, this is where to escape the tourist crowds at the Strelka.

Getting There & Away

➡**Metro** The most useful metro stations are Vasileostrovskaya on Line 3 at the island's heart and the nab Makarova/1-ya i Kadetskaya liniya exit from Sportivnaya on Line 5.

➡**Bus** The number 7 bus goes between Primorskaya to pl Vosstaniya, via Nalichnaya ul, all of Bolshoy pr and Nevsky pr. Trolleybus 10 and 11 run similar routes.

➡**Marshrutka** From Vasileostrovskaya metro station, the following *marshrutka* buses zip to the far end of Sredny pr: K30, K44, K62 and K120.

TOP SIGHT
ERARTA MUSEUM OF CONTEMPORARY ART

Erarta's superb hoard of 2300 pieces of Russian contemporary art trumps its somewhat far-flung location. Housed in an ingeniously converted neoclassical Stalinist building, the museum is spread over five floors, with the main galleries focused on the permanent collection. There are also installation spaces, plenty of temporary exhibitions, occasional shows, plus a good restaurant and gift shop.

Permanent Collection

The permanent collection is an excellent survey of the past half-century of Russian art. It's particularly strong on late-Soviet underground art. One nice curatorial touch is the frequent inclusion of objects depicted in paintings – a bowl of apples will sit, for example, in front of a painting entitled Apple Picking.

Expanded Spaces

A new wing has significantly expanded the space for temporary exhibitions. One unusual feature is the inclusion of commercial galleries, where the work on display is also for sale. These tend to feature contemporary installations, paintings, video art and sculpture by Russian artists, and are worth checking out.

Immersive Installations

Consider trying out at least one of eight 'U Space Total Installations', (R200 for up to five people), small themed rooms that immerse you in worlds ranging from childhood to outer space. An extra ticket (R250) is also required for the Theatre With No Actors, a sound-and-vision show on the 2nd floor.

DON'T MISS

➡ *USSR*, Evgeny Savrasov

➡ *Night Shift*, Nikolai Vikulov

➡ *The Great Bear*, Rinat Voligamsi

➡ *Funeral of a Commissar*, Pyotr Gorban

➡ U Spaces

PRACTICALITIES

➡ Музей современного искусства Эрарта

➡ Map p286, C4

➡ ☏812-324 0809

➡ www.erarta.com

➡ 29-ya Liniya 2

➡ adult/under 21yr R500/350

➡ ⊙10am-10pm Wed-Mon

➡ ☏

➡ Ⓜ Vasileostrovskaya

TOP SIGHT
KUNSTKAMERA

KATIE GARROD / GETTY IMAGES ©

Also known as the Museum of Ethnology and Anthropology, the Kunstkamera was the city's first museum, founded in 1714 by Peter himself. It is famous largely for its ghoulish collection of monstrosities, preserved 'freaks', two-headed mutant foetuses, deformed animals and odd body parts, all collected by Peter, who had issued an edict that such malformed, stillborn infants were sent to him from across Russia.

Babies in Bottles

Peter wanted to demonstrate that malformations were not the result of the evil eye or sorcery, but rather caused by accidents of nature. This fascinating place is an essential St Petersburg sight, although not one for the faint-hearted. Think twice about bringing young children here and consider giving the Kunstkamera a wide berth if you are pregnant yourself. Indeed, where else can you see specimens with such charming names as 'double-faced monster with brain hernia'?

Collected Curiosities

Also part of the museum's enormous collection are some wonderfully kitsch dioramas exhibiting rare objects and demonstrating cultural practices from all over the world. The 3rd floor of the museum is given over to an exhibition about polymath Mikhail Lomonosov, with a recreation of his study-laboratory.

DON'T MISS

➡ The Stuffed Pangolin
➡ Skeletons of conjoined twins
➡ Gottorp Globe
➡ Skeleton of the Giant Bourgeois

PRACTICALITIES

➡ Кунсткамера
➡ Map p286, H2
➡ ☎812-328 1412
➡ www.kunstkamera.ru
➡ Universitetskaya nab 3, entrance on Tamozhenny per
➡ adult/child R300/100
➡ ⏰11am-7pm Tue-Sun
➡ Ⓜ Admiralteyskaya

⊙ SIGHTS

ERARTA MUSEUM OF
CONTEMPORARY ART   MUSEUM
See p145.

KUNSTKAMERA   MUSEUM
See p146.

STRELKA   LANDMARK
Map p286 (Birzhevaya pl; ⓂVasileostrovskaya)
This eastern tip of Vasilyevsky Island is
where Peter the Great wanted his new city's
administrative and intellectual centre to
be. In fact, it became the focus of the city's
maritime trade, symbolised by the colonnaded Customs House (now the Institute of
Russian Literature) and the Old Stock Exchange. The Strelka is flanked by the pair of
Rostral Columns, archetypal St Petersburg
landmarks.

The Strelka has one of the best views in
the city, with the Peter and Paul Fortress to
the left and the Hermitage, the Admiralty
and St Isaac's Cathedral to the right.

NOVY MUSEUM   GALLERY
Map p286 (Новый музей; ☑812-323 5090;
www.novymuseum.ru; 6-ya liniya 29; adult/
student R200/100; ⊘noon-7pm Wed-Sun;
ⓂVasileostrovskaya) This compact contemporary art museum, with galleries on the
3rd and 4th floors, is worth visiting to see
all kinds of visual art forms created by a
group of 'non-conformist' artists working
in the Soviet Union in the latter part of the
20th century. The private collection of over
500 pieces is displayed in exhibitions that
change every three months or so.

CITY ELECTRICAL
TRANSPORT MUSEUM   MUSEUM
Map p286 (Музей городского электр-
ического транспорта; ☑812-321 9891;
http://getmuseum.ru; Sredny pr 77; adult/child
R300/100; ⊘10am-5pm Wed-Sun; ⓂVasileostro-
vskaya) A must-see if you love retro trams
and trolleybuses. A handsome brick shed
houses around 20 of these vehicles, both
originals and replicas, that used to be more
common on St Petersburg's streets. There's
also a small art gallery and exhibitions of
models, uniforms etc.

On Saturday and Sundays the museum
also runs retro tram tours (p32) across the
city to pl Turgeneva and back via the Petrograd Side; you can hop on or off the tram at
any of the stops along the route.

S-189 SUBMARINE MUSEUM   MUSEUM
Map p286 (Музей подводной лодки С-189; ☑8-
904-613 7099; www.museum-s-189.ru; cnr nab
Leytenanta Schmidta & 16-ya liniya; adult/student
R400/200; ⊘11am-7pm Wed-Sun; ⓂVasileos-
trovskaya) This Whiskey-class Soviet submarine was built in 1954, and – incredibly,
once you've looked around inside – served in
the Soviet navy until 1990. It has been renovated, repainted and can be visited if a big
cruise ship is not docked on the next door
Lieutenant Schmidt Passenger Terminal.

Inside, you can see the cramped living
quarters and the engine room, look through
the still-working periscope and see where the
torpedoes were loaded and fired.

UNIVERSITY SCULPTURE GARDEN   GARDENS
Map p286 (Universitetskaya nab 11; ⊘8am-5pm;
ⓂAdmiralteyskaya) FREE In the midst of the
university grounds is a whimsical collection
of sculptures from different artists including
monuments to figures as disparate as Ho Chi
Minh, Vladimir Nabokov, Tomáš Masaryk
and Anna Akhmatova. Look out for the one
of Major Kovalyov's nose, the character from
Gogol's *The Nose*. The leafy central courtyard
is a pleasant place to sit, but you may need to
show your passport to gain entry.

TWELVE COLLEGES   UNIVERSITY
Map p286 (Двенадцать коллегий; Mendeleevskaya liniya; ⓂVasileostrovskaya) Completed in
1744 and marked by a statue of scientist-
poet Mikhail Lomonosov (1711–65), the
400m-long Twelve Colleges is one of St Petersburg's oldest buildings. It was originally
meant for Peter's government ministries,
but is now part of the university, which
stretches out behind it. Within these walls
populist philosopher Nikolai Chernyshevsky
studied, Alexander Popov created some of
the world's first radio waves and a young
Vladimir Putin earned a degree in law.

This is also where Dmitry Mendeleev invented the periodic table of elements, and
the building now contains the small Mendeleev Museum (p149). Also of interest is the
University Sculpture Garden, which can be
accessed from the main entrance.

ROSTRAL COLUMNS   LANDMARK
Map p286 (Ростральная колонна; Birzhevaya
pl; ⓂVasileostrovskaya) The two Rostral Columns, archetypal St Petersburg landmarks,
are studded with ships' prows and four seated sculptures representing four of Russia's
great rivers: the Neva, the Volga, the Dnieper

and the Volkhov. These were oil-fired navigation beacons in the 1800s and their gas torches are still lit on some holidays, which makes for a breathtaking sight.

ICEBREAKER KRASIN MUSEUM

(Ледокол Красин; ☑812 325 354; www.krassin.ru; cnr nab Leytenanta Shmidta & 23-ya liniya; adult/student R500/200; ⊙10am-6pm Wed-Sun; Ⓜ Vasileostrovskaya) The *Krasin,* built in 1917, has a history almost as volatile as the 20th century itself. The Arctic icebreaker was decommissioned in 1971, and can now be visited on a guided tour that leaves every hour on the hour from 11am to 5pm. Call ahead to book a tour in English or French. Special tours of the engine room (over 14s only) are available at 1pm and 3pm on Saturday and Sunday.

The *Krasin* was captured by the British in 1918, returned to the Soviet Union two years later and took part in a large number of Arctic missions and rescues in her long career. The *Krasin* is also the last surviving ship of the infamous PQ-15 convoy that sent aid from Britain to the USSR during WWII.

MENSHIKOV PALACE MUSEUM

Map p286 (Государственный Эрмитаж-Дворец Меншикова; ☑812-323 1112; www.hermitagemuseum.org; Universitetskaya nab 15; admission R300; ⊙10.30am-6pm Tue, Thu, Sat & Sun, to 9pm Wed & Fri; Ⓜ Vasileostrovskaya) The first stone building in the city, the Menshikov Palace was built to the grandiose tastes of Prince Alexander Menshikov, Peter the Great's closest friend and the first governor of St Petersburg. It is now a branch of the Hermitage, and while only a relatively small part of the palace is open to visitors, its interiors are some of the oldest and best preserved in the city.

Menshikov was of humble origins (he is said to have sold pies on the streets of Moscow as a child), but his talent for both organisation and intrigue made him the second-most important person in the Russian Empire by the time of Peter's death in 1725. His palace, built mainly between 1710 and 1714, was the city's smartest residence at the time (compare it to Peter the Great's tiny Summer Palace across the river). Peter used Menshikov's palace for official functions.

The 1st floor displays some stunning Dutch tile work, intended to fortify the rooms against humidity to help ease Menshikov's tuberculosis. Original furniture and the personal effects of Menshikov are on display and each room has a fact sheet in English explaining its history. Vavara's Chamber is particularly evocative of how the aristocracy lived during Peter's time, while the impressive Walnut Study also stands out.

Also of note is the magnificent Grand Hall, where balls and banquets were held, including the infamous reception for Peter's dwarf wedding, in which Peter and his court sniggered as some 70-odd dwarfs from all over Russia attended the wedding and the subsequent drunken party of Peter's favourite.

RUSSIAN ACADEMY OF FINE ARTS MUSEUM MUSEUM

Map p286 (Музей Академии Художеств; ☑812-323 6496; www.nimrah.ru; Universitetskaya nab 17; R500, photos R500; ⊙noon-8pm Wed, 11am-7pm Thu, Sat & Sun, 1-9pm Fri; Ⓜ Vasileostrovskaya) Art lovers should not bypass the museum of this time-tested institution, which contains work by academy students and faculty dating back to its foundation in 1857. Two 3500-year-old sphinxes guard the entrance of this original location of the academy, where boys would live from the age of five until they graduated at age 15. It was an experiment to create a new species of human: the artist.

For the most part, it worked; many great Russian artists were trained here, including Ilya Repin, Karl Bryullov and Anton Losenko. But the curriculum was designed with the idea that the artist must serve the state, and this conservatism led to a reaction against it. In 1863, 14 students left to found a new movement known as the Wanderers (Peredvizhniki), which went on to revolutionise Russian art.

Nonetheless, the Academy of Arts has many achievements to show off, including numerous studies, drawings and paintings by academy members. On the 3rd floor you can examine the models for the original versions of Smolny Cathedral, St Isaac's Cathedral and the Alexander Nevsky Monastery. When you enter through the main door take the flight of stairs on your left up to the 2nd floor, where you can buy tickets.

TEMPLE OF THE ASSUMPTION CHURCH

Map p286 (Храм Успения Пресвятой Богородицы; ☑812-321 7473; http://spb.optina.ru; nab Leytenanta Shmidta 27/2; ⊙8am-8pm; Ⓜ Vasileostrovskaya) **FREE** This stunning 1895 neo-Byzantine church was built by architect Vasily Kosyakov on the site of a former monastery. It was closed during the Soviet period, and in 1957 the building became the city's first – and very popular – year-round skating rink. The 7.7m, 861kg metal cross on the roof was only replaced in 1998. Following a wonderful renovation, the church is looking superb again; do go inside to see the murals and icons covering the interior. The church runs a small, pleasant cafe (open 11am to 9pm) next door.

MUSEUM OF ZOOLOGY
MUSEUM

Map p286 (Зоологический музей; ☑812-328 0112; www.zin.ru; Universitetskaya nab 1; adult/student R250/150; ☺11am-6pm Wed-Mon; Ⓜ Admiralteyskaya) One of the biggest and best of its kind in the world, the Museum of Zoology was founded in 1832 and has some amazing exhibits, including a blue whale skeleton that greets you in the first hall. The highlight is unquestionably the stuffed skin of a 44,000-year-old woolly mammoth thawed out of the Siberian ice in 1902. There are also skeletons of a further three mammoths, including two baby ones – incredible finds.

PHARMACY MUSEUM OF DR PEL
HISTORIC BUILDING

Map p286 (Аптека Доктора Пеля; ☑812-328 1628; http://aptekapelya.ru; 7-ya liniya 16-18; ☺9am-10pm; Ⓜ Vasileostrovskaya) FREE This late-19th-century pharmacy still houses a medical clinic; it has a beautifully preserved facade as well as the original pharmacy interior on the ground floor.

OLD STOCK EXCHANGE
ARCHITECTURE

Map p286 (Birzhevaya pl; Ⓜ Vasileostrovskaya) Designed by French architect Jean-Francois Thomas de Thomon, the Greek revival–style Stock Exchange was completed in 1810. It ceased to serve its original function following the 1917 revolution and for many years housed the Central Naval Museum. Currently closed, the plan is for this to become a branch of the Hermitage to house the museum's heraldry collection.

FUTURE SITE OF KURYOKHIN CENTRE
ARTS CENTRE

Map p286 (☑812-322 0094; www.kuryokhin.net; 93 Sredny pr; Ⓜ Vasileostrovskaya) For decades the Kuryokhin Centre (p127), a hub for the contemporary arts, was based in a clapped-out but atmospheric old cinema here. At the time of research a new, excitingly designed home was being constructed with the plan to open later in 2019 when the famous SKIF festival will again be held here.

Catch bus 6 or 7, or trolleybus 10 or 11 from the opposite side of the road.

METRO MUSEUM
MUSEUM

Map p286 (Музей метро; ☑812-301 9833; www.metro.spb.ru/muzei; ul Odoevskogo 29; adult/student R300/100; ☺10am-5pm Mon-Sat; Ⓜ Primorskaya) Bring your passport with you to access this small but interesting museum, which recounts the history of St Petersburg's metro. Sadly there's no signage in English, so this is strictly for enthusiasts, but there are nice touches, such as a metro escalator taking you between floors and a metro car and cab you can enter to 'drive' your own train.

ST ANDREW'S CATHEDRAL
CATHEDRAL

Map p286 (Андреевский собор; ☑812-323 3418; http://andrew-sobor.ru/; 6-ya liniya 11; Ⓜ Vasileostrovskaya) Completed in 1786, this Baroque-style cathedral is a handsome feature of Vasilyevsky Island's skyline. The interior decoration is restrained compared to similar Russian Orthodox cathedrals.

GEOLOGICAL MUSEUM
MUSEUM

Map p286 (Геологический музей; ☑812-328 9248; www.vsegei.ru; Sredny pr 74; ☺10am-4pm Mon-Fri; Ⓜ Vasileostrovskaya) FREE Located in the upper floors of the All-Russian Geological Science and Research Institute, this huge and lovingly maintained museum contains thousands of fossils, rocks and gems. Highlights include a huge map of the Soviet Union made entirely of precious gems, which won the Paris World Exposition Grand Prix in 1937, and the giant skeleton of a mandschurosaurus.

On entering the building, call 7446 on the house phone and say you'd like to visit the museum (*ya hachoo pasyeteet moozáy*) and someone will escort you.

MENDELEEV MUSEUM
MUSEUM

Map p286 (Музей-Архив Санкт-Петербургского Университета Д.И.Менделеева; ☑812-328 9744; Universitetskaya nab 7-9; ☺11am-4pm Mon-Fri; Ⓜ Vasileostrovskaya) FREE Call ahead to arrange a tour of this small but interesting museum inside St Petersburg University and dedicated to Dmitry Mendeleev, creator of the periodic table of elements in 1869. His study has been lovingly preserved and you can see his desk (where he always stood rather than sat) and early drafts of the periodic table. Entry is via the main gate on Mendeleevskaya liniya.

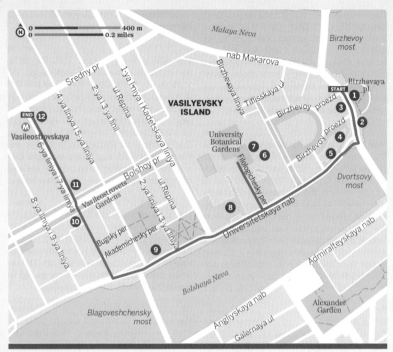

Neighbourhood Walk
Vasilyevsky Island

START STRELKA (ADMIRALTEYSKAYA)
END 6-YA LINIYA I 7-YA LINIYA (VASILEOS-
TROVSKAYA)
LENGTH 2KM; TWO HOURS

The eastern nose of Vasilyevsky Island, the
❶ Strelka (p147), boasts an unparalleled
panorama, looking out over the Peter and
Paul Fortress, the Hermitage, the Admiralty
and St Isaac's Cathedral. The red **❷ Rostral
Columns** (p147) frame the view; climb the
steps of the **❸ Old Stock Exchange** (p149)
for a raised perspective.

Continue southwest, dropping into either
the **❹ Museum of Zoology** (p149) or
the **❺ Kunstkamera** (p146), or both. The
latter was Russia's first museum, set up
by Peter to dispel common superstitions
about illness and disease and includes an
infamous collection of deformed foetuses
preserved in bottles.

At Peter's behest, Domenico Trezzini built
the magnificent **❻ Twelve Colleges** (p147),
now St Petersburg State University, in 1722.
Now part of the university, you'll find here the
small **❼ Mendeleev Museum** (p149), the
beautiful university botanical gardens and a
quirky collection of sculptures.

Peter originally gifted the entirety of
Vasilyevsky Island to his best friend, Prince
Menshikov, who proceeded to build the
fabulous **❽ Menshikov Palace** (p148) on
the north bank of the Bolshaya Neva.

Two Egyptian sphinx monuments mark the
entrance to the institutional **❾ Academy
of Arts Museum** (p148), which houses 250
years' worth of artistic expression. On display
are works created by academy students and
faculty over the years, as well as temporary
exhibitions.

Head inland up 6-ya liniya i 7-ya liniya
where you can pop briefly into the **❿ Pharmacy Museum of Dr Pelya** (p149) to view
the original 19th-century interior. Across
Bolshoy pr, the street is pedestrianised
and tree-lined, with the charming **⓫ St
Andrew's Cathedral** (p149) on the corner.
Enjoy something to eat along 6-ya liniya i 7-ya
liniya before finally checking out the modern
art of the **⓬ Novy Museum** (p147).

PUSHKIN HOUSE MUSEUM

Map p286 (Дом Пушкина; ☑812-328 0502; www.pushkinskijdom.ru; nab Makarova 4; adult/student R300/150, tour R1400; ⊙11am-5pm Mon-Fri; ⓂVasileostrovskaya) The old Customs House, topped with statues and a dome, is now home to the Institute of Russian Literature. Fondly called Pushkin House, the handsome building contains a small literary museum with dusty exhibits on Tolstoy, Gogol, Lermontov and Turgenev, as well as a room dedicated to the writers of the Silver Age. Call in advance for an English-language tour.

PEOPLE'S WILL D-2
SUBMARINE MUSEUM MUSEUM

Map p286 (Музей подводной лодки Д-2 Народоволец; ☑812-356 5277; http://eng.navalmuseum.ru/filials/narodovolec; Shkipersky protok 10; adult/student R600/400; ⊙11am-5pm Wed-Sun; ⓂPrimorskaya) The *People's Will (Narodovolets)* D-2 Submarine was one of the first six diesel-fuelled submarines built in the Soviet Union and has been wonderfully preserved in this purpose-built museum. The sub itself saw action between 1931 and 1956, and sank five German ships during WWII. Today you can wander around its supremely well-preserved (yet totally antiquated) interior and look at its equipment and weaponry. There's also a small museum containing photos, models and paintings of other submarines, including the ill-fated *Kursk*.

 EATING

MARKETPLACE CAFETERIA $

Map p286 (☑8-981-784 9814; www.market-place.me; 7-ya liniya 34/2; mains R100; ⊙8.30am-11pm Sun-Thu, until 6am Fri & Sat; Ⓢ☑; ⓂVasileostrovskaya) This chain of cafeteria-style restaurants has a popular outlet on Vasilyevsky Island's main commercial strip. With appealing, light-bathed dining areas, a large choice of excellent-value salads, soups, meat dishes and desserts, and with friendly service to boot, this spotless place is a lifeline for anyone after a low-cost lunch. There's also a cafe downstairs.

KHACHAPURI I VINO CAUCASIAN $

Map p286 (Хачапури и вино; ☑8-911-174 9007; https://vk.com/hachapuriivino; Kadetskaya liniya 29; mains R300-500; ⊙11.30am-midnight Sun-Thu, until 1am Fri & Sat; Ⓢ; ⓂVasileostrovskaya) Specialising in Adzhika cuisine from the Caucasus, this stylish place offers 10 types of *khachapuri*, the cheesy dough pies that are a bit like a thick-crust pizza. You can also sample *khinkali* (dumplings), Georgian wines and all-day breakfast dishes such as spicy scrambled eggs.

CARDAMON INDIAN $

Map p286 (Кардамон; ☑8-911-753 4741; 1-ya liniya 18; mains R250-650; ⊙noon-11pm; Ⓢ☑; ⓂVasileostrovskaya) The lacklustre decor may not instantly endear this Indian-run place to you, but its popularity with locals and visiting Indians says a great deal. The English-speaking owner will make you feel very welcome and the selection of delicious baltis, vindaloos, kadhai, biryanis and vegetarian dishes is impressive.

STOLLE RUSSIAN $

Map p286 (www.stolle.ru; 1-ya liniya 50; pies from R90; ⊙8am-10pm; ⓂVasileostrovskaya) This cosy pie shop and cafe was the first in this now nationwide chain. Aptly enough for a cafe that sells Saxon-style pies, it's located in the heart of St Petersburg's old German neighbourhood.

★BUTER BRODSKY EUROPEAN $$

Map p286 (Бутер Бродский; ☑8-911-922 2606; https://vk.com/buterbrodskybar; nab Makarova 16; mains R260-780; ⊙noon-midnight; Ⓢ; ⓂSportivnaya) Shabby chic has never looked so good as it does at this cafe-bar dedicated to the poet Joseph Brodsky (the name is a pun on *buterbrod*, the Russian word for sandwich), a super-stylish addition to Vasilyevsky Island's eating and drinking scene. The menu runs from excellent *smørrebrød* (open sandwiches; from R260) to various set meals of salads and soup.

It's also a great place for a drink as they specialise in home-made fruit-flavoured spirits and have their own very refreshing beer. The decor is particularly cool: Brodsky's (literally) chiselled features stare down on you from where they've been hammered into the cracked old walls, while elements of the historic building have been preserved and gorgeously integrated into the design.

PRYANOSTI & RADOSTI CAUCASIAN $$

Map p286 (Пряности & Радости; ☑812-640 1616; http://ginza.ru; 6-ya liniya 13; mains R550-1320; ⊙10am-1am Mon-Thu, until 3am Fri-Sun; ☑ⓘ; ⓂVasileostrovskaya) If you're travelling with young children they will love this branch of the Ginza Project–run chain for its colourful design that includes a children's room in the shape of a galleon, parrots in wall niches, an outdoor playground in summer and a real-life menagerie of animals, including a racoon, Clarissa the goat and two rabbits.

Pryanosti & Radosti (Spice and Joy) is around the back of the building, with Moko Burger (run by the same company and serving burgers, Georgian street food and craft beer) facing the street.

RESTAURANT ERARTA   INTERNATIONAL $$

Map p286 (Ресторан Erarta; ☑812-334 6896; http://erartacafe.com; 29-ya liniya 2; mains R510-810; ◐noon-11pm Mon-Sat, until 10pm Sun; Ⓜ Vasileostrovskaya) To fully take in the contemporary art collection at Erarta (p145) will take several hours, so it's handy that the museum's restaurant is a pretty good one that's worth building into your itinerary. The menu is fairly adventurous and includes well-made soups, light dishes such as barley risotto or hand-made truffle pasta, and desserts inspired by works of art.

The restaurant is also open on a Tuesday when the museum is closed.

From Vasileostrovskaya metro station, catch bus 6 or 7 to the museum, or trolleybus 10 or 11 from the opposite side of the road.

GRAD PETROV   GERMAN $$

Map p286 (Градъ Петровъ; ☑812-326 0137; www.die-kneipe.ru; Universitetskaya nab 5; meals R600-1690; ◐noon-1am; 🛜; Ⓜ Admiralteyskaya) Despite the laughable wax figure of a barely recognisable Pushkin with a quill in his hand at the entrance, 'Peter's City' is a classy German restaurant and microbrewery with an impressive menu and cosy decor. There's a separate bar where you can drink homebrewed lager, *Weizen* and *Dunkel* beers, while the menu is all about meat, and particularly sausages.

See if you can manage the metre-long Thüringer, served with onion sauce and red cabbage. Ask also for a free tour of the on-site microbrewery. There's live music Friday and Saturday from 8pm. In summer the outdoor tables offer amazing views of St Isaac's Cathedral and the Admiralty across the Neva River.

SAKARTVELO   GEORGIAN $$

Map p286 (Сакартвело; ☑812-328 0772; 12-ya liniya 13; mains R220-800; ◐11am-11pm; 🛜; Ⓜ Vasileostrovskaya) Although not flash, this is one of Vasilyevsky Island's best Georgian restaurants – a friendly place on a residential back-

street, where sumptuous Caucasian feasts are served up at any time of day, backed up by live music most evenings from 7pm.

★ RESTORAN   RUSSIAN $$$

Map p286 (Ресторанъ; ☑812-323 3031; Tamozhenny per 2; mains R700-2600; ◐noon-11pm; 🛜; Ⓜ Admiralteyskaya) Nearly 20 years on the scene and this excellent place is still going strong. Stylish and airily bright, Restoran is somehow formal and relaxed at the same time. The menu combines the best of *haute Russe* cuisine with enough modern flair to keep things interesting: try duck baked with apples or whole baked sterlet (a species of sturgeon) in white wine and herbs.

In the winter fires roar, while in the summer the thick stone walls make for an oasis from the heat. Do not miss the superb Napoleon dessert, or the interesting selection of quality Russian wines.

CASA DEL MYASO   STEAK $$$

Map p286 (Каса-дель Мясо; ☑812-320 9746; www.we-love-meat.ru; Birzhevoy proezd 6; mains R590-2950; ◐noon-midnight; 🛜; Ⓜ Sportivnaya) At this upmarket steakhouse you're guaranteed a wide selection of cuts of prime beef as well as other meats. Or you could keep it lighter with a burger, Greek-style gyros sandwich or (heaven forbid!) a salad. Its stylish, brick-walled subterranean location is a plus.

🍷 DRINKING & NIGHTLIFE

★ BEER BOUTIQUE 1516   CRAFT BEER

Map p286 (Пивной бутик 1516; ☑812-328 6066; http://butik1516.ru; 9-ya liniya 55; ◐3-10pm; Ⓜ Vasileostrovskaya) Your craft-beer cravings are sure to be satisfied at this bar-cum-bottle shop that has dedicated itself to the best local and international ales. There's usually around 17 beers on tap and 300 or so in bottles to choose from – it could be a long night.

Keeping you company will be the bar's pet white parrot Kuzhya and the friendly staff and patrons.

★ RADOSTI KOFE   CAFE

Map p286 (Радости Кофе; ☑812-925 7222; www.facebook.com/radosticoffee/; nab Makarova 28; ◐8am-11pm; 🛜; Ⓜ Sportivnaya) A leafy, relaxed ambience and river views across to the Petrograd Side make this a pleasant pit stop for coffee, other drinks and snacks while touring Vasilyevsky Island. They can make their drinks with soy, almond or hazelnut milk. The menu is available in English.

THELMA & LOUISE'S
BAR OF BROKEN HEARTS   BAR

Map p286 (Бар разбитых сердец Тельмы и Луизы; ☑812-418 3070; https://vk.com/thelma_louise; 1-ya liniya 60; ⊙11am-11pm; ⓂSportivnaya) This unpretentious, shabby-chic-verging-on-Gothic grunge bar offers live music Thursday to Saturday, 8pm to 10pm. Look for the names Thelma & Louise scratched into its black-painted door.

BIRZHA BAR   BAR

Map p286 (Биржа Бар; ☑812-925 8806; http://birjabar.ru; Birzhevoy per 4; ⊙5pm-2am Sun-Thu, until 6am Fri & Sat; 🛜; ⓂSportivnaya) A striking two-part painting of Jim Morrison hangs on the wall of this cool and spacious bar where DJs spin discs. Several beers on tap and plenty of other alcoholic concoctions will keep you in a happy mood.

BRÚGGE   PUB

Map p286 (☑812-600 2390; https://italy-group.ru/restaurants/brugge; nab Makarova 22; ⊙noon-2am; 🛜; ⓂVasileostrovskaya) If the idea of going to a 'Belgian gastronomic pub' makes your eyes roll, you're in good company, but this pleasant basement space overcomes its heavy-handed marketing with leather booths, a comfortable bar to sit at and more than 20 Belgian beers on tap. There's also a great menu (in English, if required), with fresh White Sea mussels and meaty mains.

🛍 SHOPPING

★ARTMUZA   ARTS & CRAFTS

Map p286 (Артмуза; ☑812-313 4703; http://artmuza.spb.ru; 13-ya liniya 70-72; ⊙11am-10pm; ⓂSportivnaya) This is one of the city's largest 'creative clusters' with around 13,000 sq metres of space over several floors hosting a variety of art galleries, studios, fashion boutiques and designers. On the ground floor look out for the joint atelier of **Snega Gallery** and **Slavutnitsa** where designers specialise in making clothes and accessories based on traditional Russian costumes and patterns.

Also come here to see exhibitions and theatre, and to enjoy the view from its large rooftop terrace (where there's also a cafe); sometimes events are also held here.

VASILEOSTROVSKY MARKET   MARKET

Map p286 (Василеостровский Рынок; ☑812-323 6687; www.vasryn.ru; Bolshoy pr 16-14; ⊙9am-9pm) There's been a market here since the 18th century and this modern-day version retains some retro charm. The fresh-food hall is picturesque and is a good spot to pick up fruit, vegetables, cheeses, honey and tea for a picnic or some edible souvenirs.

ERARTA   ARTS & CRAFTS

Map p286 (Эрарта; www.erarta.com; 29-aya liniya 2; ⊙10am-10pm Wed-Mon; ⓂVasileostrovskaya) The superb Erarta Museum of Contemporary Art (p145) has several shops in it, including its excellent gift shop, a well-stocked art bookshop and commercially run galleries where art is for sale. Definitely one of the best places to buy contemporary Russian art, as well as creative and unique gifts.

From Vasileostrovskaya metro station, catch bus 6 or 7 to the museum, or trolleybus 10 or 11 from the opposite side of the road.

🏃 SPORTS & ACTIVITIES

★PALACE BRIDGE WELLNESS CLUB   SPA

Map p286 (☑812-335 2214; www.pbwellnessclub.ru; Birzhevoy per 4A; before/after 4pm Mon-Fri R990/1390, 4hr/whole day Sat & Sun R1790/1990, children 3-12ye half-price, children under 3yr free; ⊙gym, sauna & pool 7am-11pm, spa 10am-10pm; ⓂSportivnaya) Attached to the Sokos Hotel Palace Bridge, there's a good gym and a variety of spa treatments here, but the highlights are the giant swimming pool (with jet fountains to massage tired backs) and the many styles of sauna (including Finnish and Russian) in which to steam away all your stresses.

It's free for hotel guests. It's a mixed-sex spa, so wear your bathing costume; towels and slippers can be rented.

IMBIR BANYA   BATHHOUSE

Map p286 (Имбирь баня; ☑8-981-851 6978; 5-ya liniya; admission R600; ⊙10am-10pm Mon-Fri, 8am-8pm Sat & Sun; ⓂVasileostrovskaya) There are several floors of baths here with the 3rd (top) floor reserved for men only. It's here that scenes from the 1997 movie *Brother* directed by Alexey Balabanov were filmed.

On the 2nd floor (closed Wednesday), it's women-only Tuesday, Friday and Sunday, and men-only Monday, Thursday, Saturday. There's also a pleasant tea room here.

Petrograd & Vyborg Sides

PETROGRADSKY ISLAND | KIROVSKY ISLANDS | VYBORG SIDE

Neighbourhood Top Five

1 **Peter & Paul Fortress** (p156) Seeing the graves of the Romanovs, climbing the bell tower for stunning views and exploring the past at museums and exhibits scattered around this historic island fortification.

2 **Street Art Museum** (p167) Taking in dazzling murals and creative art installations covering the walls of a once blighted industrial landscape.

3 **Hermitage Storage Facility** (p165) Getting a behind-the-scenes look at one of the world's top art collections.

4 **Yelagin Island** (p172) Spending a day relaxing on a charming, wooded island that's perfect for walking, picnicking, boating and sunbathing.

5 **Museum of Political History** (p159) Delving into Russian history at this sprawling collection of 20th-century artefacts in a building where Lenin once plotted.

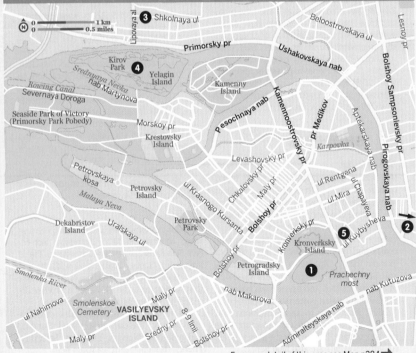

For more detail of this area see Map p284 ➡

Explore Petrograd & Vyborg Sides

Peter's city was founded on the Petrograd Side and it's a fascinating place packed with historical sites, Style Moderne architecture and a couple of great music venues. The showstopper of the area is the Peter & Paul Fortress, whose museums, soaring cathedral and panoramic views easily warrant a half- or a full-day visit. Afterwards, you could easily spend a few days taking in fascinating sights that see far fewer visitors such as the treasure-filled Hermitage Storage Facility, the sprawling Museum of Political History and insightful house museums devoted to the likes of early 20th-century opera singer Chaliapin and Soviet party boss (and Stalinist victim) Kirov.

Aside from hitting the main sights, the Petrograd Side is a fine area for exploring. The main thoroughfare of Bolshoy pr is dotted with shops, restaurants and cafes, and you'll find intriguing architecture scattered throughout the district. The wooded islands found here make a great retreat from the city streets, particularly Yelagin where you can hire boats and bicycles, and Krestovsky with its tree-lined lanes and sizeable amusement park.

Local Life

➡**Parks** If the weather's good, join locals as they take to the Kirovsky Islands (p164) for fairground rides, boating, sunbathing and cycling – it's a total escape from the city, just three metro stops from the centre.

➡**Street Art** Check out the daubs of street artists on the walls around the shuttered Red Banner Textile Factory and the giant murals near Chkalovskaya metro (p159).

➡**Strip off** Stand next to the serious sunbathers tanning against the fortress walls or on the beach at Zayachy Island. For a year-round tropical holiday, splash around with crowds at Piterland water park (p172).

Getting There & Away

➡**Metro** The Petrograd Side is served by Gorkovskaya and Petrogradskaya on Line 2, and by Sportivnaya, Chkalovskaya and Krestovsky Ostrov on Line 5. The Vyborg Side has some 20 metro stations on it, mainly serving far-flung residential areas.

➡**Bus** Bus 10 runs from the Vyborg Side at Chyornaya Rechka, down Bolshoy pr on the Petrograd Side and on into the Historic Heart.

➡**Tram** Tram 6 provides a handy link between pl Lenina and Vasilyevsky Island via Kronverksky pr on the Petrograd Side, while tram 40 is also useful for traversing the Petrograd Side to Chyornaya Rechka.

➡**Marshrutka** *Marshrutka* 346 runs the length of Bolshoy pr and then turns left onto Kamennoostrovsky pr and on to the Vyborg Side.

Lonely Planet's Top Tip

This is the real St Petersburg – a far cry from the uniform beauty of the Historic Heart. The Petrograd Side is a good place to see the everyday life of the middle classes in the city and, while the Vyborg Side around pl Lenina is a vision of a post-industrial nightmare, your average Joes live in the Soviet housing estates further along the metro line – travel to the end of lines 1 or 2 and you'll see real city life.

✕ Best Places to Eat

➡ Chekhov (p167)

➡ Koryushka (p169)

➡ Lev y Ptichka (p167)

➡ Paninaro (p167)

➡ Staraya Derevnya (p167)

For reviews, see p166 ➡

☕ Best Places to Drink

➡ Big Wine Freaks (p170)

➡ Yasli (p170)

➡ Bolshoy Bar (p170)

➡ Double B (p170)

For reviews, see p170 ➡

⊙ Best Parks & Gardens

➡ Yelagin Island (p172)

➡ Kamenny Island (p164)

➡ Botanical Gardens (p160)

➡ Maritime Victory Park (p165)

For reviews, see p159 ➡

TOP SIGHT
PETER & PAUL FORTRESS

Housing a cathedral, a former prison and various exhibitions, this large defensive fortress on Zayachy Island is the kernel from which St Petersburg grew into the city it is today. History buffs should definitely schedule a visit here. There are also panoramic views from atop the fortress walls, at the foot of which lies a sandy riverside beach, a prime spot for sunbathing.

The Fortress

Having captured this formerly Swedish settlement on the Neva, Peter set to turn the outpost into a modern Western city, starting with the Peter & Paul Fortress in 1703. It has never been utilised in the city's defence – unless you count incarceration of political 'criminals' as national defence.

Today, the fort makes for a fascinating half-day outing. The main entrance is across the **Ioannovsky Bridge** at the island's northeast end; there's also access via the **Kronwerk Bridge**, which is within walking distance of Sportivnaya metro station.

SS Peter & Paul Cathedral

All of Russia's pre-revolutionary rulers from Peter the Great onwards (except Peter II and Ivan VI) are buried inside this cathedral, which has a magnificent baroque interior quite different from other Orthodox churches. Peter I's grave is at the front on the right of the iconostasis. In 1998, the remains of Nicholas II and his family – minus Alexey and Maria – were interred in the Chapel of St Catherine, to the right of the entrance.

DON'T MISS

➡ SS Peter & Paul Cathedral

➡ Trubetskoy Bastion

➡ Commandant's House

➡ Neva Panorama

➡ The beach

PRACTICALITIES

➡ Петропавловская крепость

➡ Map p284, E7

➡ www.spbmuseum.ru

➡ grounds free, Peter & Paul Cathedral adult/child R450/250, combined ticket for 5 exhibitions R600/350

➡ ◷ grounds 8.30am-8pm, exhibitions 11am-6pm Mon & Thu-Sun, 10am-5pm Tue

➡ Ⓜ Gorkovskaya

The 122.5m-high **bell tower** (Map p284; adult/child R150/90; ⊙11am-5.30pm May-Sep; ⓂGorkovskaya) is the city's second-tallest structure after the television tower. At the base there is a small exhibition about the renovation of the tower in 1997, as well as an up-close inspection of the bell-ringing mechanism. The main reason to climb all these steps, of course, is for the magnificent 360-degree panorama. To ascend, you'll have to join a guided tour (in Russian only), which take place several times a day.

The Trubetskoy Bastion

Evocative use of the original cells for displays about the former political prisoners of **Trubetskoy Bastion** (Map p284; adult/student R200/120; ⊙10am-7pm Thu-Mon, to 6pm Tue; ⓂGorkovskaya) – who included the likes of Maxim Gorky, Leon Trotsky, Mikhail Bakunin and Fyodor Dostoevsky – make this the best of the fort's clutch of exhibitions. Short biographies in English of the various inmates are posted on the doors.

Peter the Great's son was tortured to death here and, after the 1917 revolution, the communists continued to use the prison for former aristocrats and counter-revolutionaries until 1924, when it was turned into a museum.

The Commandant's House & Neva Gate

The fascinating museum in the **Commandant's House** (Map p284; adult/student R200/120; ⊙11am-6pm Mon & Thu-Sun, to 5pm Tue; ⓂGorkovksaya) charts the history of the St Petersburg region from medieval times to 1918. What starts as a fairly standard-issue plod through the city's history really comes alive once you're upstairs, with modern, interactive exhibits, even though there's still a lack of explanations in English.

In the south wall is the **Neva Gate**, a later addition (1787), where prisoners were loaded on boats for execution or exile. Notice the plaques here showing water levels of famous (and obviously devastating) floods. Outside there are fine views of the whole central waterfront, including the Hermitage.

Along the wall, to the left, is the territory of the **Walrus Club**, the crazy crew that chops a hole in the iced-over Neva each winter so they can take a dip. Swimmers, known as *morzhi* (walruses), claim the practice eliminates muscle pains, boosts energy and even improves libido. This is not an exclusive club – all are invited to take the plunge!

PETER THE GREAT STATUE

Between the cathedral and the Senior Officers' Barracks is Mikhail Shemyakin's Peter the Great statue, which depicts him seated with strangely proportioned head and hands. When the statue was unveiled in 1991 it caused outrage among the city's citizens, for whom Peter remains a saintly figure. Local lore has it that rubbing his right forefinger will bring good luck.

Within the fortress grounds, you can grab a snack at the *stolovaya* (cafeteria) Leningradskoye Kafe (Map p284; mains R240-360; ⊙10am-8pm Thu-Tue). A far nicer option is Koryushka (p169), at the southwestern end of Zayachy Island.

POSTERN & NEVA PANORAMA

A separate ticket gains you access to both the **Postern**, a 97.4m passage hidden in the fortress walls, and the **Neva Panorama** (Map p284; Peter & Paul Fortress, Zayachy Island; adult/student R300/270; ⊙10am-8pm Thu-Tue; ⓂGorkovskaya), a walkway atop the walls, which concludes at **Naryshkin Bastion**. Every day at noon a cannon is fired from here, a tradition dating back to Peter the Great's times.

PETER & PAUL FORTRESS

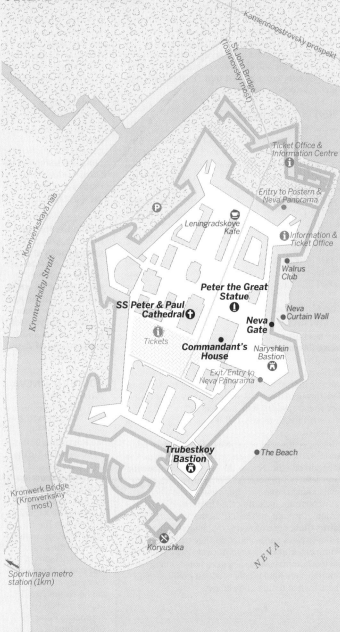

Kamennoostrovsky prospekt

St John Bridge
(Ioannovsky most)

Ticket Office &
Information Centre

Entry to Postern &
Neva Panorama

Information &
Ticket Office

Leningradskoye
Kafe

Walrus
Club

Peter the Great
Statue

SS Peter & Paul
Cathedral

Neva
Gate

Neva
Curtain Wall

Tickets

Commandant's
House

Naryshkin
Bastion

Exit/Entry to
Neva Panorama

Trubestkoy
Bastion

The Beach

Kronwerk Bridge
(Kronverkskiy
most)

Koryushka

NEVA

Sportivnaya metro
station (1km)

Kronverkskaya nab

Kronverksky Strait

◉ SIGHTS

◉ Petrograsky Island

PETER & PAUL FORTRESS
FORTRESS

See p156.

MUSEUM OF POLITICAL HISTORY
MUSEUM

Map p284 (Музей политической истории России; ☏812-313 6163; www.polithistory.ru; ul Kuybysheva 4; adult/child R200/free, audio guide R200; ⊙10am-6pm Sat-Tue, 10am-8pm Wed & Fri, closed Thu; ⓜGorkovskaya) The elegant Style Moderne Kshesinskaya Palace (1904) is a highly appropriate location for this excellent museum – one of the city's best – covering Russian politics in scrupulous detail up to contemporary times.

The palace, previously the home of Mathilda Kshesinskaya, famous ballet dancer and one-time lover of Nicholas II in his pre-tsar days, was briefly the headquarters of the Bolsheviks, and Lenin often gave speeches from the balcony.

You could spend hours exploring this museum (indeed there are two separate audio guides for the sprawling collection). Don't miss the portrait of Nicholas II, which shows the bayonet cuts made by soldiers during his night of capture on 26 October 1917. Photos show some of the horrors of the Soviet days, including 1933 street scenes in Ukraine, with the streets sprinkled with those who had died of starvation – owing to Stalin's policies. The Lenin memorial room is unchanged since Soviet days, with an almost religious atmosphere. You can visit Lenin's one-time office where he worked between the February and October Revolutions.

LEUCHTENBERG HOUSE
NOTABLE BUILDING

Map p284 (Bolshaya Zelenina ul 28; ⓜChkalovskaya) The Style Moderne gem Leuchtenberg House is so called because it once belonged to the Duke of Leuchtenberg, great-grandson of Tsar Nicholas I. Cross the street to take in the full glory of the mosaic frieze spread across the upper storey of the facade, the key decorative feature of the architect Theodor von Postels.

ROSENSHTEIN
APARTMENT BUILDING
HISTORIC BUILDING

Map p284 (Tower House; Kamennoostrovsky pr 35; ⓜPetrogradskaya) Petrogradsky Island is packed with architectural treasures, including this building, which plays with medieval themes in its stuccoed walls, lancet windows and twin castle-like towers looming over the street.

KIROV MUSEUM
MUSEUM

Map p284 (Музей Кирова; www.kirovmuseum.ru; Kamennoostrovsky pr 26/28; adult/child R150/100; ⊙11am-6pm Thu-Tue; ⓜPetrogradskaya) Leningrad party boss Sergei Kirov was one of the most powerful men in Russia in the early 1930s. His decidedly unproletarian apartment is now a fascinating museum showing how the Bolshevik elite really lived: take a quick journey back to the days of Soviet glory, including choice examples of 1920s technology, such as the first-ever Soviet-produced typewriter and a conspicuously noncommunist GE fridge, complete with plastic food inside.

Many of Kirov's personal items are on display and his office from the Smolny Institute has been fully reconstructed in one of the rooms. Kirov lived for 10 years at this flat until his murder at Stalin's behest in 1934, which sparked a wave of deadly repression in the country.

The floor above the Kirov collection has a recreated school room and shows what life was like for children in the 1930s. The 'boy's room' contains actual childhood objects belonging to Eugeny Porsin (including a cheery watercolour he painted), who was born in 1925, and was later drafted to serve in WWII. He died from wounds sustained near Vienna just 10 days before the end of fighting.

PETER'S CABIN
HISTORIC BUILDING

Map p284 (Домик Петра Великого; Petrovskaya nab 6; adult/student R200/100; ⊙10am-6pm Wed & Fri-Mon, 1-9pm Thu; ⓜGorkovskaya) This charming log cottage, protected within a stone building, is St Petersburg's oldest surviving structure. The wooden cabin itself was supposedly built in three days in May 1703 for Peter to live in while he supervised the construction of the fortress and city.

Feeling more like a shrine than a museum, the cabin confirms Peter's love for the simple life with its unpretentious, homely feel, visibly influenced by the time he spent in Holland.

It has long been a sentimental site for St Petersburg. During WWII, Soviet soldiers would take an oath of allegiance to the city here, vowing to protect it from the Germans, before disappearing to the front. After the Siege of Leningrad, this was the first museum to reopen to the public.

Look out for the bronze bust of Peter by Parmen Zabello in the garden.

ALEXANDROVSKY PARK   PARK

Map p284 (🚇; MGorkovskaya) This leafy park, laid out in 1845, wraps in an arc around the Kronwerk moat and Artillery Museum. It's too close to traffic to ensure a peaceful escape but, if you have kids in tow, it harbours a few attractions worth considering, the best of which is the Planetarium (p164), offering shows throughout the day, an observatory and several different display halls.

Also inside the park is **Mini St Petersburg** – miniature sculptures of the city's key landmarks that make for a fun photo opportunity.

CHALIAPIN HOUSE MUSEUM   MUSEUM

Map p284 (Дом-музей Шаляпина; ☏812-234 1056; www.theatremuseum.ru; ul Graftio 2B; adult/student R250/150; ⊙11am-7pm Thu-Sun, 1-9pm Wed; MPetrogradskaya) Opera buffs will want to visit this house–museum where the great singer Fyodor Chaliapin (1873–1938) lived before fleeing the Soviet Union in 1922. The kindly babushkas (clearly music lovers) will happily play some of the singer's recordings for you as you peruse his personal effects. Check online for details of concerts held here.

PETERSBURG AVANT-GARDE MUSEUM   MUSEUM

Map p284 (Музей петербургского авангарда; ☏812-234 4289; www.spbmuseum.ru/exhibits_and_exhibitions/92/1344/; ul Professora Popova 10; adult/student R150/100; ⊙11am-5pm Tue, to 6pm Thu-Mon; MPetrogradskaya) Also known as the House of Matyushin, this small museum occupies a charming grey-painted wooden cottage dating from the mid-19th century that was once the home of avant-garde artist Mikhail Matyushin (1861–1934). The exhibition here relates to Matyushin's work and that of his coterie. Entrance is free on Fridays.

BOTANICAL GARDENS   GARDENS

Map p284 (Ботанический сад; ☏812-372 5464; http://botsad-spb.com; ul Professora Popova 2; adult/child R300/200; ⊙grounds 10am-8pm Tue-Sun May-Sep; greenhouse 11am-4.30pm Tue-Sun year-round; MPetrogradskaya) On eastern Aptekarsky (Apothecary) Island, this was once a garden of medicinal plants – founded by Peter the Great himself in 1714 – that gave the island its name. Today the botanical gardens contain 26 greenhouses on a 22-hectare site. It is a lovely place to stroll around, and a fascinating place to visit – and not just for botanists.

At the turn of the 20th century, these were the second-biggest botanical gardens in the world, behind London's Kew Gardens. However, 90% of the plants died during WWII, which makes the present collection all the more impressive (you will recognise the 'veterans' by their war medals).

A highlight is the *tsaritsa nochi* (*Selenicereus pteranthus*), a flowering cactus that blossoms only one night a year, usually in mid-June. On this night, the gardens stay open until morning for visitors to gawk at the marvel and sip champagne.

Entry to the gardens is on the corner of Aptekarsky per and nab reki Karpovki. Although the grounds close from October to April, the greenhouses are open all year, with visits by guided tour (in Russian) only.

YELIZAROV MUSEUM   MUSEUM

Map p284 (Музей-квартира Елизаровых; ☏812-235 3778; ul Lenina 52, flat 24; adult/student R250/120; ⊙10am-6pm Thu-Sun, 1-9pm Wed; MChkalovskaya) Lenin's wife's family lived in this apartment-turned-museum and Vladimir Ilyich himself laid low here before the revolution while organising the workers. The delightful turn-of-the-20th-century fittings have been preserved intact, including a telephone that still bears Lenin's home phone number. By the look of things, Lenin had a very bourgeois time of it.

The apartment building, which is known locally as the 'boat house' due to its external similarities to a large cruise liner, was built in 1913 at the height of St Petersburg's lust for Style Moderne. After finding the entrance, head up the stairs to the 3rd floor to be buzzed in.

CRUISER AURORA   MUSEUM

Map p284 (Крейсер Аврора; ☎812-230 8440; www.aurora.org.ru; Petrovskaya nab; adult/child R600/400; ☻11am-6pm Wed-Sun; ♿; Ⓜ Gorkovskaya) Moored on the Bolshaya Nevka, the *Aurora* had a walk-on part in the communist revolution. On the night of 25 October 1917, its crew fired a blank round from the forward gun as a signal for the start of the assault on the Winter Palace. Restored and painted in pretty colours, it's a living museum that swarms with kids on weekends.

Launched in 1901, the *Aurora* saw action in the Russo-Japanese War and was sunk by German bombs in WWII. Inside you can view the crew's quarters as well as communist propaganda and a collection of friendship banners from around the world.

MOSQUE   MOSQUE

Map p284 (Соборная мечеть; ☎821-233 9819; http://dum-spb.ru/kontakty; Kronverksky pr 7; ☻7am-9pm; Ⓜ Gorkovskaya) This beautiful working mosque (built 1910–14) was modelled on Samarkand's Gur-e Amir Mausoleum. Its fluted azure dome and minarets are stunning and surprisingly prominent in the city's skyline. Outside of prayer times, if you are respectfully dressed (women should wear a head covering, men long trousers), you can walk through the gate at the northeast side and ask the guard for entry – the interior is equally lovely.

If you are allowed in, remove your shoes, do not talk and do not take photos.

ARTILLERY MUSEUM   MUSEUM

Map p284 (Музей Артиллерии; ☎812-232 0296; www.artillery-museum.ru; Kroneverskaya pr; adult/student R400/250; ☻11am-6pm Wed-Sun; ♿; Ⓜ Gorkovskaya) Housed in the fort's original arsenal, across the moat from the Peter & Paul Fortress, this fire-powered museum chronicles Russia's military history, with examples of weapons dating all the way back to the Stone Age. The centrepiece is Lenin's armoured car, which he rode in triumph from the Finland Station (Finlyandsky vokzal).

Even if you are not impressed by guns and bombs, who can resist climbing around on the tanks and trucks that adorn the courtyard?

CHAEV MANSION   ARCHITECTURE

Map p284 (ul Rentgena 9; ☻8am-2pm & 3-9pm Mon-Fri, 9am-2pm Sat; Ⓜ Petrogradskaya) This elegant mansion, constructed in 1907 for the engineer SN Chaev, is now occupied by a public clinic. It combines neoclassical and art nouveau motifs and has a beautifully preserved interior.

RED BANNER
TEXTILE FACTORY   NOTABLE BUILDING

Map p284 (Трикотажная фабрика "Красное Знамя»; Pionerskaya ul 53; Ⓜ Chkalovskaya) **FREE** The Red Banner Textile Factory is a grand relic of Soviet constructivist architecture. Street artists have commandeered walls around the abandoned industrial space to create an abdoor gallery of technicolour images, mainly along Korpusnaya ul.

SEASIDE PARK OF VICTORY   PARK

A leafy green park full of sports fields.

BREAD MUSEUM   MUSEUM

Map p284 (Музей хлеба; http://muzei-xleb.ru; ul Mikhailova 2; adult/student R150/100; ☻10am-6pm Tue-Sat; Ⓜ Ploshchad Lenina) This quirky little museum pays tribute to bread and the role it has played in history (of the city and of the world). A model bakery exhibits the equipment that was used to make bread for the city's poorest classes in the 19th century. A special exhibition on the Siege of Leningrad offers a chilling example of a daily ration of bread during WWII, as well as rare photographs of starving children and bread queues.

The museum's new location is a short stroll from Pl Lenina.

TOY MUSEUM   MUSEUM

Map p284 (Музей игрушки; nab reki Karpovki 32; adult/child R300/100; ☻11am-6pm Tue-Sun; Ⓜ Petrogradskaya) This privately run museum presents its pan-Russian collection in three sections – folk toys, factory toys and artisanal toys. Examples of the last include toys made in Sergiev Posad, home of the ubiquitous *matryoshka* (nesting doll), a creation often assumed to be far older than it is, being created for the first time only in the 19th century.

At the time of research, the museum was closed for renovations.

NARYSHKIN BASTION   TOWER

Map p284285 Named after Kirill Naryshkin, one of Peter the Great's commanders who oversaw the building of the original fortifications, the bastion is better known for its booming cannon, fired off daily here at noon.

Metro Art

Beautiful interior design is not just for palaces and galleries in St Petersburg – it is also found across the city's metro system. Red Line 1, the first to be opened in 1955, is particularly striking for its station designs, but other newer stations also have artistic flourishes.

Admiralteyskaya

The city's deepest metro station features mosaics about the formation of the Russian fleet under Peter the Great.

Avtovo

Marble-and-cut-glass-clad columns hold up the roof, while a relief of soldiers stands in the temple-like entrance.

Baltiyskaya

There's a wavy motif on the mouldings along the ceiling and a vivid marble mosaic at the end of the platform depicting the volley from the Aurora in 1917.

Kirovsky Zavod

The decoration takes its inspiration from oil wells and industry. A scowling bust of Lenin is at the end of the platform.

Narvskaya

Features a fantastic sculptured relief of Lenin and rejoicing proletariat over the escalators, as well as carvings of miners, engineers, sailors, artists and teachers on the platform columns.

Pl Vosstaniya

Lenin and Stalin are depicted together in the roundels at either end of the platform. Look out for Lenin on a tank and Lenin with the Kronshtadt sailors.

Pushkinskaya

A statue of the poet stands at the end of the platform and a moulding of his head is above the escalators. Nip outside to view the nearby Style Moderne Vitebsk Station.

Tekhnologichesky Institut

The southbound platform has reliefs of famous Russian scientists, the northbound one lists dates of Russia's major scientific achievements along the columns.

1. Avtovo 2. Narvskaya 3. Pushkin statue by Mikhail Anikushin in front of a mural by Maria Engelke, Pushkinskaya

SIGMUND FREUD
MUSEUM OF DREAMS   MUSEUM
Map p284 (Музей сновидений Фрейда; ☑812-456 2290; www.freud.ru; Bolshoy pr 18a; ⊙noon-5pm Tue, Sat & Sun; Ⓜ Sportivnaya) **FREE** This odd conceptual exhibition, based on abstractions and ideas, not artefacts, is an outgrowth of the Psychoanalytic Institute that houses it. The two-room exhibition aims to stimulate your subconscious as you struggle to read the display symbolising what Freud himself would have dreamt. Illustrations of Freud's patients' dreams and quotations line the dimly lit, incense-scented hall. English is spoken.

PLANETARIUM   PLANETARIUM
Map p284 (Планетарий; ☑812-233 2653; www.planetary-spb.ru; Alexandrovsky Park 4; adult/child R400/200; ⊙10.30am-6pm; Ⓜ Gorkovskaya) A crowdpleaser with the under-12 crowd, the planetarium has shows that explore the wonders of outer space.

⊙ Kirovsky Islands

This is the collective name for the three outer delta islands of the Petrograd Side – Kamenny, Yelagin (p172) and Krestovsky. Once marshy forests, the islands were granted to 18th- and 19th-century court favourites and developed into elegant playgrounds. Still mostly parkland, they are leafy venues for picnics, river sports and White Nights' cavorting, as well as home to St Petersburg's super rich.

The metro station Krestovsky Ostrov provides easy access to both Krestovsky and Yelagin Islands; for Kamenny you can walk across the bridge from metro station Chyornaya Rechka on the Vyborg Side.

YELAGIN ISLAND   ISLAND
(Елагин остров) This island is one giant park, free of traffic and a serene place to wander. It was attractively landscaped by the architect Carlo Rossi and its centrepiece, also by Rossi, is the beautifully restored **Yelagin Palace** (Map p284; http://elaginpark.org; Yelagin ostrov 1; ⊙10am-6pm; Ⓜ Krestovsky Ostrov), which Alexander I commissioned for his mother, Empress Maria. The gorgeous interiors, with detailed murals and incredible inlaid-wood floors, are furnished with antiques. Unfortunately,

the palace remains closed for long-term renovations.

Other nearby estate buildings host temporary exhibitions, too. The rest of the island is a lovely network of paths, greenery, lakes and channels. At the northern end of the island, you can rent row boats to explore the ponds or in-line skates to explore the paths; in winter it's an ideal setting for sledding, skiing and skating. At the west end, a plaza looks out to the Gulf of Finland: sunsets are resplendent from here.

KAMENNY ISLAND   ISLAND
Map p284 (Каменный остров; Ⓜ Chyornaya Rechka) Century-old dacha (country cottages) and mansions, inhabited by very wealthy locals, line the wooded lanes that twist their way around Kamenny (Stone) Island. The island is punctuated by a series of canals, lakes and ponds, and is pleasant for strolling at any time of year. At its east end, the Church of St John the Baptist (built 1776–81) has been charmingly restored.

Behind it, Catherine the Great built the big, classical Kamennoostrovsky Palace for her son; unfortunately it's visible only from the outside.

CHURCH OF
ST JOHN THE BAPTIST   CHURCH
Map p284 (Kamennoostrovsky pr; ⊙9am-6pm) An elegant red-brick church built in the 18th century.

PETER'S TREE   LANDMARK
According to legend Kamenny Island was the site where Peter the Great planted an oak tree, which stood proudly over many years. The old oak, however, died and has since been replaced with a young, healthy tree; nevertheless, it is still known as Peter's Tree.

KRESTOVSKY ISLAND   ISLAND
(Крестовский остров; 🚇; Ⓜ Krestovsky Ostrov) The biggest of the three northern islands, Krestovsky consists mostly of the vast Maritime Victory Park (p165), dotted with sports fields; at the far western end is the massive, 68,000-seat Krestovsky Stadium (p170), which will play a pivotal role in the 2018 FIFA World Cup.

At the main entrance opposite the metro station you can rent bikes and in-line skates. Also here is Divo Ostrov, a Disney-style amusement park with exciting fairground rides.

MARITIME VICTORY PARK PARK

(Приморский парк Победы; www.primpark pobedy.ru; Krestovsky pr; Ⓜ Krestovsky Ostrov) A huge leafy expanse on Krestovsky Island with ponds, walking paths and summertime food vendors.

DIVO OSTROV AMUSEMENT PARK

Map p284 (www.divo-ostrov.ru; rides R100-500; ⊙noon-7pm; 💺; Ⓜ Krestovsky Ostrov) An amusement park with thrilling rides that kids of all ages will adore. Top draws include a roller coaster with 10 loops and a vertical descent that reaches 90km per hour.

◉ Vyborg Side

SAMPSONIEVSKY CATHEDRAL CATHEDRAL

Map p284 (Сампсониевский собор; Bolshoy Sampsonievsky pr 41; ⊙9am-6pm; Ⓜ Vyborgskaya) This light-blue baroque cathedral dates from 1740, and having been repainted and restored to its original glory both inside and out, glistens like a pearl amid a gritty industrial area. Its most interesting feature is the calendar of saints, two enormous panels on either side of the nave, each representing six months of the year, where every day is decorated with a mini-icon of its saint(s).

The enormous silver chandelier above the altar is also something to behold, as is the stunning baroque, green-and-golden iconostasis. Don't miss the frieze of a young Peter the Great, on the wall behind you when you face the main iconostasis.

TOP SIGHT
HERMITAGE STORAGE FACILITY

Guided tours of the Hermitage's state-of-the-art restoration and storage facility are highly recommended. This is not a formal exhibition as such, but the guides are knowledgeable and the examples chosen for display (paintings, furniture and carriages) are wonderful.

The storage facility is directly behind the big shopping centre opposite the metro station – look for the enormous golden-yellow glass facility decorated with shapes inspired by petroglyphs.

The highlight is undoubtedly the gorgeous 17-part ceremonial tent presented to Alexander III by the Emir of Bukhara in 1893. Other treasures include an embroidered Turkish tent, presented to Catherine the Great by the Sultan Selim III one century earlier. Beside it stands an equally impressive modern diplomatic gift: a massive woodcarving of the mythical garuda bird, given by Indonesia to the city for its 300th anniversary. Another section contains gorgeous pieces from the imperial wardrobe, including the wedding gown worn by Alexandra Feodorovna (Nicholas II's wife) and dresses worn by their daughters Tatiana and Olga, Russia's last tsarinas.

Other notable displays are of ancient Russian icons and frescoes; selections from the collection of 3500 canvases by Russian artists down the ages; a hall of imperial carriages; and a depository stacked with all kinds of furniture – a veritable imperial IKEA!

Call ahead to reserve a tour in English.

DON'T MISS

➡ Turkish ceremonial tent
➡ Tapestries
➡ Medieval frescoes

PRACTICALITIES

➡ Реставрационно-хранительский центр Старая деревня
➡ Map p284, A1
➡ ☑812-340 1026
➡ www.hermitage museum.org
➡ Zausadebnaya ul 37a
➡ tours R550
➡ ⊙tours 11am, 1pm, 1.30pm & 3.30pm Wed-Sun
➡ 💺
➡ Ⓜ Staraya Derevnya

This is also believed to be the church where Catherine the Great married her one-eyed lover Grigory Potemkin in a secret ceremony in 1774.

BUDDHIST TEMPLE   TEMPLE

Map p284 (Буддистский Храм; ☑981-755 9605; www.dazan.spb.ru; Primorsky pr 91; ☉10am-6pm Mon-Fri, to 7pm Sat & Sun; Ⓜ Staraya Derevnya) Another in the city's collection of grand religious buildings is this beautiful functioning *datsan* (temple) where respectful visitors are welcome. The main prayer hall has lovely mosaic decoration and there's a cheap and cheerful **cafe** in the basement. The temple was built between 1909 and 1915 at the instigation of Pyotr Badmaev, a Buddhist physician to Tsar Nicholas II.

Money was raised from all over Russia, and as far afield as Thailand and England, by various Buddhist organisations; it even gained the support of the Dalai Lama in Lhasa.

In the 1930s the communists shut the temple, arrested many of the monks and used the building as a military radio station. In the 1960s it was taken over by the Zoological Institute and used as laboratories. Thankfully, however, the damage was not particularly profound and the *datsan* was returned to the city's small Buddhist community in 1990.

PISKARYOVSKOE CEMETERY   CEMETERY

(Пискарёвское мемориальное кладбище; www.pmemorial.ru; pr Nepokoryonnikh 72; ☉9am-9pm May-Oct, to 6pm Nov-Apr; Ⓜ Ploshchad Muzhestva) The main burial place for the victims of the Nazi blockade in WWII is a stark and poignant memorial to the tragedy. Some half a million people were laid to rest here between 1941 and 1943, during the siege.

From metro station Ploshchad Muzhestva, take *marshrutka* 123 in the direction of Ladozhskaya metro, which passes by the entrance to the cemetery.

Originally, this area was just an enormous pit where unnamed and unmarked bodies were dumped. In 1960 the remodelled cemetery was opened and has been an integral part of the city's soul ever since. Every year on Victory Day (9 May) the cemetery is packed out with mourners, many of whom survived the blockade and lost close relatives to starvation.

FINLAND STATION   HISTORIC BUILDING

Map p284 (Finlyandsky vokzal; Финляндский вокзал; pl Lenina 6; Ⓜ Ploshchad Lenina) Rebuilt in the 1970s in rectilinear Soviet style, the Finland Station (Finlyandsky vokzal) endures as a place of historical significance, where Lenin finally arrived in 1917 after 17 years in exile abroad. Here he gave his legendary speech from the top of an armoured car to a crowd who had heard of, but never seen, the man.

After fleeing a second time he again arrived here from Finland, this time disguised as a railway fireman, and the locomotive he rode in is displayed behind glass on the platform.

Walk out onto the square that still bears Lenin's name and you'll see a marvellous statue of the man himself at the far end.

SITE OF PUSHKIN'S DUEL   HISTORIC SITE

(Место дуэли Пушкина; Kolomyazhsky pr; Ⓜ Chyornaya Rechka) Russia's poetic genius, Alexander Pushkin, was fatally wounded in a duel here with the Frenchman Georges d'Anthès on 8 February 1837. A granite monument marks the alleged spot, today a small park surrounded by fast-moving traffic.

From the metro station at Chyornaya Rechka, walk down Torzhkovskaya ul and turn left at the first light on Novosibirskaya ul. Walk straight to the end of the road, cross the train tracks and enter the park.

✖ EATING

SNEZHINKA   RUSSIAN $

Map p284 (www.cafe-snezhinka.ru; Maly pr 57; mains R130-260; ☉11am-11pm) A blast from the past, Snezhinka channels Soviet-era nostalgia with its Russian-only menu of cutlets, bliny and beef Stroganoff served in a cosy, brick-walled space that's deliciously unhip.

LE MENU   RUSSIAN $

Map p284 (http://le-menu.ru; Kronverksky pr 79; mains R320-570; ☉9am-11pm; 🛜🖋; Ⓜ Gorkovskaya) This smart cafe serves a good-value menu of thoughtfully prepared fish, meat and pasta dishes, along with a good selection of vegetarian fare. The sophisticated setting has wooden floorboards and chandeliers.

WORTH A DETOUR

STREET ART MUSEUM

Street Art Museum (☑812-448 1593; http://streetartmuseum.ru; shosse Revolutsii 84, Okhta, entrance on Umansky per; adult/student R350/250; ◕noon-10pm Tue-Sun May-Sep; Ⓜ Ploshchad Lenina, then bus 28, 37, 137 or 530) It's well worth the effort making the trip out to see this magnificent collection of street art set inside a former 11-hectare industrial site. You'll find a wide variety of formats, from huge murals covering walls to mixed-media installations set inside a former boilerhouse. Every year, the exhibition changes, with top artists from around the globe invited to contribute on themes like Revolution (featured in 2017 on the 100-year anniversary of Russia's October Revolution), Migrants and Peace.

Intriguingly, parts of this industrial complex are still active, with workers at the laminated plastics factory SLOPAST surrounded by the encroaching artwork. Some of the workshops are decorated with epic works by the likes of top Russian street artists Timothy Radya, Kirill Kto and Nikita Nomerz, as well as the Spanish artist Escif. Before he died in 2013, Pasha 183 – frequently referred to as Russia's Banksy because of his anonymity – also contributed 'Walls Don't Sleep', a beautiful monochrome mural based on an image of Soviet factory workers.

Guided tours take place on weekends (at 1pm and 2pm); call ahead to ensure an English-speaking guide is on hand. The museum also hosts outdoor concerts and other big events. Check the website for the latest.

It's located in the industrial zone of Okhta, a 20-minute bus ride east of Ploshchad Lenina. Buses 28, 37 and 137 all go there.

TROITSKY MOST
VEGETARIAN $

Map p284 (Троицкий Мост; www.t-most.ru; ul Kuybysheva 33; mains R300; ◕8.30am-10.30pm; 🗷; ⓂGorkovskaya) One of the newest branches of this chain of excellent vegetarian cafes is located near Sampsonievsky Bridge. The small, handsomely designed space serves up tasty soups, salads, mushroom lasagna and vegetable tempura, plus breakfast fare like *kasha* (porridge) with fruit.

PELMENIYA
INTERNATIONAL $

Map p284 (Kronverksky pr 55; dumplings R240-520; ◕11am-11pm; 🕾; ⓂGorkovskaya) A branch of this appealing contemporary-styled dumpling bar that's good for an inexpensive, filling meal.

★CHEKHOV
RUSSIAN $$

Map p284 (Чехов; ☑812-234 4511; http://res taurant-chekhov.ru; Petropavlovskaya ul 4; mains R550-890; ◕noon-11pm; ⓂPetrogradskaya) Despite a totally nondescript appearance from the street, this restaurant's charming interior perfectly recalls that of a 19th-century dacha and makes for a wonderful setting for a meal. The menu, hidden inside classic novels, features lovingly prepared dishes such as roasted venison with bilberry sauce or Murmansk sole with dill potatoes and stewed leeks.

PANINARO
ITALIAN $$

Map p284 (Bolshaya Zelenina 28; mains R380-780; ◕9am-11.30pm Mon-Fri, from 11am Sat & Sun; 🗷) Delightfully off the beaten path, Paninaro is a gem set inside one of the Petrogradky's most striking apartment buildings (don't miss the murals up top – visible on the opposite side of the street). Stop in for tasty house-made pastas topped with grilled vegetables, creative salads and pizzas, and refreshing cocktails.

LEV Y PTICHKA
GEORGIAN $$

Map p284 (Лев и Птичка; ☑988-7069; Bolshoy pr 19; 🕾🗷) Amid big fur hats, a lion (*lev*) mural, decorative wooden chandeliers and other curious design elements, this friendly spot has a loyal local following for its delicious and reasonably priced Georgian fare, including piping hot *khachapuri* (Georgian cheese bread) fired up at the baker's oven in front. Plates are small and meant for sharing. Entrance is on ul Chaykino.

STARAYA DEREVNYA
RUSSIAN $$

Map p284 (Старая деревня; ☑812-431 0000; www.sderevnya.ru; ul Savushkina 72; mains R480-890; ◕1pm-10pm; ⓂChyornaya Rechka) This tiny, family-run hideaway offers an intimate atmosphere and delectable food. Try classic recipes such as beef in plum and nut sauce or foil-baked salmon with

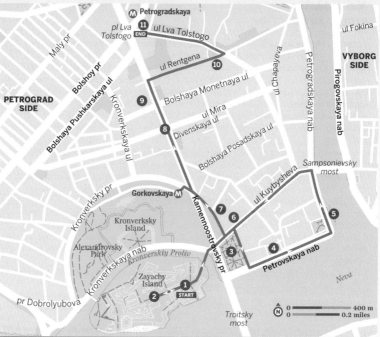

PETROGRAD & VYBORG SIDES

Neighbourhood Walk
Architectural Tour of Petrograd Side

START PETER & PAUL FORTRESS (GORKOVSKAYA)
END ROSENSHTEIN APARTMENT BUILDING (PETROGRADSKAYA)
LENGTH 1.5KM; TWO HOURS

The Petrograd Side is an architectural treasure trove with buildings ranging from St Petersburg's very inception up to contemporary times. Start with a quick tour of the city's first defensive installation, the ❶ **Peter & Paul Fortress** (p156). Don't miss the splendid ❷ **SS Peter & Paul Cathedral** (p156), the last resting place of Peter the Great and almost every tsar since.

The central square of Peter's early city, ❸ **Troitskaya pl** (Trinity Sq) formerly had as its centrepiece Trinity Cathedral, where Peter attended Mass. The cathedral was destroyed after the 1917 revolution but a small chapel remains.

Petrovskaya nab is home to two historic landmarks: ❹ **Peter's Cabin** (p159), the wooden hut that was the tsar's first modest home in the city; and, off the island's eastern tip, the ❺ **Cruiser Aurora** (p161), a legendary battleship which saw service in the Russo-Japanese War.

Return to Kamennoostrovsky pr via ul Kuybysheva, passing the Style Moderne palace of ballerina Mathilda Kshesinskaya that now houses the ❻ **Museum of Political History** (p159), and the ❼ **Mosque** (p161), coated in dazzling mosaics of aquatint tiles.

Continue north along Kamennoostrovsky pr and look closely for architectural gems around ❽ **Avstriyskaya pl**, with its castle-like edifices. Further alongyou can see the inside of a grand Style Moderne building by visiting the ❾ **Kirov Museum** (p159).

Ul Rentgena offers up more Style Moderne beauties: note the decoration on the facade of No 4 and make sure you do a full circle of the freestanding ❿ **Chaev Mansion** (p161), which exhibits great geometric precision in its design.

Follow ul Lva Tolstogo and you'll pass the turretted ⓫ **Rosenshtein Apartment Building** (p159), a whimsical mash-up of neoclassical and neo-Gothic styles.

mushrooms, peppers and olives. The small size of the restaurant guarantees personal service, but reservations are a must. From the metro, take any tram down ul Savushkina and get off at the third stop.

The restaurant lacks a liquor licence, so you're welcome to bring your own beverage of choice (no corkage fee).

BABJIB KOREAN $$

Map p284 (ul Kuybysheva 7; mains R460-840; ⊙11am-11pm; 🛜; MGorkovksaya) Be transported to contemporary Seoul at this delightful cafe serving up a tantalising menu of Korean classics such as *bibimbap* (rice with vegetables and meat), *gimbap* (sushi-style rolls) and various spicy stews. As is traditional the meals come with an assortment of hearty side dishes – so don't over order. The business lunch for R340 is a deal.

KORYUSHKA RUSSIAN, GEORGIAN $$

Map p284 (Корюшка; ☑812-640 1616; www. ginza.ru/spb/restaurant/korushka; Petropavlovskaya krepost 3, Zayachiy Island; mains R650-2400; ⊙noon-1am; 🛜🚭; MGorkovskaya) Lightly battered and fried smelt *(koryushka)* is a St Petersburg speciality every April, but you can eat the small fish year-round at this relaxed, sophisticated restaurant beside the Peter & Paul Fortress. There are plenty of other very appealing Georgian dishes on the menu to supplement the stunning views across the Neva.

MAKARONNIKI ITALIAN $$

Map p284 (Макаронники; www.makaronniki.ru; pr Dobrolyubova 16; mains R610-1200; ⊙noon-1.30am; 🛜🚭; MSportivnaya) Set on the rooftop of a business centre, this trendy spot serves up modern Italian food, from pasta and pizza to rabbit served with cabbage and osso bucco. In the summer, the outdoor tables are a great place to enjoy the views with a drink in hand from one of the picnic tables or hammocks on the roof deck.

Things get lively on Friday and Saturday nights when DJs spin until late.

JEAN-JACQUES FRENCH $$

Map p284 (Жан-Жак; www.jan-jak.com; Bolshoy pr 54/2; mains R420-710; ⊙24hr; 🛜; MPetrogradskaya) An affordable Parisian-style eatery that whips up bistro fare including breakfast (served all day on weekends), as well as a huge selection of French wines.

MESTO INTERNATIONAL $$

Map p284 (☑812-405 8799; Kronverksky pr 59; mains R600-1100; ⊙11am-midnight; 🛜; MGorkovskaya) Art deco fittings, a beautiful glass and marble counter and upholstered benches you could almost fall asleep on are a good start. The menu is eccentric but interesting: Anglophile fish pie, Japanese duck dumplings plus satisfying soups and salads. Portions are not huge but very tasty.

VOLNA INTERNATIONAL $$

Map p284 (Волна; Petrovskaya nab 5; mains R550-1050; ⊙noon-midnight; 🛜; MGorkovskaya) Opposite Peter's Cabin, this sleek, laidback lounge–restaurant has a great terrace perfect for a relaxed lunch over a bottle of wine. The menu ranges from risotto, salads and pasta to a selection of Asian dishes from the wok.

TBILISO GEORGIAN $$

Map p284 (Тбилисо; ☑812 -232 9391; Sytninskaya ul 10; mains R480-960; ⊙noon-midnight; MGorkovskaya) A beloved institution, and decidedly upscale as far as Georgian restaurants go, Tbiliso has a great interior with tiled tables and big booths, made more private by intricate latticework between them. The food is top notch, with classics such as *khachapuri* (cheese bread) and chicken *tabaka* (flattened chicken cooked in spices) sumptuously prepared, and there's a huge range of wines.

FLAMAND ROSE BELGIAN $$

Map p284 (☑812-498 5035; www.flamandrose. ru; Malaya Posadskaya ul 7/4; mains R480-780; ⊙11am-11pm; 🛜; MGorkovskaya) Above an interior-design shop, this darkly beautiful cafe-bar, dominated by a magnificent glass chandelier, specialises in Belgian cuisine and beers. The waffles are delicious, as are other sweet delights such as *tarte tatin*. Breakfast is also served up until 2pm.

PROBKA ITALIAN $$$

Map p284 (☑911-922 7727; www.probka.org; pr Dobrolyubova 6; mains R650-2490; ⊙restaurant noon-midnight, cafe 8.30am-6pm Mon-Fri; 🛜; MSportivnaya) One of the city's top Italian operations, Probka oozes Milanese sophistication and is popular with the suits from the building's Gazprom offices. Word to the wise: the Probka cafe inside the complex serves a very similar menu but is a bit cheaper.

🍷 DRINKING & NIGHTLIFE

BIG WINE FREAKS   WINE BAR

Map p284 (☎921-938 6063; Instrumentalnaya ul 3; ⏰6pm-1am Tue-Sat; 🛜) Boasting a stylish contemporary design, this aptly named place serves an excellent variety of wines from Europe and the New World, plus tasty snacks to go with those tempranillos and chardonnays. Helpful staff – all trained sommeliers – can provide tips on what to order. There's live music, along the lines of acoustic jazz, on Wednesday nights from 8pm.

DOUBLE B   CAFE

Map p284 (Дабльби; www.double-b.ru; Kronverksky pr; ⏰8am-10pm Mon-Fri, from 10am Sat & Sun; MGorkovskaya) One of Petrograd Side's best coffee spots is this hip little cafe on busy Kronverksky pr. Staff can make you a perfect brew with all the essential gadgetry. A green and grey colour scheme, geometric designs, curious lamps and a big picture window make a fine setting for a bit of caffeinated daydreaming.

YASLI   BAR

Map p284 (Ясли; www.facebook.com/yaslibar; ul Markina 1; ⏰noon-midnight Sun-Thu, to 2am Fri & Sat; 🛜; MGorkovskaya) Tucked down a narrow lane off busy Kronverksky, Yasli makes a fine retreat on chilly nights, with its excellent craft brews on tap and satisfying pub grub (like fish and chips). The setting channels a bit of Brooklyn chic with industrial fixtures and a hip but unpretentious crowd.

BOLSHOY BAR   BAR

Map p284 (Большой Бар; Bolshoy pr 45; ⏰9am-1am Sun-Tue, to 4am Wed-Sat; 🛜) A dapper boxcar-sized spot with old-time music and black-and-white films playing silently in the background, wryly named Bolshoy serves up good coffees by day and first-rate cocktails by night – though daytime drinking isn't discouraged. Slip onto a comfy bar stool and order an Aperol spritz from the talented but bristly bartender.

COFFEE ROOM ST PETERSBURG   CAFE

Map p284 (http://vk.com/coffeeroom; Kamennoostrovsky pr 22; ⏰9am-11pm Mon-Fri, from 10am Sat & Sun; MGorkovskaya) The Petrograd Side branch of this quirky chain of hipster cafe-bars – like the others it's arty and a very pleasant place to cool your feet.

VOLKONSKY   CAFE

Map p284 (www.wolkonsky.com; Kamennoostrovsky pr 8; ⏰8am-10pm; 🛜; MGorkovskaya) One of the more upmarket of the city's bakery-cafe chains, Volkonsky offers reviving brews and tempting confections.

⭐ ENTERTAINMENT

HI-HAT   LIVE PERFORMANCE

Map p284 (www.facebook.com/hihatrooftop; Aptekarsky pr 4; MPetrogradskaya) On the rooftop of an art cluster near the Botanical Gardens, Hi-Hat hosts nights of live music, DJs and open-air film screenings. The creative line-up and open-air setting draws out style mavens and a party-minded crowd. The schedule is erratic, but events typically run from 5pm or 6pm to around 1am on Fridays and Saturdays (with the odd Sunday and Thursday happening). Check the website for the schedule.

KRESTOVSKY STADIUM   STADIUM

(MKrestovsky Ostrov) Named after the island on which it stands, this huge arena seats 68,000 spectators at sporting events, and up to 80,000 at concerts. All eyes will be on Krestovsky in 2018 when it will be one of the main venues of the FIFA World Cup.

UPSALA CIRCUS   CIRCUS

(Упсала-цирк; ☎812-633 3558; http://upsala circus.ru/en/home; Sverdlovskaya nab 44; 🚸) Set up in 2000, this circus teaches performing skills to children with disabilities or from environments where they are at social risk. Unlike other circuses in Russia, there are no animals used in the acts – it's all about acrobatics, pantomime, clowning and contemporary dance. There's also a park by the circus tent that's open to all in summer.

AURORA PALACE THEATRE   PERFORMING ARTS

Map p284 (http://aurora-hall.ru; Pirogovskaya nab 5/2; MPloshchad Lenina) Named after the famed naval ship docked nearby, this place stages a mixed bag of ballets, rock and metal concerts and musical theatre.

A2
LIVE MUSIC

Map p284 (📞812-333 0379; http://a2.fm; pr Medikov 3; tickets from R500; MPetrogradskaya) With an outstanding sound system and an eclectic line-up of live music and DJs, A2 is one of the best venues for contemporary sounds in the city. It houses two concert halls (seating 1500 and 5000) and has a staggering number of bars sprinkled about the complex.

KAMCHATKA
CLUB, LIVE MUSIC

Map p284 (www.clubkamchatka.ru; ul Blokhina 15; cover R250-350; ⊙7pm-2am; MSportivnaya) A shrine to Viktor Tsoy, the late Soviet-era rocker who worked as caretaker of this former boilerhouse bunker with band mates from Kino. Music lovers flock here to light candles and watch a new generation thrash out their stuff. The line-up is varied and it's worth dropping by if only for a quick drink in this highly atmospheric place – find it tucked in a courtyard off the street.

BALTIC HOUSE
THEATRE

Map p284 (Балтийский дом; www.baltichouse. spb.ru; Alexandrovsky Park 4; MGorkovskaya) This large venue hosts an annual festival of plays from the Baltic countries, as well as Russian and European plays and a growing repertoire of experimental theatre.

SIBUR ARENA
SPECTATOR SPORT

(http://siburarena.com; Futbolnaya alleya 8, Krestovsky Ostrov; MKrestovsky Ostrov) This 7000-seat stadium is home to local basketball team BK Spartak (www.bc-spartak.ru), who play here from October to April. The complex also houses a pool, gym and hotel.

PETROVSKY STADIUM
SPECTATOR SPORT

Map p284 (Спортивный комплекс Петровский; www.petrovsky.spb.ru; Petrovsky Ostrov 2; MSportivnaya) The former home stadium of Zenit, St Petersburg's top football team, today this 21,000-seat arena is where Tosno plays many of its home games.

SHOPPING

★UDELNAYA FAIR
MARKET

(Удельная ярмарка; Skobolvesky pr, Vyborg Side; ⊙8am-5pm Sat & Sun; MUdelnaya) This treasure trove of Soviet ephemera, prerevolutionary antiques, WWII artefacts and bonkers kitsch from all eras is truly worth travelling for. Exit the metro station to the right and follow the crowds across the train tracks. Continue beyond the large permanent market, which is of very little interest, until you come to a huge area of independent stalls, all varying in quality and content.

The sheer size of the place means you'll really have to comb it to find the gems.

DAY & NIGHT
FASHION & ACCESSORIES

Map p284 (www.day-night.ru; Malaya Posadskaya ul 6; ⊙11am-9pm; MGorkovskaya) Looking like the set of *Alien* designed by Stella McCartney, this avant-garde boutique is one of St Petersburg's premier fashion experiences. Inside you'll find a top range of international designers along the lines of Comme des Garçons, Rag & Bone and Balenciaga. Bring your credit card.

There are separate entrances for the men's and women's stores, though a wildly configured interior staircase joins the two.

SYTNY MARKET
MARKET

Map p284 (Sytninskaya pl 3/5; ⊙8am-6pm; MGorkovskaya) This colourful Petrograd Side market sells everything from vegetables, fruit, meat and fish inside to electronics, clothing and knick-knacks outside. Its name means 'sated market', quite understandably.

MODEL SHOP
GIFTS & SOUVENIRS

Map p284 (Artillery Museum, Alexandrovsky Park 7; ⊙11am-6pm Wed-Sun; MGorkovskaya) Inside the Artillery Museum (though you don't need to pay for entry to get access to the shop), this is a must for model plane, train and automobile fans. There's a good range of mainly Russian models in stock.

🏃 SPORTS & ACTIVITIES

BALTIC AIRLINES
SCENIC FLIGHTS

Map p284 (📞812-611 0956; www.maxibalt tours.com; R5000; ⊙11.30am-6pm Sat, Sun & holidays, May-Oct; MGorkovskaya) For a bird's-eye view of the city, hop in a helicopter on Zayachy Island next to the Peter & Paul Fortress for 10 to 15 minute flights over the city.

They also offer flights over Peterhof taking off and landing at Kupecheskaya Gavan.

PITERLAND
WATER PARK

(http://piterland.ru; Primorsky pr 72, Vyborg Side; adult/child from R1500/900; ⊙10am-10.30pm; Ⓜ Staraya Derevnya) It's eternal summer under the giant dome of this superb aquapark accessed through a shopping mall facing onto the Gulf of Finland. The most fun is to be had slipping down the water slides twisting out of a giant pirate ship. There's also a wide range of styles of *banya* (hot baths) to sample, as well as a wave pool.

Buses and *marshrutky* run here from either Staraya Derevnya or Chyornaya Rechka metro stations.

YELAGIN ISLAND
OUTDOORS

Map p284 (Елагин остров; www.elaginpark. org; ice skating per hr R200-300; ⊙ice skating 11am-9pm; Ⓜ Krestovsky Ostrov) This car-free island becomes a winter wonderland in colder temperatures, with sledding, cross-country skiing and ice skating. Skis and skates are available for hire. In summer months, it's a great place to rent in-line skates as there is no traffic to contend with.

KRUGLIYE BANI
BATHHOUSE

(Circle Baths; ☑812-993 0808; http://batbani. ru/kruglye-bani; ul Karbysheva 29a; communal per person R60-250, luxe per person R400; ⊙communal baths 8am-10pm, luxe baths 9am-10pm Fri-Wed; Ⓜ Pl Muzhestva) One of the city's best *bani* is opposite the metro; look for the round building across the grassy traffic island. Rates at the communal baths rise towards the weekend. The luxe baths (only open to women on Wednesday and Saturday) also grant you access to the heated circular open-air pool. There are private facilities, too.

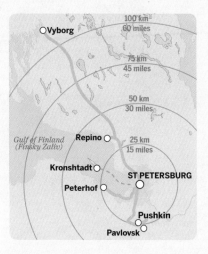

Day Trips from St Petersburg

Peterhof p174

The most popular day trip from St Petersburg is to Peter the Great's spectacular summer palace and grounds on the Gulf of Finland, easily reached from central St Petersburg by hydrofoil from outside the Admiralty.

Pushkin & Pavlovsk p179

Tsarskoe Selo (in the town of Pushkin) and Pavlovsk are two beautiful palaces and grounds next door to one another. This is a great day trip to see the summer palaces of Catherine the Great and Paul I.

Vyborg p182

Situated on the Gulf of Finland, this appealing town is features a medieval castle and an abundance of art-nouveau buildings. An easy day trip from St Petersburg, Vyborg offers enough for longer stays.

Repino p183

Part of Finland in the mid-20th-century, this village has long back in Russian hands and makes for a pleasant, outdoorsy day trip from St Petersburg.

Kronshtadt p184

Closed to foreigners until 1996, Kronshtadt's offering of history, cruises and naval might makes for a fascinating day trip destination.

TOP SIGHT
PETERHOF

The fountains are incredible, the palace is a stunner and the grounds are great for walking, so it's no surprise that Peter the Great's summer palace is usually the first-choice day trip for visitors to St Petersburg. Peterhof is no secret, however, so come early in the day or out of season to enjoy it without the crowds.

Peter's Summer Palace

Hugging the Gulf of Finland, 29km west of St Petersburg, Peterhof – the 'Russian Versailles' – is a far cry from the original cabin Peter the Great had built here to oversee construction of the Kronshtadt naval base. Peter liked the place so much he built a villa, Monplaisir, here and then a whole series of palaces and ornate gardens. Peterhof was renamed Petrodvorets (Peter's Palace) in 1944 but has since reverted to its original name. The palace and buildings are surrounded by leafy gardens and a spectacular ensemble of gravity-powered fountains.

What you see today is largely a reconstruction, as Peterhof was a major casualty of WWII. Apart from the damage done by the Germans, the palace suffered the worst under Soviet bombing raids in December 1941 and January 1942, because Stalin was determined to thwart Hitler's plan of hosting a New Year's victory celebration here.

The Lower Park

The Lower Park contains most of Peterhof's sights and is where you will arrive if you take the hydrofoil from St Petersburg to get here. Forming the lion's share of the palace grounds, it boasts an incredible symphony of gravity-powered golden fountains, beautiful waterways

DON'T MISS

➡ Grand Palace
➡ Water Avenue
➡ Monplaisir
➡ Hermitage

PRACTICALITIES

➡ Большой дворец
➡ www.peterhof museum.ru
➡ ul Razvodnaya
➡ adult/student R700/400, audio guide R600
➡ ⊘10.30am-6pm Tue-Sun, closed last Tue of month

and interesting historical buildings, making it one of St Petersburg's most dazzling attractions.

Criss-crossed by bridges and bedecked by smaller sprays, **Water Avenue** (pictured left; ☺May-Sep) is a canal leading from the hydrofoil dock to the palace. It culminates in the magnificent Grand Cascade, a symphony of over 140 fountains engineered in part by Peter himself. The central statue of Samson tearing open a lion's jaws celebrates – as so many things in St Petersburg do – Peter's victory over the Swedes at Poltava. Shooting up 62m, it was unveiled by Rastrelli for the 25th anniversary of the battle in 1735.

Grand Palace

The Grand Palace is an imposing edifice, although with 30-something rooms, it's not as large as many tsarist palaces. From the start of June to the end of September foreign tourists can visit only between 10.30am and noon, and again from 2.30pm until 4.15pm, due to guided tours being given only in Russian at other times. (While you have to enter the palace as part of a guided tour, it's quite possible to slip away.)

While Peter's palace was relatively modest, Rastrelli grossly enlarged the building for Empress Elizabeth. Later, Catherine the Great toned things down a little with a redecoration, although that's not really apparent from the glittering halls and art-filled galleries that are here today. All of the paintings, furniture and chandeliers are original, as everything was removed from the premises before the Germans arrived in WWII. The Chesme Hall is full of huge paintings of Russia's destruction of the Turkish fleet at Çesme in 1770. Other highlights include the exquisite East and West Chinese Cabinets, Peter's study and the Picture Hall, which lives up to its name, with hundreds of portraits crowding its walls. The Throne Room is the biggest in the palace, and the centrepiece is Peter's red velvet throne.

After WWII, Peterhof was largely left in ruins. Hitler had intended to throw a party here when his plans to occupy the Astoria Hotel were thwarted. He drew up pompous invitations, which obviously incensed his Soviet foes. Stalin's response was to preempt any such celebration by bombing the estate himself, in the winter of 1941–42, so it is ironic but true that most of the damage at Peterhof occurred at the hands of the Soviets.

Monplaisir

This far more humble, sea-facing villa was always Peter the Great's favourite retreat. It's easy to see why: **Monplaisir** (Монплезир; adult/student R500/300; ☺10.30am-6pm late May-early Oct) is wood panelled,

HYDROFOIL

From May to September, the **Peterhof Express** (Map p272; www.peterhof-express. com; single/return adult R800/1500, student R600/1000; ☺10am-6pm) hydrofoil departs from the jetty in front of the Admiralty every 30 minutes from 9am. The last hydrofoil leaves Peterhof at 7pm, and the trip takes 30 minutes.

The hydrofoil is fast and convenient, but rather expensive. You can save money by getting here by *marshrutka*. *Marshrutky* 300,424 and 424A (R80) leave from outside the Avtovo metro station. All pass through the town of Peterhof, immediately outside the palace. Tell the driver you want to go 'v dvaryéts' ('to the palace') and you'll be let off near the main entrance to the Upper Garden, on Sankt-Petersburgsky pr.

TRAIN

There's a reasonably frequent suburban train (R60, 40 minutes) from Baltic Station (Baltiysky vokzal) to Novy Peterhof, from where you can walk (around 30 minutes) or take any bus except 357 to the fifth stop, which will take another 10 minutes.

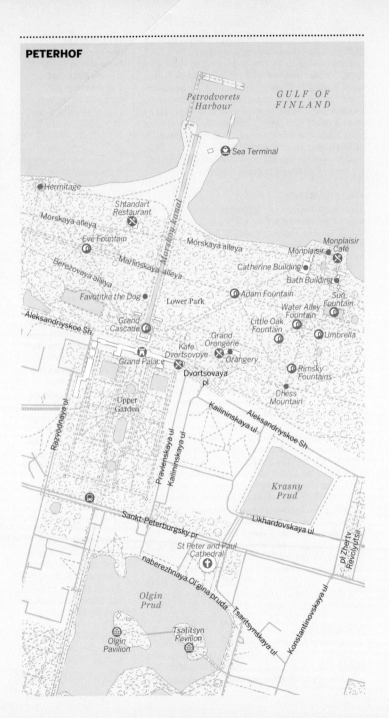

PETERHOF

Petrodvorets Harbour

GULF OF FINLAND

Sea Terminal

Hermitage

Shtandart Restaurant

Morskaya alleya

Eve Fountain

Morskaya alleya

Monplaisir Café

Monplaisir

Catherine Building

Marlinskaya alleya

Morskoy kanal

Berezovaya alleya

Bath Building

Favotitka the Dog

Lower Park

Adam Fountain

Sun Fountain

Aleksandriyskoe Sh

Grand Cascade

Water Alley Fountain

Little Oak Fountain

Umbrella

Grand Orangerie

Kafe Dvortsovoye

Grand Palace

Orangery

Rimsky Fountains

Dvortsovaya pl

Chess Mountain

Upper Garden

Kalininskaya ul

Aleksandriyskoe Sh

Razvodnaya ul

Pravlenskaya ul

Kalininskaya ul

Krasny Prud

Sankt-Peterburgsky pr

Likhardovskaya ul

St Peter and Paul Cathedral

pl Zhertv Revolyutsii

naberezhnaya Ol'gina pruda

Tsaritsynskaya ul

Konstantinovskaya ul

Olgin Prud

Olgin Pavilion

Tsatitsyn Pavilion

Cloche fountain, Monplaisir (p175)

snug and elegant, peaceful even when there's a crowd – which there used to be all the time, what with Peter's mandatory partying ('misbehaving' guests were required to gulp down huge quantities of wine).

Also in this complex is an annexe called the **Catherine Building** (Екатерининский корпус; adult/student R500/300; ☉10.30am-6pm), which was built by Rastrelli between 1747 and 1755. Its name derives from the fact that Catherine the Great was living in this building when her husband Peter III was overthrown,and it was from here that she set out for the capital to assume the Russian throne. The interior contains the bedroom and study of Alexander I, as well as the huge Yellow Hall. On the right side is the magnificent **Bath Building** (Банный корпус; adult/student R500/300; ☉10.30am-6pm Thu-Tue), built by Quarenghi in 1800, which is nothing special inside.Look out for some more trick fountains in the garden in front of the buildings.

Hermitage

Along the shore to the west, the 1725 **Hermitage** (Эрмитаж; adult/student R400/250; ☉10.30am-6pm Wed-Mon May-Oct) is a two-storey yellow-and-white box featuring the ultimate in private dining: special elevators hoist a fully laid table into the imperial presence on the 2nd floor, thereby eliminating any hindrance by servants. The elevators are circular and located directly in front of each diner, whose plate would be lowered, replenished and replaced. The device is demonstrated on Saturdays and Sundays at

NEED TO KNOW

Peterhof is 29km west of St Petersburg.

In the Lower Park itself, the best eating options are the Grand Orangerie (Lower Park; set menus R450-800; ☉11am-8pm), a cafe in the former palace orangery, or the Shtandart Restaurant (Ресторан Штандарт; www.restau rantshtandart.spb.ru; Lower Park; mains R590-1300; ☉11am-8pm), a bigger place with a terrace and views towards the Gulf of Finland. Outside the palace grounds, try the appealing Duck & Drake inside the New Peterhof Hotel (☑812-319 1010; www.new-peterhof.com; Sankt Peterburgsky pr 34; s/d from R5000/5900; ☎☒), where you can eat Russian and European fare (mains R520 to R950).

TOP TIP

Remember to bring mosquito repellent or to keep your legs and arms covered if you're here during summer; the mosquitoes on the palace grounds are fierce.

TICKETS FOR PETERHOF

On arrival, you'll need to pay to enter the grounds of the palace, known as the Lower Park, and then for each additional sight within it. Sadly, however, it's not cheap, as you're paying more than locals and the sights add up, so choose what you want to see carefully. Inexplicably, many museums also have different closing days, although all buildings are open Friday to Sunday. Nearly all tours and posted information are in Russian, so buy an information booklet at the kiosks near the entrances or, in the Grand Palace, take an English-language audio guide. Online tickets can be purchased for the Grand Palace at www.peterhofmuseum.ru, which can avoid long lines in the summer months.

1pm, 2pm and 3pm. Further west is yet another palace, Marly, inspired by the Versailles hunting lodge of the same name so loved by Louis XIV.

Park Alexandria

Even on summer weekends, the rambling and overgrown **Park Alexandria** (Парк Александрия; adult/student R300/200; ☉9am-10pm) is peaceful and practically empty. Built for Tsar Nicholas I (and named for his tsarina), these grounds offer a sweet retreat from the crowds. Originally named for Alexander Nevsky, the **gothic chapel** (adult/student R300/200; ☉10.30am-6pm Tue-Sun) was completed in 1834 as the private chapel of Nicholas I. Nearby is the **cottage** (Коттедж; adult/student R500/300; ☉10.30am-6pm Tue-Sun) that was built around the same time as his summer residence. Also part of this same ensemble is the beautifully restored **Farmer's Palace** (Фермерский дворец; adult/student R600/350; ☉10.30am-6pm Tue-Sun), built here in 1831 as a pavilion in the park and designed to reify pastoral fantasies of rural life for the royal family. It became the home of the teenage Tsarevitch Alexander (later Alexander II), who loved it throughout his life.

Peterhof Town

Outside the palace grounds is the handsome **St Peter & Paul Cathedral** (Петропавловский собор; Sankt-Petersburgsky pr; ☉9am-7pm), and, continuing around the edge of Olgin Prud (Olga's Pond), the **Tsaritsyn and Olgin Pavilions** (adult/student R700/400; ☉10.30am-6pm, last entry 4pm), two buildings sitting on islands in the middle of the pond. Nicholas I had these elaborate pavilions built for his wife (Alexandra Fyodorovna) and daughter (Olga Nikolayevna) respectively. Only recently restored and reopened, they boast unique Mediterranean architectural styles reminiscent of Pompeii.

Further down Sankt-Petersburgsky pr is the **Raketa Petrodvorets Watch Factory** (☎926-304 05 91; www.raketa.com; Sankt-Petersburgsky pr 60; ☉9am-6pm Mon-Fri) `FREE`, one of the town's biggest employers, which has an on-site shop selling very cool watches.

TOP SIGHT
PUSHKIN & PAVLOVSK

The sumptuous palaces and sprawling parks at Tsarskoe Selo and Pavlovsk (pictured) are, thanks to Catherine the Great and Pushkin, entrenched in Russian history and immortalised in literature. These two neighbouring complexes can be combined in a day's visit – although if you're not in the mood to rush, there is plenty at both of them to keep you entertained for an entire day.

DON'T MISS

➡ Catherine Palace
➡ Catherine Park
➡ Pavlovsk Great Park
➡ Pavlovsk Great Palace

The Parks

Almost adjacent yet very different in style, Tsarskoe Selo and Pavlovsk are both huge imperial estates with impressive gardens, palaces and various other embellishments. Both also have towns that have grown up around them over the centuries. (The town surrounding Tsarskoe Selo was originally called Tsarskoe Selo, too, but changed its name to Pushkin in 1937.)

Tsarskoe Selo (the 'tsar's village') is understandably the big hitter of the two thanks to the beautiful Catherine Palace and its sumptuous grounds. Pavlovsk, just a short bus ride away, is far less visited and much quieter as a result, but its grounds are wilder and arguably even more lovely, and make for a perfect place to get lost in.

Catherine Palace

The centrepiece of Tsarskoe Selo, created under Empresses Elizabeth and Catherine the Great between 1744 and 1796, is the vast baroque **Catherine Palace** (Екатерининский дворец; adult/student R1000/350, audio guide R150; ☉10am-4.45pm Wed-Sun), designed by Rastrelli and named after Peter the Great's second wife. From May to September the palace can only be visited by individuals between noon and 2pm and 4pm and 5pm, otherwise it's reserved for prebooked tour groups, such is its rightful popularity. The audio guide is well worth taking, as it gives detailed explanations of what you'll see in each room.

As at the Winter Palace, Catherine the Great had many of Rastrelli's original interiors remodelled in classical style. Most of the gaudy exterior and 20-odd rooms of the palace have been beautifully restored – compare them to the photographs of the devastation left by the Germans.

NEED TO KNOW

Pushkin is 25km south of St Petersburg, Pavlovsk 29km. The area code is ☎812.

From Moskovskaya Station, take the exit marked 'Buses for the airport', then pick up *marshrutky* 286, 299, 342 or K545 towards Pushkin (R40). These continue to Pavlovsk (R50). Look for 'Пушкин' or 'Дворец' on buses. Trains go from Vitebsk Station, but are infrequent during the week. For Pushkin, get off at Detskoe Selo (Детское село), and for Pavlovsk at Pavlovsk Station (Павловск).

EATING

In Tsarskoe Selo **Admiralty Restaurant** (☎812-465 3549; www.admiral.gutsait.ru; Parkovaya ul; mains R450-950; ☉noon-11pm; ☎) serves high-end Russian fare in an elegant brick-walled dining room. In town, try cosy **White Rabbit** (ul Moskovskaya 22; mains R490-870; ☉11am-11pm; ☎). In Pavlovsk, **Podvorye** (☎812-454 5464; www.podvorye.ru; Filtrovskoye sh 16; mains R620-1450; ☉noon-11pm) is among the best options. It's near the train station by Great Park's most eastern entrance.

The interiors are superb, with highlights including the Great Hall, the Arabesque Hall, the baroque Cavalier's Dining Room, the White State Dining Room, the Crimson and Green Pilaster Rooms, the Portrait Hall and, of course, the world-famous Amber Room. The panels used in the Amber Room were a gift given to Peter the Great, but not put to any use until 1743 when Elizabeth decided to use them decoratively, after which they were ingeniously incorporated into the walls here. What you see is a reconstruction of the original that disappeared during WWII and is believed to have been destroyed.

Catherine Park

The lovely **Catherine Park** (Екатерининский парк; May-Sep R120, Oct-Apr free; ☉9am-6pm), with its main entrance on Sadovaya ul next to the palace chapel, surrounds the Catherine Palace. It extends around the ornamental Great Pond and contains an array of interesting buildings, follies and pavilions. Near the Catherine Palace, the Cameron Gallery has rotating exhibitions. The park's outer section focuses on the Great Pond. In summer you can take a ferry to the island to visit the **Chesme Column** (adult/child R250/150; ☉11am-6pm May-Sep), a monument to Russia's victory over the Turkish fleet. Beside the pond, the blue baroque **Grotto Pavilion** (☉10am-5pm Fri-Wed) **FREE** houses temporary exhibitions in summer. A walk around the Great Pond will reveal other buildings that the royals built over the years, including the incongruous-looking Turkish Bath with its minaret-style tower, the wonderful Marble Bridge, the Chinese Pavilion and a Concert Hall isolated on an island.

Alexander Palace & Park

A short distance north of the Catherine Palace, and surrounded by the overgrown and tranquil **Alexander Park** (Александровский парк; ☉7am-11pm) **FREE**, is the classical **Alexander Palace** (Александровский дворец; Dvortsovaya ul 2). This palace, built by Quarenghi between 1792 and 1796 for the future Alexander I, was the favourite residence of Nicholas II, the last Russian tsar. Only a few rooms are open to visitors, but they're impressive, with a huge tiger-skin carpet and an extremely ropey portrait of a young Queen Victoria to boot. It's a poignant and forgotten place that doesn't get many tourists and is a welcome contrast to the Catherine Palace.

Pavlovsk Great Palace

Between 1781 and 1786, on orders from Catherine the Great, architect Charles Cameron designed the **Pavlovsk Great Palace** (Большой Павловский дворец; www.pavlovskmuseum.ru; ul Sadovaya 20; adult/

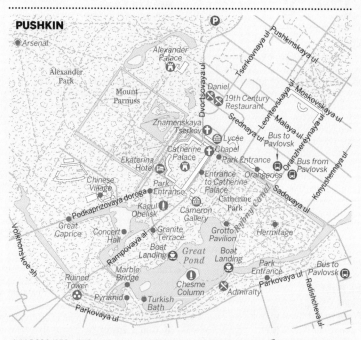

PUSHKIN

child R600/250; ⊙10am-6pm, closed Tue, Fri & 1st Mon of month) 🏊 in Pavlovsk. The palace was designated for Catherine's son Paul (hence the name, Pavlovsk), and it was Paul's second wife, Maria Fyodorovna, who orchestrated the design of the interiors. Tragically, the original palace was burnt down two weeks after the end of WWII when the cigarette of a careless Soviet soldier set off German mines (the Soviets blamed the Germans). As at Tsarskoe Selo, the restoration is remarkable.

The finest rooms are on the middle floor of the central block. Cameron designed the round Italian Hall beneath the dome and the Grecian Hall to its west, though the lovely green fluted columns were added by his assistant, Vincenzo Brenna. Flanking these are two private suites designed mainly by Brenna: Paul's along the north side of the block and Maria Fyodorovna's on the south. The Hall of War of the military-obsessed Paul contrasts with Maria's Hall of Peace, decorated with musical instruments and flowers. On the middle floor of the south block are Paul's Throne Room and the Hall of the Maltese Knights of St John, of whom he was the Grand Master.

Pavlovsk Great Park

If you decide to skip the palace, you may simply wish to wander around the serene **Pavlovsk Great Park** (Павловский парк; adult/child R150/100; ⊙6am-9pm Sat-Thu, closed 1st Mon of month) – and as you'll have to pay to enter them just to access the palace, it's worth exploring and seeing what you come across. Filled with rivers and ponds, tree-lined avenues, classical statues and hidden temples, it's a delightful place to get lost. Highlights include the **Rose Pavilion** (Розовый павильон; Pavlovsk Park; adult/student R300/150; ⊙11am-6pm Wed-Sun) and the **Private Garden** (Собственный садик; Pavlovsk Park; adult/child R250/150; ⊙11am-7pm), with its beautifully arranged flowerbeds and impressive sculpture of the Three Graces. Bike hire is available at several locations around the park and is a great way to explore, as distances are large.

Vyborg

Explore

This appealing Gulf of Finland provincial town is dominated by a medieval castle and peppered with beautiful Finnish art nouveau buildings and romantic cobblestone streets.

The border has jumped back and forth around Vyborg for most of its history. Peter the Great captured it from the Swedes in 1710. A century later it fell within autonomous Finland, and after the revolution Vyborg remained part of independent Finland. Since then the Finns have called it Viipuri. Stalin took Vyborg in 1939, lost it to the Finns during WWII, and on getting it back at the end of the war deported all the Finns. Today the Finns are back by the coachloads for sightseeing and carousing on the weekends.

The Best...

→**Sight** Vyborg Castle
→**Place to Eat** Russky Dvor
→**Scenery** Park Monrepo

Top Tip

There's a lot to see in Vyborg, so go early to make the most of your time here, or better yet stay the night and experience the city without the day trippers.

Getting There & Away

→**Train** Elektrichki (R301, 2½ hours, hourly) leave from St Petersburg's Finland Station (Finlyandsky vokzal). Of these, there are also a handful of express services (R331, 1¼ hours, four daily), or the far more expensive Helsinki-bound trains, which stop in Vyborg (R2236, one hour).

→**Bus** Services to/from St Petersburg (R280, to/from either metro stations Devyatkino or Parnas) run every 20 minutes from 6.30am to 8pm. Theoretically, travel time is around 2¼ hours, but the traffic can lengthen this, so the train remains the best option.

→**Station locations** The bus and train stations are opposite each other on Vokzalnaya pl.

Need to Know

→**Area Code** ☑81378
→**Location** 174km northwest of St Petersburg and just 30km from the Finnish border.
→**Tourist Office** The **Vyborg Tourist Information Centre** (☑905-210 5555; www.vyborg-info.ru; Vokzalnaya ul 13; ◷9am-5pm) is located near the train station.

◉ SIGHTS

★**VYBORG CASTLE**   HISTORIC BUILDING
(Выборгский замок; Zamkovy Island; grounds free, museum R100; ◷grounds 9am-7pm daily, exhibitions 10am-6pm) Rising stoutly from an islet in Vyborg Bay, this castle was built by the Swedes in 1293 when they first captured Karelia from Novgorod. Most of it now consists of 16th-century alterations. The castle contains several exhibition halls, including a mildly diverting small **museum** (R100; ◷10am-6pm Tue-Sun) on local history, but the main attraction is climbing the many steps of whitewashed **St Olaf's Tower** for commanding views over the town (closed for renovations at time of research).

ALVAR AALTO LIBRARY   ARCHITECTURE
(Biblioteka Alvara Aalto; ☑81378-24 937; www.aalto.vbgcity.ru/excursion_eng; pr Suvorova 4; guided tour in Russian/English R150/350; ◷11am-7pm Mon-Fri year-round & noon-7pm Sat Sep-May) A must-see for architecture fans is the beautifully designed public library, one of Finnish architect Alvar Aalto's iconic designs. After years of restoration, the 1935 building looks lovelier than ever, with painstaking efforts to return it to Aalto's original vision. Handmade bronze-handled doors, circular skylights in the reading room, and elegant birchwood shelves are among the many features. It's still a working public library, open to all (though oddly, it lacks wi-fi).

Call to book a guided tour in English.

★**HERMITAGE VYBORG**   MUSEUM
(Эрмитаж Выборг; ul Ladanova 1; adult/student R250/150; ◷10am-6pm) Housed in a wing of a striking building designed by Finnish architect Uno Ulberg in 1930, this small museum hosts themed exhibitions that are curated from the Hermitage's massive collection and

change every six months. The functional white building, which sits in the middle of an old defensive bastion, is shared with Vyborg's arts school, which also has a **gallery** (ul Ladanova 1; ⏰10am-6pm Mon-Fri) FREE with regularly changing exhibitions.

PARK MONREPO   PARK
(Парк Монрепо; www.parkmonrepos.org; adult/child R200/free; ⏰10am-9pm May-Sep, to 6pm Oct-Apr) This 180-hectare park facing onto tranquil Zashchitnaya Bay is a lovely place to escape the world for a few hours, if not most of the day. It's laid out in a classical style, with various pavilions, curved bridges, arbours and sculptures. Bus 1 or 6 (R30, 15 minutes) will get you here from outside the train and bus stations.

ANNINSKIE FORTIFICATIONS   FORTRESS
(Аннинские укрепления; Petrovskaya ul) At the southern end of Tverdysh Island is this double line of fortifications, built between 1730 and 1750 as protection against the Swedes and named after Empress Anna Ioanovna. Nearby, on a hill just above the restaurant Russky Dvor, a handsome statue of **Peter the Great**, erected on the bicentenary of the city's capture by Russia, surveys the town.

ACTIVITIES

BOAT STAND   BOATING
(nab 40-letiya Komsomola; boat hire per hr R250-300; ⏰10am-10pm May-Sep) In the warmer months, the best place to be is out on the water, boating peacefully, with the backdrop of old Vyborg ever at your side. A handy boat stand near the centre of town hires out row boats and paddle boats and can get you out on the water in a hurry.

EATING

★ RUSSKY DVOR   RUSSIAN $$
(Русский Двор; ☎81378-26 369; ul Shturma; meals R400-720; ⏰noon-midnight) The terrace overlooking the castle and town is an ideal spot to enjoy some traditional Russian dishes like venison with berry sauce. The chef cures his own salmon and you can drink their delicious homemade honey and horseradish *kvas* (fermented ryebread water). The high-ceilinged castle-like interior is also impressive, though sometimes ruined by blaring Russian pop music.

ROUND TOWER RESTAURANT   RUSSIAN $$
(Круглая башня; Rynochnaya pl 1; mains R420-850; ⏰noon-midnight, to 2am Fri & Sat) On the top floor of a 16th-century tower, this atmospheric and long-running place is a reliable option for traditional Russian cuisine, although it can sometimes be booked out by tour groups.

Repino

Explore
Come summer, Petersburgers stream out of the city to relax on the beaches to the north between Sestroretsk and Zelenogorsk on the Gulf of Finland. Between these two towns you'll find the village of Repino, 45km from St Petersburg. From 1918 to the end of WWII, this area was part of Finland and the village was known as Kuokkala. In 1948, back in Russian hands, the village was renamed in honour of its most famous resident, Ilya Repin.

The Best...
➡ **Sight** Penaty
➡ **Scenery** Beach Laskovy
➡ **Place to Eat** Skazka

Getting There & Away
The easiest way to get to Repino is to take the frequent *marshrutky* 400 (R105, one hour) that leaves from near Finland Station (Finlyandsky vokzal) – cross ul Komsomola, and look for the stop on the right side of pl Lenina. You can also catch bus 211 (R90, one hour) from beside Chyornaya Rechka metro station. Be sure to tell the driver that you want to get out at Penaty.

Need to Know
➡ **Area Code** ☎812
➡ **Location** 42km northwest of St Petersburg

SIGHTS

PENATY MUSEUM

(Пенаты; ☎812-432 0828; www.nimrah.ru; Primorskoe Shosse 411; adult/student R300/200; ⊙museum 10.30am-6pm Wed-Sun, grounds 10.30am-8pm Wed-Mon) The home of Ilya Repin in his later years is now a museum and park, and it's a pleasant day trip any time of year. You can also visit the nearby beach and even stay in one of the area's resort-style hotels in the summer.

Repin bought land here in 1899, named the estate after a Roman household god and designed the light-flooded house in an arts-and-crafts style. The artist produced many of his later works here, and several of his paintings still hang on the walls. The furnishings have been left just as they were during Repin's residence, which was up to his death in 1930. His grave, marked by a simple Russian Orthodox wooden cross, is in the park, along with a couple of wooden follies also designed by Repin.

BEACH LASKOVY BEACH

(Пляж Ласковый) Near the town of Repino, this long stretch of sand backed by pine forest makes a great setting for a day out of the city. The water is generally calm and perfect for a dip on those rare hot summer days. Seaside vendors dole out *kvas* (fermented rye water) and other cold drinks, as well as snacks, and there are a few sit-down restaurants overlooking the sea.

EATING

SKAZKA EUROPEAN $$

(☎812-432 1251; www.skazkarepino.ru; Primorskoe Shosse 415; mains R570-1490; ⊙11am-11pm; 🛜) A surprising find in Repino, Skazka has an attractive dining room with big picture windows and a terrace – both fine spots for enjoying eggplant parmigiano, grilled trout, duck breast with carmelised apples and other nicely executed dishes.

PENATY RUSSIAN $$

(Пенаты; ☎812-432 1125; Primorskoe Shosse 411A; mains R400-850; ⊙10am-10pm) A short stroll from Repin's estate, Penaty serves a range of Russian dishes including salads, soups and various shashlyk. Dine on the pleasant flower-trimmed terrace.

Kronshtadt

Explore

With its grand cathedral, waterfront parks and pretty canal-lined avenues, Kronshtadt makes for a fascinating half-day visit. Aside from taking in one grand neo-Byzantine church and visiting a little-visited corner of greater St Petersburg, this is a fine place for seeing Russia's mighty naval centre, and getting an overview of the bay on a boat tour.

Within a year of founding St Petersburg, Peter – desirous of protecting his new Baltic toehold – started work on the fortress of Kronshtadt on Kotlin Island, 29km out in the Gulf of Finland. It's been a pivotal Soviet and Russian naval base ever since, and was closed to foreigners until 1996.

The Best...

➡**Sight** Naval Cathedral

➡**Excursion** Reeperbahn

➡**Place to Eat** Bolshaya Cherepakha

Top Tip

The handy ring road makes it perfectly feasible to combine a trip here with a visit to either Repino or to Peterhof.

Getting There & Away

Catch bus 101 to Kronshtadt from Staraya Derevnya metro station (R40, 40 minutes). Upon exiting the metro, turn hard left and then walk past the *marshrutky* and trams until you come to a second bus park where the 101 bus begins and ends its route. Alternatively take *marshrutka* 405 from Chyornaya Rechka station (R80, 40 minutes); exit the station to your left and cross the street to find the stop.

Vehicles heading back to St Petersburg depart from both sides of the large 'Dom Byta' on the corner of ul Grazhdanskaya and pr Lenina. From there it's about a 1km walk southeast to the Naval Cathedral.

Need to Know

➡**Area Code** ☎812

➡**Location** 51km west of St Petersburg

> ## KRONSHTADT REBELLION
> ••
> In 1921 the hungry and poor Red Army sailors stationed here organised an ill-fated mutiny against the Bolsheviks. They set up a Provisional Revolutionary Committee and drafted a resolution demanding, among other things, an end to Lenin's harsh War Communism. On 16 March 1921 the mutineers were defeated when 50,000 troops crossed the ice from Petrograd and massacred nearly the entire naval force. The sailors' stand wasn't entirely in vain, as afterwards Lenin did scrap War Communism.

⊙ SIGHTS

NAVAL CATHEDRAL CHURCH
(Морской собор; Yakornaya pl; ⊙9am-6.30pm) Kronshtadt's key sight is the unusual and beautiful Naval Cathedral. Built between 1903 and 1913 to honour Russian naval muscle, this neo-Byzantine wonder stands on Yakornaya pl (Anchor Sq), where you'll also find an eternal flame for Kronshtadt's sailors, and the florid art nouveau monument of Admiral Makarov.

The cathedral underwent a thorough renovation for its centennial celebrations and is now looking breathtaking, both inside and out. Its 75m-high cupola is the highest point in town, and its enormous interior makes its use as a cinema during the Soviet period rather logical.

REEPERBAHN CRUISE
(☑821-382 0888; Middle Harbour; adult/student R550/400; ⊙departures 1.30pm, 3.30pm & 5.30pm May-Sep) From the Middle Harbour beside Petrovsky Park, you can take cruises to various forts around the island, including Fort Konstantin. Several companies offer cruises, including Reeperbahn, with three daily departures in summer.

✖ EATING

BOLSHAYA CHEREPAKHA RUSSIAN **$$**
(Большая Черепаха; www.big-turtle.com; ul Karla Libknekhta 29; mains R400-750; ⊙11am-11pm) One of Kronshtadt's better restaurants, the 'Big Turtle' serves up salads, spaghetti with seafood, perch fillet with vegetables, and grilled meats. With decent beers on tap, it's also a fine spot for an afternoon drink. It's located a short stroll from the Naval Cathedral – cross the main bridge and continue up Roshalya, where you'll see it on the right.

CAFE KASHTAN RUSSIAN **$**
(Кафе Каштан; pr Lenina 25; mains R300-500; ⊙11am-11pm) The entrance to this charming little place is actually on ul Andreevskaya, a side-street of the main shopping street, pr Lenina. It's friendly and has a wide selection of pub fare as well as coffee and desserts like tiramisu.

🛏 Sleeping

Accommodation in St Petersburg doesn't come cheap, and it pays to book well in advance as places fill up during the White Nights and throughout the summer. The hospitality industry has improved enormously in the past decade, however, with Soviet hotels now largely a thing of the past, replaced by a range of brightly decorated hostels, mini-hotels and luxury options.

Hotels

There has been a revolution in hotel accommodation in St Petersburg and a large expansion of modern, professionally run establishments. Old Soviet fleapits have been reconstructed as contemporary and appealing hotels, some of the city centre's most desperately derelict buildings have been rebuilt as boutique or luxury properties and the overall standards of service have risen enormously. That said, most hotels are still fairly expensive, with a lack of good midrange places in the city centre. Though they do exist, they tend to get booked up well in advance (particularly during the summer months), so plan ahead if you want to stay in the Historic Heart.

Mini-Hotels

Mini-hotels are a St Petersburg phenomenon. While most aspiring hoteliers are not able to pay for the renovation and conversion of entire buildings themselves, lots of small-time entrepreneurs have been able to buy an apartment or two and create a small hotel in otherwise normal residential buildings. Due to their individuality and the care that often goes into their running, mini-hotels are some of the best places to stay in the city. They also tend to be well located in the centre of the city where demand for rooms is highest. On the downside, they are by their very nature rather small places, so rooms book up quickly.

Hostels

Once a city with just a handful of very average, far-flung and depressing hostels, St Petersburg now positively spoils budget travellers with a wide range of places to sleep for well under R1000 a night. Central, well run, safe, clean and with free wi-fi, this new generation of hostels is sure to be embraced by anyone coming to Russia for the first time on a budget. Hostels here tend to be run by enthusiastic staff who themselves have travelled widely and are passionate about sharing their knowledge of their home town with travellers. Book ahead to ensure you get a place at the hostel you want.

Apartments

As hotels for individual travellers tend to be fairly expensive, even in midrange categories, renting an apartment is a great option and St Petersburg is full of large flats that are regularly rented out to tourists. Security is generally very good, with multiple locks on doors, entry phones and well-lit corridors. Many local travel agencies offer apartments, and the city's profile on the usual home-sharing websites is well established.

Lonely Planet's Top Choices

Baby Lemonade Hostel
(p189) A fun, friendly pop-art hostel with quality, hotel-style private rooms.

Soul Kitchen Hostel (p192)
Overlooking the Moyka; one of the most charming of the city's hostels.

Alexander House (p192)
Beautiful privately run place overlooking the Kryukov Canal.

Rossi Hotel (p191) Gorgeous
boutique hotel overlooking the charming Fontanka River.

Rachmaninov Antique Hotel (p189) Sublime location and
great value for money behind the Kazan Cathedral.

Best by Budget

€

Soul Kitchen Hostel (p192)
This gorgeous hostel is well located and lots of fun to stay at.

Baby Lemonade Hostel
(p189) Psychedelic design and a friendly environment with great views from the roof.

Friends by the House of Books (p190) Our favourite
of the many branches of this friendly, colourful hostel chain.

€€

Rachmaninov Antique Hotel (p189) A winner on all
fronts, this smart place is an insider's top choice.

Hotel Indigo (p194) Breathing new life into an old building,
this superb transformation is an excellent choice.

Tradition Hotel (p196) This
charming Petrograd Side hotel

is a consistent traveller favourite due to its helpful staff.

€€€

Belmond Grand Hotel Europe (p191) The classic St
Petersburg luxury hotel, the Europe is the choice of kings and presidents.

Hotel Astoria (p191) A
wonderfully modernised classic luxury hotel full of history.

Official State Hermitage Hotel (p195) An opulent offer-
ing with luxe accoutrements.

Hotel Domina Prestige
(p193) This cool place is a worthy addition to the top end of St Petersburg's hotels.

Best Small Hotels

Sovremenik (p196) Colourful
and whimsically decorated place on Petrograd Side.

Nils Bed & Breakfast
(p195) Beautifully renovated old apartment with four spacious bedrooms.

Ognivo (p194) Attractive,
well-maintained rooms with a quirky design.

Best Luxury Hotels

Kempinski Hotel Moyka 22 (p191) A superb interna-
tional luxury hotel right on the doorstep of the Hermitage.

Four Seasons Hotel Lion Palace (p191) Meticulously re-
stored palace next to St Isaac's Cathedral.

Demetra Art Hotel (p195)
The choice for lovers of art nouveau.

NEED TO KNOW

Price Ranges
The following price ranges refer to the cheapest room available during the high season (May to July).

€	less than R3000
€€	R3000–15,000
€€€	more than R15,000

Reservations
➜ It is essential to reserve at least a month in advance for accommodation during the White Nights (late May to early July).

➜ Booking online via a hotel's website is usually the cheapest method, as there are few accommodation websites worth bothering with, and most hotels post their best rates online.

Tipping
Tipping hotel staff and porters will only be expected in the very top hotels in St Petersburg, although it will always be appreciated for good service.

Breakfast
Breakfast is nearly always a buffet (shvetsky stol), and except in four- and five-star hotels, will usually be fairly unexciting, with limited choices.

SLEEPING

Where to Stay

Neighbourhood	For	Against
Historic Heart	Quite frankly, this is where you want to be if you have the chance. Everything is here, right on your doorstep, and it takes a maximum of 20 minutes to get anywhere on foot within this neighbourhood.	Accommodation here can be more expensive.
Sennaya & Kolomna	Far quieter and less busy than the Historic Heart, while still definitely historic and central itself. Great for access to the Mariinsky Theatre.	Distances on foot can be very long, especially if you're staying in Kolomna, where there's currently no metro station (one is under construction).
Smolny & Vosstaniya	Equally in the thick of things as the Historic Heart, this happening part of town around the lower half of Nevsky Pr is home to much of St Petersburg's youth culture and artistic life.	Smolny, in particular, can feel surprisingly remote from the rest of the city due to bad transport links and its own backwater ambience.
Vasilyevsky Island	A very pleasant residential area. Very well connected to the rest of the city as long as you're within easy walking distance of one of the metro stations.	If you're not near the metro, you will feel very isolated out here. If you are looking to party in St Petersburg during the summer months, this is not a good option as the bridges rise at night.
Petrograd & Vyborg Sides	The Petrograd Side is both central and very pleasant, with lots of local sights and easy transport links to the centre of town.	If you are looking to party in St Petersburg during the summer months, this is not a good option as the bridges rise at night.

📖 Historic Heart

⭐**BABY LEMONADE HOSTEL**　　　HOSTEL $
Map p272 (📱812-570 7943; http://babylemonade.
epoquehostels.com; Inzhenernaya ul 7; dm/d with
shared bathroom from R600/2500, d from R3800;
@🎧; MGostiny Dvor) The owner of Baby Lemonade is crazy about the 1960s and it shows
in the pop-art, psychedelic design of this
friendly, fun hostel with two pleasant, large
dorms and a great kitchen and living room.
However, it's worth splashing out for the bou-
tique-hotel-worthy private rooms that are in
a separate flat with great rooftop views.

FRIENDS ON BANKOVSKY　　　HOSTEL $
Map p272 (📱812-310 4950; www.en.friendsplace.
ru/druzya-na-bankovskom; Bankovsky per 3;
dm/r with shared bathroom from R580/1860;
@🎧; MSennaya Ploshchad) Social, party-
oriented hostel that's part of the ubiquitous
Friends chain. Rooms are decorated in the
chain's trademark colourful, somewhat
whimsical style.

⭐**FRIENDS HOSTEL
BY GOSTINY DVOR**　　　HOTEL $$
Map p272 (📱812-740 4720; www.en.friendsplace.
ru/druzya-na-lomonosova; ul Lomonosova 3; r from
R5200; @🎧; MGostiny Dvor) Sharing the top
floor of a renovated historic building with a
budget hotel, this is one of the best branches
of the Friends chain. There are no dorms
here and all the rooms have attached bath-
rooms, but the same cosy, quirky decorative
charm is in place – complete with cuddly
toys and flowery print curtains and linens.

There's also a good common room and
kitchen for self-catering. It's not far from
Gostiny Dvor (p102) but is actually closer to
the more common people's market Apraksin
Dvor (p103).

⭐**RACHMANINOV
ANTIQUE HOTEL**　　　BOUTIQUE HOTEL $$
Map p272 (📱812-327 7466; www.hotelrachmani
nov.com; Kazanskaya ul 5; s/d from R6300/7500;
@🎧; MNevsky Prospekt) The long-established
Rachmaninov still feels like a secret place for
those in the know. Perfectly located and run
by friendly staff, it's pleasantly old world,
with hardwood floors and attractive Russian furnishings, particularly in the breakfast salon, which has a grand piano.

Each of the 27 bedroom doors has been
painted by a different local artist, turning
the hallways into an art gallery.

SKY HOTEL　　　HOTEL $$
Map p272 (📱812-456 0789; http://skyhotel.ru;
Bolshaya Konyushennaya 17; r from R7000; ❄🎧;
MNevsky Prospekt) Wildly patterned wallpa-
per and retro theatre posters in the corridors
create an impression at this above-average
15-room hotel in a great, central location. Its
6th-floor location in a courtyard provides at-
mospheric rooftop views, particularly from
the breakfast room and lounge, which has
an outdoor balcony.

STATION HOTEL A1　　　HOTEL $$
Map p272 (Станция А1; 📱812-407 3865; https://
station-hotels.ru; Kirpichniy per 3; r from R6100;
❄🎧; MAdmiralteyskaya) The most central of a
city-wide chain of small, modern hotels that
are handy for short or business stays. Functional rooms pop with bright citrus coloured
walls and a clean Ikea vibe. Add R200 for the
buffet breakfast.

FD HOSTEL　　　HOSTEL $$
Map p272 (FD Хостел; 📱8-931-341 9652; http://
fdhostel.ru; Nevsky pr 11; r from R3000; @🎧;
MAdmiralteyskaya) Although it's called a hos-
tel there are no dorms, just plain but pleas-
ant private rooms with either double or twin
beds that share bathrooms and the rest of
the good facilities that come along with the
anti-cafe (a cafe where you pay based on
time spent there) that shares the premises.
The bonus is its brilliant location and roof-
top terrace with views all along Nevsky.

EKATERINA HOTEL　　　HOTEL $$
Map p272 (Екатерина Отель; 📱812-401 6566;
www.ekaterinahotel.com; Millionnaya ul 10; s/d
from R14,000/14,600; @🎧; MNevsky Prospekt)
Occupying part of the historic home of Andrey Stakenschnieder, chief court architect
of Alexander I, this appealing 40-room hotel
retains some of the building's original decorative features, but with largely modern furnishings in the tall-ceilinged rooms.

It's a bit of a hike to the metro but not far
from the Hermitage. Also in the building are
an antique-style teahouse and restaurant.

VODOGRAY　　　HOTEL $$
Map p272 (Водограй; 📱812-570 1717; www.vo-
dogray-hotel.ru; Karavannaya ul 2; s/d incl break-
fast from R4000/6000; 🎧; MGostiny Dvor) Its
Ukrainian country-cottage style – all pretty
patchwork quilts, pillows and dried flow-
ers – puts this well-located mini-hotel in a
grade of its own. Breakfast is served in the

even more stylised Ukranian restaurant on the ground floor.

FRIENDS BY THE HOUSE OF BOOKS

HOSTEL **$$**

Map p272 (Друзья у Дома Книги; ☑ 812-3317799; www.friendsplace.ru/druzya-na-kazanskaya/; 6th flr, nab kanala Griboyedova 19; r with shared bathroom from R4200; @ ⌖; Ⓜ Nevsky Prospekt) This appealing branch of the popular, well-designed hostel chain has a great location with a superb view of the Church of the Saviour on the Spilled Blood from its rooftop lounge. Decoration is quirky and colourful as usual.

PIO ON GRIBOYEDOV

HOTEL **$$**

Map p272 (☑ 812-571 9476; http://hotelpio.ru; nab kanala Griboyedova 35, apt 5; s/d with shared bathroom from R3400/4000, with private bathroom from R4500/5500; ⌖; Ⓜ Nevsky Prospekt) There are just six rooms here and three of them share bathrooms and toilets, but it is much more like staying in a large apartment than a hostel. The communal areas are very pleasant and the rooms are comfortable and clean. Even better is the friendly service, central location and big windows overlooking the canal.

GUEST HOUSE NEVSKY 3

HOTEL **$$**

Map p272 (☑ 812-710 6776; www.nevsky3.ru; Nevsky pr 3; s/d incl breakfast R6000/6500; ⌖; Ⓜ Admiralteyskaya) The four individually decorated rooms here sport a fridge, a TV, a safe and a fan, and overlook a surprisingly quiet courtyard just moments from the Hermitage. Guests are able to use the kitchen, making self-catering a doddle – no wonder it gets rave reviews.

Find it by going into the courtyard of Nevsky pr 3, and call apartment 10 on the intercom next to the Staraya Kniga bookshop.

3MOSTA

HOTEL **$$**

Map p272 (☑ 812-611 1188; www.3mosta.com; nab reki Moyki 3a; s/d from R5000/9000; ✳ ⌖; Ⓜ Nevsky Prospekt) Near three bridges over the Moyka River, this 26-room property is surprisingly uncramped given its wonderful location. Even the standard rooms are of a good size, with tasteful furniture, minibars and TVs. Some rooms have great views across to the Church of the Saviour on the Spilled Blood, and all guests have access to the roof for the panoramic experience.

STONY ISLAND HOTEL

HOTEL **$$**

Map p272 (☑ 812-740 1588; http://stonyisland. ru; ul Lomonosova 1; s/d incl breakfast from R6400/6600; ✳ ⌖; Ⓜ Gostiny Dvor) Right in the thick of the nightlife hot spot of ul Lomonosova (avoid front rooms if you are noise sensitive), this place offers 17 minimalist rooms in four different categories, with many of them in interesting shapes thanks to the quirky historic building. There's a fairly good stab at cool decor as well as flat-screen TVs, minibars and good bathrooms.

ANICHKOV PENSION

PENSION **$$**

Map p272 (☑ 812-314 7059; www.anichkov. com; Apt 4, Nevsky pr 64; s/d/ste incl breakfast R5500/6000/10,000; ✳ ⌖; Ⓜ Gostiny Dvor) On the 3rd floor of a handsome apartment building with an antique lift, this six-room pension takes its name from the nearby bridge. The standard rooms are fine, but the suites are well worth paying a little more for. The delightful breakfast room with a grand piano offers balcony views. Look for the entrance on Karavannaya ul.

POLIKOFF HOTEL

HOTEL **$$**

Map p272 (☑ 812-314 7809; http://polikoff hotel.ru; Nevsky pr 64/11; s/d incl breakfast from R5140/7000; ⌖; Ⓜ Gostiny Dvor) For style gurus on a budget, this quiet haven of contemporary cool is just steps away from Nevsky pr, but can be hard to find. Enter through the brown door at Karavannaya ul 11 and dial 26. You will find a soothing decor that features subdued lighting, blond-wood veneer and soft brown and cream tones.

CASA LETO

BOUTIQUE HOTEL **$$**

Map p272 (☑ 812-314 6622; http://casaleto.com; Bolshaya Morskaya ul 34; r incl breakfast from R6900; ✳ @ ⌖; Ⓜ Admiralteyskaya) A dramatically lit stone stairwell sets the scene for this stylish boutique hotel with five guest rooms named after famous St Petersburg architects. With king-sized beds, heated floors, soft pastel shades and plenty of antiques, the spacious, high-ceilinged quarters are deserving of such namesakes.

PETRO PALACE HOTEL

HOTEL **$$**

Map p272 (☑ 812-571 2880; www.petropalace hotel.com; Malaya Morskaya ul 14; r incl breakfast from R14,500; ✳ @ ⌖ ⛱; Ⓜ Admiralteyskaya) This 194-room hotel, superbly located between St Isaac's Cathedral and the Hermitage, has excellent facilities, including a great basement fitness centre with a small pool, a Finnish sauna and a full gym. Standard rooms are spacious and tastefully designed, but without any real individuality. It's popular with groups, though it rarely feels overrun.

BELVEDERE-NEVSKY
BUSINESS HOTEL $$

Map p272 (☑812-571 8338; http://belveder-nevsky.spb.ru; Bolshaya Konyushennaya ul 29; r incl breakfast from R6600; ✳@☎; ⓂNevsky Prospekt) Automatic doors open onto corridors covered with golden, diamond-patterned wallpaper, while the tired-looking decoration of the larger than average rooms also veers towards the opulent, with gold-striped wallpaper, flowing window drapes and richly patterned bedspreads.

★BELMOND
GRAND HOTEL EUROPE
HERITAGE HOTEL $$$

Map p272 (☑812-329 6000; www.belmond.com/grand-hotel-europe-st-petersburg; Mikhailovskaya ul 1/7; s/d from R26,500/31,270; ✳@☎✉; ⓂNevsky Prospekt) Since 1830, when Carlo Rossi united three adjacent buildings with the grandiose facade we see today, little has been allowed to change in this heritage building. No two rooms are the same at this iconic hotel, but most are spacious and elegant. It's worth paying extra for the terrace rooms, which afford spectacular views across the city's rooftops.

There's also a floor of suites recently redesigned with avant-garde art decoration.

★ROSSI HOTEL
BOUTIQUE HOTEL $$$

Map p272 (☑812-635 6333; www.rossihotels.com; nab reki Fontanki 55; s/d/ste from R9740/9830/15,230; ✳@☎; ⓂGostiny Dvor) Occupying a beautifully restored building on one of St Petersburg's prettiest squares, the Rossi's 65 rooms are all designed differently, but their brightness and moulded ceilings are uniform. Antique beds, super-sleek bathrooms, exposed brick walls and lots of cool designer touches create a great blend of old and new.

The best rooms have superb views over the Fontanka River. A spa with sauna and plunge pool adds to the overall cachet.

FOUR SEASONS
HOTEL LION PALACE
HERITAGE HOTEL $$$

Map p272 (☑812-339 8000; www.fourseasons.com/stpetersburg; Voznesensky pr 1; r/ste from R27,000/55,500; ✳@☎; ⓂAdmiralteyskaya) Housed in a meticulously restored palace, the Four Season's lower priced rooms fail to match the lavish promise of the lobby and grand staircase, but those fortunate enough to occupy one of the plush suites are unlikely to be disappointed.

Designed by Montferrand, the architect of next-door St Isaac's Cathedral, and formerly the home of Prince Lobanov-Rostovsky, the palace also has two attractively designed restaurants, a great bar, a winter garden for afternoon tea, and a spa with Jacuzzi pool.

HOTEL ASTORIA
HISTORIC HOTEL $$$

Map p272 (☑812-494 5757; www.roccofortehotels.com; Bolshaya Morskaya ul 39; r/ste from R34,800/76,000; ✳@☎✉; ⓂAdmiralteyskaya) What the Hotel Astoria has lost of its original Style Moderne decor, it more than compensates for in contemporary style and top-notch service. Little wonder it's beloved of visiting VIPs, from kings to rock stars. Rooms marry the hotel's heritage character with a more modern design, while the best suites are sprinkled with antiques and have spectacular views onto St Isaac's Cathedral.

The same views – at a slightly lower price – are also available next door at its sister property, the Angleterre Hotel (p190), where guests can use the gym and pool.

KEMPINSKI HOTEL MOYKA 22
HOTEL $$$

Map p272 (☑812-335 9111; www.kempinski.com; nab reki Moyki 22; r/ste with breakfast from R26,000/47,400; ✳@☎; ⓂNevsky Prospekt) Practically on the doorstep of the Hermitage, this superb hotel has all the comforts you'd expect of an international luxury chain. Rooms have a stylish marine theme, with cherry-wood furniture and a handsome navy-blue-and-gold colour scheme. The 360-degree panorama from the rooftop **Belle View** restaurant and bar is unbeatable.

W HOTEL
HOTEL $$$

Map p272 (☑812-610 6161; www.wstpetersburg.com; Voznesensky pr 6; r from R26,000; ✳@☎✉; ⓂAdmiralteyskaya) If you're familiar with the W brand, then the striking interior design at this hotel won't surprise you. Rooms in several different categories are spacious and luxurious, with contemporary styling. The lobby is also a very inviting space.

The rooftop bar W Terrace offers superb views, and breakfast is served at the connected Cococo (p94) restaurant. Another plus is the beautiful spa with sauna, Jacuzzi, treatment rooms and plunge pool.

PUSHKA INN
HOTEL $$$

Map p272 (☑812-312 0913; www.pushkainn.ru; nab reki Moyki 14; s/d incl breakfast from R9800/16,600; ❇☂➍; ⓂAdmiralteyskaya) On a particularly picturesque stretch of the Moyka River, this charming inn is housed in an historic 18th-century building. The 33 rooms are decorated in dusky pinks and caramel tones, with wide floorboards and – if you're willing to pay more – views of the Moyka.

Multi-bedroom, family-style apartments are also available from R34,200.

ANGLETERRE HOTEL
HOTEL $$$

Map p272 (☑812-494 5607; www.angleterre hotel.com; Malaya Morskaya ul 24; r/ste from R24,545/58,765; ❇@☂✉; ⓂAdmiralteyskaya) With supremely comfortable king-sized beds, huge bathrooms and a confidently understated style, the Angleterre's best rooms provide breathtaking views of St Isaac's Cathedral. More pluses are a great fitness centre, a small pool and a cinema showing original-language movies.

🛏 Sennaya & Kolomna

★SOUL KITCHEN HOSTEL
HOSTEL $

Map p280 (☑8-965-816 3470; www.soulkitchen hostel.com; nab reki Moyki 62/2, apt 9, Sennaya; dm R1500-2400, d R5700-9000; @☂➍; ⓂAdmiralteyskaya) Soul Kitchen blends boho hipness and boutique-hotel comfort, scoring perfect 10s in many key categories: private rooms (chic), dorm beds (double-width with privacy-protecting curtains), common areas and kitchen (all beautifully designed). The lounge is a fine place to hang out, with a record player, a big screen projector (for movie nights) and an artful design.

There is also bike hire, table football, free Macs to use, a toy chest for kids, free international phone calls and stunning Moyka views from a communal balcony.

★ALEXANDER HOUSE
BOUTIQUE HOTEL $$

Map p280 (☑812-334 3540; www.a-house.ru; nab kanala Kryukova 27, Kolomna; s/d/apt incl breakfast from R9000/12,200/14,600; ➌❇☂; ⓂSadovaya) This historic building opposite the Nikolsky Cathedral dates back to 1826, and contains a beautifully designed guesthouse. Each of the 14 spacious rooms are named after a city (Kyoto, Marrakesh, Venice) and contain artwork and crafts from there. Beautifully polished floors, warm colours and beamed ceilings are common throughout. There's also a lovely fireplace-warmed lounge and a vine-laden courtyard, plus a guests-only restaurant.

★ANDREY & SASHA'S HOMESTAY
APARTMENT $$

Map p280 (☑8-921-409 6701, 812-315 3330; asamatuga@mail.ru; nab kanala Griboyedova 51, Sennaya; r R5800-7300; ☂; ⓂSadovaya) Energetic Italophiles Andrey and Sasha extend the warmest of welcomes to travellers lucky enough to rent out one of their three apartments (by the room or in its entirety). All are centrally located and eclectically decorated with lots of designer touches and an eye for beautiful furniture, tiles and mirrors. Bathrooms are shared, as are kitchen facilities.

CHAO MAMA
HOTEL $$

Map p280 (☑812-570 0444; www.chaomama.ru; Grazhdanskaya ul 27; d R3600-7500; ❇☂; ⓂSadovaya) In an excellent location, Chao Mama has nine stylish rooms, each boasting a unique design, and offers excellent value for money. The best rooms have small kitchenettes and ample natural light, while the 54-sq-metre Gagarin Room has two balconies and sleeps up to four. For something a little cosier, opt for the artistically designed Jacqueline, which also boasts a fireplace.

Adjoining the hotel is the charming Julia Child Bistro (p114).

SWISS STAR
GUESTHOUSE $$

Map p280 (☑911-929 2793; www.swiss-star.ru/en; Fontanka 93; s/d with shared bathroom €55/70, with bathroom €75/90; ☂; ⓂSadovaya) This welcoming 2nd-floor guesthouse earns high marks for its spotless rooms with wood floors and its fair prices. The design is fairly minimal, though if you book the corner room with a view over the canal, you'll hardly notice. Of the eight rooms, five are en-suite, the others share a bathroom. There's a kitchen for guests, but no other common space.

The unmarked entrance on Fontanka is the first door west of Elfimova.

HOTEL GOGOL
HOTEL $$

Map p280 (☑812-571 1841; www.gogolhotel.com; nab kanala Griboyedova 69, Sennaya; s/d from R5100/6400; ➌❇☂; ⓂSadovaya) There's great value to be had at this centrally located hotel, a conversion of the house where the great writer Nikolai Gogol himself apparently once lived. The rooms are cosy and enjoy inoffensive decoration, with views of the canal or a quiet residential courtyard.

Reception is on the 2nd floor, and there's a basement restaurant.

ZOLOTAYA SEREDINA   HOTEL $$

Map p280 (Золотая Середина; ☑931-592 6413; www.retrohotel.ru; Grazhdanskaya ul 16, Sennaya; s/d with shared bathroom R2100/2500, with bathroom R2900/3400; 🛜; ⓂSadovaya) Tucked into a quiet courtyard in the narrow streets north of Sennaya pl, this friendly little hotel is a great bargain. A few antiques are scattered around to justify its 'retro' claims, but most furniture and all facilities are quite modern, with a kitchen for guest use, as well as a washing machine.

To access the hotel (which clearly has something against signage), ring 88 at the Grazhdanskaya ul 16 entry phone (even though the official street address is different) and then go up to flat 14 on the 2nd floor.

HOTEL DOM DOSTOEVSKOGO   HOTEL $$

Map p280 (☑812-314 8231; www.ddspb.ru; ul Kaznacheyskaya 61/1, Sennaya; s/d incl breakfast R4500/5000; 🛜; ⓂSennaya Ploshchad) While it's hard to imagine Fedya living anywhere so sanitary, he apparently resided in this house next to the Griboyedov Canal between 1861 and 1863. The 10 carpeted rooms here are comfortable but plain, and range from spacious to tiny, but the price is right. There's free tea and coffee throughout your stay and a fan in the room to keep you cool.

NEVSKY BREEZE HOTEL   HOTEL $$

Map p280 (☑812-570 1188; www.hon.ru; ul Galernaya 12, Kolomna; s/d R6900/8000; ⊖❄🛜; ⓂAdmiralteyskaya) This hotel is in one of the city centre's most charming streets, just one block back from the Neva River. The 33 rooms are comfortable and simple, all with private bathrooms, but without fridges. It's thoroughly contemporary inside, and little mileage is made out of the historic building, but despite this it's a popular choice.

HOTEL DOMINA PRESTIGE   HOTEL $$$

Map p280 (☑812-385 9900; www.dominarussia.com; nab Reki Moyki 99, Sennaya; r R9100-21,000; ⊖❄🛜; ⓂAdmiralteyskaya) This excellent property makes an immediate impression as its traditional Moyka embankment exterior gives way to a bright and modern atrium. Some of the decor is rather Russian in taste, but it's still stylish and fun. Rooms are comfortable and spacious, with extras such as coffee facilities and great bathrooms. There's also a sauna, gym and restaurant.

🛏 Smolny & Vosstaniya

KULTURA HOSTEL   HOSTEL $

Map p276 (☑921-870 0177; http://kulturahostel.com; ul Vosstaniya 24; dm/r with shared bathroom from R550/3000; 🛜; ⓂPloshchad Vosstaniya) Following the formula of other creative clusters around town, this one, behind the post office on ul Vosstaniya, is also home to a hostel. In this case, some thought has been applied to the design of the rooms, each of which has colourful St Petersburg–themed designs on the walls. The location is cool, with boutiques, cafes and a bar on hand.

TAIGA HOSTEL   HOSTEL $

(Тайга; ☑981-888 9983; www.taiga-hostel.com; Zagarodny pr 21; dm R700-800, d R5400, d with shared bathroom R4800; @🛜; ⓂZvenigorodskaya) Tucked down a narrow lane off busy Zagarodny pr, the Taiga is a friendly, welcoming spot with white plank floors, exposed brick walls, a small chillout lounge and touches of artwork strewn about. The rooms are cosy and some are rather small (one room also lacks windows), but guests rate Taiga highly for its helpful, English-speaking staff.

ALL YOU NEED HOSTEL   HOSTEL $

Map p276 (☑921-950 0574; www.youneedhostel.ru; ul Rubinshteyna 6, Vosstaniya; dm/d with shared bathroom from R650/2500; ⊖🛜; ⓂMayakovskaya) With a great location, this friendly hostel is basically one large apartment with a double room and two dorms sleeping six or ten. The dorm room has lockers and wooden bunks, while the private room is cramped, but still fine value for the price. You can mingle with other guests in the kitchen, and play some records in the comfy lounge.

FRIENDS ON VOSSTANIYA   HOSTEL $

Map p276 (☑812-401 6155; www.en.friendsplace.ru/friends-on-vosstaniya; ul Vosstaniya 11; dm R500-900, r with shared bathroom R1900-5000; @🛜; ⓂPloshchad Vosstaniya) Branch of the well-designed and run Friends hostel chain. The colourful private rooms are quite small (you'll have to climb across the bed to open the window), but still come with a desk, and can be excellent value for the location.

LOCATION HOSTEL   HOSTEL $

Map p276 (☑812-329 1274; http://en.location-hostel.ru; Ligovsky pr 74, Vosstaniya; dm/r from R700/1600, design rooms R9000; ⊖🛜; ⓂLigovsky Prospekt) Come and stay in St Petersburg's coolest art gallery and cultural space – the 3rd floor of Loft Project ETAGI is given over to this super-friendly hostel. Some of the dorms here are enormous (one has 20 beds in it!), but the facilities are spotless, and include washing machines and a small kitchen.

As well as the dorms there are three 'design rooms' that offer boutique hotel quality at lower prices.

HOTEL INDIGO   HOTEL $$

Map p276 (☑812-454 5577; www.indigospb. com; ul Chaykovskogo 17, Smolny; r from R10,700; ⊜❊@☎; Ⓜ Chernyshevskaya) A total overhaul of the original building – a prerevolutionary hotel in its day – paved the way for the sleek and stylish Hotel Indigo, a big step up from many St Petersburg offerings with its excellent service and handsomely designed guest rooms. The incredible atrium makes even the interior-facing rooms light filled, and touches such as rain showers and free minibars in rooms are also very welcome.

Other nice features include fine city views from the 7th-floor restaurant, a gym, sauna and small pool, plus free bikes for guest use.

OGNIVO   GUESTHOUSE $$

Map p276 (☑812-579 6295; www.ognivo-spb. com; ul Chaykovskogo 4; s/d from R4000/4800) Ognivo earns high marks for its attractive, well-maintained rooms and quiet location. There's a bit of whimsy to the design in some of the 15 rooms, with inner wooden shutters over the windows, bold wallpaper and wildly patterned tilework in the bathrooms – others have cast-iron chandeliers and wood-beamed ceilings for a more medieval look. Entrance is via a courtyard off Chaykovskogo.

ALLIANCE HOTEL   HOTEL $$

Map p276 (☑812-717 2105; www.alliancehotel.ru; Orlovsky per 5; s/d R3400/5000; ☎) A short stroll from Ploschad Vosstaniya, the Alliance is a small, well-maintained hotel that has carpeted rooms with tall ceilings, spotless bathrooms and pleasant extras (minifridges, tea and snacks available around the clock). Its deco light fixtures and lacquered furniture somehow channel a bit of old Soviet classicism. The service is friendly, though staff speak limited English.

HOTEL AZIMUT   HOTEL $$

(☑812-740 2640; www.azimuthotels.com; Lermontovsky pr 43/1, Vosstaniya; s/d from R4200/5600; ⊜☎; Ⓜ Baltiyskaya) The ambitious Azimut hotel chain has done a great job of making you forget that you're in one of St Petersburg's ugliest buildings with their clever renovation of a massive Soviet-era hotel. Prices are low, and the funky lobby and amazing top-floor Sky Bar sweeten the deal further.

GREEN APPLE HOTEL   HOTEL $$

Map p276 (☑812-272 1023; www.greenapple hotel.ru; ul Korolenko 14, Smolny; d/tr incl breakfast R4450/4950; ⊜❊☎; Ⓜ Chernyshevskaya) This modest hotel in the backstreets of Liteyny has small but adequate rooms, which are clean but lack character. Although it's nothing fancy, the Green Apple is good value for St Petersburg, particularly given the excellent location within walking distance of many restaurants and bars. Most staff don't speak much English.

ART HOTEL   HOTEL $$

Map p276 (☑812-740 7585; www.art-hotel. ru; Mokhovaya ul 27-29, Smolny; s/d/ste from R4900/5400/6300; ⊜☎; Ⓜ Chernyshevskaya) This rather misleadingly named hotel retains a straightforward elegance in its 14 rooms, but has nothing particularly arty about it. Indeed, the mood is bourgeois-on-a-budget, with heavy pleated drapes framing the windows, ruby red carpets, ceiling mouldings and crystal chandeliers. Breakfast is served to you each morning in your room.

To find it, look for the first tunnel opening south (50m) of ul Pestelya. The hotel's courtyard location ensures a peaceful night's rest.

ARBAT NORD HOTEL   BOUTIQUE HOTEL $$

Map p276 (☑812-679 9696; www.arbat-nord. ru; Artilleriyskaya ul 4, Smolny; s/d incl breakfast R8200/8900; ❊@☎; Ⓜ Chernyshevskaya) Facing an unsightly Soviet-era hotel across the street, the sleek modern Arbat Nord seems to be showing its neighbour how to run a good establishment. The 33 modern, carpeted rooms are decorated in warm hues, and even though the furniture is fairly cheap, there's plenty of space. Efficient English-speaking staff are on hand and the welcome is warm.

BROTHERS KARAMAZOV   BOUTIQUE HOTEL $$

Map p276 (☑812-335 1185; www.karamazovho tel.ru; Sotsialisticheskaya ul 11a, Vosstaniya; r incl breakfast R7650-9000; ⊜❊☎; Ⓜ Vladimirskaya) Pack a copy of Dostoevsky's final novel to read while staying at this attractive boutique hotel – the great man penned *The Brothers K* while living in the neighbourhood. In homage, the best of the hotel's 28 rooms are named after different Dostoevsky characters.

PIO ON MOKHOVAYA

B&B $$

Map p276 (🖉812-273 3585; Mokhovaya ul 39, Smolny; s/d/tr/q incl breakfast R3500/4500/5400/6100; 😊🛜📶; MChernyshevskaya) This lovely lodging is the second Pio property in St Petersburg. It's very spacious, stylish and comfortable, as well as being child friendly, with family groups warmly welcomed and provided for. It's in a quiet, residential neighbourhood a short walk from the Historic Heart. There is also a Finnish sauna on site. Call 10 on the intercom to be buzzed in.

HELVETIA HOTEL & SUITES

HOTEL $$

Map p276 (🖉812-326 5353; www.helvetiahotel.ru; ul Marata 11, Vosstaniya; r incl breakfast from R7500; 😊📶🛜; MMayakovskaya) Pass through the wrought-iron gates into a wonderfully private and professionally run oasis of calm and class. The rooms may be a little less atmospheric than the early 19th-century exterior might suggest, but they make up for it in comfort, each having a bathtub, safe and minibar. The buffet breakfast is excellent and there are two on-site restaurants.

NILS BED & BREAKFAST

HOMESTAY $$

Map p276 (🖉812-923 0575; www.rentroom.ru; 5-ya Sovetskaya ul 21, Smolny; s R3850-4600, d R4900-5600; 🛜; MPloshchad Vosstaniya) Nils Bed & Breakfast is an excellent option at a great price. Four spacious rooms share two modern bathrooms, as well as a beautiful light-filled common area and kitchen. Nils renovated this place himself, taking great care to preserve the mouldings, wooden floors and other architectural elements.

DEMETRA ART HOTEL

BOUTIQUE HOTEL $$$

Map p276 (🖉812-640 0408; www.demetra-art-hotel.com; ul Vosstaniya 44; r R16,000-24,000, ste R36,000; 📶🛜; MChernyshevskaya) In an art nouveau building dating from 1913, the Demetra Art Hotel has plush rooms with oak flooring, patterned drapes and duvets, and touches of artwork throughout (reproductions of works from the Erata Museum). Some rooms can be on the small side, though the top-notch service, stylish bar and restaurant, and great location add to the appeal.

OFFICIAL STATE
HERMITAGE HOTEL

LUXURY HOTEL $$$

Map p276 (🖉812-777 9810; www.thehermitagehotel.ru; ul Pravdy 10, Vosstaniya; r from R13,400; P😊📶🛜; MZvenigorodskaya, Vladimirskaya) Despite its incongruous location, the 126-

room Official State Hermitage Hotel is a dazzling affair with enough Italian marble and chandeliers to keep even the fussiest of Romanovs happy. Rooms are spacious and elegant without being too chintzy, and Hermès goodies stuff the bathrooms. There are some excellent dining options on site.

The Hermitage connection is fairly weak: there's a free shuttle bus to the museum every two hours, and guests who book directly through the hotel and stay for more than three nights get free entry as well.

DOM BOUTIQUE HOTEL

HOTEL $$$

Map p276 (www.domboutiquehotel.uk; Gangutskaya ul 4; r R12,000-20,000; 📶🛜; MChernyshevskaya) Just off the Fontanka River, this newish place has stylish rooms with king-sized beds, classy furniture and gilded antique-looking mirrors, plus sleek bathrooms with black subway tiles and brass fixtures. The common areas are fine spots to unwind, and there's a restaurant and bar on hand.

🛏 Vasilyevsky Island

ONLINE HOSTEL

HOSTEL $

Map p286 (🖉812-329 9594; http://online-hostel.com/; Apt 1, 6-ya liniya 27; dm/d incl breakfast from R800/2700; @📶; MVasileostrovskaya) The pick of the hostels on Vasilyevsky Island couldn't have a more convenient location, opposite the metro station. Dorms are pretty cramped but there's a welcoming and colourful vibe to the place. Fun touches include an electronic keyboard and Xbox games to play in the lounge and kitchen area.

⭐NASHOTEL

HOTEL $$

Map p286 (🖉812-323 2231; www.nashotel.ru; 11-ya liniya 50; s/d from R9500/10,600; 📶🛜; MVasileostrovskaya) This spotless, smart and stylish hotel occupies a very tall, beautifully remodelled building with a striking exterior on this quiet side street. Its rooms are blazes of colours, complete with modern furnishings, garish art and great views from the higher floors. A nice perk are the free bicycles for guests to use to get around.

SOKOS HOTEL
PALACE BRIDGE

BUSINESS HOTEL $$

Map p286 (🖉812-335 2200; www.sokoshotels.com; Birzhevoy per 4a; r from R10,900; 📶@; MSportivnaya) This is the best of several hotels in the city run by Finnish chain Sokos because of its excellent spa and fitness centre

SLEEP LIKE A TSAR

If you've always wanted to sleep in a tsarist palace, here is your chance. Peter the Great built his summer palace at Strelna, a town about 24km from St Petersburg, and now it is Putin's presidential palace, used for international meetings and state visits. Putin houses his guests on the grounds at the **Baltic Star Hotel** (☏812-438 5700; www.balticstar-hotel. ru; Beriozovaya al 3; r from R9450; 🖨 ✳ @ 🛜 🛝). If it's not otherwise occupied, you could stay here, too. Besides the 100 well-appointed rooms in the main hotel, there are 18 VIP cottages on the shore of the Gulf of Finland, each equipped with a private dining room, study, sauna, swimming pool and, of course, staff quarters for your entourage.

with a wonderful large swimming pool and saunas. The rooms are large and a bit bland, but it's a quiet location and a popular spot with business travellers.

TREZZINI PALACE HOTEL HOTEL $$$

Map p286 (☏812-313 6622; www.trezzinipalace. com; Universitetskaya nab 21; r from R16,000; ✳🛜; Ⓜ Vasileostrovskaya) This elaborately decorated hotel gives you a taste of 18th- and 19th-century imperial grandeur without compromising on modernity or convenience. The 21 rooms are spacious, with enormous bathrooms and elaborate wooden minibars that overflow with goodies. While the Trezzini teeters on the edge of being totally tasteless, its savvy staff and homogeneous style throughout miraculously reprieve it.

SOKOS HOTEL VASILYEVSKY BUSINESS HOTEL $$$

Map p286 (☏812-335 2290; www.sokoshotels. com; 8-ya liniya 11-13; r from R15,500; 🖨✳🛜; Ⓜ Vasileostrovskaya) Although this slick Finnish chain hotel offers 255 rooms, you'll hardly notice it from the street. It's a well-designed place aimed at business travellers and the upper end of the holiday market. The rooms are spacious, with nice design touches, while the large Repin Lounge downstairs takes care of all food and drink needs.

🛏 Petrograd & Vyborg Sides

SOVREMENIK HOTEL $

Map p284 (Современник; ☏812-312 9339; www.artefact-hotel.ru; ul Kronverskaya 1; dm/d/tr/q R790/2900/4300/4800; ✳🛜; Ⓜ Gorkovskaya) This small, cheerfully decorated mini-hotel has nine rooms tucked inside an apartment building a short stroll from Alexandrovsky Park. It's a colourful, some-

what whimsically decorated place, with repurposed bird cages, hats turned into lamps and bold artwork in some rooms. The friendly service and shared kitchen add to the appeal.

Note that only three rooms have private bathrooms. The other six have shared facilities.

TRADITION HOTEL HOTEL $$

Map p284 (☏812-405 8855; www.traditionhotel. ru; pr Dobrolyubova 2; r incl breakfast R9100-13,500; ✳@🛜; Ⓜ Sportivnaya) This charming small hotel is a consistent traveller favourite due to its smiling, helpful staff who really go out of their way for guests. Its spacious, carpeted rooms are comfortable and well appointed with good-size bathrooms and a vaguely antique style.

APART-HOTEL KRONVERK BUSINESS HOTEL $$

Map p284 (☏812-703 3663; www.kronverk.com; ul Blokhina 9; r incl breakfast R6820, apt from R11,080; ✳@🛜; Ⓜ Sportivnaya) If you're after something more contemporary for your lodgings, then here's a place for you. Occupying the upper floors of a slick business centre, the Kronverk offers appealing modern rooms with basic self-catering facilities. English-speaking staff are efficient and professional.

HOTEL VEDENSKY HOTEL $$$

Map p284 (☏812-332 4663; www.vedenskyhotel. ru; Bolshoy pr 37; r R8600-12,600, ste R13,600-19,500; @🛜; Ⓜ Chkalovskaya) The Vedensky is a nine-storey hotel that draws a business crowd to its 190 modern, well-equipped rooms with dark-wood furnishings and masculine colour schemes. It has a good location on Petrograd's restaurant-lined main strip, though the small top-floor terrace is also a fine spot for a drink or a bite (mains from R640 to R980).

Understand St Petersburg

St Petersburg Today

Twenty-five years of massive investment after 70 years of neglect under the Soviets has paid off: St Petersburg is once again one of Europe's most beautiful cities, its World Heritage–listed centre a virtual stage set of 300 years of architectural styles. However, like other modern metropolises, it is also prone to the ugly realities of life, including terrorist attacks, corruption scandals, and battles over cultural and political objectives.

Best on Film

Irony of Fate (1975) Perhaps the best loved Leningrad comedy of all time.
Brother (1997) Sergei Bodrov Jr fights the mafia on the mean streets of post-Soviet St Petersburg.
Russian Ark (2002) Alexander Sokurov's one-shot meditation on Russian history filmed inside the Hermitage.
The Stroll (2003) A delightfully playful film in which three friends wander from situation to situation on the streets of St Petersburg.
Onegin (1999) Pushkin's epic tale of lost love and regret, beautifully retold by Martha Fiennes.

Best in Print

Crime and Punishment (Fyodor Dostoevsky; 1866) The quintessential St Petersburg novel explores the mind of the deluded Rodion Raskolnikov.
Speak, Memory (Vladimir Nabokov; 1951) A wonderfully bittersweet literary memoir of Nabokov's own St Petersburg childhood.
The Nose (Nikolai Gogol; 1836) Follow Major Kovalyov around the city in pursuit of his errant nose.
Ten Days That Shook the World (John Reed; 1919) A remarkable first-hand account of the Russian revolution.

Terrorist Attack

There's no doubt that having the country ruled by a modern-day tsar who was born, raised, educated and cut his political teeth in the city has been a fillip to St Petersburg. As a showcase for the country, it hosts international summits and conferences, and enjoys continued federal budgetary favour, second in influence and cachet only to Moscow.

However, it has also made the city into a terrorist target. This threat became bloody reality in April 2017, when a suicide bomber exploded a device on the metro killing 15 and injuring over 50 people. When another bomb was discovered and diffused at Ploshchad Vosstaniya station, the entire metro system was shut down, leaving many commuters stranded. Locals rose to the challenge as buses and taxis drove people home for free, while others helped put up those who remained temporarily stuck in the city. It was a display of the spirit of solidarity and pluck in the face of adversity that has been ingrained in St Petersburg since its survival through the WWII siege of 900 days.

Battle for St Isaac's

A century after its citizens staged the world's first successful communist revolution, locals continue to campaign on the streets over issues they feel passionately about. A current flashpoint is the management of St Isaac's Cathedral. In January 2017, a storm of protest greeted the announcement by the city's governor Georgy Poltavchenko that the iconic golden-domed cathedral would be transferred to the Russian Orthodox Church on a free-of-charge, 49-year lease. Daily church services have been allowed in a side chapel of the Cathedral (which is a museum) since 1990, usually attended by less than 50 people. On major holidays larger services take place, too. But, for some, this was deemed insufficient.

The church plans to scrap the entry fee currently charged, laying open to question who will pay for the maintenance of a building that sees some 4 million visitors a year and is a key part of the World Heritage–listed ensemble of buildings in the city centre: answer, the city. Many of the thousands of protesters and some 200,000 who have signed an online petition are also worried about the creeping scope of the Orthodox Church's business and influence in society as it promotes traditional values that are anti-women and LGBT rights.

Krestovsky Stadium Scandal

St Petersburg is one of the key venues for the 2018 FIFA World Cup. Three years before Russia was chosen as the location for this prestigious sporting event in 2010, ground had been broken for a new city stadium to be built on Krestovsky Island. Nearly 20 years later and an estimated 550% over budget, that stadium finally opened. Touted as the most expensive stadium ever built, with an official price tag of US$700 (and an unofficial one of as much as US$1.5 billion), the stadium's construction was mired in corruption and poor design, including a leaky retractable roof and a pitch that was unstable when FIFA officials inspected it. Nevertheless, the final of the FIFA Confederation Cup was successfully held here in July 2017.

A New Highway

One of the best views of the giant spaceship-like stadium is when driving across the newly opened Gulf of Finland section of the 47km toll motorway known as the Western High-Speed Diameter. Two of Russia's largest bridge structures – a double-decker 734m span and a 620m cable-stayed bridge – make this spectacular crossing possible and allow visitors to see parts of the city as they never have before, including shipbuilding yards and docks south of the Neva that were for decades off-limits to the public. Hopefully easing traffic congestion in the city centre, the highway now enables drivers to cross the mouth of the Neva River in around 20 minutes. Along with the opening in 2018 of the Lakhta Tower, Russia's tallest building, and the construction of the major 'Golden City' development at the western tip of Vasilyevsky Island, this is one of the key infrastructure projects dragging preserved-in-amber St Petersburg into the 21st century.

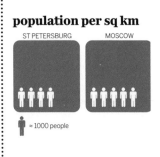

if Russia were 100 people

80 would be Russian
1 would be Belorussian
19 would be other

daily use of public transport
(% of population)

41 metro
30 bus
23 electric trams & trolleybuses
6 suburban trains

population per sq km

ST PETERSBURG   MOSCOW

= 1000 people

History

The history of St Petersburg (make that Petrograd and Leningrad, as well) is one of struggle, both for identity – is this a Russian or European city? – and for ideas, whether it be despotism versus reform, communism versus fascism, or simply democracy versus autocracy. The city, home to tsars and birthplace of Vladimir Putin, has been deeply marked by each of these struggles, making its three-century history one of the world's most eventful over such a relatively short amount of time.

Precocious Prince

For three centuries, Moscow was the home of Russia's tsars. The traditional, inward-looking capital was deep in the heart of Russia and terribly conservative. This was the place the future Peter the Great would be born into in 1672. Peter was the son of Tsar Alexey I and his second wife, Natalya Naryshkina, and was one of 16 siblings. He stood out as exceptional, however, both by his enormous height (he reached 203cm in adulthood) and by his insatiable curiosity for knowledge about the outside world. He spent long hours in the city quarter for foreign merchants, who regaled the young prince with tales of the modern age.

Once on the throne, Peter became the first tsar to venture beyond Russia's borders. Travelling in disguise, Peter and a raucous Russian entourage criss-crossed the continent, meeting with monarchs, dining with dignitaries and carousing with commoners. He recruited admirals, academics and artisans to apply their skill in his service. Having seen Western Europe in the age of the Enlightenment, Peter was more than ever convinced that Russians were still living in the dark ages and became more determined than ever to replace superstition with science, backwardness with progress and East with West.

Peter abruptly ended his European expedition when news came of a Kremlin coup. The young tsar hurried back to Moscow where he vengefully punished the plotters, sending more than a thousand to their deaths and terrorising anyone who questioned his rule. He humiliated and subdued the old elite, forcing aristocrat elders to shave their beards and wear Western clothes, while he subordinated the Orthodox Church

TIMELINE	1703	1712–14	1718
	On 27 May Peter the Great establishes the Peter & Paul Fortress on Zayachy Island, thus founding the new city of Sankt Pieter Burkh, Russia's 'window to the West'.	At the behest of Peter I, government institutions begin to move from Moscow, and St Petersburg assumes the administrative and ceremonial role as the Russian capital.	Peter the Great's son Alexey dies under torture in the Peter & Paul Fortress, where his father had him interrogated about his purported plan to depose him and reverse his reforms.

to earthly political authority, and sent the Old Believers, who cursed him as the Antichrist, into internal exile in Russia's icy north. Peter up-ended the established social order, forbidding arranged marriages and promoting the humble to high rank. He even changed the date of New Year's Day – from September to January. By now, the undisputed tsar had grown to despise Moscow, and was ready to start afresh.

The Great Northern War

Peter was anxious to turn Russia westward and he saw the Baltic Sea as the channel for change. The problem was that Sweden already domi-nated the region and it had been more than 400 years since Russia's medieval hero prince, Alexander Nevsky, had defeated the Swedes near the site of Peter's future city. In 1700 Peter put his new army to the test against the powerful Swedish Empire, and the Great Northern War was on. For the next 20 years northern Europe's modernising autocrats, Charles II and Peter, fought for supremacy over the eastern Baltic.

To Peter's dismay, his troops were badly beaten in their first engage-ment at the Battle of Narva in Estonia, by a smaller, more adept Swed-ish force. But Russia found allies in Poland, Saxony and Denmark, who diverted Charles' attention. Peter used the opportunity to revamp his army and launch his navy. He established a small Baltic foothold on tiny Hare Island (Zayachy Island) at the mouth of the Neva River, and used it as a base to rout a nearby Swedish garrison. This primitive outpost would become the kernel of Peter's northern capital.

By the time Charles tried to retake the territory, Peter commanded a formidable fighting force. Russia's first naval victory came at the Bat-tle of Hanko, where a galley fleet overwhelmed a Swedish squadron and secured Russian control over the Neva and access to the Gulf. His military chief and boyhood friend, Alexander Menshikov, led a series of impressive battlefield victories, further extending Russian presence on the Baltic coast and causing his Scandinavian foe to flee and the Swedish empire to expire. The Great Northern War shifted the balance of power to the advantage of Peter's Russia. Hostilities officially ended with the signing of the Treaty of Nystad (1721), which formally ceded Sweden's extensive eastern possessions to Russia, including its new capital city, St Petersburg.

Creating Sankt Pieter Burkh

Peter did not wait for the war to end before he started building. The wooden palisade encampment on Hare Island became the red-brick Peter & Paul Fortress. In June 1703 Peter gave the site a name – Sankt

Lindsey Hughes never pulls punches in her great Peter the Great: A Biography a detailed retelling of the tsar's less-than-laudable personal life and his often barbaric childish-ness. Hughes manages to present both the genius and failings of Peter I.

1725	1725	1727	1728
Some 13 years after St Petersburg was declared the new capital, its population is now 40,000 and as much as 90% of all foreign trade passes through its port.	Peter the Great dies of uraemia in St Petersburg, having reigned over Russia for 42 years of his 52-year life. He had anointed no successor and his wife becomes Catherine I.	Catherine I, an illiterate former housemaid, dies after ruling Russia for two years in tandem with Peter's best friend, Prince Menshikov. Peter's grandson becomes Tsar Peter II.	Following his coronation there, Peter II moves the Russian capital back to Moscow; when he dies two years later he is buried in the Kremlin.

Pieter Burkh, in his beloved Dutch tongue, and named after his patron saint, who stands guard before the gates to paradise.

There was a reason why until now the area had only attracted a few Finnish fishers for settlement: it was a swamp. The Neva River runs from nearby Lake Ladoga, Europe's largest, and flows into the Gulf of Finland through a low-lying delta of marshy, flood-prone islands, more manageable for elk than people. Although it is close to the Arctic Circle, winds and waters from the Atlantic bring moderate and moist weather. This means that winter, during which the delta freezes up, is relatively short: a matter of no small significance to Peter, who intended the city to be his naval base.

Peter's vision for the new capital was grandiose; so was the task ahead. To find enough dry ground for building, swamps were drained and wetlands filled. To protect the land from flooding, seawalls were built and canals dug. A hands-on autocrat, Peter pitched in with the hammering, sawing and joining. Thousands of fortune-seeking foreigners were imported to lend expertise: architects and engineers to design the city's intricate waterways, and craftspeople and masons to chisel its stone foundations. The hard labour of digging ditches and moving muck was performed by non-voluntary recruits. Peter pressed 30,000 peasant serfs per year into capital construction gangs, plus Russian convict labourers and Swedish prisoners of war. The work regimen was strict and living conditions were stark: more than 100,000 died. But those who survived could earn personal freedom and a small piece of land to call their own.

When he realised there wasn't enough local stone to build his city, Peter decreed a stone tax; all new arrivals had to bring a fixed amount of building materials with them in order to enter the town. (Not so unusual for a guy who previously issued a tax on beards.)

Peter's Paradise

Russia's new city by the sea began to take shape, inspired by Peter's recollections of canal-lined Amsterdam. The locus of power was the military stronghold, the Peter & Paul Fortress. Next, he ordered the chief accompaniments of tsarist authority – a church and a prison. A more impressive dwelling, the Menshikov Palace, put up by the territory's first governor-general, Alexander Menshikov, soon adorned the Vasilyevsky Island embankment.

In 1712 the tsar officially declared St Petersburg to be the capital. Inspired by the Vatican's crossed keys to paradise, he adopted a city coat of arms that presented crossed anchors topped with an imperial crown. Peter demanded the rest of Russia's ruling elite join him, or else. The tsar's royal court, the imperial senate and foreign embassies were all quickly relocated. Apprehension turned to horror when Moscow's old aristocratic families reluctantly began to arrive; to them, Peter's paradise was a peaty hell. They were ordered to bring their own stones

1730	1732	1740	1741–61
The direct male line of the Romanov dynasty ends with Peter II's death. His successor is Anna, Duchess of Courland, daughter of Peter the Great's half-brother and coruler, Ivan V.	Empress Anna switches the capital back to St Petersburg, presiding over the recommencement of the city's construction and development.	Empress Anna dies after a 10-year rule. After a series of intrigues, Peter the Great's daughter Elizabeth ascends the throne after a coup against infant Tsar Ivan VI.	Empress Elizabeth fulfils her father's goal of a grand European capital, commissioning the construction of countless sumptuous buildings and creating a glittering court.

to the party, with which to build elegant mansions and in which to start behaving like Westerners, complete with beardless faces and German dress, something that went against their conservative Orthodox beliefs.

When Peter died in 1725, at the age of 52, some thought they might get the chance to abandon his creation, but they were wrong. The wilful spirit of Peter the Great continued to possess the city and bedevil its inhabitants. Within less than a hundred years of its improbable inception, a new magnificent capital would stand on the edge of Europe.

Peter the Great's Heirs

By the end of the 18th century St Petersburg would take its place among Europe's great cities. But in the years immediately following Peter's death, the fate of the Baltic bastion was still uncertain.

While Peter's plans for his imperial capital were clear, those for his personal legacy were murky. His eldest son and heir apparent, Alexey, was estranged from his father early on, suspected of plotting against him later, and eventually tortured to death during interrogation in the Peter & Paul Fortress in 1718. The evidence for treachery was flimsy, though it was clear to Peter that his son would never be fit to rule, and that he would undo many of Peter's reforms were he ever to ascend the throne. On his death bed in 1725, Peter tried to dictate a last will, but could not name an heir before his demise. His wife Catherine I assumed the throne, with Peter's confidant and closest ally, Menshikov, acting as the power behind the throne. When Catherine died two years later, the simmering anti-Peter reaction started.

The St Petersburg–Moscow power struggle was on. The aristocracy's Old Muscovite faction seized the opportunity to influence the succession. Without his protector, the mighty Menshikov was stripped of all titles and property, and sent packing into Siberian exile. Peter's 11-year-old grandson, Peter II, was chosen as heir. Delivering to his enabling patrons, the pliable Peter II returned the capital to Moscow. St Petersburg's population halved and its public works came to rest.

Anna & Elizabeth's Contribution

The Romanovs were a delicate dynasty and the teen tsar soon succumbed to smallpox. Moscow's princely power brokers now entrusted the throne to another supposed weakling, Duchess Anna Ioanovna, Peter the Great's niece. But Anna was no pushover and she became the first in a line of tough women rulers. In 1732 Anna declared St Petersburg to be the capital once more, and bade everyone return to the Baltic. Making the offer more enticing, she recommended glamorous capital construction projects. Wary of scheming Russian elites, she

Peter's fascination with 'freaks' is well documented, but his most politically incorrect act remains the wedding he organised for his servant Iakim Volkov. All the dwarves of Moscow were rounded up and sent to St Petersburg, where a dwarf wedding was performed for the amusement of Peter and his court.

In 1737 Empress Anna celebrated victory in the Russo-Turkish War by having a palace carved in ice, complete with turrets 30m tall. Anna forced Prince Golitsyn, who had incurred her displeasure, to marry a rotund Kalmyk girl inside, before spending the night and consummating the marriage on an ice bed.

recruited talented German state administrators. Still, the city recovered slowly. A big fire in 1737 left entire neighbourhoods in ruins. Even Anna spent much time ruling from Moscow. St Petersburg remained only half built, its dynamism diminished.

Not until the reign of Peter's second-oldest daughter, the Empress Elizabeth (r 1741–62), did the city's imperial appetite return in full. Elizabeth created one of the most dazzling courts in Europe. Her baroque beauty, the Winter Palace, was meant to impress – and how could it not, with more than a quarter of a million exquisitely embellished square feet? She forbade any new building to rise higher than her 1000-room, 2000-windowed, multi-columned mansion. She loved the pomp as much as the power and her 20-year reign was a non-stop cabaret. The empress was a bit eccentric (she was certainly her father's daughter in that respect), enjoying a hedonistic lifestyle that revolved around hunting, drinking and dancing. She most loved hosting elaborate masquerade balls, at which she performed countless costume changes, apparently preferring to end the night in drag. Bawdy though she was, Elizabeth also got the Russian elite hooked on high culture. The court was graced by poets, artists and philosophers. Journalism and theatre gained popularity, and an academy of arts was founded. While her resplendent splurges may have left imperial coffers empty, Elizabeth made her father's majestic dream a reality.

Catherine the Great

Catherine the Great adopted the Russian language, and, some suggest, not always entirely successfully. One story runs that the German princess spelled the word 'ещё' (more) as истчо (sounding phonetically similar) – giving rise to the joke at court: 'How can five spelling mistakes occur in a word of three letters?'

In 1745, at the age of 16, Sophie Augusta of Prussia was betrothed to Duke Peter of Holstein: quite a score for her ambitious mother, as he was a Romanov and heir to the Imperial Russian throne. Sophie moved to St Petersburg, learned to speak Russian, delighted the court with her coy charm, and took the name Catherine when she converted to Orthodoxy.

More than just a court coquette, Catherine possessed keen political instincts and a strong appetite for power, attributes that had adverse effects on the men in her life. Her husband Tsar Peter III, as it turned out, was not terribly interested in ruling. In a plot hatched by her lover, Prince Orlov, Catherine was complicit in a coup that landed her on the throne, lifted Orlov to general-in-chief, and left her helpless husband under guard at a remote estate where he was assassinated shortly afterwards.

Despite the details of her unsavoury ascension, Catherine reigned for 34 years and presided over a golden age for St Petersburg. Relations between crown and aristocracy were never better. Empress Catherine was a charter member of a club of 18th-century monarchs known as

1796	1799	1800	1801
Upon the death of Catherine the Great, her embittered son Paul I ascends the throne. One of his first acts as tsar is to decree that women may never again rule Russia.	The birth of poet Alexander Pushkin ushers in the era of Russian romanticism and the Golden Age of Russian literature. Revered as the national bard, Pushkin's legacy endures to this day.	St Petersburg has grown exponentially in its first century, and its population reaches 220,000. By this time, the city has gained all the glory of a cosmopolitan capital.	Tsar Paul is murdered in his bedroom in Mikhailovsky Castle. The coup places his son Alexander on the throne. He vows to continue the policies of his grandmother, Catherine the Great.

the 'enlightened despots' – dictators who could hum Haydn. On the 'enlightened' side, Catherine corresponded with French philosophers, patronised the arts and sciences, promoted public education and introduced potatoes to the national cuisine. On the 'despotic' side, Catherine connived with fellow enlightened friends to carve up Poland, censored bad news, tightened serfs' bonds of servitude to their lords, and introduced potatoes to the national cuisine.

1812 Overture

The downside to becoming a great power in European politics is that you become drawn into European wars. Though, in fairness to the Hanovers and Hapsburgs, the Romanovs were pretty good at picking fights on their own. From the 19th century on, Russia was at war and St Petersburg was transformed.

It was Napoleon who coined the military maxim, 'First we engage, then we will see'. That was probably not the best tactic to take with Russia, as Napoleon himself found out when he suffered his greatest military defeat during the doomed campaign of 1812. Tsar Alexander I, Catherine the Great's successor, first clashed with Napoleon after joining an ill-fated anti-French alliance with Austria and Prussia. The Little Corporal targeted Moscow, instead of the more heavily armed St Petersburg. However, by the time he got there his army had been reduced to 100,000 and he found the city deserted and burned to the ground. With winter coming and his supply lines overstretched, Napoleon was forced to retreat.

The War of 1812 was a defining event for Russia, stirring nationalist exaltation and orchestral inspiration. Alexander I, having defeated Napoleon and led victorious Russian soldiers into Paris, presided over a period of prosperity and self-assuredness in St Petersburg. His army's exploits were immortalised in triumphal designs that recalled imperial Rome, while the Kazan Cathedral and the Alexander Column were shining symbols for a new Russian empire that stretched halfway across the globe.

St Petersburg now displayed all the features of an imperial capital: stately facade, hierarchical heart and aristocratic soul. The city's physical appearance reflected the transition. The centre of power moved across the river to the Neva's south bank. The immense Palace Square (Dvortsovaya pl) could host as many as 50 parading infantry battalions at once. Across the square an imposing semicircular structure housed the instruments of statecraft: General Staff, the Treasury and the Foreign Office. Its august archways led out to the city's central artery, Nevsky pr. The commanding Admiralty stretched along nearly 400m of

Despite her reputed fondness for anything sexual, there is little evidence that the number of Catherine the Great's lovers even went into double digits. Her long love affair with Grigory Potemkin is fascinatingly described in Simon Sebag Montefiore's *Catherine the Great and Potemkin*.

1812–14	1825	1836	1837
Alexander I oversees victory in the Napoleonic Wars and troops occupy Paris. Monuments are strewn about St Petersburg, including the Alexander Column and Narva Gates.	Alexander I dies. Reformers assemble on Senate Sq to protest the succession of conservative Nicholas I. The new tsar brutally crushes the Decembrist revolt, killing hundreds.	Construction of Russia's first railway line, from St Petersburg to Tsarskoe Selo, the imperial family's summer residence, begins. Initially trains are horse drawn.	Poet Alexander Pushkin is shot in a duel with the Frenchman Georges d'Anthès and later dies at his Moyka River house in St Petersburg, an unfathomable loss to Russian literature, still mourned today.

the south embankment, adorned with ancient heroes, including Alexander the Great, and the sea goddess Isis, and topped with golden spire.

Russia Starts to Reform

War did more than confer Great Power status on Russia: it was also a stimulus for new ideas on political reform and social change. In the 19th century, the clash of ideas spilled out of salons and into its streets.

On a frosty December morning in 1825, more than 100 soldiers amassed on Senate Sq (now Decembrists' Sq), with the intention of upsetting the royal succession. When Alexander I died unexpectedly without a legitimate heir, the throne was supposed to pass to his brother Constantine, Viceroy of Poland, but he declined, preferring not to complicate his contented life. Instead, the new tsar would be Alexander's youngest brother, Nicholas I, a cranky conservative with a fastidious obsession for barracks-style discipline. The Decembrist revolt was staged by a small cabal of officers, veterans of the Napoleonic Wars, who saw first hand how people in other countries enjoyed greater freedom and prosperity. They demanded Constantine and a constitution, but instead got exile and execution. The 'people', however, were now part of the discussion.

Russia's deeply disappointing performance in another war prompted another reform attempt, this time initiated by the tsar. In the 1850s, better-equipped British and French armies trounced Russia in a fight over the Crimean peninsula. The new emperor Alexander II concluded from the fiasco that Russia had to catch up with the West, or watch its empire unravel. A slew of reform decrees was issued, promoting public education, military reorganisation and economic modernisation. Alexander dropped the death penalty, curtailed corporal punishment and abolished serfdom, kind of – his solution that serfs pay their masters redemptive fees in exchange for freedom in fact pleased no one.

Assassination of a Tsar

By now the 'people' were becoming less abstract. Political movements that claimed to better understand and represent them were sprouting up. On a Sunday morning in March 1881, several young student members of the Peoples' Will radical sect waited nervously by the Griboyedov Canal as the tsar's procession passed. Their homemade bombs hardly dented the royal armoured coach, but badly wounded scores of spectators and fatally shredded the reforming monarch when he insisted on leaving his carriage to investigate. On the hallowed site, the magnificent and melancholy Church of the Saviour on the Spilled Blood

---

Contrary to rumour, Catherine the Great categorically did not die underneath a stallion – her death was a far more prosaic affair. She collapsed from a stroke in her bathroom and died tucked up in her bed. No horses are believed to have been present.

If you're interested in the bizarre circumstances that led to Pushkin's fatal duel with Georges d'Anthès, read *Pushkin's Buttons*, by Serena Vitale, for the definitive account.

1849	1851	1861	1866
Author Fyodor Dostoevsky is exiled to Siberia for four years of hard labour after participating in discussions with a liberal intellectual group, the Petrashevsky Circle.	Upon completion of the construction of Nikolaevsky Station (now Moscow Station), the first trains linking Moscow and St Petersburg introduce rail travel to the Russian public.	The emancipation of serfs frees up labour for the industrial revolution. The flood of workers into the capital leads to overcrowding, poor sanitation, disease epidemics and societal discontent.	Dostoevsky's classic novel of life and death in St Petersburg's poverty-stricken garrets, *Crime and Punishment*, is published, making him Russia's greatest late-19th-century author.

was constructed, its twisting onion domes trying to steady St Petersburg's uncertain present with Russia's enduring past.

Competition between Russia and Europe's other great powers compelled a state-directed campaign of economic development. St Petersburg became the centre of a robust military–industrial economy, established to fight the wars of the modern age. A ring of ugly, sooty smokestacks grew up around the still-handsome city centre. Tough times in the rural villages and job opportunities in the new factories hastened a human flood into the capital. By the 1880s, the population climbed past one million, with hundreds of thousands cramped into slummy suburban squalor. The gap between high society and the lower depths had long been manageable, but now they kept running into each other. The people had arrived.

God Save the Tsar

'We, workers and inhabitants of the city of St Petersburg, our wives, children, and helpless old parents, have come to you, Sovereign, to seek justice and protection.' So read the petition that a large group of workers intended to present to Tsar Nicholas II one Sunday in January 1905.

Nicholas II ascended the throne in 1894, when his iron-fisted autocratic father, Alexander III, died suddenly. Nicholas was of less steely stuff. Most contemporary accounts agree: he was a good guy and a lousy leader – possessive of his power to decide, but he could never make up his mind. In 1904 Nicholas followed the foolish advice of a cynical minister, who said that what Russia needed most was a 'small victorious war' to get peoples' minds off their troubles. Unfortunately, the Russo-Japanese War ended in humiliating defeat and the people were more agitated than ever.

By January 1905 the capital was a hotbed of political protest. As many as 100,000 workers were on strike, the city had no electricity and all public facilities were closed. Nicholas and the royals departed for their palace retreat at Tsarskoe Selo. In this charged atmosphere, Father Georgy Gapon, an Orthodox priest who apparently lived a double life as a police agent, organised a peaceful demonstration of workers and their families to protest against the difficult conditions. Their petition called for eight-hour work days and better wages, universal suffrage and an end to the war.

Singing 'God Save the Tsar', the crowd solemnly approached the Winter Palace, hoping to present its requests to the tsar personally. Inside, the mood was jittery: panicky guards fired on the demonstrators, at first as a warning and then directly into the crowd. More than a thousand people were killed by the gunshots or the trampling that followed.

Focusing on the colourful characters of the imperial period and the dramatic events leading up to the revolution, D Bruce Lincoln's *Sunlight at Midnight* is a definitive history of the period as well as being highly readable and academically rigorous.

1870	1881	1882	1883
After breaking from the Academy of Arts, a group of upstart artists known as the Peredvizhniki (Wanderers) starts organising travelling exhibitions to widen their audience.	A bomb kills Alexander II as he travels along Griboyedov Canal. His reactionary son, Alexander III, undoes many of his reforms, but oversees the building of the Trans-Siberian Railway.	Jews are subjected to harsh legal restrictions in retribution for their alleged role in the assassination of Alexander II. A series of pogroms provokes Jewish migration from Russia.	The dazzling Church of the Saviour on the Spilled Blood is inaugurated as a private place of mourning for the imperial family for the dead Alexander II.

THE PRIEST OF SEX

Grigory Rasputin was born in the Siberian village of Pokrovskoe in 1869. Never a monk as is frequently supposed, Rasputin experienced a vision of the Virgin while working in the fields in his mid-20s and left Pokrovskoe to seek enlightenment. On his wanderings he came to believe, as did the contemporary Khlyst (Whip) sect, that sinning (especially through sex), then repenting, could bring people close to God.

In St Petersburg Rasputin's racy brand of redemption, along with his soothing talk, compassion and generosity, made him very popular with some aristocratic women. Eventually, he was summoned by Tsaritsa Alexandra and seemed able, thanks to some kind of hypnotic power, to halt the life-threatening bleeding of her haemophiliac son, Tsarevitch Alexey, the heir to the throne. Rasputin's influence on the imperial family grew to the point where he could make or break the careers of ministers and generals. He became increasingly unpopular and many scapegoated him for Russia's disastrous performance in WWI.

In 1916 Prince Felix Yusupov and others hatched an assassination plot. According to Yusupov's own account of the murderous affair, this proved to be easier said than done: Rasputin survived poisoning, several shots and a beating, all in one evening at St Petersburg's Yusupov Palace. Apparently he died only when drowned in a nearby river. However, a 2004 BBC documentary uncovered evidence that Rasputin actually died from his bullet wounds, one of which was delivered by a British secret agent working in conjunction with the Russian plotters. For the fascinating background to this version of events read Andrew Cook's *To Kill Rasputin*.

Although Nicholas was not even in the palace at the time, the events of Bloody Sunday shattered the myth of the Father Tsar. The Last Emperor was finally able to restore order by issuing the October Manifesto, which promised a constitutional monarchy and civil rights; in fact, not much really changed.

Down with the Autocracy

At the start of WWI, nationalist fervour led St Petersburg to change its name to the more Slavic, less German-sounding Petrograd. A hundred years earlier, war with France had made the Russian Empire a great power, but now yet another European war threatened its very survival. The empire was fraying at the seams as the old aristocratic order limped onward into battle. Only the strength of the Bronze Horseman could hold it all together. But Peter's legacy rested on the shoulders of an imperial inheritor who was both half-hearted reformer and irresolute reactionary: the combination proved revolutionary.

1890	1896	1896	1899
Queen of Spades, Pyotr Tchaikovsky's opera based on the poem by Alexander Pushkin, premieres at the Mariinsky Theatre, drawing excited crowds and rave reviews.	At the coronation of Nicholas II, a stampede by the massive crowd ends with more than a thousand deaths and almost as many injuries.	Anton Chekhov's classic play *The Seagull* opens to poor reviews at the Alexandrinsky Theatre. The playwright is so unnerved by the audience's hostility that he leaves the theatre.	Vladimir Nabokov, the future author of *Lolita*, is born at his family's mansion on Bolshaya Morskaya ul. He immortalises the house in his autobiography *Speak, Memory*.

In 1917, 23 February began like most days in Petrograd since the outbreak of the war. The men went off to the metalworks and arms factories, the women went out to receive the daily bread ration. And the radical set went out to demonstrate, as it happened to be International Women's Day. Although each left their abode an ordinary individual, by day's end they would meld into the most infamous 'mass' in modern history: the Bronze Horseman's heirs let go of the reigns; the Russian Revolution, a play in three acts, had begun.

After waiting long hours in the winter chill for a little food, the women were told that there would be none. This news coincided with the end of the day shift and a sweaty outpouring from the factory gates. Activist provocateurs joined the fray as the streets swelled with the tired, the hungry and now the angry. The crowd assumed a political purpose. They marched to the river, intent on crossing to the palace side and expressing their discontent to somebody. But they were met at the bridge by gendarmes and guns.

Similar meetings had occurred previously, in July and October, on which occasions the crowd retreated. But now it was February and one did not need a bridge to cross the frozen river. First a brave few, then emboldened small groups, and finally a defiant horde of hundreds were traversing the ice-laden Neva toward the Winter Palace.

They congregated in the Palace Square, demanding bread, peace and an end to autocracy. Inside, contemptuous counts stole glances at the unruly rabble and waited for them to grow tired and disperse. But they did not go home. Instead, they went around the factories and spread the call for a general strike. By the next day a quarter of a million people were rampaging through the city centre. Overwhelmed local police took cover.

When word reached the tsar, he ordered military troops to restore order. But his troops were no longer hardened veterans: they were long dead at the front. Rather, freshly conscripted peasant youths in uniform were sent to put down the uprising. When commanded to fire on the demonstration, they instead broke rank, dropped their guns and joined the mob. At that moment, the 300-year-old Romanov dynasty and 500-year-old tsarist autocracy came to an end.

Part love story and part political thriller, Robert K Massie's *Nicholas and Alexandra* gives the nitty-gritty on the royal family, Rasputin and the resulting revolution.

All Power to the Soviets

Perhaps the least likely political successor to the tsar in February 1917 was the radical socialist Bolshevik Party. The Bolsheviks were on the fringe of the fringe of Russia's political left. Party membership numbered a few thousand, at best. Yet, in less than eight months, the

1905	1906	1914	1915
Hundreds of people are killed when troops fire on peaceful protestors presenting a petition to the tsar. Nicholas II is held responsible for the tragedy, dubbed 'Bloody Sunday'.	The first Duma (State Assembly) election is held, a decision that is made, but greatly resented, by Nicholas II on the urging of the prime minister. The Duma meets four times a year in the Tauride Palace until 1917.	Russia enters WWI, simultaneously invading Austrian Galicia and German Prussia with minimal success. St Petersburg changes its name to the less Germanic sounding Petrograd.	The first suprematist art show takes place in Petrograd, showcasing Malevich's infamous *Black Square*, creating a critical storm and putting the Russian avant-garde firmly on the map.

Bolsheviks occupied the Winter Palace, proclaiming Petrograd the capital of a worldwide socialist revolution.

In the days that followed Nicholas' abdication, the Russian Provisional Government was established. It mainly comprised political liberals, representing reform-minded nobles, pragmatic civil servants, and professional and business interests. Simultaneously, a rival political force emerged, the Petrograd Soviet. The Soviet (the Russian word for council) was composed of more populist and radical elements, representing the interests of the workers, peasants, soldiers and sailors. Both political bodies were based at the Tauride Palace.

The Provisional Government saw itself as a temporary instrument, whose main task was to create constitutional democracy. It argued over the details of organising an election and convention, rather than deal with the issues that had caused the revolution – bread and peace. At first, the Soviet deferred to the Provisional Government, but this soon changed.

On 3 April, Bolshevik leader Vladimir Lenin arrived at the Finland Station (Finlyandsky vokzal) from exile in Switzerland. Lenin's passage across enemy lines had been arranged by German generals, who hoped that he would stir things up at home, and thus distract Russia from its participation in the war. As expected, Lenin upset the political status quo as soon as he arrived. His revolutionary rhetoric polarised Petrograd. In the Soviet, the Bolshevik faction went from cooperative to confrontational. But even his radical colleagues dismissed Lenin as a stinging gadfly, rather than a serious foe. By summer's end, Lenin had proved them all wrong.

Lenin Takes Power

The Provisional Government not only refused to withdraw from the war but, at the instigation of the allies, launched a new offensive – prompting mass desertions at the front. Meanwhile, the economic situation continued to deteriorate. The same anarchic anger that fuelled the February Revolution was felt on the streets again. Lenin's Bolsheviks were the only political party in sync with the public mood. September elections in the Petrograd Soviet gave the Bolsheviks a majority.

Lenin had spent his entire adult life waiting for this moment. For 20 years he did little else than read, write and rant about revolution. He enjoyed Beethoven, but avoided listening to his music from concern that the sentiment it evoked would make him lose his revolutionary edge. A successful revolution, Lenin observed, had two preconditions: first, the oppressed classes were politically mobilised and ready to act; and, second, the ruling class was internally divided and questioned its

Top Historic Sites

....

Peter & Paul Fortress (Petrograd & Vyborg Sides)

....

Winter Palace (Hermitage, Historic Heart)

....

Alexander Nevsky Monastery (Smolny & Vosstaniya)

....

Tsarskoe Selo (Pushkin)

1916	1917	1918	1920
After evoking the ire of aristocrats, Grigory Rasputin is invited to Yusupov Palace for cyanide-laced tea by a group of plotters, who eventually drown him in the icy Moyka River.	The February Revolution results in the abdication of Nicholas II, followed by the Bolshevik coup in October. Vladimir Ilych Lenin seizes power and civil war ensues.	Lenin pulls Russia out of WWI and moves the capital to Moscow. Civil war continues throughout the country, and Petrograd enters a period of political and cultural decline.	The ongoing civil war and the change of capital take their toll on St Petersburg. The population falls to 722,000, one-third of the pre-revolutionary figure.

will to continue. This politically explosive combination now existed. If the Bolsheviks waited any longer, he feared, the Provisional Government would get its act together and impose a new bourgeois political order, ending his dream of socialist revolution in Russia.

On 25 October (7 November in the Gregorian calendar), the Bolsheviks staged their coup. Bolshevik Red Guards seized a few buildings and strategic points. The Provisional Government was holed up in the tsar's private dining room in the Winter Palace, protected by a few Cossacks, the Petrograd chapter of the Women's Battalion of Death, and the one-legged commander of a bicycle regiment. Before dessert could be served, their dodgy defences cracked. Mutinous mariners fired a window-shattering salvo from the cruiser *Aurora* to signal the start of the assault; and the Red Guards – led by Lenin – moved in on the Winter Palace. Three shells struck the building, bullet holes riddled the square side of the palace and a window was shattered on the 3rd floor before the Provisional Government was arrested in the Small Dining Room behind the Malachite Hall. This largely bloodless battle would be celebrated for 70 years as the most glorious moment in history.

At the Tauride Palace the Soviet remained in emergency session late into the night when Lenin announced that the Provisional Government had been arrested and the Soviet was now the supreme power in Russia. Half the deputies walked out in disgust. Never one to miss an opportunity, Lenin quickly called a vote to make it official. It passed. Incredibly, the Bolsheviks were now in charge.

Consolidating Communism

Nobody believed the Bolsheviks would be around for long. Even Lenin said that, if they could hold on for just 100 days, their coup would be a success by providing future inspiration. It was one thing to occupy a few palaces in Petrograd, but across the empire's far-flung regions Bolshevik-brand radicalism was not so popular. From 1918 to 1921 civil war raged in Russia: between monarchists and socialists, imperialists and nationalists, aristocrats and commoners, believers and atheists. When it was over, somehow Soviet power was still standing. In the final act of the Russian Revolution, the scene shifted from the Petrograd stage. The imperial capital would never be the same.

In December 1917, an armistice was arranged and peace talks began with the Germans. The Bolsheviks demanded a return to prewar imperial borders, but Germany insisted on the liberation of Poland, where its army was squatting. Leon Trotsky, the foreign affairs commissar, defiantly walked out of negotiations, declaring 'neither war, nor peace'. The German high command was a bit confused and not at all amused –

Simon Sebag Montefiore's *The Romanovs* is a fast paced and gossip filled account of the dynasty that created St Petersburg.

HISTORY CONSOLIDATING COMMUNISM

Vsevolod Pudovkin's 1927 silent film *The End of St Petersburg* was produced to commemorate the 10th anniversary of the October Revolution and it remains a landmark for Soviet realist cinema.

1921	1924	1930	1934
Kronshtadt sailors and soldiers rebel against the increasingly dictatorial regime. They are brutally suppressed in the last major uprising against Communist rule until the Soviet collapse.	Lenin dies without designating a successor. The city is renamed Leningrad in his honour. Power is assumed by a 'triumvirate' but Stalin increasingly takes control.	Dmitry Shostakovich's satirical opera *The Nose* premieres at Maly Operny (the current Mikhailvosky Theatre). He is accused of 'formalism' by Stalinist critics and the opera is not performed again until the 1970s.	Leningrad party boss Sergei Kirov is murdered as he leaves his office at the Smolny Institute. The assassination kicks off the Great Purge, ushering in Stalin's reign of terror.

THE SWITCH IN CALENDARS

Until 1918 Russian dates followed the Julian calendar, which lagged behind the Gregorian calendar (used by pretty much every other country in the world) by 13 days. The new Soviet regime brought Russia into line by following 31 January 1918 with 14 February (skipping 1 to 13 February). This explains why, in Russian history, the revolution was on 25 October 1917 while in the West it occurred on 7 November 1917. The Julian calendar is still used in Russia by the Orthodox Church, which is why Christmas Day is celebrated on 7 January instead of 25 December.

hostilities immediately resumed. Lenin had vowed never to abandon the capital, but that was before a German battle fleet cruised into the Gulf of Finland. Exit stage left. In 1918 the Bolsheviks vacated their new pastel digs in Petrograd and relocated behind the ancient red bricks of Moscow. It was supposed to be temporary (Lenin personally preferred St Petersburg). But Russia was turning inward, and Peter's window to the West was closing.

Along with the loss of its capital political status, St Petersburg had also lost its noble social status: the aristocratic soul lost its control of the proletarian body following the February Revolution. In March 1917 Nicholas II and his family were placed under house arrest in the Alexander Palace at Tsarskoe Selo, and were later imprisoned and executed in Yekaterinburg by the Bolsheviks. The more fortunate families fled with the few valuables they could carry; the less fortunate who stayed were harassed, dispossessed and killed.

The revolution began in Petrograd and ended there in March 1921 when Kronshtadt sailors staged a mutiny. These erstwhile Bolshevik boosters demanded the democracy they had been promised now that the civil war was won. But Lenin, who had since renamed his political party 'the Communists', was reluctant to relinquish political power. The sailors' revolt was brutally suppressed in a full-scale military assault across the frozen bay, confirming the historical adage that revolutions eat their children.

Soviet Second City

Moscow finally reclaimed its coveted ancient title with the caveat that it was now the world's first communist capital. Petrograd consoled itself as the Soviet second city.

The redesignation of the capital prompted the departure of the bureaucracies: the government ministries, the military headquarters, the party apparatus, which took with them a host of loyal servants and

1937–38	1940	1941	1942
The height of Stalin's great purge, Yezhovshchina, terrorises the whole of Russia, but particularly Leningrad, liquidating much of its local intelligentsia and party organisation.	Rapid industrialisation shows results: the population of the city has rebounded, reaching 3.1 million, and Leningrad is now responsible for 11% of Soviet industrial output.	The Nazis invade the Soviet Union and Leningrad is surrounded, blocking residents from all sources of food and fuel, as the city comes under attack.	The Leningrad Radio Orchestra performs the Seventh Symphony by Dmitry Shostakovich. Musicians are given special rations so they can perform, and the music is broadcast throughout the city.

servile lackeys. The population dropped by two-thirds from its prewar count. Economic exchange was reduced to begging and bartering. To make matters worse, the food shortages that first sparked the revolution during the war continued well afterwards. Fuel was also in short supply – homes went unheated, factory gates stayed shut and city services were stopped.

Leningrad was eventually revived with a proletarian transfusion. At the beginning of the 1930s the socialist state launched an intensive campaign of economic development, which reinvigorated the city's industrial sector. New scientific and military research institutes were fitted upon the city's strong higher-education foundations. On the eve of WWII, the population had climbed to over three million. Public works projects for the people were undertaken – polished underground metro stations, colossal sports complexes and streamlined constructivist buildings muscled in next to the peeling pastels and cracked baroque of the misty past.

The Leningrad Purges

Though no longer the capital, Leningrad still figured prominently in Soviet politics. A position in the party machine, headquartered in the Smolny Institute, was a plum post in the Communist Party. The First Secretary, head of the Leningrad organisation, was always accorded a seat on the Politburo, the executive board of Soviet power. In the early years Leningrad was a crucial battlefront in the bloody intra-party competition to succeed Lenin.

Lenin died from a stroke at the age of 53, without designating a successor. He was first replaced by a troika of veteran Bolsheviks, including Leningrad party head, Alexander Zinoviev. But their stay at the top was brief; they were outmanoeuvred by the most unlikely successor to Lenin's mantle, Josef Stalin, a crude, disaffected Georgian bureaucrat.

In 1926 Zinoviev was forced to relinquish his Leningrad seat to Sergei Kirov, a solid Stalin man. In high-profile Leningrad, Kirov soon became one of the most popular party bosses. He was a zealous supporter of Stalin's plans for rapid industrialisation, which meant heavy investment in the city. But the manic-paced economic campaign could not be sustained, causing famine and food shortages. Kirov emerged as a proponent of a more moderate course instead of the radical pace that Stalin still insisted on. The growing rift in the leadership was exposed at a 1934 party congress, where a small cabal of regional governors secretly connived to remove Stalin in a bureaucratic coup and replace him with Kirov. It was an offer that Kirov flatly refused.

1944	1953	1955	1956
The Germans retreat. Leningrad emerges from its darkest hour, but more than one million are dead from starvation and illness. The city's population has dropped to an estimated 600,000.	Stalin dies in Moscow, marking the end of decades of terror, and the eventual liberalisation of Soviet society.	The first seven stations of the city's metro open 15 years after construction began, hampered initially by war and then by the marshy earth under the city, making the metro a technical marvel.	Party leader Nikita Khrushchev makes a 'Secret Speech' denouncing Stalin, thus commencing the de-Stalinisation of the Soviet Union, a period of economic reform and cultural thaw.

But it was hard to keep a secret from Stalin. Wary of Kirov's rising appeal, Stalin ordered that he be transferred to party work in Moscow, where he could be watched more closely. Kirov found reasons to delay the appointment and remained in Leningrad. On 1 December 1934, as he left a late-afternoon meeting, Kirov was shot from behind and killed in the corridor outside his Smolny office – on orders from Stalin.

Kirov's murder was the first act in a much larger drama. According to Stalin, it proved that the party was infiltrated by saboteurs and spies and the ensuing police campaign to uncover these hidden enemies became known as the Great Purges, which consumed nearly the entire post-revolutionary Soviet elite. Leningrad intellectuals were especially targeted. More than 50 Hermitage curators were imprisoned, including the Asian art specialist, accused of being an agent of Japanese imperialism, and the medieval armour specialist, accused of harbouring weapons. Successive waves of arrest, exile and execution effectively transformed the Leningrad elite, making it much younger, less assertive and more Soviet. When it was finally over, Stalin stood as personal dictator with unrivalled power – even by tsarist standards.

The Siege

On 22 June 1941 Leningraders were basking in the summer solstice when Foreign Minister Molotov interrupted state radio to announce an 'unprecedented betrayal in the history of civilised nations'. That day, German Nazi forces launched a full-scale military offensive across the Soviet Union's western borders. Stalin's refusal to believe that Hitler would break their nonaggression pact left Leningrad unprepared and vulnerable.

Symphony for the City of the Dead: Dmitri Shostakovich and the Siege of Leningrad by MT Anderson is a gripping account for young adult readers both of the WWII siege of the city and how Shostakovich's Seventh Symphony came to be played there in 1942.

The German code-name for its assault on Leningrad was Operation Nordlicht (Operation Northern Lights). The Führer ordered his generals to raze the city rather than incur the cost of feeding and heating its residents in winter. By July German troops had reached the suburbs, inflicting a daily barrage of artillery bombardment and aerial attacks. All Leningraders were mobilised around the clock to dig trenches, erect barricades and board up buildings. The city's factories were dismantled, brick by brick, and shipped to the other side of the Urals. Hermitage staff crated up Catherine's collection for a safer interior location; what they did not get out in time was buried on the grounds of the Summer Garden. The spires of the Admiralty and Peter & Paul Fortress were camouflaged in coloured netting, which was changed according to the weather and season. The youngest and oldest residents were evacuated; everybody else braced themselves.

1960	1964	1975	1979–80
The remodelled Piskaryovskoe Cemetery opens in northern Leningrad; here are buried almost 500,000 civilian and military casualties from the blockade.	A coup against Khrushchev brings Brezhnev to power; the Years of Stagnation begin. Future Nobel laureate Joseph Brodsky is sentenced to five years' hard labour.	Vladimir Putin, who was born in the city in 1955, graduates from St Peterburg University and joins the KGB; 16 years later he returns to the city to start his political career.	Russia invades Afghanistan to support its communist regime against US-backed Islamic militants. Relations between the superpowers deteriorate.

At the end of August the Germans captured the east-bound railway: Leningrad was cut off. Instead of a bloody street fight, the Nazi command vowed to starve the city to death. Food stocks were low to begin with but became almost nonexistent after napalm bombs burned down the warehouse district. Moscow dispatched tireless and resourceful Dmitry Pavlov to act as Chief of Food Supply. Pavlov's teams ransacked cellars, broke into box cars and tore up floorboards in search of leftover cans and crumbs. The city's scientists were pressed to develop something edible out of yeast, glue and soap. As supplies dwindled, pets and pests disappeared. A strict ration system was imposed and violators were shot. Workers received 15 ounces (425g) of bread per day; everyone else got less. It was not enough. The hunger was relentless, causing delirium, disease and death. Hundreds of thousands succumbed to starvation, corpses were strewn atop snow-covered streets, mass graves were dug on the outskirts.

Relief finally arrived in January, when food supplies began to reach the city from across the frozen Lake Ladoga lifeline. Trucks made the perilous night-time trek on ice roads, fearing the Luftwaffe above and chilled water below. Soviet military advances enabled the supply route to stay open in the spring when the lake thawed. Leningrad survived the worst; still the siege continued. The city endured the enemy's pounding guns for two more years. At last, in January 1944, the Red Army arrived in force. They pulverised the German front with more rockets and shells than were used at Stalingrad. Within days, Leningrad was liberated. The 900 days marked history's longest military siege of a modern city. The city was badly battered but not beaten. The St Petersburg spirit was resilient.

Harrison Salisbury's *The 900 Days: The Siege of Leningrad* is a fascinating forensic reconstruction of the Nazi blockade. It's not for those with a passing interest in the blockade, but for those who want to vicariously suffer through the darkest hours of the city.

From Dissent to Democracy

Throughout the Soviet period, Moscow kept suspicious eyes trained on Leningrad. After WWII, Stalin launched the 'Leningrad Affair', a sinister purge of the Hero City's youthful political and cultural elite, who were falsely accused of trying to create a rival capital. Several thousand were arrested, several hundred were executed. Kremlin apparatchiks were committed to forcing conformity onto the city's free-thinking intellectuals and keeping closed the window to the West. They ultimately failed.

Leningrad's culture club was irrepressible. Like in tsarist times, it teased, goaded and defied its political masters. Stalin terrorised, Khrushchev cajoled and Brezhnev banished, yet the city still became a centre of dissent. As from Radishchev to Pushkin, so from Akhmatova to Brodsky. By the 1970s the city hosted a thriving independent

HISTORY FROM DISSENT TO DEMOCRACY

1982	1985	1991	1997
The Leningrad musical underground is lit up by the arrival of Viktor Tsoy's band Kino, who begin to perform live and release their first album, *45*.	Reformer Mikhail Gorbachev defeats Leningrad boss Grigory Romanov and is elected general secretary of the party with policies of *perestroika* (restructuring) and *glasnost* (openness).	On Christmas Day, Gorbachev announces the dissolution of the Soviet Union. Leningrad's name reverts to St Petersburg after a referendum on the issue.	Mikhail Manevich, vice-governor of the city, is assassinated by a sniper in the middle of town as he travels to work, marking the height of St Petersburg's lawlessness.

underground of jazz and rock musicians, poets and painters, reformists and radicals. Like the Neva in spring, these cultural currents overflowed when Mikhail Gorbachev finally came to power in 1985 and declared a new policy of openness and reform. The Leningrad democratic movement was unleashed.

Gorbachev forced long-time Leningrad party boss Grigory Romanov and his communist cronies into retirement. He held elections for local office that brought to power liberal-minded Anatoly Sobchak, the darling of the progressive intelligentsia and the first popularly elected mayor in the city's history. Leningrad was at the forefront of democratic change, as the old regime staggered towards the exit.

Whereas Gorbachev sought to reform Soviet socialism, his rival Boris Yeltsin was intent on killing it off for good. Just two months after Sobchak's historic election, anti-reform hardliners staged a coup. While Yeltsin mollified Moscow, a hundred thousand protestors filled Palace Square in Leningrad. The ambivalent soldiers sent to arrest Sobchak disobeyed orders, and instead escorted him to the local TV station where the mayor denounced the coup and encouraged residents to do the same. Anxiously waiting atop flimsy barricades, anticommunist demonstrators spent the evening in fear of approaching tanks. But the inebriated coup plotters lost their nerve, thanks in large part to the people of Leningrad.

The Lawless 1990s

In 1991, by popular referendum, the citizens of Leningrad voted to change their city's name once more, restoring its original name, St Petersburg.

As reviled as the communist regime may have been, it still provided a sufficient standard of living, a predictable day at the office and a common target for discontent. The familiar ways of life suddenly changed. The communist collapse caused enormous personal hardship; economic security and social status were put in doubt. Mafia gangs and bureaucratic fangs dug into the emerging market economy, creating contemptible crony capitalism. The democratic movement splintered into petty rivalries and political insignificance. One of its shining stars, Galina Starovoytova, social scientist turned human rights advocate, was brazenly shot dead in the foyer of her St Petersburg apartment in 1998. Out on the street, meanwhile, prudish reserve gave way to outlandish exhibitionism. Uncertainty and unfairness found expression in an angry and sometimes xenophobic reaction.

With the old order vanquished, the battle to define the new one was on. The symbols of the contending parties were on display throughout

1998	1998	2000	2003
The bodies of the last tsar, Nicholas II, and most of his family are finally buried in the SS Peter & Paul Cathedral after their murders by the Bolsheviks 80 years earlier.	St Petersburg politician and human rights activist Galina Starovoitova is murdered outside her apartment by hitmen, another blow to Russia's reputation as a free and safe society.	St Petersburg native Vladimir Putin is elected President of Russia, beginning a new era of far greater central control and 'managed democracy'.	Putin's favoured candidate, Valentina Matvienko, prevails in local elections. Winning 63% of votes, she becomes the governor of St Petersburg.

the city. The nouveaux riches quickly claimed Nevsky pr for their Milano designer get-ups and Bavarian driving machines. The disaffected youth used faded pink courtyard walls to spray-paint Zenit football insignias, swastikas and the two English words they all seemed to know. Every major intersection was adorned with gigantic billboard faces of prima ballerinas and pop singers sipping their favourite cups of coffee. And, like all their St Petersburg predecessors, the new ruling elite aimed to leave its own distinctive mark, as witnessed by a slew of ugly office blocks that were built in the city centre.

The Rise of Putin

When St Petersburg native Vladimir Putin was elected president in 2000, speculation was rife that he would transfer the Russian capital back to his home town. That never happened, but with Putin in power – followed for four years in 2008 by another St Petersburg son Dmitry Medvedev – the city has certainly benefited.

Born in 1952, Putin spent his childhood in the Smolny district. Little Vlad went to school in the neighbourhood and took a law degree at Leningrad State University, before working in Leningrad, Moscow and East Germany for the KGB. In 1990 he returned to his home town, where he was promptly promoted through the ranks of local politics. By 1994 he was deputy to St Petersburg mayor Anatoly Sobchak. In his office in the Smolny Institute, Putin famously replaced the portrait of Lenin with one of Peter the Great.

As the city economy slowly recovered from collapse and shock, Sobchak was voted out of office in 1996. Putin was then recruited by fellow Leningrader, Anatoly Chubais, to join him in the capital in the Kremlin administration. Rising rapidly through the ranks, he took over the FSB (the postcommunist KGB) in 1998 and was made prime minister the following year. On New Year's Eve that same year, the ailing Yeltsin resigned and Putin was appointed acting president.

Putin went on to win two presidential elections, before resigning to become prime minister in 2008, due to constitutionally mandated term limits. Before the 2012 election changes were made to the consitution to allow Putin to be re-elected and for the presidential terms to be extended from four to six years; at the time of writing he is expected to stand once again for the presidency (and win, since there is no credible opposition) in 2018.

Reconstructing Piter

Under the appointed governorships of Putin loyalitsts Valentina Matvienko (2003–11) followed by current incumbent Georgy Poltavchenko,

A Soviet census-taker stops a man along Nevsky pr:

Where were you born? St Petersburg.

Where did you go to school? Petrograd.

Where do you live now? Leningrad.

Where would you like to live? St Petersburg.

2006	2008–09	2010	2011
Putin hosts the G8 Summit in St Petersburg, the most significant international political event ever held in the city, marking its reinvention as a ceremonial showpiece for Putin's Russia.	A worldwide financial crisis hits Russia hard. The economic recession is exacerbated by the falling price of oil and military entanglements with Georgia.	Governor Matvienko announces that after years of protests and international criticism, the controversial 400m-high Okhta Centre will no longer be built in the city centre.	Valentina Matvienko is moved sideways out of the governor's seat in St Petersburg to become the speaker of the Federation Council by President Dmitry Medvedev.

considerable and much-needed investment has been made in St Petersburg's infrastructure and cultural facilities.

Neglected and sidelined under the Soviets and then forced for the first two decades after the end of communism to concentrate on urgent conservation rather than development, St Petersburg has recently completed several huge engineering projects. These include the construction of a new ring road around the city, a flood barrier, the new M5 metro line and the Marine Facade cruise port on Vasilyevsky Island. Other recent important prestige projects include the opening of the Mariinsky II Theatre in 2013, and the transformation of the General Staff Building into a branch of the Hermitage.

All are significant, and herald the city's determination to be taken seriously as a business and tourism destination. To this end the city has hosted the prestigious St Petersburg International Economic Forum (www.forumspb.com) since 1997 and is one of the key venues for the 2018 FIFA World Cup.

2011	2013	2014	2017
Former KGB officer and Putin loyalist Georgy Poltavchenko is appointed governor of St Petersburg.	The Mariinsky II opens after a decade of planning and construction, giving St Petersburg a state-of-the-art ballet and opera theatre.	St Petersburg hosts Manifesta 10, the European Biennial of Contemporary Art, despite critics calling for a boycott due to Russia's annexation of Crimea.	In April a Russian suicide bomber on the city's metro kills 15 people and injures at least another 45.

Architecture

Peter the Great's intention was to build a city that rivalled Paris and Rome for architectural splendour. He envisioned grand avenues, weaving waterways and magnificent palaces. His successors, especially Empresses Anna, Elizabeth and Catherine the Great, carried out their own even more elaborate versions of their forebear's plan. Today, the historic centre of St Petersburg is a veritable museum of 18th- and 19th-century architecture, with enough baroque, neoclassical and empire-style extravagances to keep you ogling indefinitely.

Petrine Baroque

The first major building in the city was the Peter & Paul Fortress (p156), completed in 1704 and still intact today. Peter recruited Domenico Trezzini from Switzerland to oversee early projects. It was Trezzini, more than any other architect, who created the style known as Petrine Baroque, which was heavily influenced by Dutch architecture, of which Peter was enamoured. Trezzini's buildings included the Alexander Nevsky Monastery (p123), the SS Peter & Paul Cathedral (p156) within the fortress and Twelve Colleges (p147) on Vasilyevsky Island.

Initially, most funding was diverted to the war against Sweden, meaning there wasn't enough money to create the European-style city that Peter dreamed of. Once Russia's victory was secured in 1709, the city began to see feverish development. In 1711, the Grand Perspective (later Nevsky pr) was initially built as a road to transport building supplies from Russia's interior. Nevsky pr was supposed to be a perfectly straight avenue heading to Novgorod. The existing kink (at pl Vosstaniya) is attributed to a miscalculation by builders.

Stone construction was banned outside the new capital, in order to ensure that there would be enough masons free to work on the city. Peter ordered Trezzini to create a unified city plan designed around Vasilyevsky Island. He also recruited Frenchman Jean Baptiste Alexandre LeBlond from Paris. The two architects focused their efforts on Vasilyevsky Island, even though most people preferred to live across the river on the higher ground of Admiralty Island. The eponymously named Menshikov Palace, the home of Peter's best friend and St Petersburg's first governor, was the finest in the city, and far grander than Peter's Winter Palace.

The Age of Rastrelli

Empress Anna oversaw the completion of many of Peter's unfinished projects, including the Kunstkamera (p146) and Twelve Colleges (p147). Most significantly, she hired Italian Bartolomeo Rastrelli as chief architect, a decision that more than any other influenced the city's look today. His major projects under Anna's reign were the Manege Central Exhibition Hall (p112) and the Third Summer Palace (since destroyed). Rastrelli's greatest work, however, was yet to come.

Anna left her mark on the face of St Petersburg in many ways. She ordered all nobles to pave the street in front of their properties, thus

Top Five Architectural Sights

Winter Palace (Historic Heart)

Singer Building (Historic Heart)

Chesme Church (Smolny & Vosstaniya)

Smolny Cathedral (Smolny & Vosstaniya)

House of Soviets (Smolny & Vosstaniya)

While wandering down Nevsky pr, don't miss the beautiful equestrian sculptures on Anichkov Bridge and check out for yourself the local legend that the sculptor portrayed a man he didn't like (some say it was Napoleon, others that it was his wife's lover) on the testicles of one of the stallions.

ensuring the reinforcement of the Neva Embankment and other major thoroughfares. A massive fire in 1737 wiped out the unsightly and run-down wooden housing that surrounded the Winter Palace, thus freeing the historic centre for the centralised city planning that would be implemented under Elizabeth.

Elizabethan St Petersburg was almost entirely the work of Rastrelli, whose Russian baroque style became synonymous with the city. His crowning glory, of course, was the construction and remodelling of the Winter Palace (p56), completed in 1762, shortly after Elizabeth's death.

Rastrelli's second major landmark was Anichkov Palace (p91). After that creation, he became the city's most fashionable architect. Commissions soon followed to build the Stroganov Palace (p84), Vorontsov Palace (p91), Kamennoostrovsky Palace, Catherine Palace (p179) at Tsarskoe Selo and the extension of LeBlond's Grand Palace at Peterhof (p174). The sumptuous Smolny Cathedral (p126) is another Rastrelli landmark. His original design included a massive bell tower that would have been the tallest structure in Russia. The death of Empress Elizabeth in 1761 (1762 by the Gregorian calendar) prevented him from completing it, however.

Rastrelli's baroque style would go out of fashion quickly after Elizabeth's death. But his legacy would endure, as he created some of the most stunning facades in the city, thus contributing to the Italianate appearance of St Petersburg today.

Catherine's Return to Classicism

Despite her fondness for Elizabeth personally, Catherine the Great was not a fan of her predecessor's increasingly elaborate and sumptuous displays of wealth and power. Catherine's major philosophical interest was the Enlightenment, which had brought the neoclassical style to the fore in Western Europe. As a result, she began her long reign by departing from baroque architecture and introducing neoclassicism to Russia.

The first major neoclassical masterpiece in Catherine's St Petersburg was the Academy of Arts (p148) on Vasilyevsky Island, designed by Jean-Baptiste-Michel Vallin de la Mothe. Catherine employed a wide range of architects, including foreigners such as Vallin de la Mothe, Charles Cameron, Antonio Rinaldi and Giacomo Quarenghi, as well as home-grown architects such as Ivan Starov and Vasily Bazhenov.

Catherine's plan was to make the palace embankment the centrepiece of the city. To this end, she commissioned the Small Hermitage by Vallin de la Mothe, followed by the Large (Old) Hermitage and the Hermitage Theatre (p99) on the other side of the Winter Canal. These buildings on Dvortsovaya pl were followed by Quarenghi's magnificent Marble Palace (p84). Catherine also developed the embankment west of the Winter Palace, now the English Embankment (Angliyskaya nab), creating a marvellous imperial vista for those arriving in the city by boat.

The single most meaningful addition under Catherine's reign was the Bronze Horseman (p85) by Etienne-Maurice Falconet, an equestrian statue dedicated to Peter the Great. It is perched atop an enormous 1500-tonne boulder, known as Thunder Stone, which is from the Gulf of Finland and is supposedly the largest stone ever moved.

Other notable additions to the cityscape during Catherine's reign included the new Gostiny Dvor (p102), one of the world's oldest surviving shopping centres. Elizabeth had commissioned Rastrelli to rebuild an arcade that had burned down in 1736, but Catherine removed Rastrelli from the project and had it completed by Vallin de la Mothe, who created a more subtle and understated neoclassical facade. The purest classical construction in St Petersburg was perhaps Ivan Starov's Tauride Palace (p128), built for Prince Potemkin and surrounded by William Gould's expansive English-style gardens.

Russian Empire Style

Alexander I (r 1801–25) ushered in the new century with much hope that he would see through Catherine's reforms, becoming the most progressive tsar yet. His most enduring architectural legacy would be the new Alexandrian Empire style, a Russian counterpart of the style that had become popular in prewar Napoleonic France. This style was pioneered by a new generation of architects, most famously Carlo Rossi.

Before the Napoleonic Wars, the two most significant additions to the cityscape were the Strelka (p147), the 'tongue of land' at the tip of Vasilyevsky Island, and Kazan Cathedral (p83), prominently placed on Nevsky pr by Andrei Voronikhin. The Strelka had long been the subject of designs and proposals as a centrepiece to St Petersburg. Thomas de Thomon finally rebuilt Quarenghi's Stock Exchange and added the much-loved Rostral Columns to the tip of the island. The result was a stunning sight during summer festivities when the columns lit the sky with fire, a tradition that still continues today. Kazan Cathedral is a fascinating anomaly in St Petersburg's architectural history. It was been commissioned by Tsar Paul I and reflected his tastes and desire to fuse Catholicism and Orthodoxy. As such it is strikingly un-Russian, borrowing many of its features from the contemporaneous Italian architecture of Rome and Florence.

Following the Napoleonic wars, Carlo Rossi initiated several projects of true genius. This Italian architect defined the historic heart of St Petersburg with his imperial buildings – arguably even more so than Rastrelli. On Palace Square, he created the sumptuous General Staff Building (p72), which managed to complement Rastrelli's Winter Palace without outshining it. The building's vast length, punctuated by white columns, and its magnificent triumphal arch make Palace Square one of the most awe-inspiring urban environments in the world. The final touch to Palace Square was added by Auguste Montferrand, who designed the Alexander Column, a monument to the 1812 trouncing of Napoleon. Rossi also completed the Mikhailovsky Palace (now the Russian Museum (p74)) as well as the gardens behind it and pl Iskusstv (Arts Sq; p91) in front of it.

Rossi's genius continued to shine through the reactionary rule of Nicholas I. In fact, Nicholas was the last of the Romanovs to initiate mass municipal architecture, and so Rossi remained in favour, despite Nicholas' personal preference for the Slavic Revival style that was very popular in Moscow at the time.

Rossi's largest projects under Nicholas were the redesign of Senate Sq (now pl Dekabristov) and Alexandrinskaya Sq (now pl Ostrovskogo), including the Alexandrinsky Theatre and Theatre St (now ul Zodchego Rossi). The Theatre St ensemble is a masterpiece of proportions: its width (22m) is the same height as its buildings, and the entire length of the street is exactly 10 times the width (220m).

Imperial St Petersburg

Although Rossi continued to transform the city, the building that would redefine the city's skyline was Montferrand's St Isaac's Cathedral (p82). An Orthodox church built in a classical style, it is the fourth-largest cathedral in Europe. Montferrand's unique masterpiece took over three

Arthur George's *St Petersburg* is the first comprehensive popular history of St Petersburg and is a superb read for anyone interested in the city's architectural development. Taking the reader from Petrine Baroque to Stalinism, George is an expert guide to the differing styles that so define the city.

ST PETERSBURG GOES STYLE MODERNE

Industrialisation during the latter part of the 19th century brought huge wealth to St Petersburg, which resulted in an explosion of commissions for major public buildings and mansions, many in the much-feted style of the time – art nouveau, known in Russia as Style Moderne.

You only have to walk down Nevsky Prospekt to see several of the key results of this daring architectural departure: the **Singer Building** (p102) and **Kupetz Eliseevs** (p102), both of which have been restored to their full glory in recent years, are ostentatious in their decorative details. Also in the Historic Heart, search out **Au Pont Rouge** (p101), a revival of the old department store Esders and Scheefhaals, which combines Moderne and Italianate features, and **DLT** (p101), finished in 1909 as the department store for the elite Petersburg Guards regiments, and still operating as the city's most luxurious fashion house. The romantic interior of the Vitebsk Station (Vitebsky vokzal), crafted at the turn of the 19th century, offers up stained glass, sweeping staircases and beautiful wall paintings in its spacious waiting halls.

But it is over on the Petrograd Side, the most fashionable district of the era, that the majority of Style Moderne buildings can be found. Highlights include the Troitsky Bridge, the fabulous mansion of the ballet dancer Mathilda Kshesinskaya (now the **Museum of Political History** (p159)) and much of Kamennoostrovsky pr, which is lined with prime examples. Poke around the district's backstreets to discover many gems from the early 20th century, including **Chaev Mansion** (p161) and **Leuchtenberg House** (p159).

decades to construct and remains the highest building in central St Petersburg.

Nicholas I's reign saw the construction of St Petersburg's first permanent bridge across the Neva, Blagoveshchensky Most (Annunciation Bridge), and Russia's first railway (linking the capital to Tsarskoe Selo to get the royal family to their summer palace quickly). A more useful line to Moscow began service in 1851, and the Nikolaevsky Station, now known as the Moscow Station (Moskovsky vokzal), was built to accommodate it.

The reigns of Alexander II and Alexander III saw few changes to the overall building style in St Petersburg. Industrialisation under Alexander II meant filling in several canals, most significantly the Ligovsky Canal (now Ligovsky pr). A plan to fill in Griboyedov Canal thankfully proved too expensive to execute and the canal remains one of the city's most charming.

The main contribution of Alexander III was the Church of the Resurrection of Christ, better known as the Church of the Saviour on the Spilled Blood (p81), built on the site of his father's 1881 assassination. Alexander III insisted the church be in the Slavic Revival style, which explains its uncanny similarity to St Basil's Cathedral on Red Square in Moscow. Architects Malyshev and Parland designed its spectacular multicoloured tiling, the first hints of Russian Style Moderne, which by the end of the 19th century would take the city by storm. Painters such as Mikhail Nesterov and Mikhail Vrubel contributed to the interior design.

Soviet Leningrad

As in all other spheres of Russian culture, the collapse of the tsarist regime in 1917 led to huge changes in architecture. In the beleaguered city, all major building projects stopped; the palaces of the aristocracy and the mansions of the merchant classes were turned over to the state or split up into communal apartments. The title of capital returned to Moscow and the city went into a decline that was to last until the 1990s.

The architectural form that found favour under the Bolsheviks in the 1920s was constructivism. Combining utilitarianism and utopianism, this modern style sought to advance the socialist cause, using technological innovation and slick unembellished design. Pl Stachek is rich with such buildings, such as the Kirov Region Administrative Building on Kirovskaya pl and the incredibly odd Communication Workers' Palace of Culture on the Moyka Canal.

Stalin considered the opulence of the imperial centre of renamed Leningrad to be a potentially corrupting influence on the people. So, from 1927, he began to relocate the centre to the south of the city's Historic Heart. His traditional neoclassical tastes prevailed. The prime example of Stalinist architecture is the vast House of Soviets (p130), which was meant to be the centrepiece of the new city centre. Noi Trotsky began this magnificent monstrosity in 1936, although it was not finished until after the war (by which time Trotsky had died). With its columns and bas-reliefs, it is a great example of Stalinist neoclassical design – similar in many ways to the imperial neoclassicism pioneered a century earlier. The House of Soviets was never used as the Leningrad government building, as the plan to relocate the centre was shelved after Stalin's death in 1953.

WWII saved many buildings of great importance: the Church of the Saviour on the Spilled Blood, for example, was slated for destruction before the German invasion of the Soviet Union intervened. Many other churches and historical buildings, however, were destroyed.

During the eras of Khrushchev and Brezhnev, St Petersburg's imperial heritage was cautiously respected, as the communist leadership took a step back from Stalin's excesses. Between the 1950s and 1970s, a housing shortage led to the construction of high-rise Soviet apartment buildings, which would cover huge swaths of the city outside the historic centre. For many visitors, this is their first and last view of the city. Examples of archetypal post-Stalinist Soviet architecture include the massive Grand Concert Hall, near pl Vosstaniya, and the classically inspired Finland Station (p166) (Finlyandsky vokzal), on the Vyborg Side.

Contemporary St Petersburg

Following the demise of the Soviet Union in the early 1990s, efforts were focused on the reconstruction of imperial-era buildings, many of which were derelict and literally falling down due to 70 years of neglect. Between 1991 and St Petersburg's tercentennial celebrations in 2003, much of the historic heart was restored at vast expense. Efforts are ongoing, and include the total regeneration of New Holland.

The governorship of Valentina Matvienko (2003–11) was marked by a shift from preservation to construction, and the city saw a large growth in new building projects during this time, not always to the delight of campaigners for the protection of St Petersburg's architectural heritage, or Unesco, who awarded St Petersburg's historic centre World Heritage status in 1990.

The most noteworthy of contemporary architecture projects in St Petersburg are the Mariinsky II Theatre, the airy, light-filled New Stage of the Alexandrinsky Theatre, the Krestovsky Stadium and the 462m Lakhta Center (http://lakhta.center) which, when it's completed in 2018, will be both the tallest building in Russia and Europe. This twisted spire, funded by the petrochemical company Gazprom, replaced a controversial plan for the Okhta Centre which was slated to be built opposite Smolny Cathedral. After worldwide condemnation and a strong local protest movement the project was relocated to the north of the city facing the Gulf of Finland.

The best view of the Lakhta Tower and of Krestovsky Stadium are when you're driving over the suspension bridges of the Western High Speed Diameter, arguably the city's most impressive recent infrastructure project.

1. Catherine Palace (p179), Pushkin 2. Academy of Arts (p148)
3. House of Soviets (p130) 4. Singer Building (p102)

ROMAN SIBIRIYAKOV / SHUTTERSTOCK ©

Architectural Styles

St Petersburg will fascinate anyone with even a passing interest in architectural forms of the past three centuries. From baroque to austere Soviet via neoclassicism, Russian Empire style and Style Moderne, here are the more prominent styles you'll encounter.

Baroque

Best epitomised by Bartolomeo Rastrelli's **Smolny Cathedral** (p126), the baroque style in St Petersburg reached its zenith under Empress Elizabeth, and can be seen most prominently in the **Winter Palace** (p56). Other examples are the **Stroganov Palace** (p84) and the **Catherine Palace** (p179).

Neoclassical

The **Academy of Arts** (p148) is the most obvious example of the neoclassical style popular with Catherine the Great. With its references to the colonnaded architecture of ancient Greece and Rome, this is one of the most recognisable styles of the city and can also be seen in **Bolshoy Gostiny Dvor** (p102) and in the **Tauride Palace** (p128).

Russian Empire Style

Having defeated Napoleon, Russia under Alexander I and Nicholas I was ready for an architectural style of its own. Russian Empire style is best represented by the **General Staff Building** (p72), built by Carlo Rossi.

Style Moderne

Perhaps the style most associated with St Petersburg, Style Moderne remains one of its richest architectural legacies. One of its best examples is the **Singer Building** (p102).

Soviet Style

There are many different eras of Soviet architecture in the city, but there's no better example of this bombastic, intimidating and regimented style than the **House of Soviets** (p130).

Arts

Despite the evident European influences, St Petersburg's Russian roots are a more essential source of inspiration for its artistic genius. Musicians and writers have long looked to Russian history, folk culture and other national themes. That St Petersburg has produced so many artistic and musical masterpieces is in itself a source of wonder for the city's visitors and inhabitants today, and it's no coincidence that St Petersburg is often referred to as Russia's cultural capital.

Ballet

Above: Mikhailovsky Castle (p85), a branch of the Russian Museum (p74)

First introduced in the 17th century, ballet in Russia evolved as an off-shoot of French dance combined with Russian folk and peasant dance techniques. In 1738, French dance master Jean Baptiste Lande established the Imperial Ballet School in St Petersburg – a precursor to the famed Vaganova School of Choreography.

The French dancer and choreographer Marius Petipa (1819–1910) is considered the father of Russian ballet, acting as principal dancer and premier ballet master of the Imperial Theatres and Imperial Ballet. All told, he produced more than 60 full ballets, including the classics *Sleeping Beauty* and *Swan Lake*.

In 1907, Petipa wrote in his diary, 'I can state that I created a ballet company of which everyone said: St Petersburg has the greatest ballet in all Europe'. At the turn of the 20th century, the heyday of Russian ballet, St Petersburg's Imperial Ballet School rose to world prominence, producing superstar after superstar. Names such as Vaslav Nijinsky, Anna Pavlova, Mathilda Kshesinskaya, George Balanchine, Michel Fokine and Olga Spessivtzeva turned the Mariinsky Theatre into the world's most dynamic display of the art of dance.

Sergei Diaghilev graduated from the St Petersburg Conservatory in 1892, but he abandoned his dream of becoming a composer when his professor, Nikolai Rimsky-Korsakov, told him he had no talent for music. Instead he turned his attention to dance, and his Ballets Russes took Europe by storm. The Petipa-inspired choreography was daring and dynamic, and the stage decor was painted by artists such as Alexander Benois, Mikhail Larionov, Natalya Goncharova and Leon Bakst. The overall effect was an artistic, awe-inducing display unlike anything taking place elsewhere in Europe.

Under the Soviets, ballet was treated as a natural resource. It enjoyed highly privileged status, which allowed schools such as Vaganova and companies such as the Kirov (as the Mariinsky was renamed) to maintain a level of lavish production and no-expense-spared star-searches. Still, the story of 20th-century Russian ballet is connected with the West, to where so many of its brightest stars emigrated or defected. Anna Pavlova, Vaslav Nijinsky, Rudolf Nureyev, Mikhail Baryshnikov, George Balanchine, Natalya Makarova, Mathilda Kshesinskaya, to name a few, all found fame in Western Europe or America, and most of them ended up living there.

The Kirov is once again known by its pre-revolutionary name and has its home at the Mariinsky Theatre (p117) where it has been rejuvenated under the fervent directorship of artistic director Valery Gergiev. The Mariinsky's calling card has always been its flawless classical ballet, but in recent years names such as William Forsythe and John Neumeier have brought modern choreography to this establishment. The Mariinsky's credibility on the world stage has been bolstered by the 2013 opening of the Mariinsky II (p118), built adjacent to the original theatre on the Kryukov Canal.

Music

St Petersburg has a rich musical legacy, dating back to the days when the Group of Five (Mily Balakirev, Alexander Borodin, César Cui, Modest Mussorgsky and Nikolai Rimsky-Korsakov) and Pyotr Tchaikovsky composed here. Opera and classical music continue to draw crowds, and the three Mariinsky theatres and Philharmonia regularly sell out their performances of home-grown classics. Surprisingly, earlier music, such as baroque and medieval, is not as well known or as well loved, though the city's Early Music Festival has long campaigned to change that.

Music lovers come in all shapes and sizes, however. Even when rock-and-roll was illegal it was played in basements and garages. In the post Soviet world, St Petersburg is the centre of *russky rok*, a magnet for musicians and music lovers, who are drawn to its atmosphere of innovation and creation.

ARTS MUSIC

Of the huge range of productions it's possible to see at the Mariinsky Theatre, Prokofiev's thoroughly modernist ballet *Romeo and Juliet* is perhaps one of the most enjoyable. It premiered on this very stage in 1940 and has changed little since – a true classic.

Best Artist House-Museums in St Petersburg

Rimsky-Korsakov Flat–Museum (Smolny & Vosstaniya)

Chaliapin House–Museum (Petrograd & Vyborg Sides)

Anna Akhmatova Museum at the Fountain House (Smolny & Vosstaniya)

Brodsky House–Museum (Historic Heart)

Classical Music & Opera

As the cultural heart of Russia, St Petersburg was a natural draw for generations of composers, its rich cultural life acting as inspiration for talent from throughout Russia. Mikhail Glinka is often considered the father of Russian classical music. In 1836 his opera *A Life for the Tsar* premiered in St Petersburg. While European musical influences were evident, the story was based on Russian history, recounting the dramatic tale of a peasant, Ivan Susanin, who sacrificed himself to save Mikhail Romanov.

In the second half of the 19th century, several influential schools formed in the capital, from which emerged some of Russia's most famous composers and finest music. The Group of Five looked to folk music for uniquely Russian themes. They tried to develop a distinct sound using unusual tonal and harmonic devices. Their main opponent was Anton Rubinstein's conservatively rooted Russian Musical Society, which became the St Petersburg Conservatory in 1861. The competition between the two schools was fierce. Rimsky-Korsakov wrote in his memoirs: 'Rubinstein had a reputation as a pianist, but was thought to have neither talent nor taste as a composer.'

Pyotr Tchaikovsky (1840–93) seemed to find the middle ground, embracing Russian folklore and music as well as the disciplines of the Western European composers. In 1890 Tchaikovsky's *The Queen of Spades* premiered at the Mariinsky. His adaptation of the famous Pushkin tale surprised and invigorated the artistic community, especially as his deviations from the original text – infusing it with more cynicism and a brooding sense of doom – tied the piece to contemporary St Petersburg.

Tchaikovsky is widely regarded as the doyen of Russian national composers and his output, including the magnificent *1812 Overture,* his concertos and symphonies, ballets (*Swan Lake, Sleeping Beauty* and *The Nutcracker*), and opera *(Yevgeny Onegin)* are among the world's most popular classical works.

Following in Tchaikovsky's romantic footsteps was the innovative Igor Stravinsky (1882–1971). He fled Russia after the revolution, but his memoirs credit his childhood in St Petersburg as having a major effect on his music. *The Rite of Spring* (which created a furore at its first performance in Paris), *Petrouchka* and *The Firebird* were all influenced by Russian folk music. The official Soviet line was that Stravinsky was a 'political and ideological renegade'; but he was rehabilitated after he visited the USSR and was formally received by Khrushchev himself.

Similarly, the ideological beliefs and experimental style of Dmitry Shostakovich (1906–75) led to him being alternately praised and condemned by the Soviet government. As a student at the Petrograd conservatory, Shostakovich failed his exams in Marxist methodology, but still managed to write his first symphony before he graduated in 1926. He wrote brooding, bizarrely dissonant works, as well as accessible traditional classical music. After official condemnation by Stalin, his seventh symphony (Leningrad Symphony) brought him honour and international standing when it was performed during WWII. The authorities changed their mind and banned his anti-Soviet music in 1948, then 'rehabilitated' him after Stalin's death. These days he is held in high esteem as the namesake of the acclaimed Shostakovich Philharmonia (p99).

Since becoming its artistic director in 1988, Valery Gergiev has revitalised the Mariinsky (p117). The Russian classics still top the list of performances, but Gergiev is also willing to be a little adventurous, taking on operas that had not been performed in half a century or more.

For an engaging account of how culture and politics became intertwined during the early Soviet period, read Solomon Volkov's *Shostakovich and Stalin,* which examines the fascinating relationship between two of the main representatives of each field.

Mariinsky Theatre (p106)

Gergiev is also responsible for initiating the Stars of White Nights Festival, an annual event that showcases the best and brightest dancers and musicians.

Rock

Russian music is not all about classical composers. Ever since the 'bourgeois' Beatles filtered through in the 1960s, Russians both young and old have supported the rock revolution. Starved of decent equipment and the chance to record or perform to big audiences, Russian rock groups initially developed underground. By the 1970s – the Soviet hippy era – rock music had developed a huge following among the disaffected, distrustful youth in Leningrad.

Although bands initially imitated their Western counterparts, a real underground sound emerged in Leningrad in the 1980s. Boris Grebenshchikov and his band Akvarium (Aquarium; www.aquariumband.com) caused sensations wherever they performed; his folk rock and introspective lyrics became the emotional cry of a generation. Yury Shevchuk and his band DDT emerged as the country's main rock band. The god of Russian rock was Viktor Tsoy and his group Kino. His early death in a 1990 car crash ensured his legend would have a long life. On the anniversary of Tsoy's death (15 August), fans still gather to play his tunes and remember the musician, especially at his grave at the Bogoslovskoe Cemetery, which is located a short distance from the Piskaryovskoe Cemetery (p166). A former boilerhouse bunker where Tsoy and his Kino bandmates once worked as caretakers is now a shrine-cum-concert-venue (Kamchatka (p171)) on the Petrograd Side.

One local band to watch out for is Leningrad (http://leningrad.top), who play contemporary rock and dance music with a strong brass section.

Five Classic Petersburg Albums

Kino – Gruppa Krovi

Leningrad – Piraty XXI Veka

Akvarium – Peski Peterburga

DDT – Chorny Pyos Peterburg

Dva Samolyota – Ubitsy Sredi Nas

Visual Arts

It should come as no surprise that St Petersburg is an artistic place, having been designed by the leading artists of the day. In the early years, aristocrats and emperors filled their palaces with endless collections of paintings and applied arts, guaranteeing a steady stream of artistic production. These days, millions of visitors come here to see the masterpieces that hang in the Hermitage (p56) and the Russian Museum (p74).

But St Petersburg's artistic tradition is not only historical. The city's winding waterways, crumbling castles and colourful characters continue to inspire creative types and in recent years the city has become a nurturing space for artists to work, with plentiful studios, gallery spaces and new museums interested in modern work. Anyone interested in the state of contemporary art in the city should head to Erarta Museum of Contemporary Art (p145), the Kuryokhin Centre (p127) (in temporary digs at present) and the Street Art Museum (p167). St Petersburg has always been a city of artists and poets, and that legacy endures.

One of the city's top rock bands in recent decades has been Leningrad (http://leningrad.top), a 14-piece ensemble led by Sergey Shnurov and playing what has been described as gypsy punk.

Academy of Arts

This state-run artistic institution was founded in 1757 by Count Ivan Shuvalov, a political adviser, education minister and longtime lover of Empress Elizabeth. It was Catherine the Great who moved the Academy out of Shuvalov's home, commissioning the present neoclassical building on Vasilyevsky Island (p148).

The Academy was responsible for the education and training of young artists. It focused heavily on French-influenced academic art, which incorporated neoclassicism and romanticism. Painters such as Fyodor Alexeyev and Grigory Chernetsev came out of the Academy of Arts.

The Wanderers

In the 19th century, artist Ivan Kramskoy led the so-called 'revolt of 14' whereby a group of upstart artists broke away from the powerful but conservative Academy of Arts. The mutineers considered that art should be a force for national awareness and social change, and they depicted common people and real problems in their paintings. The Wanderers (*Peredvizhniki*), as they called themselves, travelled around the country in an attempt to widen their audience (thus inspiring their moniker).

The Wanderers included Vasily Surikov, who painted vivid Russian historical scenes, and Nicholas Ghe, who favoured both historical and biblical landscapes. Perhaps the best-loved of all Russian artists, Ilya Repin has works that range from social criticism (*Barge Haulers on the Volga*) to history (*Cossacks Writing a Letter to the Turkish Sultan*) and portraits.

By the end of the 19th century, Russian culture was retreating from Western influences and looking instead to nationalistic themes and folk culture for inspiration. Artists at this time invented the *matryoshka,* the quintessential Russian nesting doll. One of the world's largest collections of *matryoshki* is on display at the Toy Museum (p161).

Mikhail Vrubel was inspired by Byzantine mosaics and Russian fairy tales. Painters such as Nikolai Roerich and Mikhail Nesterov incorporated mystical themes, influenced by folklore and religious traditions. All of these masters are prominently featured at the Russian Museum (p74).

Top: Performance of
Tchaikovsky's *Swan Lake*
Bottom: Novy Museum
(p147)

The Hermitage (p56)

Avant-Garde

From about 1905 Russian art became a maelstrom of groups, styles and 'isms', as it absorbed decades of European change in a few years. It finally gave birth to its own avant-garde futurist movements.

Mikhail Larionov and Natalya Goncharova were the centre of a Cézanne-influenced group known as the Knave of Diamonds. This husband-and-wife team went on to develop neo-primitivism, based on popular arts and primitive icons. They worked closely with Sergei Diaghilev, the founder of the Ballets Russes, designing costumes and sets for the ballet company that brought together some of the era's greatest dancers, composers and artists.

The most radical members of the Knave of Diamonds formed a group known as Donkey's Tail, which exhibited the influences of cubism and futurism. Larionov and Goncharova were key members of this group, as well as Marc Chagall and Kazimir Malevich.

In 1915 Malevich announced the arrival of suprematism. His abstract geometrical shapes (with a black square representing the ultimate 'zero form') freed artists from having to depict the material world and made art a doorway to higher realities. See one of his four *Black Square* paintings, and other examples of Russian avant-garde, at the General Staff Building (p72).

Soviet Art

Futurists turned to the needs of the revolution – education, posters, banners – with enthusiasm. They had a chance to act on their theories of how art shapes society. But at the end of the 1920s abstract art fell out of favour. The Communist Party wanted socialist realism. Images abounded of striving workers, heroic soldiers and healthy toiling peasants, some of which are on display at the Russian Museum (p74). Two million sculptures of Lenin and Stalin dotted the country; Malevich ended up painting portraits and doing designs for Red Square parades.

After Stalin, an avant-garde 'Conceptualist' underground group was allowed to form. Ilya Kabakov painted, or sometimes just arranged, the debris of everyday life to show the gap between the promises and realities of Soviet existence. Erik Bulatov's 'Sotsart' pointed to the devaluation of language by ironically reproducing Soviet slogans or depicting words disappearing over the horizon. In 1962 artists set up a show of 'unofficial' art in Moscow: Khrushchev called it 'dog shit' and sent it back underground. Soviet underground art is particularly well represented in the collections of the excellent Erarta Museum of Contemporary Art (p145) and Novy Museum (p147), both on Vasilyevsky Island.

Neo-Academism & Non-Conformist Art

As the centre of the avant-garde movement in Russia at the turn of the last century, St Petersburg never gave up its ties to barrier-breaking, gut-wrenching, head-scratching art. After the end of communism the city rediscovered its seething artistic underbelly.

Much of St Petersburg's post-Soviet contemporary art revolved around the artistic collective at Pushkinskaya 10 (p127), where artists and musicians continue to congregate and create. This place was 'founded' in the late 1980s, when a bunch of artists and musicians moved into an abandoned building near pl Vosstaniya. The centre has since developed into an artistic and cultural institution that is unique in Russia, if not the world, even if its heyday has long now passed.

In the early 1990s Timur Novikov founded the Neo-Academic movement as an antidote to 'the barbarism of modernism'. This return to classicism (albeit with a street-level, junk-shop feel) culminated in his foundation of the Museum of the New Academy of Fine Arts, which is housed at Pushkinskaya 10. Although he died in 2002, he continues to cast a long shadow on the city's artistic scene.

More commercial ventures currently dominate the St Petersburg art scene, however, with such so-called 'creative spaces' as Loft Project ETAGI (p131), Tkachi (p141) and Artmuza (p153) blurring the lines between commerce and art. Smaller, private galleries in the centre of town also showcase contemporary art, while the commerical galleries at the Erarta Museum remain the best place to look at St Petersburg's current artistic output.

SERGEI KURYOKHIN

A key figure in the Leningrad undergound and a national star of the avant-garde in post-Soviet Russia, Sergei Kuryokhin (1954–96) is little known outside his homeland, but he casts a long shadow over St Petersburg's music and art scene. As an accomplished musician, activist, actor, artist and writer Kuryokhin became a big star during the years of *glasnost,* even collaborating with local supergroup Akvarium on several albums, and starring in several popular countercultural films. He remains perhaps best known for scandalising Soviet society during the last days of the USSR by claiming on a TV show to have evidence that Lenin had been a mushroom. He died suddenly in 1996 from a heart condition, but his legacy of nonconformism and artistic originality is continued at the **Kuryokhin Centre** (p127), temporarily located in the city centre while its original home in an old cinema on Vasilyevsky Island is rebuilt, and in the annual Sergei Kuryokhin International Festival (SKIF), a celebration of avant-garde music, performing and visual arts.

Cinema

The Lenfilm studio on the Petrograd Side was a centre of the Soviet film industry, producing many much-loved Russian comedies and dramas – most famously, Sergei Eisenstein's *October* (1928). Lenfilm has continued in the post-communist era to work with some success as a commercial film studio both for cinema and television.

Ever since *Russian Ark* (2002), St Petersburg native Alexander Sokurov has been recognised as one of Russia's most talented contemporary directors. The world's first unedited feature film, *Russian Ark* was shot in one unbroken 90-minute frame. Sokurov's films have tackled a wide range of subjects, most significantly the corrupting influence of power, which was explored in a tetralogy of films observing individual cases, including Hitler *(Molokh),* Lenin *(Taurus),* Japanese Emperor Hirohito *(The Sun)* and Faust *(Faust).* Another Sokurov production that was critically acclaimed is *Alexandra* (2007), the moving tale of an elderly woman who visits her grandson at an army base in Chechnya. The title role is played by Galina Vishnevskaya, opera doyenne and wife of composer–conductor Mstislav Rostropovich.

Another star of the St Petersburg film industry was Alexey German, who gained attention with his 1998 film *Khrustalyov, My Car!* Based on a story by Joseph Brodsky, the film tells the tale of a well-loved military doctor who was arrested during Stalin's 'Doctors' Plot'. German died in 2013, leaving his final film, *Hard to Be a God,* which tells the story of a planet trapped in the dark ages, almost finished. It was completed with the help of his son and wife, and garnered excellent reviews from critics.

Other Lenfilm successes include Alexey Balabanov's *Of Freaks and Men* (1998), the joint project of Boris Frumin and Yury Lebedev, *Undercover* (2005), and Andrei Kravchuk's *The Italian* (2005), all of which enjoyed some critical acclaim in the West. They also worked on the international co-production of *Anna Karenina,* directed by Bernard Rose, in 1996.

A charming and whimsical film, Alexey Uchitel's *The Stroll* (Progulka, 2003), follows three young Petersburgers as they wander around the city getting into all sorts of situations, from a soccer riot to an argument between friends and a rainstorm. Great for St Petersburg local colour.

Theatre

While it may not be completely accessible to most travellers due to language barriers, theatre plays a major role in St Petersburg performing arts. At least a dozen drama and comedy theatres dot the city streets, not to mention puppet theatres and musical theatres. As in all areas of the performing arts, contemporary playwrights do not receive as much attention as well-known greats and adaptations of famous literature. Nonetheless, drama has a long history in Russia, and St Petersburg, as the cultural capital, has always been at the forefront.

In the early days, theatre was an almost exclusive vehicle of the Orthodox Church, used to spread its message and convert believers. In the 19th century, however, vaudeville found its way to Russia. More often than not, these biting, satirical one-act comedies poked fun at the rich and powerful. Playwrights such as Alexander Pushkin and Mikhail Lermontov decried the use of their art as a tool of propaganda or evangelism. Other writers – Nikolai Gogol, Alexander Griboyedov and Alexander Ostrovsky – took it a step further, writing plays that attacked not just the aristocracy but the bourgeoisie as well. Anton Chekhov wrote for St Petersburg newspapers before writing one-act, vaudevillian works. Yet it is his full-length plays that are his legacy.

Towards the end of the 19th century Maxim Gorky represented an expansion of this trend in anti-establishment theatre. His play *The Song of the Stormy Petrel* raised workers to a level superior to that of the intellectual. This production was the first of what would be many socialist

For a surreal night at the opera, treat yourself to tickets to the Mariinsky's production of Shostakovich's *The Nose,* based on the satirical short story by Nikolai Gogol about a socially aspirant bureaucrat who wakes up one morning to find his nose has left him and is gadding around town.

realist performances, thus earning its author the esteem of the Soviet authorities.

The futurists had their day on the stage, mainly in the productions of the energetic and tirelessly inventive director Vsevolod Meyerhold, who was one of the most influential figures of modern theatre. His productions of Alexander Blok's *The Fair Show Booth* (1906) and Vladimir Mayakovsky's *Mystery-Bouffe* (1918) both caused a sensation at the time. Both Anna Akhmatova and Dmitry Shostakovich cited Meyerhold's 1935 production of *The Queen of Spades* by Tchaikovsky as one of the era's most influential works.

During the Soviet period, drama was used primarily as a propaganda tool. When foreign plays were performed, it was for a reason – hence the popularity in Russia of *Death of a Salesman,* which showed the inevitable result of Western greed and decadence. However, just after the revolution, theatre artists were given great, if short-lived, freedom to experiment – anything to make theatre accessible to the masses. Avant-garde productions flourished for a while, notably under the mastery of poet and director Igor Terentyev. Artists such as Pavel Filonov and Kazimir Malevich participated in production and stage design.

Even socialist theatre was strikingly experimental: the Theatre of Worker Youth, under the guidance of Mikhail Sokolovsky, used only amateur actors and encouraged improvisation, sudden plot alterations and interaction with audience members, striving to redefine the theatre-going experience. Free theatre tickets were given out at factories; halls that once echoed with the jangle of upper-class audience's jewellery were now filled with sailors and workers. The tradition of sending army regiments and schoolchildren to the theatre continues to this day.

Today theatre remains important to the city's intellectuals, but it isn't at the forefront of the arts, receiving little state support and, unlike the ballet or opera, unable to earn revenues from touring abroad. If you're interested in the state of contemporary Russian theatre, the Maly Drama Theatre (p140), Baltic House (p171) and the Priyut Komedianta Theatre (p100) are particularly worth checking out.

For a comprehensive rundown of the history of drama from classical staging to the revolutionary works of Meyerhold and Mayakovsky, see Konstantin Rudnitsky's excellent *Russian and Soviet Theatre: Tradition and the Avant-Garde.*

ARTS THEATRE

Literature

St Petersburg's very existence, a brand new city for a brand new Russia, seems sometimes to be the stuff of fiction. Indeed, its early history is woven into the fabric of one of Russia's most famous epic poems, Pushkin's *The Bronze Horseman*, which muses on the fate of the city through the eyes of Falconet's famous equestrian statue of Peter the Great. In just three centuries the city has nurtured more great writers than many cities do over a millennium.

Romanticism in the Golden Age

Among the many ways that Peter and Catherine the Great brought Westernisation and modernisation to Russia was the introduction of a modern alphabet. Prior to this time, written Russian was used almost exclusively in the Orthodox Church, which employed an archaic and incomprehensible Church Slavonic. During the Petrine era, it became increasingly acceptable to use popular language in literature and this development paved the way for two centuries of Russian literary prolificacy, with St Petersburg at its centre.

Romanticism was a reaction against the strict social rules and scientific rationalisation of previous periods, exalting emotion and aesthetics. This was the dawn of what is known as the Golden Age of Russian literature. Nobody embraced Russian romanticism more than the national bard, Alexander Pushkin (1799–1837), who lived and died in St Petersburg. Most famously, his last address on the Moyka River is now a suitably hagiographic museum (p86), its interior preserved exactly as it was at the moment of his death. The duel that killed him is also remembered with a monument on the likely site (p166).

Pushkin's epic poem *Yevgeny Onegin* (*Eugene Onegin* in English) is partly set in the imperial capital. Pushkin savagely ridicules its foppish aristocratic society, despite being a fairly consistent fixture of it himself for most of his adult life. The wonderful short story *The Queen of Spades* is set in the house of a countess on Nevsky pr and is the weird supernatural tale of a man who uncovers her Mephisthophelean gambling trick. Published posthumously, *The Bronze Horseman* is named for the statue of Peter the Great that stands on pl Dekabristov (p85). The story takes place during the great flood of 1824. The main character is the lowly clerk Yevgeny, who has lost his beloved in the flood. Representing the hopes of the common people, he takes on the empire-building spirit of Peter the Great, represented by the animation of the *Bronze Horseman*.

Four Statues of Pushkin in St Petersburg

....

pl Iskusstv (Historic Heart)

....

Pushkin House (Vasilyevsky Island)

....

Pushkinskaya ul (Smolny & Vosstaniya)

....

Site of Pushkin's Duel (Petrograd & Vyborg Sides)

Dostoevsky & Gogol

No other figure in world literature is more closely connected with St Petersburg than Fyodor Dostoevsky (1821–81). He was among the first writers to navigate the murky waters of the human subconscious, blending powerful prose with psychology, philosophy and spirituality. Born in Moscow, Dostoevsky moved to St Petersburg to study in 1838, aged 16, and he began his literary and journalistic career there, living

THE SEXUAL LABYRINTH OF NIKOLAI GOGOL

If you want to get inside the mind of St Petersburg's most surreal writer, try Simon Karlinsky's explosive *The Sexual Labyrinth of Nikolai Gogol,* which argues that the key is understanding that the writer was a self-hating homosexual. Strongly supported by textual analysis, the book is convincing, if rather polemical.

at dozens of addresses in the seedy and poverty-stricken area around Sennaya pl, where many of his novels are set.

His career was halted – but ultimately shaped – by his casual involvement with a group of young freethinkers called the Petrashevsky Circle, some of whom planned to overthrow the tsar. Nicholas I decided to make an example of some of these liberals by having them arrested and sentencing them to death. After a few months in the Peter & Paul Fortress prison, Dostoevsky and his cohorts were assembled for execution. As the guns were aimed and ready to fire, the death sentence was suddenly called off and the group was committed instead to a sentence of hard labour in Siberia. After Dostoevsky was pardoned by Alexander II and returned to St Petersburg, he wrote *Notes from the House of the Dead* (1861), a vivid recounting of his prison sojourn.

The ultimate St Petersburg novel and literary classic is Dostoevsky's *Crime and Punishment* (1866). It is a tale of redemption, but also acknowledges the 'other side' of the regal capital: the gritty, dirty city that spawned unsavoury characters and unabashed poverty. It's a great novel to read before visiting St Petersburg, as the Sennaya district in which it's largely set retains its dark and sordid atmosphere a century-and-a-half later.

In his later works, *The Idiot, The Possessed* and *The Brothers Karamazov,* Dostoevsky was explicit in his criticism of the revolutionary movement as being morally bankrupt. A true believer, he asserted that only by following Christ's ideal could humanity be saved. An incorrigible Russophile, Dostoevsky eventually turned against St Petersburg and its European tendencies. His final home near Vladimirskaya pl now houses the Dostoevsky Museum (p129), and he is buried at Tikhvin Cemetery within the walls of the Alexander Nevsky Monastery (p123), a suitably Orthodox setting for such a devout believer.

Amid the epic works of Pushkin and Dostoevsky, the absurdist short-story writer Nikolai Gogol (1809–52) sometimes gets lost. But his troubled genius created some of Russian literature's most memorable characters, including Akaki Akakievich, tragicomic hero of *The Overcoat,* and the brilliant social climber Major Kovalyov, who chases his errant nose around St Petersburg in the absurdist masterpiece *The Nose.* Gogol came to St Petersburg from his native Ukraine in 1829, and wrote and lived here for a decade before spending his final years abroad. He was not impressed by the legendary capital: in a letter to his mother he described it as a place where 'people seem more dead than alive' and complained endlessly about the air pressure, which he believed caused illness. He was nevertheless inspired to write a number of absurdist stories, collectively known as *The Petersburg Tales,* which are generally recognised as the zenith of his creativity.

Symbolism in the Silver Age

The late 19th century saw the rise of the symbolist movement, which emphasised individualism and creativity, purporting that artistic endeavours were exempt from the rules that bound other parts of society. This was the start of Russian literature's Silver Age and the outstanding figures of this time were the philosopher–poet Vladimir Solovyov (1853–1900), novelist Andrei Bely (1880–1934) and poet Alexander Blok (1880–1921) as well as the poets Sergei Yesenin (1895–1925), Nikolai Gumilev (1886–1921) and Anna Akhmatova (1889–1966). The Stray Dog Café, an underground bar just off pl Iskusstv (Arts Sq), was a popular meeting place where symbolist writers, musicians and artists exchanged ideas and shared their work; it's still there today.

Blok and Bely, who both lived in St Petersburg, were the most renowned writers of the symbolist movement. While Bely was well known and respected for his essays and philosophical discourses, it is his mysterious novel *Petersburg* for which he is remembered. The plot, however difficult to follow, revolves around a revolutionary who is hounded by the *Bronze Horseman* (the same statue that harasses Pushkin's Yevgeny) and is ordered to carry out the assassination of his own father, a high-ranking tsarist official, by his revolutionary cell. Many critics see Bely's masterpiece as a forerunner of Joyce's far later modernist experiments in *Ulysses,* even though *Petersburg* wasn't even translated into English until the 1950s.

Blok took over where Dostoevsky left off, writing of prostitutes, drunks and other characters marginalised by society. Blok sympathised with the revolutions and he was praised by the Bolsheviks once they came to power in 1917. His poem *The Twelve,* published in 1918, is pretty much a love letter to Lenin. However, he later became disenchanted with the revolution and consequently fell out of favour; he died, sad and lonely, in 1921, before his fall out with the communists could have more serious consequences. In one of his last letters, he wrote, 'She did devour me, lousy, snuffling dear Mother Russia, like a sow devouring her piglet'. The flat where he spent the last eight years of his life is now a museum (p113).

> *Crime and Punishment* may be on everyone's reading list before they head to the northern capital, but another (far shorter) St Petersburg work from Dostoevsky is *White Nights,* a wonderful short story that has been adapted for cinema by no less than nine different directors.

Revolutionary Literature

The immediate aftermath of 1917 saw a creative upswing in Russia. Inspired by social change, writers carried over these principles into their work, pushing revolutionary ideas and ground-breaking styles.

The trend was temporary, of course. The Bolsheviks were no connoisseurs of culture; and the new leadership did not appreciate literature unless it directly supported the goals of communism. Some writers managed to write within the system, penning some excellent poetry and plays in the 1920s; however, most found little inspiration in the prevailing climate of art 'serving the people'. Stalin later announced that writers were 'engineers of the human soul' and as such had a responsibility to write in a partisan direction.

The clampdown on diverse literary styles culminated in the early 1930s with the creation of socialist realism, an art form created to promote the needs of the state, praise industrialisation and demonise social misfits. While Stalin's propaganda machine was churning out novels with titles such as *How the Steel Was Tempered* and *Cement,* St Petersburg's literary community was secretly writing about life under tyranny. The tradition of underground writing, which had been long established under the Romanovs, once again flourished.

Literature of Dissent & Emigration

Throughout the 20th century, many talented writers were faced with silence, exile or death as a result of the Soviet system. Many accounts of Soviet life were *samizdat* (literally 'self-publishing') publications, secretly circulated among the literary community. The Soviet Union's most celebrated writers – the likes of Boris Pasternak, Alexander

Solzhenitsyn, Mikhail Bulgakov and Andrei Bitov – were silenced in their own country, while their works received international acclaim. Others left Russia in the turmoil of the revolution and its bloody aftermath, including perhaps St Petersburg's greatest 20th-century writer, Vladimir Nabokov.

Born to a supremely wealthy and well-connected St Petersburg family in 1899, the 18-year-old Nabokov was forced to leave St Petersburg in 1917 due to his father's previous role in the Provisional Government. Leaving Russia altogether in 1919, Nabokov was never to return to his homeland and died in Switzerland in 1977. His fascinating autobiography, *Speak, Memory,* is a wonderful recollection of his idyllic Russian childhood amid the gathering clouds of revolution, and the house he grew up in now houses the small, but very worthwhile, Nabokov Museum (p111).

No literary figure is as inextricably linked to the fate of St Petersburg-Petrograd-Leningrad as Anna Akhmatova (1889–1966), the long-suffering poet whose work contains bittersweet depictions of the city she loved. Akhmatova's family was imprisoned and killed, her friends were exiled, tortured and arrested, and her colleagues were constantly hounded – but she refused to leave her beloved city and died there in 1966. Her former residence in the Fountain House now contains the Anna Akhmatova Museum (p125), a fascinating and humbling place.

Akhmatova was well travelled, internationally feted and an incorrigible free spirit who, despite having the chance after the revolution, decided not to leave Russia and go abroad. This decision sealed her fate: within a few years her ex-husband would be shot by the Bolsheviks, and decades of harassment and proscription would follow as Akhmatova's work was denounced by Communist Party officials as 'the poetry of a crazed lady, chasing back and forth between boudoir and chapel'.

However, as a reward for her cooperation with the authorities in the war effort, Akhmatova was allowed to publish again after WWII. Nonetheless, she was cautious, and she worked in secret on masterpieces such as *Requiem,* her epic poem about the terror. Through all this, her love for her city was unconditional and unblinking. Despite unending official harassment, Akhmatova outlived Stalin by over a decade. Her sad life is given a very poignant memorial (p129) opposite the Kresty Holding Prison, where the poet queued up for days on end to get news of her son following one of his many arrests.

When Nikita Khrushchev came to power following Stalin's death in 1953, he relaxed the most oppressive restrictions on artists and writers. As this so-called 'thaw' slowly set in, a group of young poets known as 'Akhmatova's Orphans' started to meet at her apartment to read and discuss their work. The star of the group was the fiercely talented Joseph Brodsky (1940–96), who seemed to have no fear of the consequences of writing about what was on his mind. In 1964 he was tried for 'social parasitism' (ie being unemployed) and was exiled to the north of Russia. His sentence was shortened after concerted international protests led by French philosopher Jean-Paul Sartre. He returned to Leningrad in 1965, only to immediately resume his thorn-in-the-side activities.

During Brodsky's absence, Khrushchev had been overthrown and replaced by a more conservative Brezhnev. It was Brezhnev who came up with the plan to silence troublemaking writers by sending them into foreign exile. Brodsky was put on a plane to Germany in 1972, and the second wave of Russian émigré writers began.

An original interpretation of Gogol can be found in Vladimir Nabokov's wonderful 1944 biography, *Nikolai Gogol.* Written in English by the polyglot Nabokov, it discusses in English the impact of much of Gogol's Russian language – something quite inaccessible to most readers!

Postcommunist St Petersburg Writing

The post-*glasnost* era of the 1980s and 1990s uncovered a huge library of work that had been suppressed during the Soviet period. Authors such as Yevgeny Zamyatin, Daniil Kharms, Anatoly Rybakov, Venedict Erofeev and Andrei Bitov – banned in the Soviet Union – are now recognised for their cutting-edge commentary and significant contributions to world literature.

Surprisingly, however, St Petersburg is not a magnet for Russian writers in the 21st century (unlike artists and musicians). The contemporary literary scene is largely based in Moscow, and, to some degree, abroad, as émigré writers continue to be inspired and disheartened by their motherland.

Action-packed thrillers and detective stories have become wildly popular in the 21st century, with Darya Dontsova, Alexandra Marinina and Boris Akunin ranking among the best-selling and most widely translated authors. Realist writers such as Tatyana Tolstaya and Ludmilla Petrushevskaya engage readers with their moving portraits of everyday people living their everyday lives.

Hearteningly, love of literature is an integral part of St Petersburg culture: ask any Petersburger what books they like to read and they'll no doubt begin to wax rhapsodical on the Russian classics without any hesitation. Anyone with any degree of education in the city will be able to quote freely from Pushkin or Akhmatova, and reference a clutch of Dostoevsky novels or Nabokov short stories they've read.

Survival Guide

Transport

ARRIVING IN ST PETERSBURG

St Petersburg is well connected to the rest of Europe by plane, train, ferry and bus. The vast majority of travellers arrive in St Petersburg by air at Pulkovo Airport. Flight time from London and Paris to St Petersburg is three hours, from Berlin it's a two-hour flight, and from Moscow it's under an hour.

Train is also a popular way to get here – from Moscow there are pleasantly slow overnight sleeper trains as well as six to eight fast four-hour daytime Sapsan trains. See www.rzd.ru for details. From Helsinki there are four daily Allegro express trains that take you from the Finnish capital to St Petersburg in an impressive 3½ hours. See www.vr.fi for prices and timetables.

An increasing number of travellers arrive at one of St Petersburg's five cruise and ferry terminals. There are regular connections between St Petersburg and Stockholm (22 to 24 hours), Tallinn (14 hours) and Helsinki (10 hours). Those who arrive this way also have the option of 72-hour visa-free travel. See **St Peter Line** (☑812-702 0777; https://st peterline.com) for prices and timetables.

Flights, cars and tours can be booked online at lonelyplanet.com.

Pulkovo Airport

Most travellers arrive in St Petersburg at **Pulkovo International Airport** (LED; ☑812-337 3822; www. pulkovoairport.ru; Pulkovskoye sh), 23km south of the city. This terminal building, which opened in 2014, and is confusingly still referred to as Terminal 1, handles all domestic and international flights and is St Petersburg's only airport.

Taxi

Taking a taxi from the airport to the city centre has never been easier or safer. Leave the terminal building and outside you'll find an official taxi dispatcher who will ask you for your destination's address, indicate which taxi to go to and write you a price on a slip of official paper that you can then give to your driver. Prices vary, but expect to pay between R800 and R1000 to reach the centre, depending on where exactly you're headed. Drivers usually won't speak much English, so just hand over the money on arrival – you don't need to tip. It's also possible to book a trip into the city via a taxi app for around R700.

Marshrutka & Bus

For those on a budget, *marshrutka* (minibus) K39 shuttles you from outside the terminal building to the nearest metro station, Moskovskaya (R35, every five minutes, from 7am to 11.30pm). The bus terminates at the Moskovskaya metro station, so you don't need to worry about where to get off, and you can connect to the rest of the city from there.

There's also bus 39 (R40, every 15 minutes, from 5.30am to 1.30am) that runs the same route over longer hours, but trundles along somewhat more slowly.

Moscow Station

If you're arriving from Moscow, you'll come to the **Moscow Station** (Moskovsky vokzal; Московский вокзал; Map p276; www.moskovsky-vokzal. ru; Nevsky pr 85; ⓂPloshchad Vosstaniya) (Moskovsky vokzal), in the centre of the city. There are two metro stations close by: pl Vosstaniya (Line 1) and Mayakovskaya (Line 3). To get here (you can enter both stations through one building) turn left outside the main entrance to the Moscow Station, and the exit is in one side of the building on Ligovsky pr.

Finland Station

Trains from Helsinki arrive at the **Finland Station** (Финляндский вокзал; Map p284; www.finlyandsky.dzvr. ru; pl Lenina 6; ⓂPloshchad

CLIMATE CHANGE & TRAVEL

Every form of transport that relies on carbon-based fuel generates CO_2, the main cause of human-induced climate change. Modern travel is dependent on aeroplanes, which might use less fuel per kilometre per person than most cars but travel much greater distances. The altitude at which aircraft emit gases (including CO_2) and particles also contributes to their climate change impact. Many websites offer 'carbon calculators' that allow people to estimate the carbon emissions generated by their journey and, for those who wish to do so, to offset the impact of the greenhouse gases emitted with contributions to portfolios of climate-friendly initiatives throughout the world. Lonely Planet offsets the carbon footprint of all staff and author travel.

Lenina) (Finlyandsky vokzal). From here you can connect to anywhere in the city by metro from the Ploshchad Lenina station (Line 1) on the square outside the station.

Ladoga Station

Some trains from the Leningradskaya Oblast and those from Helsinki to Moscow stop en route in St Petersburg at the **Ladoga Station** (Ladozhsky vokzal; Ладожский вокзал; http://lvspb.ru; Zanevsky pr 73; ⓂLadozhskaya) (Ladozhsky vokzal). It's served by the Ladozhskaya metro station (Line 4).

Bus Station

St Petersburg's main bus station, **Avtovokzal** (Автобусный вокзал; ☎812-766 5777; www.avokzal.ru; nab Obvodnogo kanala 36; ⓂObvodny Kanal), has bus connections to cities all over western Russia, including Veliky Novgorod, but most travellers won't use it. If you do happen to arrive here, it's a short walk along the canal to the metro station Obvodny Kanal (Line 5).

Sea Ports

There are a number of places where cruise ships arrive in St Petersburg, while all ferries from elsewhere in the Baltic arrive at the Sea Port on Vasilyevsky Island.

Anyone on a river cruise from Moscow will arrive at the **River Passenger Terminal** (Речной вокзал; ☎812-262 6321, 812-262 0239; Obukhovskoy Oborony pr 195; ⓂProletarskaya) in the south of the city, which is a short walk away from the Proletarskaya metro station (Line 3). Upon leaving the metro turn right onto pr Obukhovskoy Oborony and it's five minutes up the road.

Marine Facade Terminal

The **Marine Facade Terminal** (Пассажирский Порт Санкт-Петербург Морской Фасад; ☎812-303 6740; www.portspb.ru; 1 Bereg Nevskoy gubi; ⓂPrimorskaya) at the far end of Vasilyevsky Island is a relatively new facility. It's not in the city centre, but all shore excursion operators have buses or cars for their passengers, and the journey to the Hermitage can be done in 30 minutes. The nearest metro station is Primorskaya, from where it's just two stops to Gostiny Dvor (Line 3) in the Historic Heart, but it's a good 30-minute walk away and you'd be advised to arrange a taxi. Head down the main road from the Marine Facade, then once you've crossed Nalichnaya ul, take Novosmolenskaya nab and you'll reach the station.

For taxis, an official dispatch stand is in the arrivals area, with fixed rates to various places around

town. You'll be given a slip of paper with the price you need to pay the driver: prices average from R200 to R400 depending on where in the centre you want to go.

Sea Port

If you're arriving by ferry from Stockholm, Tallinn or Helsinki then you'll disembark at the **Sea Port** (Морской вокзал; ☎812-337 2060; www.mvokzal.ru; pl Morskoy Slavy 1) in the southern corner of Vasilyevsky Island. It's not served by the metro, so your easiest way into the city centre is to take a taxi. Drivers wait outside the terminal or you can order a taxi by phone app; prices average from R200 to R400 depending on where in the centre you want to go.

An alternative option is to take bus 7 (R40) from the main road outside. The bus should have pl Vosstaniya (Пл Восстания) written on it, and it goes all the way down Sredny pr, crosses the Neva at the Hermitage and then goes down Nevsky pr to pl Vosstaniya.

St Peter Line (☎812-702 0777; https://stpeterline.com) offers a €25 'tour package' bus service that shuttles passengers to St Isaac's Cathedral and back again every hour.

Other Ports

There are three other docks where cruise ships sometimes arrive in St Petersburg. Smaller cruise ships usually dock on either the **English**

Embankment Passenger Terminal (Map p280) or the **Lieutenant Schmidt Passenger Terminal** (Map p286). Neither terminal has much in the way of facilities, but both are centrally located and you're within easy walking distance of the sights in the Historic Heart.

One far less attractive possibility is docking at the **St Petersburg Sea Port** (Морской порт Санкт-Петербурга; www.seaport.spb. ru; Mezhevoy kanal 5), which is the main commercial and industrial port in the city. It's on Gutuyevsky Island and a long way from anything. It's technically possible to walk out of the port to the Narvskaya metro station, but reckon on a 30-minute walk through a fairly miserable industrial area. If you decide to walk, head up Obvodny Canal and then turn right onto Staropetrogovsky pr and you'll see Narvskaya metro station on pl Stachek.

GETTING AROUND

Metro Fastest way to cover long distances. Has around 70 stations and runs from approximately 5.45am to 12.45am.

Bus, Trolleybus & Marshrutky Buses are best for shorter distances in areas without good metro coverage; they can be slow going, but the views are good. Trolleybuses are slower still, but are cheap and plentiful. *Marshrutky* are the private sector's contribution – fast fixed-route minibuses that you can get on or off anywhere along their routes.

Tram Largely obsolete and little used, but still useful in areas such as Kolomna and Vasilyevsky Island where there is little else available.

Metro

The St Petersburg **Metro** (☑800 350 1155; www.metro. spb.ru; ◷6am-12.45am) is a very efficient five-lined system. The network of some 70 stations is most usefully employed for travelling long distances, especially connecting the suburbs to the city centre. New stations are being added and it's possible that the one at Teatralnaya, next to the Mariinsky Theatre, will be operational by 2020.

Look for signs with a big blue 'M' signifying the entrance to the metro. The flat fare for a trip is R45; you will have to buy an additional ticket if you are carrying a significant amount of baggage. If you wish to buy a single journey, ask for '*adin proyezd*' and you will be given a *zheton* (token) to put in the machine.

If you are staying more than a day or two, however, it's worth buying a smart card (R60), which is good for multiple journeys to be used over the course of a fixed time period – for example, 10 trips in seven days for R355. Their main advantage is that you won't have to line up to buy tickets – the ticket counters can have very long lines during peak hours.

The metro system is fully signed in English, so it's quite easy to use, even for first-timers in Russia.

Bus, Marshrutka & Trolleybus

Buses and, particularly *marshrutky* (minibuses), are a very handy way to

---

BUYING TICKETS IN ST PETERSBURG

You'll most likely have your onward travel tickets when you arrive in St Petersburg, but if not it's easy to purchase tickets for boat, bus, train and plane travel. First of all, try online – you can buy train tickets (www.rzd.ru), bus tickets (www.luxexpress.eu) and, of course, airline tickets via websites.

Buying train tickets in person can be done at any train station (even at a different terminus from where your train departs), although waiting time can be long if you buy them at a counter. Far quicker are the new ticket machines, which all work in English and where you can usually pay with either cash or credit card. Another option is the centrally located **Train Tickets Centre** (Кассы ЖД; Map p272; nab kanala Griboyedova 24; ◷8am-8pm Mon-Sat, until 6pm Sun; Ⓜ Gostiny Dvor), where there are also ticket machines, which makes waiting in line unnecessary.

You can buy ferry tickets for nearly all boats at the **Ferry Centre** (Паромный центр; Map p276; ☑812-327 3377; www.paromy.ru; ul Vosstaniya 19; ◷10am-7pm Mon-Fri; Ⓜ Ploshchad Vosstaniya), a short walk from the Moscow Station. Alternatively, it's possible to buy ferry tickets in the **Sea Port** (Морской вокзал; ☑812-337 2060; www.mvokzal.ru; pl Morskoy Slavy 1) at the far-flung end of Vasilyevsky Island, as well as online through the ferry companies themselves.

If time is tight, then nearly all travel agencies can organise onward travel tickets for you, although of course there's usually a markup on the cost and a delivery fee.

get around the city and they tend to cover routes that the metro doesn't, making them essential for certain parts of town. Most travellers find taking them a bit daunting, however, as there's little signage in English. On both buses and trolleybuses, you get on and then pay a conductor; the fare is R40.

Marshrutky can be flagged down anywhere along their route (there are no bus stops for *marshrutky*). Open the door yourself and jump in, then once you've taken your seat you pay the driver (pass the money via your fellow passengers if you're not sitting within reaching distance); the rates are usually posted on the inside of the bus near the driver. You'll also need to request the stop you want – usually announcing to the driver the name of the street or the place you're going to shortly before you get there. Alternatively, when you want to get off, simply say (or shout!): *'AstanavEEtye pazhalsta!'* ('Stop please!') and the driver will pull over as soon as possible.

Taxi

Taxi apps, such as Gett and Yandex Taxi, are all the rage in St Petersburg and they've brought down the prices of taxis in general, while improving the service a great deal.

Aside from the apps, the best way to get a taxi is to order it by phone. Operators will usually not speak English, so unless you speak Russian, ask your hotel reception to call a taxi for you. It also remains possible to flag down a random car in the street and negotiate the price, keeping in mind all security caveats.

Peterburgskoe Taksi 068 (☑812-324 7777, in St Petersburg 068; www.taxi068.ru)

Taxi-4 (☑812-333 4333; www.taxi-4.ru)

BRIDGE TIMETABLE

From mid-April until late November major bridges across the Neva rise at the following times overnight to allow ships to pass through the city. It's rare that the Grenadersky, Kantemirovsky and Sampsonievsky Bridges over the Bolshaya Nevka River (connecting the Vyborg and Petrograd Sides) are raised and, if so, two days' notice is given beforehand. You can check the full, up-to-date timetable at www.razvodka-mostov.ru (in Russian only).

Because of the new fixed suspension bridges on the Western High Speed Diameter highway across the mouth of the Neva you will not be stuck either side of the river when the bridges go up. Note also that between May and the end of November the M5 metro line shuttles every 20 minutes back and forth between Admiralteyskaya and Sportivnaya stations between 1am and 3am on Saturday and Sunday and the eve of public holidays, creating an easy way to get between the islands and the Historic Heart.

BRIDGE	UP	DOWN	UP	DOWN
Alexandra Nevskogo	2.20	5.10		
Birzhevoy	2.00	2.55	3.35	4.55
Blagoveshchensky	1.25	2.45	3.10	5.00
Bolsheokhtinsky	2.00	5.00		
Dvortsovy (Palace)	1.10	2.50	3.10	4.55
Liteyny	1.40	4.45		
Troitsky	1.20	4.50		
Tuchkov	2.00	2.55	3.35	4.55
Volodarsky	2.00	3.45	4.15	5.45

Taxi Blues (Такси-Блюз; ☑812-321 8888; www.taxiblues.ru)

Taxi 6000000 (☑812-600 0000; http://6-000-000.ru) Has operators and drivers who speak English.

Bicycle

Despite the local traffic being still in the learning stages about basic respect for cyclists, this is a great way to get around this huge and flat city.

➡ Some youth hostels and bike shops, such as **Rentbike** (☑812-981 0155; www.rentbike.org; Naberezhnaya fontanki 77; per hr/day from R100/500; ☺10am-10pm; Ⓜ Sennaya

Ploshchad) and **Skladnye Velosipedy** (Складные Велосипеды; Map p276; ☑812-748 1407; www.shulzbikes.ru; Goncharnaya ul 20; bike hire per day/24 hr R700/1000; ☺11am-9pm), hire bikes for as little as R500 per day.

➡ If you're keen to do a lot of cycling, bring a helmet, bike lights and a good lock from home, as these are hard to come by.

➡ **Velogorod** (☑812-648 2100; http://spb.velogorod.org; ride/day pass R45/129) is a handy bike-sharing system with 56 stations across the city. You'll need to use the website or download the app to hire one of their bicycles.

Directory A–Z

Customs Regulations

Customs controls in Russia are relatively relaxed these days. Searches beyond the perfunctory are quite rare. Apart from the usual restrictions, you are limited by the amount of cash you can bring in. If you are carrying more than US$3000 – or valuables worth that much – you must declare it and proceed through the red channel.

Otherwise, on entering Russia, you can pick up your luggage and go through the green channel, meaning 'nothing to declare'.

If you want to take home anything 'arty' (manuscripts, instruments, coins, jewellery) it must be assessed by the **Cultural Security Department** (Map p272; ☑812-311 5196; Malaya Morskaya ul 17; ⊙11am-5pm Mon-Fri; Ⓜ Admiralteyskaya). Take your passport, a sales receipt and the item. Experts will issue a receipt for tax paid and a certificate stating that the item is not an antique. It's illegal to export items over 100 years old.

Discount Cards

If you're a student, bring an International Student Identity Card (ISIC) to get discounts – cards issued by non-Russian universities will not always be accepted. The Hermitage is the blissful exception, where anyone with a student card from any country gets in for free. Senior citizens (usually anyone over the age of 60) are often also eligible for discounts, so bring your passport with you as proof of age.

The St Petersburg Card (https://petersburgcard.com) is sold online and by the **St Petersburg Tourist Centre** (Map p272; http://eng.ispb.info; Sadovaya ul 14/52; ⊙10am-7pm Mon-Sat; Ⓜ Gostiny Dvor). It gives discounts on tours and sights such as the Hermitage, Peterhof and Tsarskoe Selo (savings aren't huge), as well as acting as a card for public transport.

Electricity

Electricity in Russia is supplied at 220v/50hz, and European-style plugs are used.

Type C
220V/50Hz

PRACTICALITIES

Newspapers & Magazines There is no English-language newspaper but the free bi-monthly In Your Pocket (www.inyourpocket.com) magazine is worth picking up for events listings and other background information.

Smoking Russia introduced a comprehensive smoking ban in 2014. It is no longer legal to smoke inside except in your own home.

TV As well as the main state TV channels, St Petersburg has several local channels. Satellite TV is available at most top-end hotels.

Weights & Measures The metric system is used.

TO DRINK OR NOT TO DRINK

Reports about the harmful effects of drinking tap water in St Petersburg have been widely publicised and greatly exaggerated. The city's water supplier, Vodokanal (www. vodokanal.spb.ru), insists that the water is safe to drink, as many local residents do. Nonetheless, the pipes are antiquated, so the water may contain some metal pollutants. Furthermore, traces of the parasite *Giardia lamblia* have been found on a very small scale; the parasite causes unpleasant stomach cramps, nausea, bloated stomach, diarrhoea and frequent gas – and there is no preventative drug, so it is worth taking precautions against contracting it.

To be absolutely safe, only drink water that has been boiled for 10 minutes or filtered through an antimicrobial water filter. It's safe to accept tea or coffee at someone's house, and all restaurants and hotels will have filtration systems. Bathing, showering and brushing your teeth cause no problems at all.

If you develop diarrhoea, be sure to drink plenty of fluids, preferably including an oral rehydration solution. Imodium is to be taken only in an emergency; otherwise it's best to let the diarrhoea run its course and eliminate the parasite from the body. Metronidazole (brand name Flagyl) or Tinidazole (known as Fasigyn) are the recommended treatments for *Giardia lamblia*.

Embassies & Consulates

Despite not being a capital city, St Petersburg has a good level of consular representation. If your country is not represented here, contact your embassy in Moscow in an emergency.

Australian Consulate (Map p284; ☑812-325 7334; www. russia.embassy.gov.au; 14 Petrovsky pr; Ⓜ Sportivnaya)

Belarusian Embassy (Map p276; ☑812-274 7212; www. embassybel.ru; ul Bonch-Bruevicha 3a; Ⓜ Chernyshevs-kaya)

Chinese Consulate (Посольство Китая; Map p280; ☑812-714 7670; http:// saint-petersburg.chinesecon sulate.org/rus/; nab kanala Griboyedova 134; Ⓜ Sadovaya, Sennaya Ploshchad)

Finnish Consulate (Map p276; ☑812-331 7600; www.finland. org.ru; Preobrazhenskaya pl 4; Ⓜ Chernyshevskaya)

French Consulate (Map p272; ☑812-332 2270; https:// ru.ambafrance.org; 5th fl, Nevsky pr 12; Ⓜ Admiraltey-skaya)

German Consulate (Map p276; ☑812-320 2400; www. germania.diplo.de; Furshtat-skaya ul 39; Ⓜ Chernyshevs-kaya)

Japanese Embassy (Посольство Японии; Map p272; ☑812-314 1434; www.st-petersburg.ru.emb-japan.go.jp; nab reki Moyki 29; Ⓜ Admiral-teskaya)

Kazakhstani Consulate (Map p276; ☑812-335 2546; http:// kazconsulate.spb.ru; Vilensky per 15; Ⓜ Chernyshevskaya)

Lithuanian Consulate (Map p276; ☑812-327 2681; http:// consulate-stpetersburg.mfa.lt/ stpetersburg/lt/; ul Ryleeva 37; Ⓜ Chernyshevskaya)

Netherlands Consulate (Map p272; ☑812-334 0200; www. niderlandy-i-vy.nl; nab reki Moyki 11; Ⓜ Admiralteyskaya)

UK Consulate (Map p276; ☑812-320 3200; pl Proletar-skoy Diktatury 5; Ⓜ Cherny-shevskaya)

US Consulate (Map p276; ☑812-331 2600; www.st petersburg.usconsulate.gov; Furshtatskaya ul 15; Ⓜ Cherny-shevskaya)

Emergency

Ambulance	☑03
Fire Department	☑01
Police	☑02

Health

Health insurance for any trip to St Petersburg is necessary. Note also that, officially at least, most Russian embassies issuing visas require you to purchase travel insurance. This isn't strictly implemented, however; but by all means send them details of your policy if you already have one.

Health care in the city is very good if you're going private. Using public hospitals is not something you should consider, so even if your local Russian embassy doesn't require valid health insurance, you should definitely purchase it.

Internet Access

Internet access is excellent and practically universal. Nearly all hotels have free wireless internet. Many restaurants, cafes, bars and clubs also have wi-fi. You may have to ask for a password *(parol)* to get online, and also input your mobile phone number. Sometimes this will need to be a Russian number (ie one starting with 7); if you don't have one, ask a local if you can use their number.

Legal Matters

It's not unusual to see police officers randomly stopping people on the street to check their documents. This checking tends to be directed at those with darker skin colour, but the police have the right to stop anyone. In the past travellers have complained about police pocketing their passports and demanding bribes, but reports of this nature have decreased of late as the Russian police slowly become more professional and accountable. The best way to avoid such unpleasantness is to carry a photocopy of your passport, visa and registration, and present that when a police officer demands to see your *dokumenty*. A photocopy is sufficient for such enquiries, despite what the officer may argue. Threatening to phone your consulate usually clears up any such misunderstandings.

LGBT Travellers

While St Petersburg is liberal by Russian standards, it is still far behind the rest of Europe. It should be no problem at all to book a double room for same-sex couples, although outside top-end hotels you can expect some curiosity from staff. Same-sex public displays of affection are never a good idea, however: always err on the side of caution.

Sadly, homophobia has been steadily growing, stoked by first a local, then a national law prohibiting 'gay propaganda'. While having few legal ramifications for most people, this has unleashed some latent homophobia in a country where so-called 'non-traditional orientations' were previously little discussed and thus largely ignored.

There is a busy and growing gay scene, but it remains fairly discreet. Gay pride marches are routinely attacked by far right groups and the police often harass protesters. Coming Out (www.comingoutspb.com) is the site of a St Petersburg–based support organisation.

A few other useful links:

english.gay.ru The English version of this site includes club listings and tour guides, plus information on gay history and culture in Russia.

www.lesbi.ru An active site for lesbian issues; Russian only.

www.xs.gay.ru The local gay and lesbian portal. Russian only.

Medical Services

Clinics

These private clinics have facilities of an international standard and are pricey, but generally accept major international insurance policies, including direct billing.

American Medical Clinic (Map p280;☎812-740 2090; www.amclinic.ru; nab reki Moyki 78; ⏱24hr; Ⓜ Admiralteyskaya)

Euromed (Map p276;☎812-327 0301; www.euromed.ru; Suvorovsky pr 60; ⏱24hr; Ⓜ Chernyshevskaya)

Medem International Clinic & Hospital (Map p276;☎812-336 3333; www.medem.ru; ul Marata 6; ⏱24hr; Ⓜ Mayakovskaya)

Pharmacies

Look for the sign АПТЕКА *(apteka)* or the usual green cross to find a pharmacy.

A chain of 24-hour pharmacies called **36.6 Pharmacy** (www.366.ru) has many branches around the city, including in the **Historic Heart** (Map p272; ☑812-324 2666; Gorokhovaya ul 16; ⏱9am-9pm Mon-Fri, 10am-9pm Sat & Sun; Ⓜ Admiralteyskaya). Other convenient pharmacies include Raduga, with branches in the **Petrograd Side** (Радуга; Map p284; Bolshoy pr 62; ⏱9am-10pm Mon-Fri, from 10am Sat & Sun; Ⓜ Petrogradskaya) and **Smolny** (Map p276; ☑812-275 8189; Nevsky pr 98, Smolny; ⏱24hr; Ⓜ Mayakovskaya).

Money

The Russian currency is the rouble (рубль), abbreviated as 'p' in Russian or R in English. There are 100 kopeks in a rouble and these come in coin denominations of one (rarely seen), five, 10 and 50. Also issued in coins, roubles come in amounts of one, two, five and 10, with banknotes in values of 10, 50, 100, 200, 500, 1000, 2000 and 5000 roubles.

ATMs

ATMs linked to international networks such as Amex, Maestro, Eurocard, MasterCard and Visa can be found everywhere in St Petersburg. Look for the sign БАНКОМАТ (bankomat). Using a credit or debit card, you can always obtain roubles, although US dollars and euros are sometimes available, too.

Changing Money

US dollars and euros are easy to change around St Petersburg, but other currencies will undoubtedly cause more hassle than they are worth. Whatever currency you bring should be in good condition, as banks and exchange bureaus (обмен валют) do not accept old, tatty bills with rips or tears.

Be prepared to show your passport when exchanging money.

Credit & Debit Cards

Credit cards, especially Visa and MasterCard, and various debit cards are widely accepted in hotels, restaurants and shops. You can also use your credit card to get a cash advance at most major banks in St Petersburg. You may be asked for photo ID when you use a credit card in a shop or restaurant, but this is increasingly rare as their use becomes more and more common.

Opening Hours

Banks 9am–6pm Monday to Friday, some open 9am–5pm Saturday

Bars & clubs 6pm–2am Monday to Thursday, 6pm–6am Friday to Saturday

Cafes 8am–10pm

Museums Hours vary widely, as do their weekly days off. Nearly all shut their ticket offices an hour before closing time. Many close for a *sanitarny den* (cleaning day), during the last week of every month.

Restaurants noon–midnight

Shops 10am–8pm

Supermarkets & food stores 24 hours

Post

Although service has improved dramatically in recent years, warnings about delays and disappearances of incoming and outgoing mail apply to St Petersburg. Airmail letters and postcards take up to two or three weeks to Europe, and up to three or four weeks to the USA or Australasia.

To send parcels home, head to the elegant **main post office** (Map p280; Pochtamtskaya ul 9; ⓂAdmi-

ralteyskaya). Smaller post offices may refuse to send parcels internationally; most importantly, your package is more likely to reach its destination if you send it from the main post office. You will need to provide a return address in St Petersburg – your hotel name will be fine.

Public Holidays

New Year's Day 1 January

Russian Orthodox Christmas Day 7 January

Defenders of the Motherland Day 23 February

International Women's Day 8 March

Easter Monday April/May (varies)

International Labour Day/ Spring Festival 1 May

Victory Day 9 May

Russian Independence Day 12 June

Unity Day 4 November

Safe Travel

You can disregard the dated horror stories you may have heard about the mafia in Russia. A far bigger threat is petty theft, especially pickpocketing in the city centre. Take care among the crowds on Nevsky pr and in the metro. Be cautious about taking taxis late at night, especially near bars and clubs that are in isolated areas. It's always best to call a taxi rather than get one on the street if you're alone and don't speak Russian. Never get into a car that already has two or more people in it.

One far grimmer problem is the rise of the skinhead and neo-Nazi movement in St Petersburg. You are unlikely to encounter these thugs, but you will undoubtedly read about some acts of violence that have been committed against people

from the Caucasus and Central Asia and other darker-skinned or foreign-looking residents of the city. Non-white travellers should therefore exercise caution when wandering around the city after dark and at any-time of day in the suburbs. While this violence peaked around 2005 and has since declined, it's still a very real, if unlikely, threat.

Telephone

Russia's international code is ☑7. The international access code from landline phones in Russia is ☑8 followed by 10 after the second tone, then the country code and number. From mobile phones, however, just dial +[country code] to place an international call.

Mobile Phones

Mobile phone numbers start interchangeably with either the country code (☑7) or the internal mobile code (☑8), plus three digits that change according to the service provider, followed by a seven-digit number. Nearly all Russians will give you their mobile number with an initial 8, but if you're dialling from a non-Russian number, replace this 8 with a 7.

To call a mobile phone from a landline, the line must be enabled to make paid calls (all local numbers are free from a landline anywhere in Russia). To find out if this is the case, dial 8, and then if you hear a second tone you can dial the mobile number in full. If you hear nothing, hang up – you can't call anywhere but local landlines from here.

Main mobile providers include Beeline, Megafon, MTS and Sky Link. You can buy a local SIM card at any mobile phone shop, which you can slot into your home handset during your stay. SIM cards cost as little as R200, and usually include free internet data, meaning you only pay to make calls. You'll need to bring your passport to buy one.

Topping up your credit can be done either via pre-paid credit cards bought from kiosks or mobile phone shops or, more commonly, via paypoint machines found in shopping centres, underground passes, and at metro and train stations. Choose your network, input your telephone number and the amount of credit you'd like, insert the cash and it's done, minus a 3% to 10% fee for the transaction. Confirmation of the top-up comes via a text message (in Russian) to your phone. You can also use the websites of mobile phone companies to top up your phone with a credit card.

Time

St Petersburg is GMT +3 hours, the same as Moscow time.

Toilets

Around nearly all metro stations and tourist attractions there's at least one blue Portakabin-type toilet staffed by an attendant who will charge you around R35 for the honour of using it. There are also pay toilets in all main-line train stations and free ones in museums. As a general rule, it's far better to stop for a drink in a cafe or duck into a fancy hotel and use their cleaner facilities.

Tourist Information

Tourist information is half-way decent in St Petersburg, and in addition to the Tourist Information Bureau's main office, just off Nevsky pr in the Historic Heart, there is an office in **Smolny** (Map p276; pl Vosstaniya; ⊙10am-7pm; Ⓜ Ploshchad Vosstaniya), and kiosks at **Palace Square** (Map p272; ☑931-326-5744; Dvortsovaya pl; ⊙10am-7pm; Ⓜ Admiralteyskaya), **St Isaac's Cathedral** (Map p272; Isaakievskaya pl; ⊙10am-7pm; Ⓜ Admiralteyskaya) and **Pulkovo Airport** (⊙9am-8pm).

Travellers with Disabilities

Inaccessible transport, lack of ramps and lifts, and no centralised policy for people with physical limitations make Russia a challenging destination for travellers with restricted mobility.

Toilets are frequently accessed from stairs in restaurants and museums; distances are great; public transport can be extremely crowded; and many footpaths are in a poor condition and are hazardous even for the fully mobile.

This situation is changing (albeit slowly), as buildings undergo renovations and become more accessible. Most upmarket hotels (especially Western chains) offer accessible rooms and have lifts, and the Hermitage is also now fully accessible.

Download Lonely Planet's free Accessible Travel guide from http://lptravel.to/AccessibleTravel.

Visas

Nearly all visitors need a visa, which will require an invitation. Tourist visas are generally single entry and valid for up to 30 days. See p29 for more information.

Women Travellers

Foreign women are likely to receive some attention, mostly in the form of genuine, friendly interest. An interested stranger may approach you and ask: *'Mozhno poznakomitsa?'* ('May we become acquainted?'). Answer with a gentle, but firm, *'Nyet'* ('No') and it usually goes no further, although drunken men may persist. The best way to lose an unwelcome suitor is to enter an upmarket hotel or restaurant, where ample security will come to your aid. Women should avoid taking non-official taxis alone at night.

Russian women dress up and wear lots of make-up on nights out. If you are wearing casual gear, you might feel uncomfortable in a restaurant, club or theatre.

Language

Russian belongs to the Slavonic language family and is closely related to Belarusian and Ukrainian. It has more than 150 million speakers within the Russian Federation and is used as a second language in the former republics of the USSR, with a total number of speakers of more than 270 million people.

Russian is written in the Cyrillic alphabet (see the next page), and it's well worth the effort familiarising yourself with it so that you can read maps, timetables, menus and street signs. Otherwise, just read the coloured pronunciation guides given next to each Russian phrase in this chapter as if they were English, and you'll be understood. Most sounds are the same as in English, and the few differences in pronunciation are explained in the alphabet table. The stressed syllables are indicated with italics.

BASICS

Hello.	Здравствуйте.	zdrast·vuy·tye
Goodbye.	До свидания.	da svi·da·nya
Excuse me.	Простите.	pras·ti·tye
Sorry.	Извините.	iz·vi·ni·tye
Please.	Пожалуйста.	pa·zhal·sta
Thank you.	Спасибо.	spa·si·ba
You're welcome.	Пожалуйста.	pa·zhal·sta
Yes.	Да.	da
No.	Нет.	nyet

WANT MORE?

For in-depth language information and handy phrases, check out Lonely Planet's *Russian phrasebook*. You'll find it at **shop. lonelyplanet.com**, or you can buy Lonely Planet's iPhone phrasebooks at the Apple App Store.

How are you?

Как дела?	kak di·la

Fine, thank you. And you?

Хорошо, спасибо. А у вас?	kha·ra·sho spa·si·ba a u vas

What's your name?

Как вас зовут?	kak vas za·vut

My name is ...

Меня зовут ...	mi·nya za·vut ...

Do you speak English?

Вы говорите по-английски?	vi ga·va·ri·tye pa·an·gli·ski

I don't understand.

Я не понимаю.	ya nye pa·ni·ma·yu

ACCOMMODATION

Where's a ...?	Где ...?	gdye ...
boarding house	пансионат	pan·si·a·nat
campsite	кемпинг	kyem·ping
hotel	отель	o·tel
youth hostel	хостел	ho·stel

Do you have a ... room?	У вас есть ...?	u vas yest' ...
single	одно-местный номер	ad·na·myest·nih no·mir
double (one bed)	номер с двуспальной кроватью	no·mir z dvu·spal'·noy kra·va·tyu

How much is it for ...?	Сколько стоит за ...?	skol'·ka sto·it za ...
a night	ночь	noch'
two people	двоих	dva·ikh

The ... isn't working.	... не работает.	... ne ra·bo·ta·yit
heating	Отопление	a·ta·plye·ni·ye
hot water	Горячая вода	ga·rya·cha·ya va·da
light	Свет	svyet

CYRILLIC ALPHABET

Cyrillic	Sound	
А, а	a	as in 'father' (in a stressed syllable); as in 'ago' (in an unstressed syllable)
Б, б	b	as in 'but'
В, в	v	as in 'van'
Г, г	g	as in 'god'
Д, д	d	as in 'dog'
Е, е	ye	as in 'yet' (in a stressed syllable and at the end of a word);
	i	as in 'tin' (in an unstressed syllable)
Ё, ё	yo	as in 'yore' (often printed without dots)
Ж, ж	zh	as the 's' in 'measure'
З, з	z	as in 'zoo'
И, и	i	as the 'ee' in 'meet'
Й, й	y	as in 'boy' (not transliterated after ы or и)
К, к	k	as in 'kind'
Л, л	l	as in 'lamp'
М, м	m	as in 'mad'
Н, н	n	as in 'not'
О, о	o	as in 'more' (in a stressed syllable);
	a	as in 'hard' (in an unstressed syllable)
П, п	p	as in 'pig'
Р, р	r	as in 'rub' (rolled)
С, с	s	as in 'sing'
Т, т	t	as in 'ten'
У, у	u	as the 'oo' in 'fool'
Ф, ф	f	as in 'fan'
Х, х	kh	as the 'ch' in 'Bach'
Ц, ц	ts	as in 'bits'
Ч, ч	ch	as in 'chin'
Ш, ш	sh	as in 'shop'
Щ, щ	shch	as 'sh-ch' in 'fresh chips'
Ъ, ъ	–	'hard sign' meaning the preceding consonant is pronounced as it's written
Ы, ы	ih	as the 'y' in 'any'
Ь, ь	'	'soft sign' meaning the preceding consonant is pronounced like a faint y
Э, э	e	as in 'end'
Ю, ю	yu	as the 'u' in 'use'
Я, я	ya	as in 'yard' (in a stressed syllable);
	ye	as in 'yearn' (in an unstressed syllable)

DIRECTIONS

Where is ...?
Где ...? — gdye ...

What's the address?
Какой адрес? — ka·koy a·dris

Could you write it down, please?
Запишите, пожалуйста. — za·pi·shih·tye pa·zhal·sta

Can you show me (on the map)?
Покажите мне, пожалуйста (на карте). — pa·ka·zhih·tye mnye pa·zhal·sta (na kar·tye)

Turn ...	Поверните ...	pa·vir·ni·tye ...
at the corner	за угол	za u·gal
at the traffic lights	на светофоре	na svi·ta·fo·rye
left	налево	na·lye·va
right	направо	na·pra·va

behind ...	за ...	za ...
far	далеко	da·li·ko
in front of ...	перед ...	pye·rit ...
near	близко	blis·ka
next to ...	рядом с ...	rya·dam s ...
opposite ...	напротив ...	na·pro·tif ...
straight ahead	прямо	prya·ma

EATING & DRINKING

I'd like to reserve a table for ...
Я бы хотел/ хотела заказать столик на ... (m/f) — ya bih khat·yel/ khat·ye·la za·ka·zat' sto·lik na ...

two people	двоих	dva·ikh
eight o'clock	восемь часов	vo·sim' chi·sof

What would you recommend?
Что вы рекомендуете? — shto vih ri·ka·min·du·it·ye

What's in that dish?
Что входит в это блюдо? — shto fkho·dit v e·ta blyu·da

That was delicious!
Было очень вкусно! — bih·la o·chin' fkus·na

Please bring the bill.
Принесите, пожалуйста счёт. — pri·ni·sit·ye pa·zhal·sta shot

I don't eat ...
Я не ем ... — ya nye yem ...

eggs	яйца	yay·tsa
fish	рыбу	rih·bu
poultry	птицу	ptit·su
red meat	мясо	mya·so

Key Words

bottle	бутылка	bu·*tihl*·ka
bowl	миска	*mis*·ka
breakfast	завтрак	*zaf*·trak
cold	холодный	kha·*lod*·nih
dinner	ужин	*u*·zhihn
dish	блюдо	*blyu*·da
fork	вилка	*vil*·ka
glass	стакан	sta·*kan*
hot (warm)	горячий	go·*rya*·chiy
knife	нож	nosh
lunch	обед	ab·*yet*
menu	меню	min·*yu*
plate	тарелка	tar·*yel*·ka
restaurant	ресторан	ris·ta·*ran*
spoon	ложка	*losh*·ka
with/without	с/без	s/byez

Meat & Fish

beef	говядина	gav·*ya*·di·na
caviar	икра	i·*kra*
chicken	курица	*ku*·rit·sa
duck	утка	*ut*·ka
fish	рыба	*rih*·ba
herring	сельдь	syelt'
lamb	баранина	ba·ra·ni·na
meat	мясо	*mya*·sa
oyster	устрица	*ust*·rit·sa
pork	свинина	svi·*ni*·na
prawn	креветка	kriv·*yet*·ka
salmon	лосось	la·*sauce*
turkey	индейка	ind·*yey*·ka
veal	телятина	til·*ya*·ti·na

Fruit & Vegetables

apple	яблоко	*yab*·la·ka
bean	фасоль	fa·*sol'*
cabbage	капуста	ka·*pu*·sta
capsicum	перец	*pye*·rits
carrot	морковь	mar·*kof'*
cauliflower	цветная капуста	tsvit·*na*·ya ka·*pu*·sta
cucumber	огурец	a·gur·*yets*
fruit	фрукты	*fruk*·tih
mushroom	гриб	grip

Signs

Вход	Entrance
Выход	Exit
Открыто	Open
Закрыто	Closed
Информация	Information
Запрещено	Prohibited
Туалет	Toilets
Мужской (М)	Men
Женский (Ж)	Women

nut	орех	ar·*yekh*
onion	лук	luk
orange	апельсин	a·pil'·*sin*
peach	персик	*pyer*·sik
pear	груша	*gru*·sha
plum	слива	*sli*·va
potato	картошка	kar·*tosh*·ka
spinach	шпинат	shpi·*nat*
tomato	помидор	pa·mi·*dor*
vegetable	овощ	*o*·vash

Other

bread	хлеб	khlyep
cheese	сыр	sihr
egg	яйцо	yeyt·*so*
honey	мёд	myot
oil	масло	*mas*·la
pasta	паста	*pa*·sta
pepper	перец	*pye*·rits
rice	рис	ris
salt	соль	sol'
sugar	сахар	*sa*·khar
vinegar	уксус	*uk*·sus

Drinks

beer	пиво	*pi*·va
coffee	кофе	*kof*·ye
(orange) juice	(апельсиновый) сок	(a·pil'·*si*·na·vih) sok
milk	молоко	ma·la·*ko*
tea	чай	chey
(mineral) water	(минеральная) вода	(mi·ni·*ral'*·na·ya) va·*da*
wine	вино	vi·*no*

EMERGENCIES

Help!	Помогите!	pa·ma·gi·tye
Call ...!	Вызовите ...!	vih·za·vi·tye ...
a doctor	врача	vra·cha
the police	полицию	po·li·tsih·yu

Leave me alone!
проваливай! pro·va·li·vai

There's been an accident.
Произошёл pra·i·za·shol
несчастный случай. ne·shas·nih slu·chai

I'm lost.
Я заблудился/ ya za·blu·dil·sa/
заблудилась. (m/f) za·blu·di·las'

Where are the toilets?
Где здесь туалет? gdye zdyes' tu·al·yet

I'm ill.
Я болен/больна. (m/f) ya bo·lin/bal'·na

It hurts here.
Здесь болит. zdyes' ba·lit

I'm allergic to (antibiotics).
У меня алергия u min·ya a·lir·gi·ya
на (антибиотики). na (an·ti·bi·o·ti·ki)

SHOPPING & SERVICES

I need ...
Мне нужно ... mnye nuzh·na ...

I'm just looking.
Я просто смотрю. ya pros·ta smat·ryu

Can you show me?
Покажите, pa·ka·zhih·tye
пожалуйста? pa·zhal·sta

How much is it?
Сколько стоит? skol'·ka sto·it

That's too expensive.
Это очень дорого. e·ta o·chen' do·ra·ga

There's a mistake in the bill.
Меня обсчитали. min·ya ap·shi·ta·li

bank	банк	bank
market	рынок	rih·nak
post office	почта	poch·ta
telephone office	телефонный пункт	ti·li·fo·nih punkt

Question Words

What?	Что?	shto
When?	Когда?	kag·da
Where?	Где?	gdye
Which?	Какой?	ka·koy
Who?	Кто?	kto
Why?	Почему?	pa·chi·mu

TIME, DATES & NUMBERS

What time is it?
Который час? ka·to·rih chas

It's (10) o'clock.
(Десять) часов. (dye·sit') chi·sof

morning	утро	ut·ra
day	день	den
evening	вечер	vye·chir
yesterday	вчера	vchi·ra
today	сегодня	si·vod·nya
tomorrow	завтра	zaft·ra

Monday	понедельник	pa·ni·dyel'·nik
Tuesday	вторник	ftor·nik
Wednesday	среда	sri·da
Thursday	четверг	chit·vyerk
Friday	пятница	pyat·ni·tsa
Saturday	суббота	su·bo·ta
Sunday	воскресенье	vas·kri·syen·ye

January	январь	yan·var'
February	февраль	fiv·ral'
March	март	mart
April	апрель	ap·ryel'
May	май	mai
June	июнь	i·yun'
July	июль	i·yul'
August	август	av·gust
September	сентябрь	sin·tyabr'
October	октябрь	ak·tyabr'
November	ноябрь	na·yabr'
December	декабрь	di·kabr'

1	один	a·din
2	два	dva
3	три	tri
4	четыре	chi·tih·ri
5	пять	pyat'
6	шесть	shest'
7	семь	syem'
8	восемь	vo·sim'
9	девять	dye·vyat'
10	десять	dye·syat'
20	двадцать	dva·tsat'
30	тридцать	tri·tsat'
40	сорок	so·rak
50	пятьдесят	pi·dis·yat
60	шестьдесят	shihs·dis·yat
70	семьдесят	syem'·dis·yat

80	восемьдесят	*vo·sim'·di·sit*
90	девяносто	*di·vi·no·sta*
100	сто	*sto*
1000	тысяча	*tih·si·cha*

TRANSPORT

Public Transport

A ... ticket (to Novgorod).	Билет ... (до Новгорода).	*bil·yet ...* (do *nov·ga·rat·a*)
one-way	в один конец	*v a·din kan·yets*
return	туда-обратно	*tu- da ob·rat·no*
bus	автобус	*af·to·bus*
train	поезд	*po·ist*
tram	трамвай	*tram·vai*
trolleybus	троллейбус	*tra·lyey·bus*
first	первый	*pyer·vih*
last	последний	*pas·lyed·ni*
platform	платформа	*plat·for·ma*
(bus) stop	остановка	*a·sta·nof·ka*
ticket	билет	*bil·yet*
Podorozhnik (SPB travel pass)	Подорожник	*Pa·da·rozh·nik*
ticket office	билетная касса	*bil·yet·na·ya ka·sa*
timetable	расписание	*ras·pi·sa·ni·ye*

When does it leave?
Когда отправляется?   *kag·da at·prav·lya·it·sa*

How long does it take to get to ...?
Сколько времени   *skol'·ka vrye·mi·ni*
нужно ехать до ...?   *nuzh·na ye·khat' da ...*

Does it stop at ...?
Поезд останав-   *po·yist a·sta·nav·*
ливается в ...?   *li·va·yit·sa v ...*

Please stop here.
Остановитесь здесь,   *a·sta·na·vit·yes' zdyes'*
пожалуйста.   *pa·zhal·sta*

Driving & Cycling

I'd like to hire a ...	Я бы хотел/ хотела взять ... напрокат. (m/f)	*ya bih kha·tyel/ kha·tye·la vzyat' ... na pra·kat*
4WD	машину с полным приводом	*ma·shih·nu s pol·nihm pri·vo·dam*
bicycle	велосипед	*vi·la·si·pyet*
car	машину	*ma·shih·nu*
motorbike	мотоцикл	*ma·ta·tsikl*

KEY PATTERNS

To get by in Russian, mix and match these simple patterns with words of your choice:

When's (the next bus)?
Когда (будет   *kag·da* (*bu·dit*
следующий   *slye·du·yu·shi*
автобус)?   *af·to·bus*)

Where's (the station)?
Где (станция)?   *gdye* (*stant·sih·ya*)

Where can I (buy a padlock)?
Где можно (купить   *gdye mozh·na* (ku·*pit'*
навесной замок)?   *na·ves·noy za·mok*)

Do you have (a map)?
У вас есть (карта)?   *u vas yest'* (*kar·ta*)

I'd like (the menu).
Я бы хотел/   *ya bih khat·yel/*
хотела (меню). (m/f)   *khat·ye·la* (min·*yu*)

I'd like to (hire a car).
Я бы хотел/   *ya bih khat·yel/*
хотела (взять   *khat·ye·la* (vzyat'
машину напрокат).   *ma·shih·nu na·pra·kat*)

Can I (come in)?
Можно (войти)?   *mozh·na* (vey·*ti*)

Could you please (write it down)?
(напишите),   (*na·pi·shi·te·*mne)
пожалуйста?   *pa·zhal·sta*

Do I need (a visa)?
Мне нужна (виза)?   *mne nuzh·na* (*vi·*za)

I need (assistance).
Мне нужна   *mnye nuzh·na*
(помощь).   (*po·*mash)

diesel	дизельное топливо	*di·zil'·na·ye to·pli·va*
regular	бензин номер 93	*ben·zin no·mir di·vi·no·sta tri*
unleaded	очищенный бензин	*a·chi·shi·nih bin·zin*

Is this the road to ...?
Эта дорога ведёт в ...?   *e·ta da·ro·ga vid·yot f ...*

Where's a petrol station?
Где заправка?   *gdye za·praf·ka*

Can I park here?
Здесь можно стоять?   *zdyes' mozh·na sta·yat'*

I need a mechanic.
Мне нужен   *mnye nu·zhihn*
автомеханик.   *af·ta·mi·kha·nik*

The car has broken down.
Машина сломалась.   *ma·shih·na sla·ma·las'*

I have a flat tyre.
У меня лопнула шина.   *u min·ya lop·nu·la shih·na*

I've run out of petrol.
У меня кончился   *u min·ya kon·chil·sa*
бензин.   *bin·zin*

GLOSSARY

(m) indicates masculine gender, (f) feminine gender and (n) neuter gender

aeroport – airport
alleya – alley
apteka – pharmacy
avtobus – bus
avtomaticheskie kamery khranenia – left-luggage lockers
avtovokzal – bus station

babushka – grandmother
bankomat – ATM
banya – bathhouse
bolshoy/bolshaya/bolshoye (m/f/n) – big, great, grand
bulvar – boulevard
bylina – epic song

dacha – country cottage
datsan – temple
deklaratsiya – customs declaration
dom – house
duma – parliament
dvorets – palace

elektrichka – suburban train; also *prigorodnye poezd*

galereya – gallery
glasnost – openness; policy of public accountability developed under the leadership of Mikhail Gorbachev
gorod – city, town
kafe – cafe
kamera khranenia – left-luggage office or counter
kanal – canal
kladbische – cemetery
kolonnada – colonnade
kon – horse
korpus – building within a building
koryushki – freshwater smelt
kruglosutochno – open 24 hours

lavra – most senior grade of Russian Orthodox monastery
letny sad – summer garden
liteyny – foundry

maly/malaya/maloye (m/f/n) – small, little
marshrutka – minibus that runs along a fixed route; diminutive form of *marshrut-noye taxi*
Maslenitsa – akin to Mardi Gras; fete that celebrates the end of winter and kicks off Lent
matryoshka – nesting doll; set of painted wooden dolls within dolls
mekh – fur
mesto – seat
morskoy vokzal – sea port
morzh – literally walrus, but the name commonly given to ice swimmers in the Neva
most – bridge
muzey – museum

naberezhnaya – embankment
novy/novaya (m/f) – new
Novy God – New Year

ostrov – island

parilka – steam room (at a *banya*)
Paskha – Easter
passazhirskiy poezd – passenger train
perekhod – transfer
pereryv – break, recess
perestroika – reconstruction; policy of reconstructing the economy developed under the leadership of Mikhail Gorbachev
pereulok – lane, side street
pivnaya – beer bar
ploshchad – square
politseyskiy – police officer
politsiya – police
prigorodnye poezd – suburban train; also *elektrichka*

proezd – passage
prospekt – avenue

rechnoy vokzal – river port
reka – river
restoran – restaurant
Rozhdestvo – Christmas
rynok – market
ryumochnaya – equivalent of the local pub

samizdat – underground literary manuscript during the Soviet era
sanitarny den – literally 'sanitary day'; a day during the last week of every month on which establishments such as museums shut down for cleaning
shosse – highway
skory poezd – fast train; regular long-distance service
sobor – cathedral
stary/staraya/staroye (m/f/n) – old
stolovaya – cafeteria

tapochki – slippers
teatralnaya kassa – theatre kiosk; general theatre box office scattered about the city
troika – sleigh drawn by three horses
tserkov – church

ulitsa – street

vagon – carriage (on a train)
veniki – bundle of birch branches used at a *banya* to beat bathers to eliminate toxins and improve circulation
vokzal – station
vyshaya liga – Russia's premier football league

zal – hall
zamok – castle

MENU DECODER

bliny – pancakes блины
borsch – beetroot soup борщ
buterbrod – open-faced sandwich бутерброд

garnir – garnish, or side dish гарнир

ikra (chyornaya, krasnaya) – caviar (black, red) икра (чёрная, красная)

kartoshki – potatoes картошки
kasha – porridge каша
kefir – sour yoghurt drink кефир
khleb – bread хлеб
kvas – mildly alcoholic fermented-rye-bread drink квас

lapsha – noodle soup лапша
losos – salmon лосось

mineralnaya voda (gazirovannaya, negazirovannaya) – water (sparkling, still) минеральная вода (газированная, негазированная)

moloko – milk молоко
morozhenoye – ice cream мороженое
myaso – meat мясо

obed – lunch обед
okroshka – cold cucumber soup with a *kvas* base окрошка
ovoshchi – vegetables овощи
ovoshnoy salat – tomato and cucumber salad, literally 'vegetable salad' овошной салат

pelmeni – dumplings filled with meat or vegetables пельмени
pirog/pirogi (s/pl) – pie пирог/пироги
pivo (svetloe, tyomnoe) – beer (light, dark) пиво (светлое, тёмное)
ptitsa – poultry птица

ris – rice рис
ryba – fish рыба

salat olivier – see *stolichny salat* салат Оливье

seld pod shuboy – salad with herring, potatoes, beets and carrots, literally 'herring in a fur coat' сельдь под шубой
shashlyk (myasnoy, kuriny, rybnoy) – kebab (meat, chicken, fish) шашлык (мясной, куриный, рыбной)
shchi – cabbage soup щи
sok – juice сок
solyanka – a tasty meat soup with salty vegetables and hint of lemon солянка
stolichny salat – 'capital salad', which contains beef, potatoes and eggs in mayonnaise; also called *salat olivier* столичный салат
svekolnik – cold beet soup свекольник

tvorog – soft sweet cheese similar to ricotta творог

uzhin – dinner ужин

zakuski – appetisers закуски
zavtrak – breakfast завтрак

Behind the Scenes

SEND US YOUR FEEDBACK

We love to hear from travellers – your comments keep us on our toes and help make our books better. Our well-travelled team reads every word on what you loved or loathed about this book. Although we cannot reply individually to your submissions, we always guarantee that your feedback goes straight to the appropriate authors, in time for the next edition. Each person who sends us information is thanked in the next edition – the most useful submissions are rewarded with a selection of digital PDF chapters.

Visit **lonelyplanet.com/contact** to submit your updates and suggestions or to ask for help. Our award-winning website also features inspirational travel stories, news and discussions.

Note: We may edit, reproduce and incorporate your comments in Lonely Planet products such as guidebooks, websites and digital products, so let us know if you don't want your comments reproduced or your name acknowledged. For a copy of our privacy policy visit lonelyplanet.com/privacy.

OUR READERS

Many thanks to the travellers who used the last edition and wrote to us with helpful hints, useful advice and interesting anecdotes: Adi Eyal, Andrew Tranent, Ines Schihab, Juyoung Hwang, Karin Unterstrasser, Lisi Beiter, Marie-Maude Cossette, Peter Glossop, Sarper Unen, Sassoon Grigorian, Steven Warriner, Sue Simmons, Veronica Choroco.

WRITER THANKS

Regis St Louis

Many thanks to Tatiana and Vlad for the warm welcome in Petersburg; Peter Kozyrev for Chkalovsky knowledge and the late-night strolling seminar; Darina Gribova for the street art tour; Vladimir, Yegor and Natasha of Wild Russia for many local recommendations; and friend and fellow author Simon Richmond for his many helpful tips. Warm thanks to Cassandra and daughters Magdalena and Genevieve for all their support.

Simon Richmond

Many thanks to my fellow author Regis and to Peter Kozyrev, Andrey and Sasha, Yegor Churakov, Vladimir Stolyarov, Dima Alimov, Konstantin Yurganov and Darina Gribova.

ACKNOWLEDGEMENTS

Cover photograph: Catherine Palace, Pushkin; Danita Delimont/AWL ©.

Illustration pp58-9 by Javier Zarracina

THIS BOOK

This 8th edition of Lonely Planet's *St Petersburg* guidebook was researched and written by Simon Richmond and Regis St Louis. The previous edition was written by Simon Richmond and Tom Masters. This guidebook was produced by the following:

Destination Editor Brana Vladisavljevic

Product Editors Joel Cotterell, Anne Mason
Senior Cartographer Julie Sheridan
Book Designer Wibowo Rusli
Assisting Editors Judith Bamber, James Bainbridge, Michelle Bennett, Nigel Chin, Michelle Coxall, Melanie Dankel, Andrea Dobbin, Samantha Forge, Emma Gibbs, Jennifer Hattam, Gabby Innes, Christopher Pitts, Sarah Reid, Fionnuala Twomey, Maja Vatrić, Sam Wheeler
Assisting Cartographer Valentina Kremenchutskaya
Cover Researcher Naomi Parker
Thanks to Grace Dobell, Elizabeth Jones, Kate Kiely, Wayne Murphy, Martine Power, Rachel Rawling, Kira Tverskaya

See also separate subindexes for:

🍴 **EATING P264**

🍷 **DRINKING & NIGHTLIFE P265**

☆ **ENTERTAINMENT P265**

🔒 **SHOPPING P265**

🏃 **SPORTS & ACTIVITIES P266**

🛏 **SLEEPING P266**

Index

NOTES

St Petersburg Maps

Sights

- Beach
- Bird Sanctuary
- Buddhist
- Castle/Palace
- Christian
- Confucian
- Hindu
- Islamic
- Jain
- Jewish
- Monument
- Museum/Gallery/Historic Building
- Ruin
- Shinto
- Sikh
- Taoist
- Winery/Vineyard
- Zoo/Wildlife Sanctuary
- Other Sight

Activities, Courses & Tours

- Bodysurfing
- Diving
- Canoeing/Kayaking
- Course/Tour
- Sento Hot Baths/Onsen
- Skiing
- Snorkelling
- Surfing
- Swimming/Pool
- Walking
- Windsurfing
- Other Activity

Sleeping

- Sleeping
- Camping
- Hut/Shelter

Eating

- Eating

Drinking & Nightlife

- Drinking & Nightlife
- Cafe

Entertainment

- Entertainment

Shopping

- Shopping

Information

- Bank
- Embassy/Consulate
- Hospital/Medical
- Internet
- Police
- Post Office
- Telephone
- Toilet
- Tourist Information
- Other Information

Geographic

- Beach
- Gate
- Hut/Shelter
- Lighthouse
- Lookout
- Mountain/Volcano
- Oasis
- Park
- Pass
- Picnic Area
- Waterfall

Population

- Capital (National)
- Capital (State/Province)
- City/Large Town
- Town/Village

Transport

- Airport
- Border crossing
- Bus
- Cable car/Funicular
- Cycling
- Ferry
- Metro station
- Monorail
- Parking
- Petrol station
- S-Bahn/Subway station
- Taxi
- T-bane/Tunnelbana station
- Train station/Railway
- Tram
- Tube station
- U-Bahn/Underground station
- Other Transport

Routes

- Tollway
- Freeway
- Primary
- Secondary
- Tertiary
- Lane
- Unsealed road
- Road under construction
- Plaza/Mall
- Steps
- Tunnel
- Pedestrian overpass
- Walking Tour
- Walking Tour detour
- Path/Walking Trail

Boundaries

- International
- State/Province
- Disputed
- Regional/Suburb
- Marine Park
- Cliff
- Wall

Hydrography

- River, Creek
- Intermittent River
- Canal
- Water
- Dry/Salt/Intermittent Lake
- Reef

Areas

- Airport/Runway
- Beach/Desert
- Cemetery (Christian)
- Cemetery (Other)
- Glacier
- Mudflat
- Park/Forest
- Sight (Building)
- Sportsground
- Swamp/Mangrove

Note: Not all symbols displayed above appear on the maps in this book

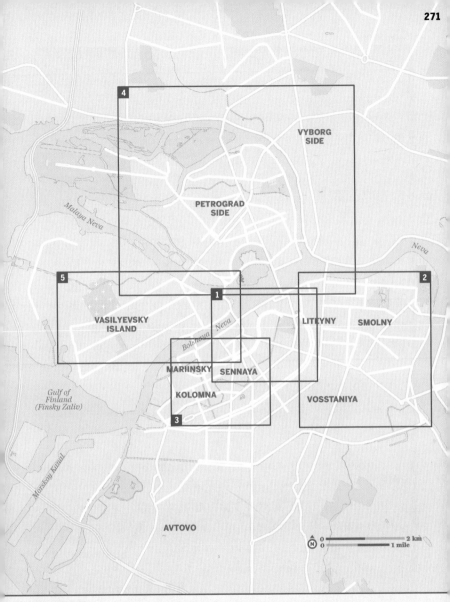

MAP INDEX

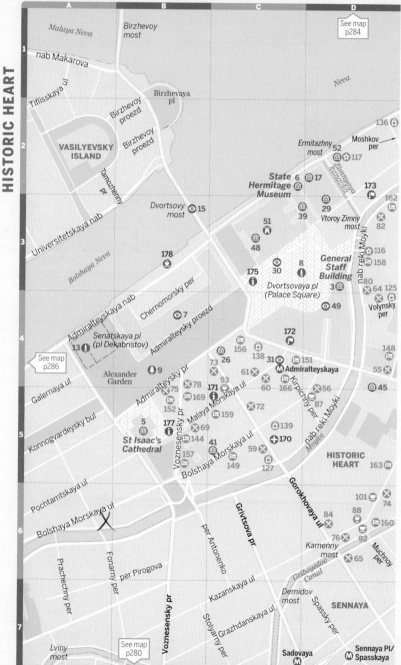

See map
p284

See map
p286

See map
p280

Malaya Neva

Birzhevoy
most

nab Makarova

Tiflisskaya ul

Birzhevaya
pl

Neva

Birzhevoy
proezd

Birzhevoy
proezd

VASILYEVSKY
ISLAND

Tamozhenny per

Universitetskaya nab

Bolshaya Neva

Dvortsovy
most

15

136

Ermitazhny
most   52

Moshkov
per

117

State
Hermitage
Museum

6   17

173

162

29

39

Vtoroy Zimny
most

82

51

116

48

158

nab reki Moyki

178

175

30   8

General
Staff
Building

3

80

64   125

Dvortsovaya pl
(Palace Square)

Volynsky
per

Chernomorsky per

7

49

Admiralteyskaya nab

Senatskaya pl
(pl Dekabristov)

13

Admiralteysky proezd

172

148

156

138   31

151

Admiralteyskaya

55

Alexander
Garden

9

73 26

Kirpichny per

45

61

Galernaya ul

75 78

171

93

60   166   56

87

152

169

72

Malaya Morskaya ul

159

Konnogvardeysky bul

5

177

69

144   41

59

139

170

nab reki
Moyka

Voznesensky pr

157

Bolshaya Morskaya ul

149

127

HISTORIC
HEART

163

Pochtamtskaya ul

Gorokhovaya ul

101

74

Bolshaya Morskaya ul

84

88

160

Prachechny per

Fonarny per

per Pirogova

per Antonenko

Grivtsova pr

76   92

Kamenny
most

65

Muchnoy
per

Kazanskaya ul

Griboyedov
Canal

Demidov
most

SENNAYA

Lviny
most

Voznesensky pr

Stolyarny per

Grazhdanskaya ul

Spassky per

Sadovaya

Sennaya Pl/
Spasskaya

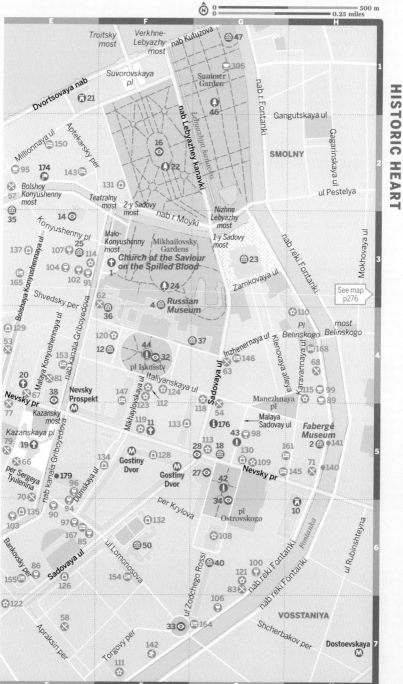

0   500 m
0   0.25 miles

E

Troitsky most

Verkhne-Lebyazhy most

nab Kutuzova   47 105

Dvortsovaya nab

Suvorovskaya pl

21

Summer Garden

SMOLNY

Millionnaya ul   150   Aptekarsky per

95   174   143

131   16

22   46

nab r Fontanki

Gangutskaya ul

Gagarinskaya ul

ul Pestelya

57   Bolshoy Konyushenny most   Teatralny most   2-y Sadovy most   nab r Moyki   Nizhne-Lebyazhny most

35   14   Konyushenny pl   25

Malo-Konyushenny most   Mikhailovsky Gardens   I-y Sadovy most

137   107   114   Church of the Saviour on the Spilled Blood   23   Zamkovaya ul   nab reki Fontanki   Mokhovaya ul

104   102   91   1   24

165   Shvedsky per   Bolshaya Konyushennaya ul   62   36   Russian Museum   4

129   153   120   12   44   32   37   Inzhenernaya ul   146   110   Pl Belinskogo   most Belinskogo   See map p276

53   81   pl Iskusstv   63   168   68

20   38   Nevsky   Italyanskaya ul   124   118   Karavannaya ul   115   99

67   Prospekt   147   123   112   54   Manezhnaya pl   89

Nevsky pr   119   11   133   176   Malaya Sadovay ul   Faberge Museum

77   Kazansky most   134   128   28   18   43   98   2   141

19   Kazanskaya pl   113   130   161   71   140

79   66   Gostiny Dvor   27   42   109   145   10

70   179   96   Gostiny Dvor   34   Nevsky pr

135   90   94   132   per Krylova   pl Ostrovskogo   Fontanka

103   97   167   85   108

86   Sadovaya ul   126   50   40   100   ul Rubinshteyna

155   58   ul Lomonosova   154   121   83   nab reki Fontanki   VOSSTANIYA

122   Apraksin per   Torgovy per   33   164   106   Shcherbakov per   Dostoevskaya

142   111

HISTORIC HEART *Map on p272*

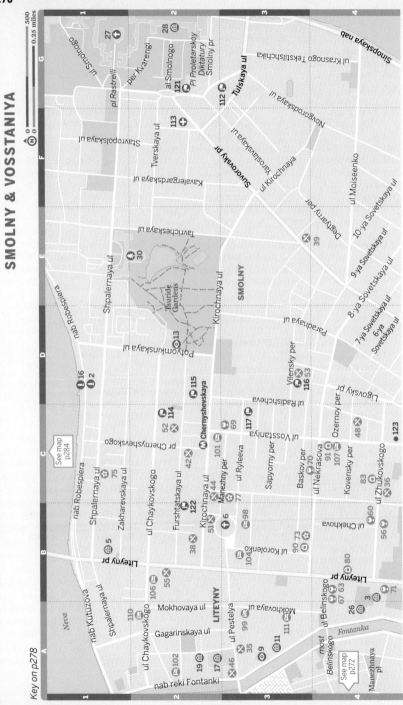

500 m
0.25 miles

See map p284

See map p272

Neva

nab Kutuzova

nab reki Fontanki

Fontanka

Manezhnaya pl

most Belinskogo

LITEYNY

SMOLNY

Sinopskaya nab

ul Krasnogo Tekstilshchika

Tulskaya ul

pl Proletarskoy Diktatury

Smolny pr

al Smolnogo

pl Rastrelli

ul Smolnogo

per Kvarengi

Stavropolskaya ul

Tverskaya ul

Kavalergardskaya ul

Novgorodskaya ul

Yaroslavskaya ul

Kirochnaya ul

Tavricheskaya ul

Shpalernaya ul

Taurida Gardens

Potyomkinskaya ul

Kirochnaya ul

ul Moiseenko

10-ya Sovetskaya ul

9-ya Sovetskaya ul

8-ya Sovetskaya ul

7-ya Sovetskaya ul

6-ya Sovetskaya ul

Degtyarny per

Paradnaya ul

Vilensky per

Ligovsky pr

Ozerny per

ul Radishcheva

ul Vosstaniya

Sapyorny per

Baskov per

ul Nekrasova

Kovensky per

ul Zhukovskogo

ul Chekhova

ul Korolenko

ul Ryleeva

Manezhny per

ul Pestelya

Mokhovaya ul

Gagarinskaya ul

Mokhovaya ul

ul Belinskogo

ul Chaykovskogo

Furshtatskaya ul

Kirochnaya ul

Zakharevskaya ul

Shpalernaya ul

nab Robespiera

pr Chernyshevskogo

Liteyny pr

Liteyny pr

Chernyshevskaya

27

28

121

112

113

30

13

16

2

115

114

52

42

53

116

69

117

101

51

44

122

77

6

98

104

90 73

70

91

107

83

48

36

123

60

56

80

67 63

3

71

26

111

99

35

9

11

46

17

19

102

5

38

55

106

110

39

75

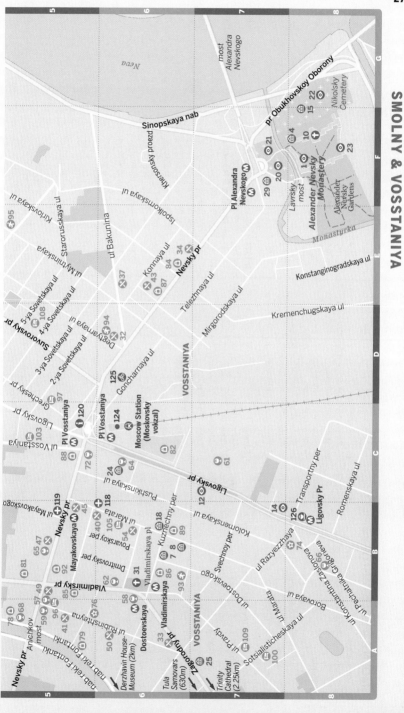

Neva

most
Alexandra
Nevskogo

Sinopskaya nab

pr Obukhovskoy Oborony

Nikolsky
Cemetery

15 22

4

10

21

Konstanginogradskaya ul

Kremenchugskaya ul

29

20

Pl Alexandra
Nevskogo

23

Lavrsky
most

Alexander Nevsky
Monastery

Alexander
Nevsky
Gardens

Monastyrka

Kirovskaya ul

Ispolkomskaya ul

ul Bakunina

Khrestovsky proezd

Starorusskaya ul

ul Myrtinskaya

95

37

Konnaya ul

34

43

87

Nevsky pr

Telezhnaya ul

Mirgorodskaya ul

VOSSTANIYA

Suvorovsky pr

5-ya Sovetskaya ul

4-ya Sovetskaya ul

3-ya Sovetskaya ul

2-ya Sovetskaya ul

Degtyarnaya ul

108

94

32

125

Goncharnaya ul

Grechesky pr

Ligovsky pr

97

ul Vosstaniya

Pl Vosstaniya

120

124

Pl Vosstaniya

Moscow Station
(Moskovsky
vokzal)

103

88

82

72

24

64

12

Ligovsky pr

61

Transportny per

Romenskaya ul

119

Nevsky pr

ul Mayakovskogo

Mayakovskaya

45

118

105

40

54

Pushkinskaya ul

ul Marata

Kuznechny per

Povarskoy per

18

7 8

89

Kolomenskaya ul

Svechnoy per

14

126

Ligovsky Pr

74

81

92

Dmitrovsky per

Vladimirskaya pl

31

86

93

ul Dostoevskogo

ul Konstantina Zaslonova

66

ul pechatnika Grigoreva

Vladimirsky pr

85

62

Vladimirskaya

58

33

VOSSTANIYA

25

ul Marata

ul Pravdy

Borovaya ul

109

100

Satsialisticheskaya ul

Nevsky pr

Anichkov
most

nab reki Fontanki

78

68

57

49

59

96

41

50

79

76

ul Rubinshteyna

Derzhavin House-
Museum (2km)

Tula
Samovars
(630m)

Trinity
Cathedral
(2.25km)

Zagorodny pr

Dostoevskaya

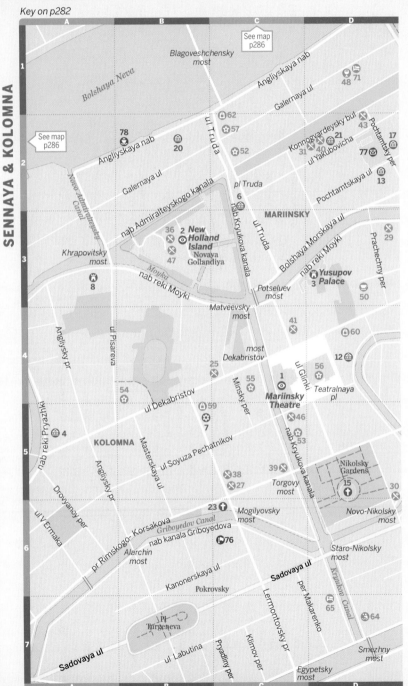

Key on p282

See map p286

See map p286

Blagoveshchensky most

Bolshaya Neva

Angliyskaya nab

Galernaya ul

48 71

ul Truda

62
57

78

20

52

Konnogvardeysky bul

43

17

31 40 21

ul Yakubovicha

77

13

Galernaya ul

Angliyskaya nab

Novo-Admiralteysky Canal

nab Admiralteyskogo kanala

pl Truda

6

MARIINSKY

Pochtamtsky per

Pochtamtskaya ul

Khrapovitsky most

36 2 **New Holland Island**
Novaya Gollandiya

47

nab Kryukova kanala

ul Truda

Bolshaya Morskaya ul

nab reki Moyki

29

Moyka
nab reki Moyki

8

3 **Yusupov Palace**

Prachechny per

Potseluev most

Matveevsky most

50

most Dekabristov

41

60

Angliysky pr

ul Pisareva

25

ul Glinki

12

56

Teatralnaya pl

54

55

1

Mariinsky Theatre

ul Dekabristov

Minsky per

46

59

53

7

KOLOMNA

nab reki Pryazhki

4

Masterskaya ul

ul Soyuza Pechatnikov

38

39

27

Torgovy most

Nikolsky Gardens

15

30

Novo-Nikolsky most

Angliysky pr

Drovyanoy per

pr Rimskogo-Korsakova

23

Mogilyovsky most

76

nab kanala Griboyedova

Griboyedov Canal

Staro-Nikolsky most

ul V Ermaka

Alarchin most

Kanonerskaya ul

Pokrovsky

Sadovaya ul

Lermontovsky pr

per Makarenko

Kryukov Canal

65

64

pl Turgeneva

Sadovaya ul

ul Labutina

Pryadilny per

Klimov per

Egyptsky most

Smezhny most

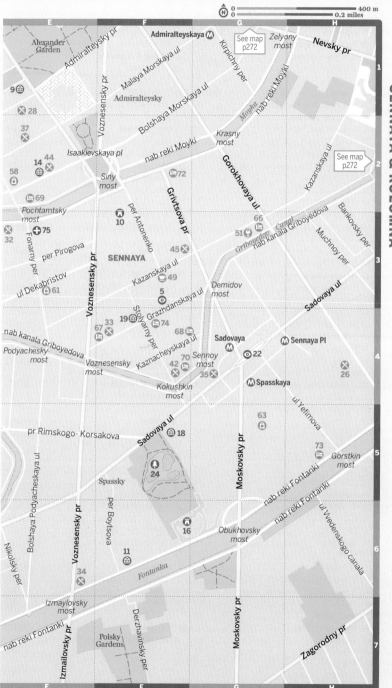

SENNAYA & KOLOMNA *Map on p280*

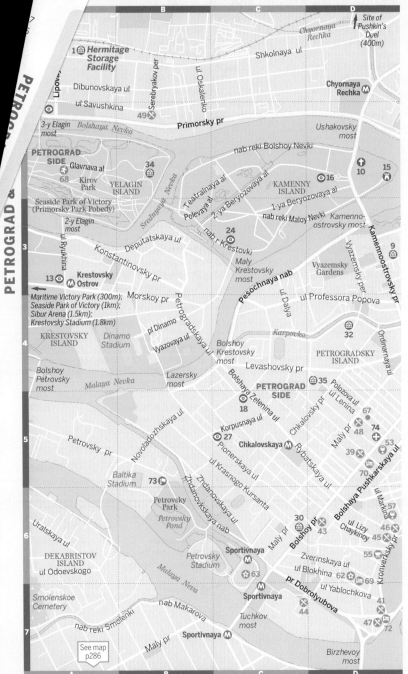

PETROGRAD &

PETROGRAD & ...

Site of
Pushkin's
Duel
(400m)

Chyornaya
Rechka

Shkolnaya ul

1 🏛 **Hermitage
Storage
Facility**

Chyornaya
Rechka Ⓜ

Dibunovskaya ul

Lipovaya

Serebryakov per

ul Oskalenko

ul Savushkina

Ushakovsky
most

49

Primorsky pr

3-y Elagin
most

Bolshaya Nevka

nab reki Bolshoy Nevki

15

**PETROGRAD
SIDE**

Glavnaya al

34

Teatralnaya al

KAMENNY
ISLAND

16

10

68

Kirov
Park

YELAGIN
ISLAND

Polevaya al

2-ya Beryozovaya al

1-ya Beryozovaya al

Seaside Park of Victory
(Primorsky Park Pobedy)

nab reki Maloy Nevki

Kamenno-
ostrovsky most

2-y Elagin
most

Srednyaya Nevka

nab r. Krestovki

24

ul Ryukhina

Deputatskaya ul

Maly
Krestovsky
most

Vyazemsky
Gardens

Vyazemsky per

9

Kamennoostrovsky pr

13 Ⓜ **Krestovsky
Ostrov**

Konstantinovsky pr

Morskoy pr

Pesochnaya nab

ul Dalya

ul Professora Popova

Maritime Victory Park (300m);
Seaside Park of Victory (1km);
Sibur Arena (1.5km);
Krestovsky Stadium (1.8km)

Petrogradskaya ul

pl Dinamo

Karpovka

32

Ordinarnaya ul

KRESTOVSKY
ISLAND

Dinamo
Stadium

Vyazovaya ul

Bolshoy
Krestovsky
most

PETROGRADSKY
ISLAND

Bolshoy
Petrovsky
most

Malaya Nevka

Lazersky
most

Levashovsky pr

**PETROGRAD
SIDE**

35

Polozova ul

ul Lenina

67

Petrovsky pr

Novoladozhskaya ul

Bolshaya Zelenina ul

18

Chkalovsky pr

Maly pr

48

74

53

Korpusnaya ul

Rybatskaya ul

39

70

Bolshaya Pushkarskaya ul

ul Markina

57

27

Chkalovskaya Ⓜ

73

Zhdanovskaya ul

ul Krasnogo Kursanta

Pionerskaya ul

46

45

Baltika
Stadium

Zhdanovskaya nab

30

Bolshoy pr

43

ul Lizy
Chaykinoy

Kronverksky pr

55

Uralskaya ul

Petrovsky
Park

Petrovsky
Pond

Maly pr

Zverinskaya ul

ul Blokhina

62

69

DEKABRISTOV
ISLAND

ul Odoevskogo

Sportivnaya Ⓜ

63

ul Yablochkova

41

47

72

Smolenskoe
Cemetery

Petrovsky
Stadium

Sportivnaya

pr Dobrolyubova

44

nab reki Smolenki

nab Makarova

Malaya Neva

Tuchkov
most

Sportivnaya Ⓜ

Maly pr

Birzhevoy
most

See map
p286

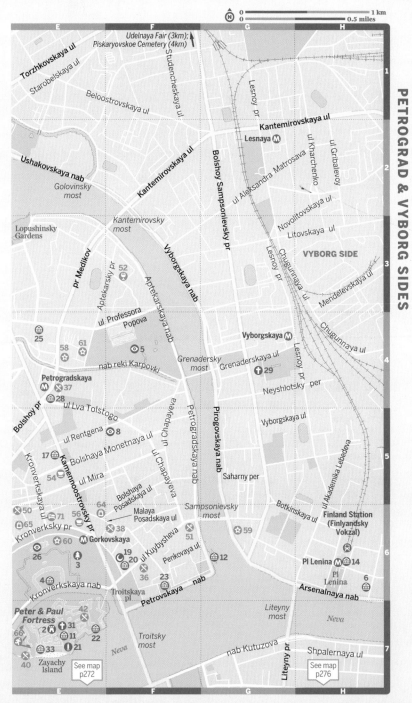

0   1 km
0   0.5 miles

Udelnaya Fair (3km);
Piskaryovskoe Cemetery (4km)

Torzhkovskaya ul
Starobelskaya ul
Beloostrovskaya ul
Studencheskaya ul

Kantemirovskaya ul
Lesnoy pr
Kantemirovskaya ul
Lesnaya Ⓜ

ul Aleksandra Matrosava
ul Kharchenko
ul Gribalevoy

Ushakovskaya nab
Golovinsky most
Bolshoy Sampsonievsky pr

Kantemirovsky most
Novolitovskaya ul
Litovskaya ul

Lopushinsky Gardens
Kantemirovsky most

Vyborgskaya nab

VYBORG SIDE

Chugunnaya ul
Lesnoy pr
Mendelevskaya ul

pr Medikov
52
Aptekarsky pr
Aptekarskaya nab

ul Professora Popova

Chugunnaya ul

25
58   61
Ⓜ 5

nab reki Karpovki

Vyborgskaya Ⓜ
Grenaderskaya ul
Grenadersky most
Ⓘ 29

Petrogradskaya
Ⓜ ✕37
▥28

Neyshlotsky per

Bolshoy pr
ul Lva Tolstogo

Petrogradskaya nab
Pirogovskaya nab

Vyborgskaya ul

ul Rentgena   Ⓜ 8

17 ▥
54

Bolshaya Monetnaya
ul Mira

ul Chapayeva

Saharny per

ul Akademika Lebedeva

Kronverkskaya ul
Kamennoostrovsky pr

Bolshaya Posadskaya ul
64

Malaya Posadskaya ul

Sampsonievsky most

Botkinskaya ul

Finland Station (Finlyandsky Vokzal)

50   71   56
65

38

51
59

Kronverksky pr
Ⓜ Gorkovskaya
60
26

19   20
ul Kuybysheva
Penkovaya ul
12

Pl Lenina Ⓜ ▥14
Pl Lenina

3
36   23

Petrovskaya nab
Arsenalnaya nab

6

4 ▥
Kronverkskaya nab
Troitskaya pl

Liteyny most
Liteyny pr

Peter & Paul Fortress
42

2   31
66   11
33   21
22

40
Zayachy Island

Troitsky most

Neva

Troitsky most

Neva

nab Kutuzova

Shpalernaya ul

nab Kutuzova

See map p272

See map p276

E   F   G   H

VASILEVSKY ISLAND

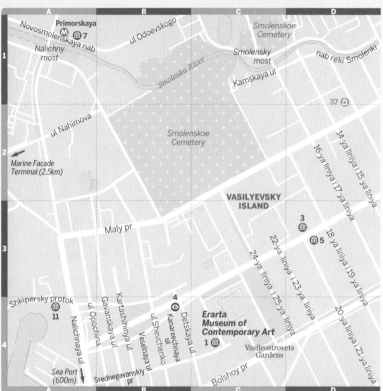